N
0
25
MILES

Wavell

XMAS. 1987.

Collins Pocket Guide to British Birds

from Marilyn. x

COLLINS POCKET GUIDE TO

BRITISH BIRDS

by

R. S. R. FITTER

Illustrated by

R. A. RICHARDSON

REVISED EDITION

CHANCELLOR
PRESS

George Moore stopped me in the hall one day: 'Oh! Praeger, I'm sure you can tell me the name of a little brown bird . . .' and he attempted to describe it. 'I am not an ornithologist,' I said, 'and there are a lot of little brown birds; but I fancy it was a Meadow Pipit.' Six months later I met him in the street; he stopped me. 'Oh! Praeger, can you tell me the name of a little brown bird . . .' and he ran over its points again. 'I believe it was a Meadow Pipit,' I answered. He wrote the name on his cuff and thanked me. Later on I met him again. 'Oh! Praeger . . .' 'I know,' I said, 'it's about the little brown bird. I'm sure it was a Meadow Pipit.' And as a Meadow Pipit, I believe, it appeared in one of his books.

R. LLOYD PRAEGER

I find pipits in the field almost hopeless and not much better in the hand.

T. A. COWARD

An ornithologist . . . the sort of man who can tell at a glance the difference between a ring dotterel, a whimbrel and a skua.

HAROLD NICOLSON

First published in Great Britain in 1952 by
William Collins Sons & Co. Ltd.
Revised edition published 1966.

This edition published in 1986 by
Chancellor Press
59 Grosvenor Street
London W1

ISBN 1 85152 026 0

Printed in Hungary

CONTENTS

DESCRIPTIONS OF BIRDS

CONTENTS

NOTE: A list of the plates in colour and black-and-white is to be found on pp. 22-5. The plates in colour are to be found between pages 128-9, and those in black-and-white between pages 160-1.

PREFACE TO REVISED EDITION

It is 14 years since the first edition of the *Pocket Guide*, and in that time, although the plumage of the birds has not changed their distribution has. Britain has acquired one completely new breeding bird, the collared dove, as I forecast in the first edition, and many other scarce or rare visitors have become more frequent, among them the melodious and icterine warblers, the Mediterranean gull and a number of American waders. In addition the breeding distribution of certain birds, especially the wryneck, red-backed shrike and little ringed plover, has changed considerably.

In completely revising the book, therefore, I have had to change little in the descriptions of birds and their habits, and not a great deal in the introductory material on bird watching, but a fair amount under the heading of 'Range and Status.' The collared dove is now fully described, and shorter descriptions of 20 less common species have been added. Two plates have been revised, to accommodate the collared dove and Mediterranean gull, and 9 line drawings of rarer species, such as Caspian tern and dowitcher, have been added. The list of rare birds which have occurred fewer than 20 times in the British Isles has been brought up to date; as many as 31 of these have appeared in the British Isles for the first time since the first edition.

ACKNOWLEDGMENTS

It would be impossible for any one man to supply all, or even the bulk, of the information in such a book as this out of his personal experience. I am therefore most indebted both to a multitude of published sources and to many kind friends who have helped in innumerable ways.

First, the manuscript was read by my wife, Bruce Campbell, James Fisher and Richard Richardson. For all their invaluable comments I am extremely grateful. Those who have looked at and helpfully criticised one or more of the plates are too numerous to mention, and the artist and I must apologise for not being able to thank them all by name. I owe a special degree of thanks to Peter Scott, who placed the unrivalled facilities of the Wildfowl Trust at our disposal during the painting of the waterfowl plates; and to Mrs. R. F. Meiklejohn, for innumerable acts of kindness while the plates were being painted, which almost qualify her to rank as the book's godmother.

Among many others who have helped at various stages in the book, by supplying information of one kind or another, and whom both author and artist would like to thank, are: R. P. Bagnall-Oakeley, Phyllis Barclay-Smith, John Barrett, the Duke of Bedford, W. Bishop, C. D. Borrer, British Waterfowl Association, Philip Brown, Major Anthony Buxton, John Buxton, G. S. Cansdale, Peter Clarke, Peter Conder, the Hon. H. M. Douglas-Home, E. A. Ellis, R. High, P. A. D. Hollom, Peter Jackson, S. T. Johnstone with other members of the staff of the Wildfowl Trust, G. T. Kay, Captain C. W. R. Knight, Dr. and Frü Løvenskiold, Dr. Lief Natvig, John Parrinder, Cyril Pease, Richard Perry, M. L. Ridgway, B. B. Riviere, Dr. K. B. Rooke, Ronald Stevens, P. O. Swanberg, G. Tallon with H. Lomont and the *gardes* of the Société d'Acclimatation's reserves in the Camargue, Alan Thompson, B. W. Tucker, Captain and Mrs. H. R. H. Vaughan, Dr. G. M. Vevers, Reg Wagstaffe, J. Walpole-Bond, George Warner, Ken Williamson, G. K. Yeates and members of the staff of the Zoological Society of London.

I have left till last my greatest single debt, to *The Handbook of British Birds*. In particular, I should like to pay tribute to the plumage descriptions of H. F. Witherby, and the field characters supplied by Bernard Tucker, whose tragically early death dealt such a blow to the progress of British ornithology. Other books to whose authors I am also indebted, include: T. A. Coward's *Birds of the British Isles and their Eggs*, H. E. Dresser's *A Manual of Palaearctic Birds*, James Fisher's *Bird Recognition*, vol. I, F. H. Kortright's *The Ducks, Geese and Swans of North America*, Roger Tory Peterson's *A Field Guide to the Birds*, Peter Scott's *Key to the Wildfowl of the World* and *The Swans, Geese and Ducks of the British Isles*, and many notes and papers in the journal *British Birds*, especially the two admirable discussions of the identification of glaucous and Iceland gulls by G. T. Kay.

All or part of the proofs have been read by my wife, Philip Brown, James Fisher, Theo Kay, Richard Richardson and Peter Scott, all of whom I must thank again for weeding out imperfections. It would be too much to hope that in a work of this character no error had escaped the notice of even all these skilled eyes, and I shall be glad to hear from any reader who spots anything amiss.

HOW TO USE THE BOOK

HOW TO FIND THE BIRD YOU WANT

If you want to look up a bird whose name you know, there is an index beginning on page 279.

If you want to identify a bird there are three main lines of approach:

DESCRIPTIVE SECTION, pages 31-216. All the birds you are likely to see in Britain are arranged in order of SIZE, grouped under the main headings of *Land*, *Waterside*, and *Water*. The section begins with our smallest land bird, the Goldcrest, and ends with our largest water bird, the Mute Swan. The size classifications are based on the relative sizes of such well-known birds as, for instance, the sparrow and the pheasant.

THE ILLUSTRATIONS, 64 colour plates between text pages 128 and 129, and 48 black-and-white plates between text pages 160 and 161, provide you with the means of identifying a bird *visually*, for here the birds are grouped first by colour and then by size, e.g. all the brown birds are together in order of size. In fact, you just flick over the pages until you get near the appearance of the bird you are looking for.

THE KEY, pages 217-64. This affords a special method for easy identification if you have only caught sight of one or two features—the bird's general colouring, for example, a white patch on its wing, or a forked tail. The Key is divided as follows:

Plumage. Between pages 219 and 251 you can seek the bird under its general colouring, or look under sub-headings for spots, streaks, etc.

Structural Features. Between pages 251 and 255 you can look for any distinctive feature you may have noticed, such as a crossed bill, a forked tail, or a crest.

Behaviour. Between pages 255 and 259 you have a chance to look up any peculiarities of behaviour that may have struck you, such as hovering, diving, singing in flight, or flocking.

Habitat. Between pages 259 and 264 you can find out if the bird may be expected to occur in any one of 29 different types of habitat, such as built-up areas, sea cliffs, or reed-beds.

Migrants. If the bird is a migrant, the table on pages 265-271 will tell you whether it is the right time of year to see it.

The System of the Key. The system is, in fact, simply to find the common denominator, the only bird which tallies with all the features you have been able to see, and the time and place in which you saw it. An example is given on page 218.

The great majority of bird books arrange their birds according to the systematic scientific classification, but as this is apt to be confusing to bird-watchers in their early stages, a break has been made with tradition and the birds arranged in a way which it is hoped will prove more helpful to the beginner. They are first divided into three broad habitat groups (Land, Waterside, Water), and within each habitat group the birds are set out in ascending order of size in eight main groups based on the length of the bird. The text therefore constitutes a broad identification key in itself, for if, say, a small land bird about the size of a sparrow is seen, all the birds which it is likely to be will be found within a few pages of each other.

THE HABITAT GROUPINGS

The three main categories used throughout the book are defined as follows:

Land: Found predominantly on land away from water.

Waterside: Generally found in the neighbourhood of water, but not normally swimming on it.

Water: Normally flying over or swimming on water.

All water birds and many land birds may, of course, be seen temporarily at the water's edge, as water birds must come to land to nest, and land birds go to water to drink and bathe. Cross-references have been given in the appropriate place in the text wherever a bird can be classed as normally both 'Land' and 'Waterside' (e.g. lapwing), or 'Land' and 'Water' (e.g. common gull).

THE LENGTH GROUPS

Within each habitat grouping the birds are arranged in eight length groups, as nearly as possible in ascending order of size, starting with the smallest and ending with the largest. Thus, the book begins with the smallest British bird, the goldcrest, and ends with the largest, the mute swan. The eight groups are based on the overall length of the bird from the tip of the bill to the tip of the tail, and each is represented by a common bird.

Where cock and hen birds differ significantly in size, the smaller has been described first in the text, with a cross-reference in the appropriate size-position of the other. Where immature birds are markedly shorter than the adults, however, as with the skuas, the main description is given under the adult. (All young birds, of course, are smaller than adults in their early life, and this should be borne in mind in using the text; fortunately, young birds usually remain in family parties until they are more or less fully grown.) Certain birds vary considerably in size even in the adult state—the curlew is a good example—and here it has sometimes also been necessary to give cross-references to the main size-position.

To facilitate the use of the text, the habitat groupings and length groups, e.g. LAND-Short, or WATER-Long, are shown on the running headline at the top of the page. Within each length group, birds of the same family have been kept as close together as possible, without interrupting the size gradient.

Length Groups

Length Group	*Abbreviation*	*Type Bird*
1. Very Short	VS	Blue Tit
2. Short	S	House Sparrow
3. Medium Short	MS	Starling
4. Medium	M	Lapwing
5. Medium Long	ML	Rook
6. Long	L	Mallard
7. Very Long	VL	Cock Pheasant
8. Huge	H	Mute Swan

SOME DEFINITIONS

Throughout the text the words 'British' or 'in the British Isles' are to be understood as qualifying every statement, while such assertions as that 'the crossbill is the only bird with a crossed bill' must be understood to mean 'the only bird out of those mentioned in this book'. It is clearly impracticable so qualify such statements to cover all vagrant or escaped birds that might possibly be seen. Exceptions to this rule are indicated individually.

The word *juvenile* applies to plumages up to the first autumn moult; *immature* to plumages between the first autumn moult and assumption of full adult plumage; *young* to the juvenile and immature stages taken together; *eclipse* to the moult plumages of drakes (and occasionally ducks and game-birds) in the late summer and early autumn; *summer* to breeding plumages, which may in fact be assumed in late winter and lost in early summer; and *winter* to plumages assumed after the breeding season, i.e. in the converse period to the summer plumage. Thus, in the terns, for instance, Arctic terns may arrive on their breeding grounds with traces of their black winter bill-tip remaining, while Sandwich terns can regularly be seen at their colonies towards the end of their breeding season with the white foreheads which are characteristic of their winter plumage.

NAMES

The great majority of the English names used are those to be found in *The Handbook of British Birds* and other standard works, but changes have been made in a few cases where the current book-names either do not conform with general usage among bird-watchers or are needlessly cumbrous or misleading. All alternative names in current use, whether book-names or folk-names, are given as well, but it has not been easy to find out which folk-names are still in current use. For the benefit of bird-watchers from across the Atlantic, I have added the vernacular name from Roger Tory Peterson's *A Field Guide to the Birds*, where this differs from the British name for any bird, even where it is applied to a different geographical race. I have not, however, indicated where, as with the robin, the English name is applied to two quite different birds on opposite sides of the Atlantic. In the body of the text the need for compression has led to the omission of the group name when birds belonging to a particular group are being discussed, and then the specific name is italicised, e.g. in dealing with gulls, *common* and *herring* stand for the common gull and herring gull respectively.

The scientific name of a bird is part of the international language of science, enabling bird watchers in one country to know what those in another country are talking about, despite the language difficulty. A scientific name consists of two parts, a generic name, which comes first and is spelt with a capital initial, and a specific or trivial name, which follows it and is spelt with a small initial. For instance, the scientific name of the rook is *Corvus frugilegus*, which indicates that the rook belongs to the group or genus of true crows (*Corvus*), from other species of which it is sufficiently distinct to have been given the specific name of *frugilegus*. The scientific names in this book are those used in the British Ornithologists' Union's official list, with any necessary late amendments.

The further complication of geographical races is dealt with in Appendix II (p. 272-3). The various genera are grouped by systematists into larger groupings called families and orders. A list of the families represented in this book will be found in Appendix III (p. 274) in the correct systematic order. In the text, where the English name of a bird corresponds to the English name given to the family in the Appendix, the family is not shown; but where there is no such clue, the family to which the bird belongs is given.

PLUMAGE

A general description of all plumages likely to be seen in the British Isles is given, together with the colour of the bare parts (bill, legs, eyes). Feet are assumed to be the same colour as legs. Where the colour of the eye is not stated, it may be taken to be black or dark brown. See also under 'Some Definitions', above.

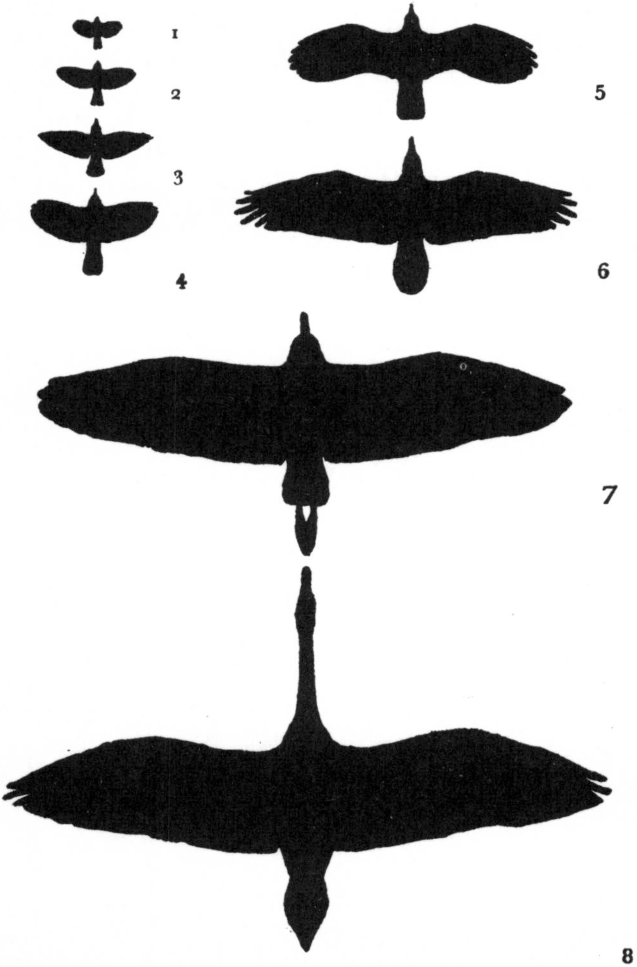

Wing-lengths (see p. 14)

STRUCTURE

This section contains coded information on the absolute length of the wing, and on the relative length of the wing, tail, neck, bill and legs. Some attempt has been made to define such usually vague terms as 'long' and 'short' by dividing each category up into a number of groups, represented by a type bird.

The eight *wing-length* or wing-span groups are based on the length of the wing from the carpal joint (which appears to be the elbow, but is actually the wrist of the bird) to the wing-tip. This is not a completely accurate representation of the wing-span, but is near enough to indicate which birds appear larger on the wing than they do at rest, e.g. swift, short-eared owl, shearwaters. Broadly speaking, if a bird ranks one group lower in wing-length than in overall length, it will appear smaller on the wing than at rest, and if it appears one group higher, it will appear larger on the wing than at rest.

Wing-Length Group	*Abbreviation*	*Type Bird*
1. Very Short	VS	Blue Tit
2. Short	S	House Sparrow
3. Medium Short	MS	Wheatear
4. Medium	M	Blackbird
5. Medium Long	ML	Lapwing
6. Long	L	Rook
7. Very Long	VL	Heron
8. Huge	H	Mute Swan

The *wing-ratio* groups need to be carefully distinguished from the wing-length groups. They indicate the relative length of a bird's wings to its body, as distinct from their absolute length. Thus the swift, a small bird with unusually long wings, is classed as 'medium long' on absolute wing-length, but as 'long' on relative wing-ratio. The wing-ratic represents the proportion of the wing-length to the overall length, and there are five size groups, viz.:

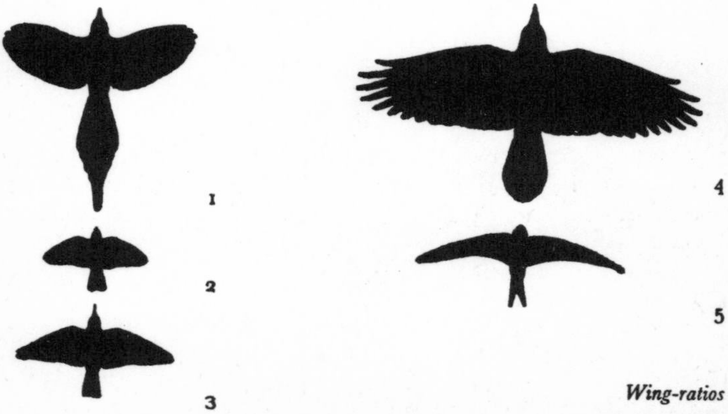

Wing-ratios

Wing-ratio Group	*Abbreviation*	*Type Bird*
1. Short	S	Magpie
2. Medium Short	MS	House Sparrow
3. Medium	M	Starling
4. Medium Long	ML	Rook
5. Long	L	Swift

The *tail-ratio* is again a measurement of relative rather than absolute length, and represents the length of the tail proportionately to the overall length of the bird minus the length of the bill. There are seven size groups, viz.:

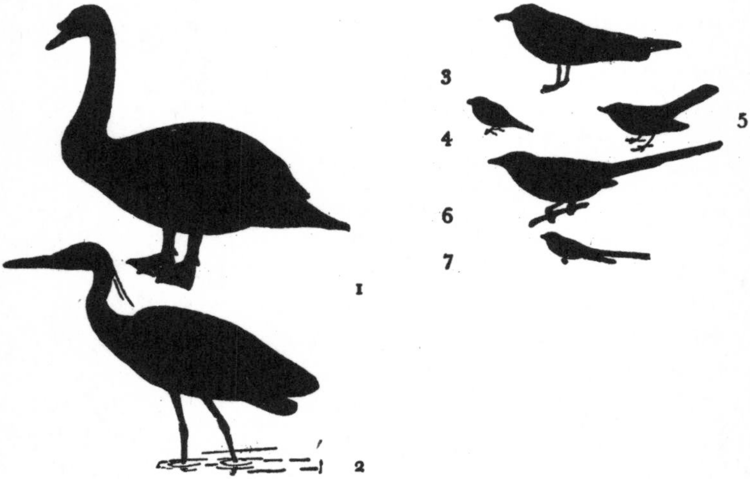

Tail-Ratio Group	*Abbreviation*	*Type Bird*
1. Very Short	VS	Mute Swan
2. Short	S	Heron
3. Medium Short	MS	Black-headed Gull
4. Medium	M	House Sparrow
5. Medium Long	ML	Blackbird
6. Long	L	Magpie
7. Very Long	VL	Swallow (adult)

The *neck-ratio* is the proportion of the head and neck together, including the hill, to the rest of the overall length. There are five size groups, viz.:

Neck-Ratio Group	*Abbreviation*	*Type Bird*
1. Short	S	House Sparrow
2. Medium Short	MS	Woodpigeon
3. Medium	M	Mallard
4. Long	L	Cormorant
5. Very Long	VL	Heron

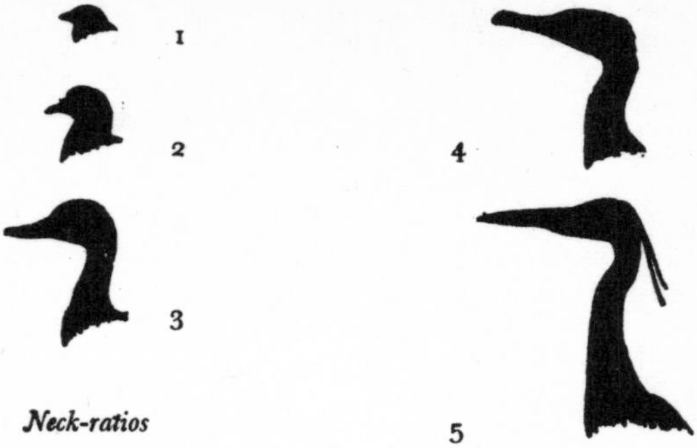

Neck-ratios

The *leg-ratio* represents the proportion of the tarsus plus the unfeathered portion of the tibia immediately above it (see p. 28) to the overall length minus the bill. Shearwaters, divers and grebes are regarded as having no legs, as they do not stand upright on them; note also that some of the auks often crouch rather than stand. It has proved impossible to arrive at a satisfactory set of size groups that take into account the longer necks and tails of many long-legged birds, so that many of them are classified as less long-legged than they appear. There are six size groups, viz.:

Leg-Ratio Group	*Abbreviation*	*Type Bird*
1. Very Short	VS	Kingfisher
2. Short	S	House Sparrow
3. Medium	M	Starling
4. Medium Long	ML	Heron
5. Long	L	Common Crane
6. Very Long	VL	Avocet

The final set of size groups is based not on overall length but on the length of the head and bill. The *bill-ratio* represents the proportion of the bill to a line drawn from the tip of the bill back through the eye to the back of the head. There are seven size groups, viz.:

Bill-Ratio Group	*Abbreviation*	*Type Bird*
1. Very Short	VS	Blue Tit
2. Short	S	House Sparrow
3. Medium Short	MS	Robin
4. Medium	M	Starling
5. Medium Long	ML	Heron
6. Long	L	Woodcock
7. Very Long	VL	Curlew

Leg-ratios

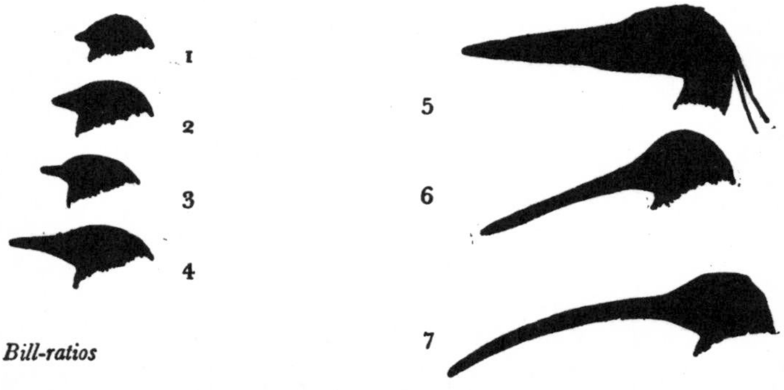

Bill-ratios

MOVEMENT

Details of flight and gait. Diving is assumed to be from the surface of the water unless otherwise stated.

VOICE

This is one of the most important aspects of bird identification, the call being often the only way of identifying, say, finches flying overhead in a poor light. Only calls and songs likely to be heard in the British Isles are given. To avoid confusion the notation adopted in *The Handbook of British Birds* has been used, except in a few cases where this is felt to be misleading. The songs or calls of 195 of the birds in this book can be found in *Witherby's Sound-Guide to British Birds*, by Myles North and Eric Simms (2 vols., £5 10*s.* each). The dozen excellent records offered by the Royal Society for the Protection of Birds (The Lodge, Sandy, Beds.) at 12*s.* each also cover 116 of these birds.

FIELD MARKS

This section contains various hints on field identification. Since a bird's voice is nearly always distinctive, this has not usually been repeated under 'Field Marks'.

FLOCKING

Where this section is omitted, the bird may be assumed to be solitary, and where no associates are given, it may be assumed that it does not normally consort with other species. 'Flocks' are taken to mean aggregations of a dozen or more birds, 'parties' consisting of groups from three to a dozen.

HABITAT

Definitions of general terms used throughout the text include: *coniferous woods*, woods consisting predominantly of cone-bearing trees, such as Scots pine, larch and spruce; *freshwater margins*, the edges of all kinds of fresh water, ponds, pools, lakes, rivers, streams and marshes; *coastal migration stations*, observatories on the coast for the study in particular of migration—the principal ones are the Fair Isle (Shetland), Isle of May (Firth of Forth), Spurn Head (Yorkshire), Gibraltar Point (Lincolnshire), Bradwell (Essex), Dungeness (Kent), St. Agnes (Scilly), Lundy (Bristol Channel), Skokholm (Pembrokeshire), and Bardsey (Caernarvonshire). Cley (Norfolk) and the Farne Islands (Northumberland) are also important points for the observation of migration.

RANGE AND STATUS

As a general rule the distribution as affecting the Scottish isles has been omitted, but any range which is given as 'almost throughout the British Isles' may be taken as indicating that some or all of the Scottish isles are the exception. References to the 'northern isles' are to Orkney and Shetland. Autumn immigration on the east coast may be assumed to be from the Continent (especially Scandinavia, the Baltic, N. Germany and the Low Countries); on the west coast, from Greenland, Iceland and the Faeroes. Details of the normal dates of arrival and departure of migrants will be found in Appendix I (p. 265).

Part III of the author's *Guide to Bird Watching* (Collins) consists of a comprehensive topographical guide, county by county, to suitable localities for bird watching throughout the British Isles.

NESTING

Details of the nests, eggs, young and breeding seasons of all British birds will be found in a companion volume, the author's *Pocket Guide to Nests and Eggs* (Collins).

THE BIRDS IN THE BOOK

In a book designed especially for those in the early stages of a bird-watching career it is clearly out of place to describe and illustrate every bird on what is usually called 'the British List'. This list, which is officially drawn up by the British Ornithologists' Union, the central representative body of British ornithology, includes all birds which are believed to have reached the British Isles unaided on at least one occasion, together with a handful of well-established birds that have been introduced by human agency, such as the Canada goose, pheasant and red-legged partridge. As at present constituted, the 'British List' includes many birds which have been recorded only once, or on a handful of occasions. Many more have been rejected on the grounds that they had probably escaped from captivity or must have rested on a vessel on their way across the Atlantic.

To eliminate all these stragglers, most of which the average bird watcher is highly unlikely ever to see in Britain, almost all birds which have been recorded in the British Isles on fewer than fifty occasions are omitted both from the main text and from the illustrations. Brief notice is accorded in the text to those species that have turned up between twenty and fifty times, and to a number of escapes of various kinds.

The aim of the present book, as has been stated already, is to enable a bird watcher to identify any bird he or she is reasonably likely to see on his walks in town or country. 'Any bird' is treated literally, so that a good many birds not ordinarily found in the pages of bird books appear here. For instance, a selection of ornamental waterfowl has been included, because not only are they liable to escape from zoos and other collections and turn up in unexpected places—indeed the Wildfowl Trust at the New Grounds in Gloucestershire pursues a deliberate policy of allowing certain full-winged waterfowl their liberty—but many people are obliged to limit their bird-watching to town parks, where ornamental waterfowl are the most conspicuous and attractive birds. The choice of these waterfowl was difficult and inevitably arbitrary, but all birds known to be at large or especially liable to escape have been included, with a few more known to be numerous in captivity.

Also included are a few cage birds that frequently escape (canary, budgerigar, Barbary dove), and a small number of the most confusing domestic birds likely to be encountered away from the farmyard on a country walk (Chinese goose, Khaki Campbell duck, Muscovy duck). The only birds whose identity is here assumed to be unmistakable are the farmyard fowl, duck, goose and turkey, other than the specialised forms of duck and goose just mentioned. To give some indication of the likelihood of encountering these domestic and ornamental birds at large, the author has himself met with the following in the British Isles during the past forty years: canary, budgerigar (nine times), black swan, bar-headed goose, Chinese goose, grey-headed and paradise shelducks, Khaki Campbell (on the Thames at Twickenham), farmyard duck (on the Solway), rosy-bill, Chiloe wigeon, ruddy duck, Bahama pintail and Muscovy duck. The majority of these ornamental waterfowl are treated only briefly in the text, but most of them are fully illustrated because of the difficulty of finding coloured pictures of them anywhere else. A few, such as the Canada and Egyptian geese and the mandarin duck, which are now well established as breeders in certain areas, and the ruddy shelduck, red-crested pochard and ferruginous duck, which are vagrants in their own right, are included in the main text.

A few other birds appear in the main text through elasticity in the strict application of the rules. The great black woodpecker, for instance, has been seen or shot on well over fifty occasions, some quite recent, but the authorities have not yet been satisfied that these birds had not been introduced by human agency. Since one of the difficulties in identifying the great black woodpecker has been the relative inaccessibility of coloured plates and field notes against which observations could be checked, it is included here as a British bird *manqué*. Some other birds that have genuinely occurred on fewer than fifty occasions are included in the main text and illustrations on various grounds: the serin, for instance, because it is spreading north-westwards in Europe and may perhaps become a more frequent visitor.

Finally, a word must be said on behalf of Britain's most neglected bird, the semi-domesticated or London pigeon. Though it has been living in a wild state in London for half a millennium and is to be found living quite wild in most of our largest towns to-day, the majority of bird books ignore it almost completely. I know of no published illustrations of any of its interesting range of plumages except on Plates 24 and 68 of this book.

A NOTE ON THE ILLUSTRATIONS

The illustrations are in two continuously numbered series, one in colour and one in black and white. The broad principle has been to give portraits in colour, except in a few cases where the bird's plumage is wholly black and white, and flight pictures in black and white, except in a few cases where colour is an important element in identifying the bird in flight. The aim has been to illustrate all plumages which are sufficiently distinct in the field to be identifiable on a reasonably good view. The only important exception to this rule has been in the case of the eclipse (moult) plumages assumed by drakes in the late summer and early autumn. These are mostly so similar to the normal plumages of the ducks (apart from the retention of the drakes' wing-pattern) that it has not been considered necessary to show them separately, except for the mallard (the most likely to be seen) and the eider (the least like the duck, and one of the most puzzling of all waterfowl plumages). With a few of the rarer vagrants the plumage of the immature bird only is shown, as adults are so rare as to fall outside the category of birds reasonably likely to be seen.

Flight pictures have been given of the majority of the commoner large birds, as so many of them are more often seen in flight than at rest, but not for the majority of the smaller land birds, many of which cannot be satisfactorily identified in flight unless they are calling.

The illustrations have been arranged in key form in both the colour and the black-and-white series. Each is divided broadly into the same three habitat groups as are used in the text, viz.: Land, Waterside, Water. Within each group, the plates consist of birds which are roughly similar in colour. With the flight-pictures of ducks and waders it has been possible to go further and to group them under categories, dependent on the colour of the rump or head, or the presence or absence of a wing-bar, which should be of assistance in making a first approximation to identifying a strange bird seen.

Scale is indicated on each plate by a black outline of a house sparrow. On plates 29, 30, 33, 34, 35, 41, 45, 55, 59, 60, 65, 66, 73, 77 and 83 this silhouette is unfortunately very slightly too large.

LIST OF PLATES

Birds are arranged in three broad habitat groupings (Land, Waterside, Water), with some unavoidable overlappings. For general notes on the arrangement of the plates, see page 21; and for explanation of code indicating size (vs, s, etc.), see page 11.

♂ signifies male; ♀ signifies female

COLOUR PLATES
(between pages 128-129)

LAND BIRDS

See also starred plates under Waterside birds
** Indicates some Waterside birds included*

WATERSIDE BIRDS

See also starred plates under Land and Water Birds
** Indicates some Land birds included*

WATER BIRDS

** Indicates some Waterside birds included*

BLACK-AND-WHITE PLATES

(in flight, except where indicated. Between pages 160-161)

LAND BIRDS

See also starred plates under Waterside Birds
** Indicates some Waterside birds included*

WATERSIDE BIRDS

See also starred plates under Land and Water Birds
** Indicates some Land birds included*

WATER BIRDS

* *Indicates some Waterside birds included*

INTRODUCTION TO BIRD-WATCHING

The aim of this book is to enable anybody who is interested in birds to identify any bird he or she is reasonably likely to see in the British Isles without any prior knowledge except the relative sizes of a handful of common birds, viz. blue tit, house sparrow, starling, lapwing, rook, mallard, cock pheasant and mute swan. The whole arrangement of the book is built up on eight groupings based on the lengths of these eight birds. For fuller details, see the section 'How to Use the Book' on p. 9.

Though bird-watching is becoming an increasingly popular pastime, many are still deterred from taking it up by the initial difficulty of telling one bird from another. 'One little brown bird', as Jefferies said, 'at a casual glance is so much like another little brown bird', and he added that there is no way of getting to know them except by learning them one by one as they come into song in the spring. This is indeed a better way than turning over the pages of a bird book till you come across a picture that looks like the bird you have just seen. Even so, it calls for some basic knowledge that you can only get in the first place from books or from a knowledgeable friend. There is, indeed, no primrose path to bird-watching proficiency, no short cut that does not involve the expenditure of much—extremely pleasurable—time and patience. But there is no reason at all why anybody with a pair of sharp eyes, a reasonably good ear and a capacity to sit and wait should not get a great deal of enjoyment from bird-watching in his leisure hours. If he has the integrity to record only what he is sure he has seen, he may also have the satisfaction of adding to the stock of known facts about birds.

It is most important not to start out with the idea that you should expect to be able to identify every bird you see, or even to know what it is doing. All honest bird-watchers, including (perhaps especially) the most eminent, must quite often fail to put a name to a bird because they do not have a good enough view of it. Naturally, however, with increasing experience the proportion of birds thus unidentified may be expected to diminish. The beginner may well be baffled at the way an old hand is able to pick out a bird at a distance and identify it with confidence before any details of its plumage can be seen. It is all a matter of practice and knowing what you are looking for.

Some birds have highly characteristic features—for instance, the hovering of the kestrel and the plummet-diving of the gannet—by which they can be identified with certainty when they are scarcely more than specks in the distance. Others, such as the chiffchaff and willow warbler or the marsh and willow tits, are so alike that even experts cannot be confident about them until they hear them call. Knowing what to look for does not, of course, mean that you should give full rein to your wishful thinking. It does mean, however, that you should start out with some idea in your mind of which parts of the bird to concentrate on in the few seconds that may be all you have before it passes out of range or behind a tree. In observing a wader in flight, for instance, it is useful to know that wing-bars and rumps are keys to the identity of many of this group. In the smaller birds of prey, on the other hand, the shape of the wing and the colour of the mantle are more important. To have seen that a small falcon has no wing-bar does not get you anywhere, but a note that it had a blue-grey head and tail and a chestnut mantle fixes it at once as a male kestrel.

THE USE OF FIELD GLASSES

By such devices as a bird-table it is often possible to lure birds near enough to the observer for them to be both identified and enjoyed with the use of the naked eye alone. But for general field purposes, when the observer is moving about the countryside or along the sea-shore, a pair of binoculars is essential. As there is now an excellent short booklet by J. R. Hebditch on *Binoculars and Telescopes for Field Use* (British Trust for Ornithology, Tring, 3*s*.), here it need only be said that the best magnifications for normal bird-watching purposes are 7 × and 8 ×. A 6 × glass is just adequate for the nearer distances, but lower than this cannot be advised. Nor are the 9 × and even larger magnifications now favoured by many bird-watchers necessary for the beginner. The most important quality of a pair of binoculars for bird-watching is its light-gathering power, measured by the figure that represents the diameter of the object-glass and is engraved on most binoculars after the magnification, e.g. 6 × 30, 7 × 40 or 8 × 50. The key figure is obtained by dividing the magnification into the diameter, and any result between 4 and 7 may be regarded as satisfactory, e.g. a 6 × 30 gives 5 and a 7 × 50 gives 7. Most people prefer binoculars that focus in the centre, which can be refocused more quickly than those in which each eyepiece is focused separately.

Telescopes are fashionable and much used by bird-watchers who spend much of their time visiting reservoirs and estuaries, where birds can often be seen only as specks away out on the water or on a distant tideline. In such places, of course, telescopes are very desirable, if not indispensable. In ordinary country, however, they are merely an additional burden on the back. With telescopes a magnification of 30 × or 40 × should be aimed at.

This and other technical aspects of bird-watching are discussed at greater length in Part 1 of the author's *Guide to Bird Watching* (Collins).

MAKING NOTES

If you have seen an unfamiliar bird and want to find out what it is, either by consulting a book yourself or by referring to a knowledgeable friend, it is essential to make accurate notes on what you have seen and not just to rely on your memory. The first and most important rule of note-taking is that it should be done on the spot. The unreliability of the human memory is such that by the time you have looked up a book or been cross-examined by a friend, what you have actually seen is likely to have become thoroughly scrambled up with the ideas later put into your head. Therefore a pencil and notebook are musts. If you can, make a sketch as well as written notes. Of course, it is better still to take the knowledgeable friend to see the bird, so try not to frighten it away.

What facts to note down is the next question that arises. Some people favour a system in which the main items are keyed into a code word, such as SECTOR recommended by the late Commander Robertson in the excellent chapter on bird-spotting in his *Birds Wild and Free* (1950), viz.:

- S Size and shape
- E Environment
- C Call-note, colouring and company
- T Tail and beak
- O Occupation
- R Remarks

Many, however, will prefer to devise their own code word, and it is certainly easier to remember the significance of each letter if you do. One way of setting about it is to run rapidly through the principal parts of the bird: upperparts, underparts, head, wings, tail, bill, legs and so forth. This is an excellent plan if the bird stays in front of you long enough for detailed notes to be taken, and in this connection it will probably be found helpful to memorise the drawing below.

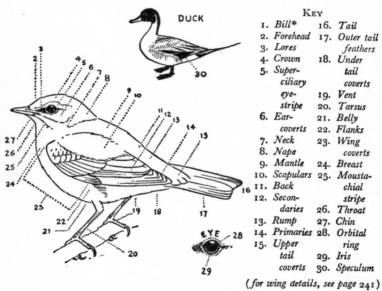

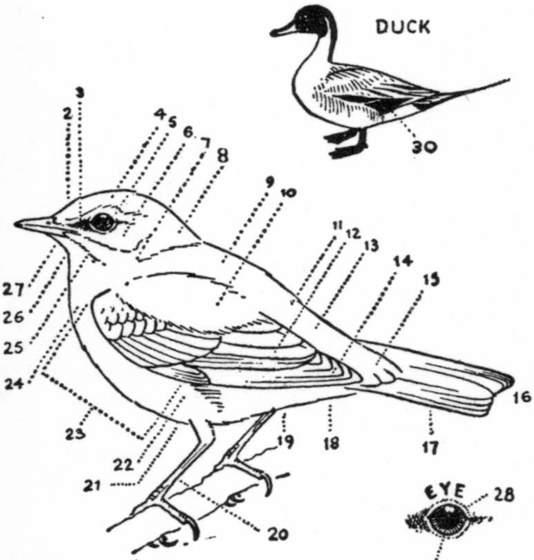

KEY

1. *Bill**
2. *Forehead*
3. *Lores*
4. *Crown*
5. *Super-ciliary eye-stripe*
6. *Ear-coverts*
7. *Neck*
8. *Nape*
9. *Mantle*
10. *Scapulars*
11. *Back*
12. *Secon-daries*
13. *Rump*
14. *Primaries*
15. *Upper tail coverts*
16. *Tail*
17. *Outer tail feathers*
18. *Under tail coverts*
19. *Vent*
20. *Tarsus*
21. *Belly*
22. *Flanks*
23. *Wing coverts*
24. *Breast*
25. *Mousta-chial stripe*
26. *Throat*
27. *Chin*
28. *Orbital ring*
29. *Iris*
30. *Speculum*

(*for wing details, see page* 241)

* Birds of prey and doves have a cere, a bare patch of skin containing the nostrils, at the base of the bill.

† Above the tarsus is the tibia, connected to it by the knee-like joint which is actually the bird's ankle.

All too often, however, you have only a matter of seconds in which to see what you can, and on such occasions the following headings are useful to bear in mind when making your notes after the bird has gone:

1. Size and general shape.
2. Size and shape of bill, legs, wings, tail, neck and other conspicuous parts of the body.
3. General colour above and below.
4. Any conspicuous marks or patches, their colour and approximate position on the bird.
5. Colour of bill, legs, feet and eye.
6. Actions and character of flight, and the characteristic cut or rig, which T. A. Coward used to call the 'jizz' of the bird.
7. Any call-notes or song.
8. Comparisons with any other bird that suggest themselves.
9. Habitat and general surroundings, e.g. in a tree, in a garden, in a village, or at a pool, on a salt-marsh, on an estuary.

These nine points, in the compilation of which I have consulted the published advice of those fine field ornithologists H. G. Alexander, the late B. W. Tucker and the late H. F. Witherby, should, when taken into consideration with the season and the geographical location, suffice to determine the identity of any common bird. Naturally, you cannot expect to be able to fill in details under each heading every time, and it need hardly be said that it is better to record nothing than something of which you are not sure. Should you have any reason to suspect that the bird you have seen is an uncommon one—and it is best not to give way to such suspicions until every possibility of a commoner species has been eliminated—then certain additional details should be recorded before the observation is submitted for the opinion of an expert. These may be briefly summarised as follows:

1. Date, time, place, weather.
2. Distance of bird from observer, and whether glasses used or not.
3. Angle of vision and conditions of light.
4. Whether bird was at rest, swimming or in flight.
5. Whether notes written down at the time, or later.
6. Whether the bird was seen by any other person.

Records of uncommon birds should be sent in the first place to the bird recorder of the appropriate county society or bird club, whose name and address may be obtained from the Intelligence Unit of the Council for Nature, c/o Zoological Society of London, Regent's Park, London, N.W.1. If the bird is thought to be a real rarity, a vagrant or rare vagrant, the record should be sent also to the Secretary of the Rarities Committee of *British Birds* (c/o 61 Watling St., London, E.C.4).

Many bird-watchers have contracted the habit of keeping a 'life list' of all the birds they have seen, and some also keep annual lists in the same way. Useful pocket lists of British birds can be obtained from the British Trust for Ornithology (Beech Grove, Tring, Herts). These 'field lists' can be used not only for annual and life lists but on day trips and holidays, and are a useful way of quickly noting down what you have seen.

DESCRIPTIONS OF BIRDS

For the plan of arrangement, and detailed notes on general points relating to the sub-headings under each bird, see pp. 9-19. If you want to find any particular bird quickly, use the index on p. 279.

LAND BIRDS: Very Short

RED-EARED WAX-BILL *Estrilda astrild*

Sparrow Family

A small finch-like cage bird from Africa, with whitish breast, pink belly, wax-red bill and conspicuous red eyestripe, frequently escaping but not establishing itself.

Red-eared Waxbill

GOLDCREST *Regulus regulus* Plate I — Kinglet Family

Golden-crested Wren; Kinglet.

PLUMAGE. Yellowish-green, with two whitish bars and a dark mark on wing; adult has black-bordered crest, orange in cock, yellow in hen and occasionally in cock. Thin blackish bill; brown legs.

STRUCTURE. *Wing length* vs. *Ratios:* wing M; tail ML; neck S; bill VS; legs M.

MOVEMENT. Undulating tit-like flight; rarely on ground.

VOICE. Call-note a thin 'zi' or 'zi-zi-zi', very liable to confusion with similar cries of treecreeper and tits, especially coal tit, except when uttered in intensified form, 'zi-zi-zi-zeee-zeee-zeee-zeee-zi-zi'. High-pitched song has distinctive pattern, 'cedar-cedar-cedar-cedar-sissu-pee'.

FIELD MARKS. Tiny size (3½ in.) marks it out from all other small yellowish-green birds, except firecrest and yellow-browed warbler, both of which are rare and have a white eyestripe; the commoner leaf warblers are all at least ¾ in. longer, and lack both wing-markings and crest.

FLOCKING. Often in small parties after breeding. especially accompanying winter tit flocks.

HABITAT. Woods, large gardens and other places with scattered trees, especially conifers, in which it almost invariably breeds; after breeding also on bushy heaths and commons, and hedgerows, where conifers not present.

RANGE AND STATUS. Resident, breeding almost throughout British Isles; often scarce after hard winters; many arrive E coast in autumn.

FIRECREST *Regulus ignicapillus* Plate 1 Kinglet Family

Fire-crested Wren.

PLUMAGE AND STRUCTURE. As goldcrest (above), but with a white stripe above the eye, a black line through it and a white mark under it; crest of both sexes orange like cock goldcrest; bronze patch on side of neck.

MOVEMENT. Undulating, tit-like flight; rarely on ground.

VOICE. Like goldcrest, but not so 'wiry' and intense; 'peep' or 'peep-peep'.

FIELD MARKS. Can be told from goldcrest by black and white eyestripes, and from other small yellowish-green birds also by tiny size and double wing-bar; note, however, that rare yellow-browed warbler (below) has both a stripe above the eye and a double wing-bar.

FLOCKING. Often in mixed parties of tits and goldcrests.

HABITAT. As goldcrest, but no special preference for conifers, and often in thickets and bramble-brakes.

RANGE AND STATUS. Annual winter visitor in very small numbers to coastal counties, Norfolk to Cornwall; much less often inland and elsewhere. Now breeds in Hampshire.

WREN *Troglodytes troglodytes* Plate 3

Jenny Wren; Winter Wren (N America).

PLUMAGE. Rufous brown barred darker, especially on wings, tail and flanks. Thin brownish bill, flesh-brown legs.

STRUCTURE. *Wing length* vs. *Ratios:* wing MS; tail M; neck S; bill S; legs M.

MOVEMENT. Flight whirring; hops; often creeps among undergrowth like mouse; almost always has tail cocked up.

VOICE. Usual call-note an irritable 'tic-tic-tic', often prolonged into a scolding trill. Vigorous, clear warbling song is louder than would be expected from so small a bird, and is usually delivered from a perch.

FIELD MARKS. The smallest warm-brown bird, its barred plumage and cocked-up tail make it almost unmistakable; in flight rufous tail contrasts strongly with darker brown wings.

HABITAT. Almost universal on land, from rocky mountain tops to marine islands, but not in centre of large cities; prefers areas with low scrub, brambles and bushes, but is satisfied with rocks and stone walls; a common suburban bird.

RANGE AND STATUS. Resident, breeding throughout British Isles; may be scarce after very hard winters; migratory movements on E coast.

RED AVADAVAT *Amandava amandava* Sparrow Family

Tiger Finch or Strawberry Finch

A small cage bird from India and SE Asia, with bright red bill and black tail; cocks are red with rufous brown wings, hens and out-of-colour cocks are fawn with red rumps; frequently escaping but not establishing itself.

YELLOW-BROWED WARBLER *Phylloscopus inornatus* Plate I

A leaf warbler.

PLUMAGE. Greenish-brown, with paler underparts; pale stripe over eye and double wing-bar. Thin brown bill; brownish legs.

Red Avadavat (♂ in breeding 'red')

STRUCTURE. *Wing length* VS. *Ratios:* wing MS; tail M; neck S; bill S; legs M.

MOVEMENT. Restless, flitting flight; rather skulking; hops.

VOICE. Call-note an intense, penetrating 'swee'.

FIELD MARKS. Can be told from other leaf warblers by small size, light eyestripe and double wing-bar; from goldcrest and firecrest by slightly larger size, lack of crest and of dark mark on wing; goldcrest has no eyestripe, and firecrest has triple one.

HABITAT. Mostly seen at coastal migration stations.

RANGE AND STATUS. Passage migrant in small numbers on E coast, regular on Fair Isle and probably overlooked elsewhere; a Siberian bird, which migrates westwards in small numbers every year.

WILLOW WARBLER *Phylloscopus trochilus* Plate I

Willow Wren; a leaf warbler.

PLUMAGE. Greenish olive-brown, with paler underparts tinged yellow, especially in juvenile. Thin brown bill; dark brown to flesh-coloured legs.

STRUCTURE. *Wing length* S. *Ratios:* wing M; tail ML/L; neck S; bill S; legs M.

MOVEMENT. Restless, flitting flight; hops.

VOICE. Call-note a gentle disyllabic 'hooeet' like common redstart. Song, a fluent series of rather similar wistful descending notes, is quite different from chiffchaff, and is commonest bird-song in woods from April to June.

FIELD MARKS. Can only safely be separated from chiffchaff by song, unless at close range yellow tinge of underparts can be made out (this is most obvious in juveniles in autumn). Chiffchaffs usually look less green above and whiter below, but position is complicated by existence of two colour forms of migrant Northern race of *willow*, one identical with breeding birds, the other much browner above and whiter below. Until recently it was thought that chiffchaffs could always be told from willow warblers by their darker legs, but intensive trapping has shown that some willow warblers also have dark legs; it is still, however, safe to say that a bird with flesh-coloured legs is a *willow*. Larger *wood* has yellow eyestripe, throat and breast, and white underparts; smaller *yellow-browed* has a prominent yellowish eyestripe and a double wing-bar.

FLOCKING. Not gregarious, but will accompany foraging parties of tits in autumn.

HABITAT. Woods, and other well-timbered and bushy places, such as heaths, commons, shrubberies and large gardens; no special preference for willows.

RANGE AND STATUS. Summer visitor, breeding almost throughout the British Isles, and passage migrant; Northern race is also passage migrant, probably regular.

CHIFFCHAFF *Phylloscopus collybita* Plate 1 Warbler Family

A leaf warbler.

PLUMAGE. Greenish olive-brown, paler beneath; inclined to be less green above and whiter below than willow warbler. Thin, blackish bill; dark brown legs.

STRUCTURE. As willow warbler (above), but wing length vs/s.

MOVEMENT. A restless flitting flight; hops.

VOICE. Call-note a monosyllabic 'hweet' not unlike willow warbler, but song is totally different, consisting of a monotonous 'chiff-chaff' or 'zip-zap', repeated several times and sometimes interspersed with a guttural little 'chirr-chirr', which is only audible at close range.

FIELD MARKS. See above for distinctions from *willow* and other leaf warblers; the Scandinavian and Siberian races cannot be separated from each other in the field, but both differ from the breeding form by greyer upperparts and much whiter underparts, and Siberian bird has a distinctive, 'sad' single note.

FLOCKING. As willow warbler.

HABITAT. As willow warbler, but in breeding season needs trees at least 15 ft. high to sing from, and brambles or other undergrowth to nest in, so usually in more wooded areas.

RANGE AND STATUS. Summer visitor, except in Scotland, where only breeds locally as far N as Firth of Forth; also passage migrant; very small numbers winter in SW England and S Wales; Scandinavian and Siberian races are passage migrants on E coast, regular on Fair Isle, and probably overlooked elsewhere.

GREENISH WARBLER *Phylloscopus trochiloides*

Like a chiffchaff (above) with a conspicuous pale eyestripe and wing-bar; rare but increasing visitor, mainly to E coast, and in autumn.

COAL TIT *Parus ater* Plate 2

Cole Tit.

PLUMAGE. Olive-grey above and buff beneath, with black crown and throat, and white cheeks and nape. Juvenile and Irish race are yellowish on the white parts. Black bill; grey-blue legs.

STRUCTURE. *Wing length* vs. *Ratios:* wing MS; tail M; neck S; bill VS; legs M.

MOVEMENT. As blue tit (below), but even more prone to creep up trees.

VOICE. Like other tits has a varied range of notes, many resembling more or less closely those of other tits and only distinguishable by experience; characteristic notes include 'tsüü', 'tsüi', 'ticha, ticha', and a thin 'tsee', easily confused with goldcrest. Song is a miniature of great tit's (p. 52) saw-sharpening note.

FIELD MARKS. The smallest tit; can be told at once from other black-capped tits (great, marsh, willow) by prominent white patch on nape; in juvenile this patch is yellowish and must not be confused with yellowish patch on nape of larger, black-bibbed great tit; blue tit also has white nape-patch, but no black on head; *coal* can also be told from marsh and willow tits by its double white wing-bar.

FLOCKING. As blue tit (below), but less predominant in flocks; in conifer woods associates particularly with goldcrest.

HABITAT. Woods, and places with scattered trees, with especial preference for conifers; less often in gardens and city parks and at bird-tables than great and blue tits.

RANGE AND STATUS. Resident almost throughout Great Britain; Irish race breeds throughout Ireland.

CRESTED TIT *Parus cristatus* Plate 2

PLUMAGE. Brown above and paler below, prominent black and white crest, white cheeks, no wing-bar. Black bill, greyish-olive legs.

STRUCTURE. *Wing length* VS/S. *Ratios:* wing M; tail M/ML; neck S; bill S; legs M.

MOVEMENT. As coal tit (above).

VOICE. Unlike other tits, has only a characteristic short trill and the usual 'si-si-si' contact-note.

FIELD MARKS. Can be told from all other small birds by crest and trill, from coal tit also by lack of wing-bar.

FLOCKING. As coal tit, with which it especially consorts.

HABITAT. Confined to pine forests.

RANGE AND STATUS. Resident, breeding only in the Scottish Highlands, especially Strathspey and Strathnairn.

BLUE TIT *Parus caeruleus* Plate 2

Tom Tit, Pick-cheese.

PLUMAGE. Bright blue on head, wings and tail; white cheeks and patch on nape, yellowish-green mantle, yellow underparts with dark line down belly. Juvenile is duller with yellowish cheeks and nape patch. Black bill; dark blue-grey legs.

STRUCTURE. *Wing length* VS/S. *Ratios:* wing M; tail M/ML; neck S; bill VS; legs M.

MOVEMENT. Flight weak, and undulating when at all prolonged; hops; will creep up tree-trunks like a treecreeper.

VOICE. Characteristic note is cheerful, scolding, 'tsee-tsee-tsee, tsit', but has many others, mostly akin to those of other tits, and its vocabulary must be learnt the hard way. Song may be rendered 'tsee-tsee-tsütsühühühühühü'. Hen has explosive hissing throat-display on nest.

FIELD MARKS. The only small bird which appears predominantly blue; white patch on nape must not be confused with white patch on nape of black-capped coal tit.

FLOCKING. Very sociable after breeding, often forming the bulk of tit parties, and accompanied by goldcrests and leaf warblers.

HABITAT. Woods, copses, gardens, orchards and other places with scattered trees; common in city parks and squares, also often in winter in reed-beds and dykes overgrown with reed or sedge.

RANGE AND STATUS. Resident, but scarce and local in NW Scotland; migration sometimes observed on E coast in autumn, apparently partly of Continental origin.

MARSH TIT *Parus palustris* Plate 2

PLUMAGE. Brown, with black crown and chin, and paler cheeks and underparts. Black bill; blue-grey legs.

STRUCTURE. *Wing length* VS. *Ratios:* wing MS; tail M; neck S; bill VS; legs M.

MOVEMENT. Flight weak, and undulating when at all prolonged; hops.

VOICE. Has the wide range of notes usual with tits, and two or three characteristic ones which are the best means of telling it from willow tit, viz. 'pitchüü', a scolding 'chickabeebeebeebee', and a harsh 'tchay', not unlike *willow* but less nasal and usually preceded by 'pitchüü'. Song, usually rendered 'schip-schip-schip' or 'schüppi-schüppi-schüppi' is also quite distinct from *willow*.

FIELD MARKS. Can be told from great tit by size; from *great, blue* and *coal* by lack of white patch on nape; from *blue* also by black crown; and from all three by lack of wing-bar and pale, not white, cheeks. Can best be told from willow tit by voice (see below), but also in good light by no pale patch on wing and glossy, not sooty, black crown (but note that in some *willow* pale patch is very faint, and that young *marsh* also have sooty caps). Is distinctly smaller and less grey than cock blackcap, which has longer bill and no black chin.

FLOCKING. Odd birds accompany many tit parties in winter.

HABITAT. Woods, copses and places with scattered trees, but not often in parks and gardens, and rarely in urban or suburban areas; has no special preference for marshy areas.

RANGE AND STATUS. Resident in England and Wales, but very local in Cornwall, Cumberland, Northumberland and N Wales; only Berwickshire in Scotland.

WILLOW TIT *Parus montanus* Plate 2

PLUMAGE. Almost identical with marsh tit (above), except for light patch on wing (edges to secondaries) and sooty black cap.

STRUCTURE. *Wing length* VS/S. *Ratios:* wing MS; tail M; neck S; bill VS; legs M.

MOVEMENT. Flight weak, and undulating when at all prolonged; hops.

VOICE. Most characteristic note is very harsh, nasal 'tchay', or 'aig', usually uttered in triplicate, sometimes preceded by 'chick' or 'chichit', but never by the marsh tit's 'pitchüü'; once the observer has learnt to recognise the almost grating quality of this note compared with the *marsh's* 'tchay', it can confidently be used to separate the two species. Another call-note which the *marsh* lacks is the *willow's* thin 'eez-eez-eez', not to be confused with the high-pitched 'si-si-si' common to most tits. Song is also distinctive, but is not often heard; full song comprises a series of strikingly liquid garden-warbler-like notes, quite unlike those of any other tit, interspersed with high-pitched, almost squeaky, notes, and uttered with a blackcap's spasmodic delivery; an alternative and commoner song consists of full-throated 'piu-piu' notes, not unlike the plaintive call of the wood warbler.

FIELD MARKS. See marsh tit (above), and Voice.

FLOCKING. Less prone to join winter tit parties than marsh tit.

HABITAT. Very similar to marsh tit, but even less partial to neighbourhood of human settlement; often breeds in marshy areas with rotten trees where it can excavate nesting-holes (*marsh* seldom makes its own hole), but has no special preference for willows; in winter odd birds and pairs often frequent hedges, commons, heaths, etc.

RANGE AND STATUS. Resident, but range still imperfectly worked out because not discovered in Britain till 1897; local in most parts of England and Wales. commonest in SE and part of N England; in Scotland even more local as far N as Ross, and commonest in Lanark.

RED-BREASTED FLYCATCHER *Muscicapa parva* Plates 4, 7, 10

PLUMAGE. Ashy-brown above, paler below; cock has red throat and upper breast; hen and immature have whitish underparts; all have prominent white patches at base of tail. Typical flattish flycatcher bill is brown; legs dark brown.

STRUCTURE. *Wing length* S. *Ratios:* wing M; tail ML; neck S; bill S; legs M.

MOVEMENT. Much as spotted flycatcher, but more skulking.

VOICE. Has a loud 'pfiff' call, and a wren-like chattering or scolding note.

FIELD MARKS. Can be told from all other small brown birds by flycatching habits, coupled with striking white marks at base of tail, and cock's red throat and breast; tail is frequently flicked up, revealing the white marks, so that no bird seen at close range should remain long in doubt; it is a full inch shorter than *spotted* (which has no white in tail), and lacks the white wing-bar of the slightly larger *pied*; neither of these has red on the breast. Whinchat is streaked above and has creamy eyestripe.

HABITAT. Mostly at coastal migration stations.

RANGE AND STATUS. Irregular passage migrant, most often on E coast, especially Norfolk, where half the specimens recorded in England have occurred.

SUBALPINE WARBLER *Sylvia cantillans*

Like a small pale Dartford warbler (p. 42), with a conspicuous white moustachial stripe, unspotted throat and whiter edging to shorter tail; increasing but still rare vagrant, especially in spring and in Irish Sea area.

ARCTIC WARBLER *Phylloscopus borealis*

Like a large willow warbler (p. 33), nearly wood warbler (p. 41) size, with pale whitish underparts, wing-bar and eyestripe; rare but increasing autumn visitor to E coast, especially Fair Isle.

SAND MARTIN See *Waterside: Very Short*, p. 117

SERIN and CANARY *Serinus canarius* Plate 12 Finch Family

PLUMAGE. Serin is yellowish-green with darker streaks and bright yellow rump, cock being bright yellow on head and breast, but hen duller. Canary varies from plumages like serin or siskin, the so-called 'mules', through various patterns of yellow and white, to completely yellow. Both have cleft tail, dark brown to flesh-brown bill, and flesh-brown legs.

STRUCTURE. *Wing length* s. *Ratios:* wing M; tail M/ML; neck s; bill s; legs s/M.

MOVEMENT Flight bounding; hops.

VOICE. Serin has flight-note 'tirrilillit' and curious, whispering, jingling song, like miniature corn bunting but more sustained. Canary has call-note 'tsooeet', and song of same basic pattern as serin, but sweet and lyrical.

FIELD MARKS. Serin can be told from siskin by lack of yellow at base of tail and much more prominent yellow rump, and cock serin from cock siskin also by lack of black on head and chin; from greenfinch by smaller size and lack of yellow wing-bar.

Any completely yellow or yellow and white small bird with a shortish tail is most likely to be an escaped canary, but beware possibility of cock siskin (black on head and chin, yellow at base of tail), cock yellow wagtail (longish tail), or cock yellowhammer (chestnut rump). Mule canaries present more difficulty, and careful comparison needs to be made with field characters of serin, siskin, female and juvenile yellowhammer and cirl bunting, in conjunction with habits of any bird in doubt. Extreme variability of plumage of domesticated canaries makes exact guidance impossible.

FLOCKING. Serin might occur in flocks of other finches; escaped canaries often join flocks of sparrows and finches.

HABITAT. Serin should be listened for in well-timbered urban areas in spring; in autumn as other finches. Escaped canaries most likely to be seen near towns and villages.

RANGE AND STATUS. Serin is a vagrant, recorded in British Isles only 60-70 times, but as it has spread NW in Europe during past century and now breeds all along Channel and North Sea coasts from France to Denmark, it may well attempt to colonise SE England. Canary is an escaped cage bird, not infrequently to be seen at large.

GOLDFINCH *Carduelis carduelis* Plates 11, 12, and p. 56
Draw-water; King Harry.

PLUMAGE. A striking mixture of red, white, black, yellow and brown. Juvenile is streaked and lacks the adult's red face, but has the yellow wing-bar. Tail cleft; legs and stout bill are pale flesh-coloured.

STRUCTURE. *Wing length* s. *Ratios:* wing ML; tail M; neck s; bill MS; legs s.

MOVEMENT. Flight bounding and buoyant, flocks seeming to dance in the air like stringless puppets; hops.

VOICE. Flight-note a liquid 'tswitt-witt-witt', also a rather harsh 'geez'. Song, uttered from tree or in air, consists of tinkling variations on the flight-note.

FIELD MARKS. Adult is the only bird with a red face and a yellow wing-bar; whitish rump conspicuous when flying away; juvenile can also be told from young greenfinch by white tips to wing-feathers and lack of yellow in tail.

FLOCKING. Gregarious, but usually only in parties of a score or less; often with redpolls and siskins on alders and birches, and with other seed-eaters on stubbles.

HABITAT. Breeds mostly in large gardens and orchards, but also in open woodland and thick hedgerows; habitually feeds on thistles and other tall weeds, also alders and birches, and will visit stubbles and other places favoured by seed-eaters.

RANGE AND STATUS. Resident but local, and absent from much of Scottish Highlands; regular migrant along E coast in autumn.

SISKIN *Carduelis spinus* Plate 12 Finch Family

PLUMAGE. Cock mainly yellowish-green, streaked darker, with yellow rump and black chin and crown. Hen and juvenile much less yellow and more streaked, with no black on head. Tail cleft; legs and stout bill, dark brown.

STRUCTURE. *Wing length* S. *Ratios:* wing M; tail M; neck S; bill S; legs S.

MOVEMENT. Flight bounding, also a bat-like circular display flight; hops.

VOICE. Most frequent calls are 'tsüü' and 'tsyzing'. Sweet, twittering song is uttered from tree or in display flight.

FIELD MARKS. In good light, cock much yellower than any other finch except canary, from which can be told by black crown and chin; in poor light hard to tell from redpolls in mixed flocks except by somewhat shorter tail and dumpier appearance; a yellow wing-bar shows in flight; at all ages can be told from all finches except larger greenfinch by yellow at base of tail.

FLOCKING. Gregarious, habitually with redpolls and sometimes with goldfinches in winter.

HABITAT. Breeds mainly in coniferous woods, but also in other woods and even gardens with conifers; in winter often feeds in birches and alders.

RANGE AND STATUS. Resident, breeding over most of Scottish Highlands, locally on either side of Solway and in Ireland, and very occasionally in S; in winter also rather local in England and Wales.

REDPOLL *Carduelis flammea* Plates 10, 11 Finch Family

PLUMAGE. Brownish, streaked darker; adult has red forehead and black chin, and breeding cock also pink breast and rump. Juvenile lacks all red and pink. Cleft tail; stout, yellowish bill; dark brown legs.

STRUCTURE. *Wing length* S. *Ratios:* wing M; tail ML; neck S; bill S; legs S.

MOVEMENT. Flight bounding and nearly as buoyant as goldfinch, also a circular display flight, rather less bat-like than greenfinch and siskin; hops.

VOICE. Characteristic flight-note, 'chuch-uch-uch-uch', alternating with 'errrr', which often enables bird to be picked up when flying at a distance, also forms basis of somewhat primitive song, delivered from tree or bush or more often in display flight; also a 'tsooeet' note like other finches.

FIELD MARKS. Can always be told from other small brown finches by black or blackish chin; adult can also be told from all except cock linnet (which has chestnut upperparts and much redder breast) by red forehead; slightly longer tail marks out redpolls from siskins in mixed flocks even in poor light when lack of yellow in plumage cannot be seen.

Far the commonest form of redpoll in Britain is the resident lesser redpoll, but the paler mealy and the larger Greenland redpolls also occur; those who are thoroughly familiar with the range of variation in the *lesser* may pick out the slightly larger *mealy* by its paler plumage with whiter wing-bar and much paler rump showing in flight (see also Arctic redpoll, below); *Greenland* is a trifle larger than *mealy*, but is as dark as *lesser* in plumage, and has three or four bold streaks on flanks.

FLOCKING. Gregarious, and often with other finches in winter, especially siskins and goldfinches at alders and birches.

HABITAT. Breeds on heaths and in copses with birch and alder, also among conifers, in large gardens and shrubberies; not uncommon in some suburban areas; in winter most often feeds on birches and alders, but also in other places favoured by seed-eaters, including salt-marshes (*mealy*).

RANGE AND STATUS. *Lesser* is local resident over most of England and Wales, commoner in parts of Scotland, and general in Ireland; flocks of redpolls, sometimes including *mealies*, arrive E coast in autumn; *Greenlands* arrive at same time from NW and appear to be annual passage migrants in Fair Isle and probably elsewhere in Scotland and Ireland; in winter redpolls are more generally distributed.

ARCTIC REDPOLL (including Coues's, Hornemann's and Hoary Redpolls) (*Carduelis hornemanni*); Finch family. Similar to mealy and lesser redpolls, but can be told by unstreaked white rump and underparts. Rare vagrant from Greenland and Lapland.

TREECREEPER *Certhia familiaris* Plate 4 Creeper Family
Brown Creeper (N America).

PLUMAGE. Brown with paler streaks above, silvery-white below. Curved brown bill; pale brown legs.

STRUCTURE. *Wing length* vs/s. *Ratios:* wing MS; tail ML; neck S; bill MS; legs M.

MOVEMENT. Flight weak and undulating, and rarely sustained, except for curious bat-like display flight, which is not often seen; creeps up trees and along branches, when it looks at first sight more like a mouse than a bird.

VOICE. Call-note a very high-pitched and rather prolonged 'tsee', also a tit-like 'tsit'. Song, delivered always from a tree, is also very high-pitched, and may be rendered 'tee-tee-tee-tititidooee'; once the 'tseee' and the song are learnt it will be found that the bird is much more often heard than seen.

FIELD MARKS. The only small land bird with a curved beak, and apart from the wryneck, the only small brown bird that habitually creeps about tree-trunks. (N.B.—It is virtually impossible to differentiate it in the field from the Continental short-toed treecreeper (*C. brachydactyla*), except by voice, the latter having a loud piping call-note, sometimes uttered as a trill, and a quite distinct song; the short-toed treecreeper has never been recorded in Britain, but it seems unlikely that vagrants never get blown across the Channel, so that any treecreeper making an unfamiliar sound should be sharply scrutinised for the rather greyer appearance and slightly longer bill of the short-toed.)

FLOCKING. Never in more than family parties, but one or two accompany many winter foraging parties of tits and goldcrests.

HABITAT. Exclusively in trees, mostly in woods and copses, but also in well-timbered parks and gardens and occasionally in trees in hedgerows and town streets.

RANGE AND STATUS. Resident almost throughout British Isles.

PIED FLYCATCHER *Ficedula hypoleuca* Plates 4, 5, 16

PLUMAGE. Breeding cock is strikingly pied, being black above with white forehead; hen and winter cock are olive-brown above, cock retaining white forehead; juvenile is olive-brown above, spotted paler; all have white underparts, wing-bars and outer tail-feathers. Legs and typical flattish flycatcher bill are black.

STRUCTURE. *Wing length* S. *Ratios:* wing M; tail M/ML; neck S; bill S; legs M.

MOVEMENT. Much as spotted flycatcher (p. 49), but nearly always returns to a different perch after catching its fly. Constantly flicks wings and tail.

VOICE: Call-notes, 'whit' like swallow, and 'whit-tic' like chats and redstarts. Song, usually delivered from perch, is rather varied, not unlike redstart in one phase, and has been aptly rendered as 'tree, tree, tree, once more I come to thee'.

FIELD MARKS. Cock looks very white from front, and no other small black and white bird has its flycatching habit; hen and juvenile are rather like small hen chaffinch without white shoulder-patch, and can also be told by flycatching habit, coupled with white wing-bar. Spotted flycatcher is larger and has no wing-bar; red-breasted flycatcher is smaller and has white at base of tail and no wing-bar.

FLOCKING. Not gregarious, but travels in loose parties on migration, often accompanying common redstarts.

HABITAT. Woods, and all well-timbered places, including parks, orchards and large gardens; especially fond of wooded combes and cloughs in hill country; on migration also in treeless places on coast.

RANGE AND STATUS. Summer visitor to parts of Wales, W and N England and S Scotland; breeds commonly in Forest of Dean (Glos.) and thinly on English side of Welsh border N to S Salop; also on N York Moors and on both sides of Scottish border from NW Yorks N to Dumfries and Midlothian; very local in the Highlands, elsewhere a passage migrant, regular on E coast, but rather sporadic elsewhere.

WOOD WARBLER *Phylloscopus sibilatrix* Plate 1

Wood Wren; a leaf warbler.

PLUMAGE. Greenish-brown above, with yellow breast and white underparts; a noticeable yellow eyestripe. Thin brownish bill; yellowish legs.

STRUCTURE. *Wing length* S. *Ratios:* wing M; tail M; neck S; bill S; legs M.

MOVEMENT. Restless, flitting flight; hops.

VOICE. Anxiety note, a mellow, plaintive 'dee-ur' or 'püü', sometimes recalling the bullfinch's pipe. Has two quite different and distinctive songs, a long, quivering trill, and a plangent repetition of the anxiety note.

FIELD MARKS. Can be told from other leaf warblers by larger size, eyestripe and yellow and white underparts, and of course voice; see also icterine warbler (p. 47).

FLOCKING. Family parties only.

HABITAT. Exclusively woodland, especially woods with sparse undergrowth, such as beechwoods on the chalk and limestone, and the valley oakwoods and birchwoods of Wales and W Scotland, which are also favoured by the pied flycatcher and common redstart; occasionally in coniferous woods.

RANGE AND STATUS. Summer visitor, widespread, but rather local in S and E England, Midlands and NW Scotland; extremely scarce and local in Ireland; irregular passage migrant on E coast.

GRASSHOPPER WARBLER *Locustella naevia* Plate 3

Reel Bird; Reeler.

PLUMAGE. Brown, with upperparts streaked darker, and paler underparts; tail graduated, thin brownish bill, pink legs.

STRUCTURE. *Wing length* VS/S. *Ratios:* wing MS; tail M/ML; neck S; bill S; legs M.

MOVEMENT. Has a typical flitting warbler flight, but rarely takes wing, and then dives quickly into cover, where it skulks and creeps through the undergrowth like a mouse.

VOICE. Call-note 'tchick'; song is much more like an angler's reel or a loud free-wheel on a bicycle than any British grasshopper; may be delivered from thick cover or an exposed spray, or even in flight, and often at night.

FIELD MARKS. A very retiring bird, which is usually detected by its unmistakable reeling song (much more high-pitched than the nightjar); can be told from other warblers by the dark streaks on the upperparts combined with the graduated, elliptical tail (which looks heavy in flight), and in particular from sedge warbler by streaked rump and lack of prominent eyestripe.

HABITAT. Heaths, commons, sites of felled woodland, osier-beds and other places, both damp and dry, where there are scattered bushes and bramble-brakes, and a good deal of coarse vegetation growing up among them.

RANGE AND STATUS. Summer visitor, but remarkably local, and absent from N Scotland; passage migrant on both E and W coasts.

MARSH WARBLER See *Waterside: Very Short*, p. 118

DARTFORD WARBLER *Sylvia undata* Plate 4

Furze Wren.

PLUMAGE. Dark brown, with dark grey head, pale-spotted throat, pinkish-brown underparts and pale edging to graduated tail. Thin blackish bill; yellow legs; reddish-brown eye with bright-red orbital ring.

STRUCTURE. *Wing length* VS. *Ratios:* wing S; tail L; neck S; bill S; legs M.

MOVEMENT. Flies in typical flitting warbler fashion, but is extremely skulking, except when cock is singing from bush-top or in dancing song-flight.

VOICE. Call-notes similar to common whitethroat (p. 48), but perhaps more grating; also a scolding 'jer-jit'; song like common whitethroat.

FIELD MARKS. Combination of dark plumage, pinkish-brown underparts, and long, graduated, white-edged tail is unique among small birds, but all too often all that can be seen is a small dark bird with a longish tail rapidly disappearing into a gorse bush.

FLOCKING. In small parties out of breeding season.

HABITAT. Heaths and commons, especially on Greensand, with tall heather or thick gorse, also on gorsy downs.

RANGE AND STATUS. Resident, though almost exterminated by severe winter of 1963; breeds only in S and SE England, except for an outlying colony in SW England; rare vagrant elsewhere in S England and Midlands.

WHINCHAT *Saxicola rubetra* Plates 5, 7, 10 Thrush Family

PLUMAGE. Brownish, streaked darker above; underparts buff, deepest on breast, and streaked in juvenile; eyestripe white in cock, buffish in hen and juvenile; white chin and wing-patch, most prominent in cock. Black bill and legs.

STRUCTURE. *Wing length* S. *Ratios:* wing M; tail M; neck S; bill S; legs M.

MOVEMENT. Flitting flight, frequently flycatching; hops; fond of perching prominently on low bush or tall plant.

VOICE. Chief call-note is 'tic-tic' or 'u-tic', usually uttered while flicking tail. Song, usually delivered from a low perch, is a brief squeaky warble, similar to wheatear and stonechat, and sometimes mimetic.

FIELD MARKS. The only small brown bird with a prominent white eyestripe that habitually perches conspicuously on a low eminence (sedge warbler, which also has light eyestripe, is rather skulking); white sides to base of tail are additional distinction from hen and juvenile stonechat; cock seen from front in bright sunshine can appear to have breast almost as red as a cock linnet.

FLOCKING. Family parties only.

HABITAT. All kinds of rough grassland, including hillsides, valley floors, derelict building sites, railway embankments, reservoir banks, heaths and commons; bushes are not essential so long as there are tall plants such as bracken or thistles, or even tangled coils of barbed wire.

RANGE AND STATUS. Summer visitor, breeding almost throughout British Isles, but very local in some areas, e.g. SE England, Cornwall, Scottish Isles, Ireland; commonest in moorland areas of Wales, N England and Scotland; also passage migrant.

STONECHAT *Saxicola torquata* Plates 5, 7, 10 Thrush Family

PLUMAGE. Summer cock is very black and tan in appearance, with black head, chestnut underparts, and white patches on neck, wing and rump; winter cock has black somewhat obscured by brown fringes. Hen and juvenile are brown, streaked darker. Black bill and legs.

STRUCTURE. *Wing length* VS/S. *Ratios:* wing MS; tail M; neck S; bill S; legs M.

MOVEMENT. As whinchat (above).

VOICE. Commonest note a harsh, grating 'tsak, tsak' or 'hwee-tsak-tsak', usually accompanied by tail-flicks. Squeaky, chat-like song, delivered from low perch or in dancing song-flight, may also resemble hedgesparrow.

FIELD MARKS. The only other small bird with a black-and-white head pattern which habitually perches in prominent places is the cock reed bunting, which normally has quite different habitat, is larger and has white outer tail-feathers; hen and juvenile are like whinchats with no eyestripe or white at base of tail; white wing-bars are prominent in flight; beware north-country name 'stonechat' for wheatear.

FLOCKING. Family parties only.

HABITAT. Breeds especially in gorsy places, heaths, commons, downs, hillsides and cliffs, also in tall heather and rough grassland with low bushes; in winter also on rough ground generally, railway embankments, building sites, etc., especially near the sea.

RANGE AND STATUS. Resident, breeding throughout British Isles, but decreasing and very local, especially in Midlands and SE England, and commonest near the sea; usually affected by hard winters; many move S in autumn, some emigrating.

HOUSE MARTIN *Delichon urbica* Plates 9, 65 and p. 227

Swallow Family

PLUMAGE. Blue-black above (juvenile brownish), with white rump; white below. Forked tail; short black bill; legs and feet feathered white.

STRUCTURE. *Wing length* MS/M. *Ratios:* wing L; tail ML; neck S; bill VS; legs S.

MOVEMENT. As swallow (p. 73), but flight often alternates stiff gliding with quick fluttering.

VOICE. Usual call-note, 'chirrrp' or 'chichirrrp'; alarm-note, 'tseeep'; gentle, twittering, budgerigar-like song, delivered on wing or from perch.

FIELD MARKS. Prominent white rump is outstanding feature, and together with completely white underparts distinguishes at once from swallow, sand martin and swift, the only other small aerial birds with long wings and forked tails. Adult can also be told from sand martin by blue-black upperparts; in brownish juvenile these appear blue-black only at certain angles. Adult swallow's tail streamers are much longer; note also that house martins are the birds which nest in rows under the closed eaves on the outside of modern houses, and that swallows never do this, though they used to nest on the old-fashioned open eaves; see comparative pictures on pp. 45 and 74.

FLOCKING. Even more gregarious than the swallow, nesting in colonies; on migration often flies with swallow, sand martin and swift, and gathers on telegraph wires.

HABITAT. Aerial; breeds in country towns, suburbs, villages, isolated houses and farms, also sometimes cliffs and quarries; feeds over open country, lakes and rivers.

RANGE AND STATUS. Summer visitor, breeding almost throughout British Isles, but local in Ireland; also passage migrant.

House Martin's nest

LAND BIRDS: Short

LINNET *Carduelis cannabina* Plates 10, 11, 14 and p. 55 Finch Family
Brown Linnet.

PLUMAGE. Brownish, streaked darker, but breeding cock has crimson forehead and breast, greyish head and chestnut back. Cleft tail; stout, dark brown bill; dark flesh-brown legs.

STRUCTURE. *Wing length* S. *Ratios:* wing M; tail M; neck S; bill S; legs M.

MOVEMENT. Flight bounding or dancing; hops.

VOICE. Flight-note like greenfinch, but more high-pitched, and quite distinct from redpoll; also typical finch 'tsooeet' anxiety call. Song, a pleasant medley of twittering notes, usually delivered from a tree, but sometimes in the air, and often in chorus.

FIELD MARKS. Breeding cock is only small brown bird with grey head as well as red forehead and breast; always much more chestnut above than twite or redpolls, and can be told from twite by brown bill and from redpolls by lack of black chin; a prominent whitish wing-bar shows both at rest and in flight.

FLOCKING. Gregarious at all seasons; often nests in small loose colonies, and cocks will sing in chorus; in winter often with other seed-eaters.

HABITAT. Breeds on gorsy commons and heaths, gardens, sandhills and all kinds of rough ground, low bushes being chief requirement; in winter feeds on stubbles and other places favoured by seed-eaters, and is especially common on sea-walls, salt-marshes and other rough ground near coast.

RANGE AND STATUS. Resident, widespread but absent from much of Scottish Highlands; many breeding birds move S in autumn, some crossing the Channel, while many more arrive on E coast.

TWITE *Carduelis flavirostris* Plates 11, 14 Finch Family
Mountain Linnet.

PLUMAGE. Brown, streaked darker; cock has pink rump. Cleft tail; stout bill is grey in summer, yellow in winter; legs dark brown.

STRUCTURE. *Wing length* S. *Ratios:* wing M; tail M; neck S; bill S; legs M.

MOVEMENT. Flight bounding; hops.

VOICE. Flight-note and song (delivered from low song-post or in air) resemble linnet; nasal 'tsooeek' or 'twa-it' call, from which it gets its name, is distinctive.

FIELD MARKS. Closely resembles juvenile linnet and redpolls, but at close range can be told from adult linnet and in summer also from redpolls by bill colour; can be told from redpolls at all ages by yellowish-buff chin. Cock is the only small brown bird with pink on rump but not on breast or forehead; shows a whitish mark on the wing in flight like linnet.

FLOCKING. Habitually flocks after breeding, often with other finches.

HABITAT. Breeds on heather-, bracken- and grass-covered uplands, also on lowland mosses and other rough, open ground; some stay in breeding areas in winter, but most move to coast, feeding on stubbles, rickyards, sea-walls, salt-marshes and other places favoured by seed-eaters.

RANGE AND STATUS. Resident; breeds very locally in Pennines N from Staffordshire, rather more widely in S Scotland, commonly in W Highlands and islands of Scotland, and in Ireland, except central plain; some autumn immigrants arrive E coast, and small numbers appear on S and E coasts England in winter.

REDPOLLS See *Land: Very Short*, p. 39

LITTLE BUNTING *Emberiza pusilla* Plate 13 Finch Family

PLUMAGE. Chestnut and brown, streaked black, with rufous cheeks, paler underparts and white outer feathers in cleft tail. Stout blackish-brown bill, pale brown legs.

STRUCTURE. *Wing length* S. *Ratios:* wing MS; tail M; neck S; bill S; legs S/M

MOVEMENT. As other buntings (below).

VOICE. Call-note 'tsew' like reed bunting; alarm-note 'pwick' or 'tip, tip', distinct from reed bunting.

FIELD MARKS. Closely resembles a small hen reed bunting (p. 121), but can be told by small size and rufous cheeks at close range; see rustic bunting (p. 56).

HABITAT. Bare windswept islands and other coastal migration stations.

RANGE AND STATUS. Passage migrant in very small numbers, especially on E coast; regular on Fair Isle and probably often overlooked elsewhere.

MELODIOUS and ICTERINE WARBLERS *Hippolais polyglotta* and *H. icterina*

Like rather large, round-headed wood warblers (p. 41), but yellow (not white) on belly, and with bluish-grey legs and quite different songs; immatures are less yellow. *Melodious* has rather brighter plumage, and shorter, more rounded wings than *icterine*, but best field characters are more conspicuous pale patch on wing of *icterine* and songs. *Melodious* has liquid, musical song, with sparrow-like, chattering call-note; *icterine's* harsh varied song recalls croaking of an indifferent nightingale, with 'dideroid' call-note. Both have rather long pinkish bills, giving them a somewhat reed-warbler-like look. Both are scarce passage migrants from W Europe, *melodious* now regular in S England and around Irish Sea, and *icterine* fairly regular along both E and S coasts Great Britain.

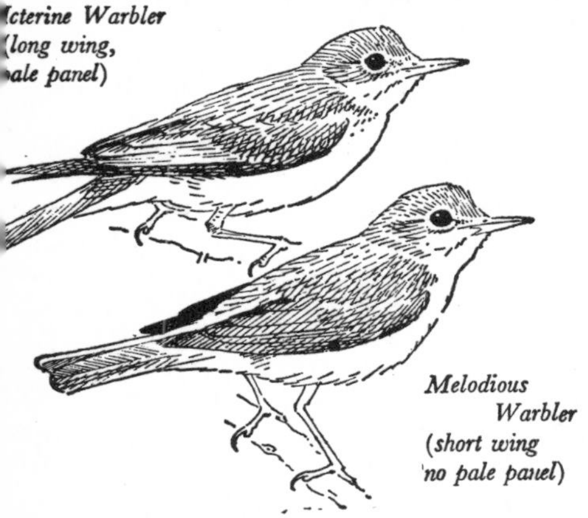

LESSER WHITETHROAT *Sylvia curruca* Plate 4 Warbler Family

PLUMAGE. Grey-brown above and whitish below, with whiter throat, darker ear-coverts and white feathers in tail. Thin blackish bill; grey-blue legs.

STRUCTURE. *Wing length* VS/S. *Ratios:* wing MS; tail M; neck S; bill S; legs M.

MOVEMENT. Typical flitting warbler flight, but more skulking than common whitethroat, and has no song-flight.

VOICE. Call-notes 'tacc' and 'charr' resemble common whitethroat (below), but song, usually delivered from a well-concealed perch, is quite different, a tuneless rattle repeating a single note, somewhat reminiscent of cirl bunting; at close quarters a pleasant quiet warbling can also often be heard.

FIELD MARKS. Combination of greyish-brown appearance, white throat and dark ear-coverts distinguishes from all other warblers; from common whitethroat in particular separable by lack of rufous wings.

HABITAT. As common whitethroat, but prefers places with more trees and taller hedges and bushes, such as shrubberies and large gardens.

RANGE AND STATUS. Summer visitor, breeding not uncommonly in S England, Midlands and E Wales, but local in N England and Isle of Man, and not at all in Cornwall, W Wales and Scotland; passage migrant E coast and N isles, rare vagrant in Ireland.

COMMON WHITETHROAT *Sylvia communis* Plate 3.

Nettle Creeper. Warbler Family

PLUMAGE. Brown, with white throat, rufous wings and white feathers in tail; cock in summer is more greyish-brown and has grey head. Juvenile has less markedly white throat. Thin greyish-brown bill; pale brown legs.

STRUCTURE. *Wing length* S. *Ratios:* wing MS; tail M/ML; neck S; bill S; legs S/M.

MOVEMENT. Typical flitting warbler flight, also special song-flight; skulks much in thick vegetation.

VOICE. Has a harsh churring note, also a 'tacc' and a 'wheet' or 'whit'. Brief, staccato song, not unlike chaffinch's final flourish, is usually delivered in a short dancing song-flight, but also from a perch.

FIELD MARKS. Can be told from all other warblers at all ages by rufous wings; cock can also be told from all other warblers by combination of grey head (without lesser whitethroat's dark ear-coverts) and conspicuous white throat.

FLOCKING. Sometimes with foraging parties of leaf warblers, after breeding.

HABITAT. Areas with tangled coarse vegetation, brambles, briars, bushes, hedgerows, etc., including heaths, commons, country lanes, clearings in and edges of woods; after breeding will also visit gardens, especially soft fruit and vegetable patches.

RANGE AND STATUS. Summer visitor, breeding throughout British Isles, but local in N Scotland; passage migrant on both E and W coasts.

GARDEN WARBLER *Sylvia borin* Plate 3

PLUMAGE. Uniform brown, paler below. Thin brown bill; grey-brown legs.

STRUCTURE. *Wing length* S. *Ratios:* wing MS; tail M; neck S; bill S; legs S/M.

MOVEMENT. Jerky, flitting flight; spends most of time skulking in cover; hops.

VOICE. Has a churr and a hard 'tacc'. Song, delivered from a perch that is often well concealed, is a very even warble, mellower, lower-pitched and more sustained than blackcap; garden warbler sometimes, however, sings in short snatches, while some tiresome blackcaps have song extremely similar to garden warbler; nevertheless typical songs of both species are very distinct.

FIELD MARKS. Uniform plumage lacking any distinctive feature is most important visual field character; can be told from whitethroats, reed and marsh warblers by lack of white or whitish throat; from blackcap can be told at once by absence of dark cap, and this must always be the decisive point when any doubtful song is heard.

HABITAT. Woods, copses, commons, heaths and other places with a plentiful undergrowth of brambles, rose briars, etc.; not specially a garden bird, and uncommon in small and medium-sized ones.

RANGE AND STATUS. Summer visitor, breeding almost throughout England and Wales, local in S Scotland up to Highland line, and very local in Ireland; passage migrant on E coast.

BLACKCAP *Sylvia atricapilla* Plates 3, 4 Warbler Family

PLUMAGE. Cock greyish-brown with black crown; hen and juvenile a warmer brown, with red-brown crown; all paler beneath. Thin blackish bill; grey-black legs.

STRUCTURE. *Wing length* S. *Ratios:* wing MS; tail M/ML; neck S; bill S; legs S/M.

MOVEMENT. As garden warbler (above).

VOICE. Call-notes as garden warbler; normal song, usually delivered from well concealed perch, is higher pitched and generally less sustained than garden warbler, but a variant is very hard to distinguish from the latter's more indifferent performances; more mimetic than garden warbler, and possibility of occasional mimicry of each species by the other must be borne in mind.

FIELD MARKS. Hen and juvenile can be told from all other small birds by red-brown cap; cock can be told from all except smaller marsh and willow tits (which both have black chins) by black cap; especial care is needed when willow tit is singing its rather warbler-like song.

HABITAT. As garden warbler, but is perhaps rather more particular about the presence of trees and more partial to overgreen shrubs, especially rhododendrons.

RANGE AND STATUS. As garden warbler, but breeds locally farther N in Scotland; occasional individuals winter in S and W England and S Ireland.

SAVI'S WARBLER *Locustella luscinioides*

Like a rather large reed warbler (p. 117), with a reeling voice like a loud grasshopper warbler (p. 42), uttered in shorter bursts; a skulking bird distinguished from *grasshopper* by its unstreaked plumage; formerly bred in the Fens, now breeds in Kent.

SPOTTED FLYCATCHER *Muscicapa striata* Plates 4, 5

PLUMAGE. Mousy grey-brown, with paler underparts and dark streaks on head and breast. Juvenile has a more spotted appearance. Blackish bill is flattened at base; legs black.

STRUCTURE. *Wing length* S. *Ratios:* wing M; tail M/ML; neck S; bill S; legs S.

MOVEMENT. Typically darts out from a perch to catch a fly and back again, but more sustained flight is undulating; hops, but is seldom on ground, except to fly down and pick an insect off the grass.

VOICE. Call-note a shrill, robin-like 'tzee'; alarm-note a chat-like 'whee-tucc-tucc'. Song consists of some half-dozen shrill and rather grating and squeaky notes, which do not carry far, and sound at first as if uttered by several birds engaged in a somewhat spasmodic conversation; indeed it may take an observer several seasons to realise that he has been hearing the spotted flycatcher's song all the time.

FIELD MARKS. Can be told from other flycatchers by lack of any distinctive feature in plumage, and flycatchers can be told from all other birds by habit of persistent sallies from a perch (other birds will do this, but not so persistently); forehead appears rather steep.

HABITAT. Gardens, parks, riverside trees and the edges of and clearings in woods; common in suburbs, coming far into the built-up area, even in London.

RANGE AND STATUS. Summer visitor, breeding almost throughout British Isles; also passage migrant.

SHORT-TOED LARK

Calandrella cinerea

Like a small skylark (p. 70), but paler, especially beneath, and with a distinctive dark patch on the side of the breast which is not always easy to see in the field; lark-like in flight, pipit-like on ground. Rare but increasing vagrant.

Short-toed Lark

COMMON REDSTART *Phoenicurus phoenicurus* Plates 5, 6

Firetail. Thrush Family

PLUMAGE. Summer cock is very striking, with white forehead, black throat, grey mantle and fiery chestnut tail and underparts. Winter cock, hen and immature are each browner than the next on mantle and less black on throat, and lack white forehead (winter cock retains a trace of this). Juvenile is speckled paler, but still has red tail. Black bill and legs.

STRUCTURE. *Wing length* S. *Ratios:* wing MS; tail M/ML; neck S; bill MS; legs M.

MOVEMENT. Flitting flight, with frequent flycatching sallies; hops; has curious habit of shivering tail.

VOICE. Chief notes are chat-like 'hwee-tucc-tucc' and loud, willow warbler-like 'hooeet'. Song is usually an inconsequent, squeaky little warble, recognisably similar to the chats, but sometimes a more finished performance, and frequently mimetic; usually delivered fairly high up in a tree.

FIELD MARKS. Except for black redstart, the only small bird with a fiery reddish-chestnut tail, though both nightingale and bluethroat have rather dull brownish-chestnut tails; *common* can be told from all plumages of *black* by its chestnut-red or orange-buff underparts; white forehead of cock *common* also marks it out, as does white wing-patch of cock *black*; juvenile *common* has a generally speckled appearance in contrast to the generally smoky appearance of juvenile *black*.

FLOCKING. Family parties only; on migration is often associated with pied flycatcher.

HABITAT. Breeding localities largely determined by choice of nest site (hole in tree, rock or ground, or nest-box), usually woods, parks with old timber, orchards and large gardens, also river- and stream-sides with old pollards, hill districts with stone walls, and old quarries; on migration occurs in more open country, especially near the coast.

RANGE AND STATUS. Summer visitor, breeding throughout Great Britain, except Cornwall; distinctly local in SE England, Devon and Scotland; also a passage migrant, but scarce in Ireland, where has bred.

BLACK REDSTART *Phoenicurus ochrurus* Plates 5, 6, 23 Thrush Family

PLUMAGE. Summer cock is predominantly black, and winter cock greyish-black, with more or less prominent white wing-patch; hen and young are smoky grey-brown (juvenile obscurely speckled darker) above and below; all have reddish-chestnut rump and tail. Bill and legs black.

STRUCTURE. *Wing length* S/MS. *Ratios:* wing M; tail ML; neck S; bill MS; legs M.

MOVEMENT. As common redstart (above).

VOICE. Has an obvious family resemblance to common redstart; most frequent notes are 'tsip' or 'tic' and 'tucc-tucc'. Song is a staccato warble, rather like the poorer efforts of the *common*, with frequent interjections of a remarkable sound which has been aptly likened to the grinding together of little metal balls; usually delivered from a building, often at a great height.

FIELD MARKS. Red tail prevents confusion with any species except common redstart (which see for warning as to bluethroat and nightingale); jet-black plumage with white wing-patch of adult cock *black* could not be confused with any plumage of *common*, but cocks often breed in immature plumage, when almost indistinguishable from hens; for distinctions of hen and young *black* from corresponding plumages of *common*, see that species.

FLOCKING. Family parties only.

HABITAT. One of the few really urban birds; has a strong preference for broken and rubbly ground, such as waste and building sites, boulder-strewn shores, derelict industrial areas, brickfields and rubbish dumps; breeds in a building, ruined or occupied, or in cliffs; on migration and in winter usually either near buildings or on shore above high-water mark.

RANGE AND STATUS. Summer visitor, a few pairs breed annually in Central London and in coastal towns from Norfolk to Sussex, occasionally in industrial towns inland; non-breeding cocks may occupy territories in summer in places where has not yet bred. Otherwise passage migrant on both E and W coasts, and occasionally inland, and winter visitor in rather small numbers, mostly to S and SW England, W Wales and S Ireland.

BLUETHROAT See *Waterside: Short*, p. 120

ROBIN *Erithacus rubecula* Plates 5, 10 Thrush Family

Redbreast.

PLUMAGE. Olive-brown above, with orange-red face, throat and breast; bluish-grey flanks, whitish belly. Juvenile is brown speckled paler all over. Thin brown bill; brown legs.

STRUCTURE. *Wing length* S. *Ratios:* wing MS; tail M/ML; neck S; bill MS; legs M.

MOVEMENT. Flitting flight; hops; very confiding and will approach close to man; often perches in bush with head on one side watching, and on sighting prey darts down and flies quickly back with it.

VOICE. Commonest note is 'tic, tic', also a thin 'tsit' and a high-pitched 'tsweee'; pleasant, rather thin, warbling song is normally delivered from a perch, often quite high up, almost throughout the year.

FIELD MARKS. Red face as well as breast distinguishes adult from all other red-breasted birds; juvenile closely resembles speckled juvenile nightingale and chats, but is easily the most confiding of them all.

HABITAT. Woods, copses, spinneys, shrubberies, gardens, town parks and hedgerows; in open country away from cover only on migration; a common suburban bird; will enter buildings in hard weather.

RANGE AND STATUS. Resident almost throughout British Isles, but scarce in N Scotland; many, especially in N, move S in autumn, and some emigrate; substantial autumn immigration on E coast.

NUTHATCH *Sitta europaea* Plates 2, 20

PLUMAGE. Blue grey above, buff and chestnut below, with a black stripe through the eye. Thin grey bill; yellowish-brown legs.

STRUCTURE. *Wing length* S. *Ratios:* wing M; tail MS; neck S; bill MS; legs M.

MOVEMENT. Flight undulating; climbs up and down tree-trunks with a jerky motion quite distinct from treecreeper's mouselike gait; the only bird that habitually goes down trees head downwards (treecreeper does this, but much less often).

VOICE. Has a most remarkable range of notes, most of them loud ringing or piping calls, viz. 'chwit-chwit' or 'chwit-it-it', the most usual note; a tit-like 'tsit'; a sibilant 'tsirrp' distinctly reminiscent of the long-tailed tit; and breeding-season calls, two or three loud piping repetitions of 'twee', 'chü' or 'pee', one of which is very like a boy whistling, and another not unlike the bullfinch's pipe.

FIELD MARKS. No other small bird which is blue-grey above and buff or chestnut below climbs trees.

FLOCKING. Sometimes accompanies winter foraging parties of tits and goldcrests.

HABITAT. Exclusively in trees, mostly in woods, copses and well-timbered parks and gardens; will visit bird-tables.

RANGE AND STATUS. Resident; fairly common in England S of Humber and Mersey and in most of Wales, but local in N England and vagrant only in Isles of Wight and Man, Lakeland, Northumberland, Scotland and Ireland.

GREAT TIT *Parus major* Plate 2

Ox-eye Tit.

PLUMAGE. Black on crown, nape and throat and down centre of yellow underparts; white cheeks, wing-bar and outer tail-feathers; yellowish-green mantle and patch on nape, blue-grey rump. Juvenile much yellower, especially on cheeks, and has black parts brownish. Black bill, grey-blue legs.

STRUCTURE. *Wing length* S. *Ratios:* wing MS; tail M/ML; neck S; bill VS; legs S/M.

MOVEMENT. Flight weak, and undulating when at all prolonged; hops.

VOICE. Has many calls, including a 'pink' almost indistinguishable from the chaffinch, most of which are louder versions of notes also made by other tits, so that great care is needed until the observer is thoroughly familiar with the main range of vocabulary of the commoner tits. High-pitched 'song', often rendered 'teacher, teacher', has been likened to sharpening of a saw and pumping of a bicycle tyre. Hen has an explosive hissing threat display on nest.

FIELD MARKS. Black and white head, coupled with broad black bib down middle of bright yellow underparts, makes adult different from any other small bird, and even juvenile, which has black brownish and white yellowish, is distinctive; appreciably bulkier than any other tit, so that there should be no confusion with juvenile coal tit which also has yellowish patch on nape.

FLOCKING. Very sociable after breeding, often in mixed flocks of tits, goldcrests and leaf warblers.

HABITAT. Mainly in trees, but more often feeds on grounds than other tits; in woods, copses, well-timbered gardens, orchards, heaths, commons, parks and hedgerows; often at bird-tables even in well built-up areas.

RANGE AND STATUS. Resident, but scarce and local N and W Scotland; some immigration on E coast in autumn and winter.

LONG-TAILED TIT *Aegithalos caudatus* Plate 2, 17

Bottle Tit (from shape of nest).

PLUMAGE. White on crown and underparts, black and pink elsewhere; juvenile lacks pink. Black bill; legs blackish-brown in adult, dull flesh-colour in juveniles; eyelids and orbital ring pink.

STRUCTURE. *Wing length* vs/s. *Ratios:* wing S; tail L; neck S; bill VS; legs S.

MOVEMENT. Flight weak and undulating, a string of birds flying from tree to tree being a very characteristic sight; rarely on ground.

VOICE. Chief call-note is a spluttering 'tsirrup', also 'tupp' and the usual tit 'si-si-si'.

FIELD MARKS. The only small bird with a long tail and black, white and pink plumage.

FLOCKING. As great tit (above), but more often in family parties.

HABITAT. More exclusively woodland than other tits, especially in winter, but at all times also on bushy heaths and commons and along well-grown hedgerows; rare in town parks, gardens and suburban areas.

RANGE AND STATUS. Resident almost throughout British Isles.

TREE SPARROW *Passer montanus* Plate 15

PLUMAGE. Chestnut with darker streaks above (crown uniform chestnut), pale greyish or buffish white below; black bib and patch on cheek. Stout black or blackish bill; legs pale brown.

STRUCTURE. *Wing length* s. *Ratios:* wing MS; tail M; neck S; bill S; legs S/M.

MOVEMENT. Flight direct or bounding; hops.

VOICE. Like house sparrow (below), but shriller, and has a quick 'chip, chip' and a flight-note 'teck, teck' which are distinctive. Song, a simple chirpy affair, is delivered from a tree and sometimes sung in chorus.

FIELD MARKS. Both sexes resemble cock house sparrow, but can be told at once by chestnut crown, yellowish-brown rump, smaller black bib, black patch on cheek, and slight double wing-bar; in poor light can be told from all finches and buntings by square tail.

FLOCKING. Always gregarious, breeding in small loose colonies, and flocking in winter, often with house sparrows and their associates.

HABITAT. Hard to define, but nests in tree-holes, so prefers areas with old and pollard trees, such as parks, derelict orchards, river banks and even large gardens, especially when enticed by nest-boxes; breeds less commonly in old buildings, quarries and rocky cliffs of windswept marine islands; in winter in rickyards, stubbles and other places favoured by seed-eaters.

RANGE AND STATUS. Resident, breeding locally, chiefly on E side Great Britain and in Midlands; very local in Ireland; substantial immigration on E coast in autumn.

HOUSE SPARROW *Passer domesticus* Plates 14, 15

English Sparrow (N America).

PLUMAGE. Brownish, streaked darker, with paler underparts and a light wing-bar; cock has chestnut mantle, grey crown and rump, and black chin and throat. Stout horn-coloured bill; legs pale brown.

STRUCTURE. *Wing length* S. *Ratios:* wing MS; tail M; neck S; bill S; legs M.

MOVEMENT. Flight direct or bounding; hops.

VOICE. Various chirps and cheeps, with a double note 'chissick', sometimes strung together to form a rudimentary song, delivered usually from a house-top, often in chorus.

FIELD MARKS. Cock can be told from tree sparrow by grey crown and rump, more extensive black bib, no black spot on cheek and only single wing-bar; grey rump conspicuous when flying away; hen and juvenile can be told from hen chaffinch by lack of white shoulder-patch and wing-bar, and are larger or smaller than all other nondescript brownish streaked seed-eaters that lack white in the tail; sparrows differ from all finches and buntings in having square, not cleft, tails.

FLOCKING. Gregarious at all times, breeding in small colonies and afterwards collecting in large flocks, often with other seed-eaters, especially greenfinches, chaffinches, yellowhammers and tree sparrows.

HABITAT. Breeds exclusively on or near occupied human habitations, from isolated farmsteads to centres of large cities; in autumn also in cornfields, rickyards and other places favoured by seed-eaters.

RANGE AND STATUS. Resident throughout British Isles; some rather obscure migratory movements occur on E and S coasts England, but no evidence that residents undertake anything but quite local movements.

GREENFINCH *Chloris chloris* Plate 12

Green Linnet.

PLUMAGE. Yellowish-green, with yellower rump and bright yellow leading edge to wing and patches at base of cleft tail. Juvenile is streaked darker. Stout flesh-coloured bill; pale flesh-coloured legs.

STRUCTURE. *Wing length* S/MS. *Ratios:* wing M; tail M; neck S; bill MS; legs S.

MOVEMENT. Flight bounding; also a bat-like circular display flight; hops.

Greenfinch (left) and Linnet in flight

VOICE. Flight-note 'chichichichichit', canary-like 'tsooeet' (shared by several other finches), and in spring and summer characteristic nasal 'dzweee' are commonest notes. Song, a medley of twittering sounds, is delivered from a tree or in display flight.

FIELD MARKS. Can be told from all other yellowish-green finches (several of which also have a yellow rump) by bright yellow patches on wing, and from all except markedly smaller siskin by yellow at base of tail.

FLOCKING. Sociable even in the breeding season, when loose colonies may nest in adjacent bushes; afterwards flocks with other seed-eaters, especially the chaffinch, yellowhammer and house sparrow.

HABITAT. Breeds in bushy places near human settlements, such as gardens, shrubberies and roadside hedges; afterwards flocks on stubbles or waste ground, in rickyards, along sea-walls, and other places favoured by seed-eaters.

RANGE AND STATUS. Resident almost throughout British Isles; many immigrants arrive E coast in autumn.

BULLFINCH *Pyrrhula pyrrhula* Plates 10, 11 and p. 56

PLUMAGE. Cock has bright pink cheeks and underparts; black chin, crown, nape, wings and tail; white rump, under tail-coverts and wing-bar; and grey mantle. Hen and juvenile are similar but much duller. Cleft tail; stout black bill; brown legs.

STRUCTURE. *Wing length* S. *Ratios:* wing M; tail M; neck S; bill MS; legs S.

MOVEMENT. Flight bounding, but not dancing like goldfinch; hops.

VOICE. Usually reveals its presence by penetrating, plangent, low whistle, 'deu': also a feeble, creaky, often trisyllabic, piping song.

FIELD MARKS. The only small bird with both a black cap and red or pink underparts, and apart from brambling (below) the only small woodland bird with a white rump, conspicuous when flying away; rear view of bird at rest is predominantly grey; the northern race is perceptibly larger and brighter.

FLOCKING. After breeding, in small parties and occasionally sizeable flocks, but shuns the company of other birds.

HABITAT. A markedly woodland bird, favouring also copses, shelter-belts, shrubberies and overgrown hedgerows; visits gardens and orchards in spring to feed on fruit-buds.

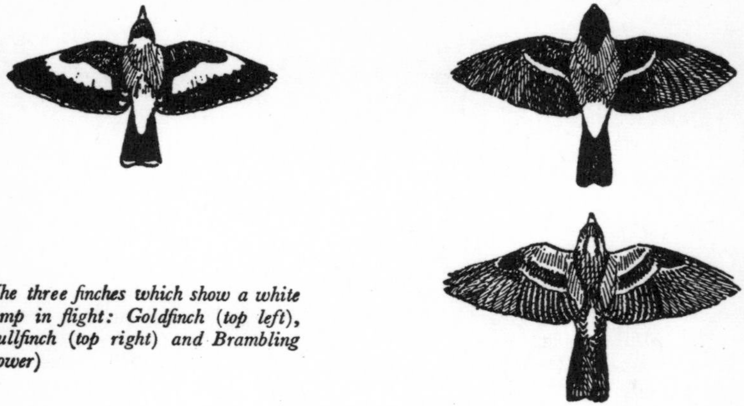

The three finches which show a white rump in flight: Goldfinch (top left), Bullfinch (top right) and Brambling (lower)

RANGE AND STATUS. Resident, but local in Scotland and Ireland; northern race is irregular immigrant on E coast in autumn, most often seen Scotland, especially Shetland and Fair Isle.

SCARLET GROSBEAK *Carpodacus erythrinus* Plate 14 Finch Family

PLUMAGE. Cock dark brownish, with bright red head, breast and rump. Hen and immature, brown, streaked darker, with a pale double bar on the wing. Tail cleft; stout brown bill; dark brown legs.

STRUCTURE. As bullfinch (above).

MOVEMENT. Flight bounding; hops.

VOICE. Call-note 'twee-eek' resembles cross between those of twite and chaffinch.

FIELD MARKS. Cock can be told from crossbill by uncrossed bill; hen and immature resemble slim juvenile bullfinch or corn bunting in general build; at all ages can be told by double wing-bar.

HABITAT. Usually seen on migration on bare, windswept islands.

RANGE AND STATUS. Irregular autumn visitor to Scottish isles, particularly Fair Isle; very rare vagrant elsewhere; red cocks are extremely rare.

TWO-BARRED CROSSBILL or White-winged Crossbill *Loxia leucoptera* Finch family. Similar to crossbill (p. 65), but with a double white wing-bar. Can be told from chaffinch by crossed bill and different call-note. Rare vagrant from N Europe.

RUSTIC BUNTING *Emberiza rustica* Finch Family

Like a smallish reed bunting (p. 121) with white underparts, the cock also distinguished by white facial streak and chestnut instead of black breast; rare but increasing autumn visitor to E coast.

BRAMBLING *Fringilla montifringilla* Plates 14, 15 and p. 56 Finch Family
Bramble Finch.

PLUMAGE. Brownish; cock has head black in summer and blackish-brown in winter, and orange-buff shoulders. Both sexes have orange-buff breast, white rump and cleft tail. Stout bill is blue-black in spring and yellow in winter; legs flesh-brown.

STRUCTURE. *Wing length* S/MS. *Ratios:* wing M; tail M; neck S; bill MS; legs S.

MOVEMENT. Flight bounding; hops or walks.

VOICE. Commonest call-note is 'tsweek', flight-note 'chucc-chucc'; cock's spring song, sometimes heard from wintering birds, resembles greenfinch's 'dzweee'.

FIELD MARKS. White rump picks bramblings out quickly among mixed finch flocks; cock can also be told from cock chaffinch by orange-buff shoulder-patch and black or blackish head, and hen from hen chaffinch by orange-buff breast and no white on shoulders; orange-buff breast at once distinguishes from bullfinch, which also has a more conspicuous white rump.

FLOCKING. Very gregarious, usually with chaffinches under beeches and with same associates as chaffinches on stubbles.

HABITAT. As winter chaffinch (below); occasional in birchwoods in NW Highlands in spring.

RANGE AND STATUS. Winter visitor, rather local; most regular where there are beeches, e.g. on the chalk and limestone hills of S England; may have bred occasionally in N Scotland, but this only proved once.

CHAFFINCH *Fringilla coelebs* Plates 10, 14

PLUMAGE. Cock has slate-blue head and nape, chestnut mantle and pinkish-brown underparts; hen and juvenile are yellowish-brown above and greyish below; all have prominent white shoulder-patch, white wing-bar and white in cleft tail. Stout bill is grey-blue in summer cock, pale brown in winter cock, brown in hen and juvenile; legs pale brown.

Chaffinch in flight and in profile, showing effect of prominent white shoulder-patches

STRUCTURE. *Wing length* S/MS. *Ratios:* wing M; tail ML; neck S; bill MS; legs S.

MOVEMENT. Flight bounding; hops or walks.

VOICE. Commonest note, 'pink, pink', is virtually indistinguishable from similar note of great tit, even to practised ears; also has 'wheet', 'tsit' and a flight-note, 'tsup'; a rare but confusing call is 'tsweeee', like a cross between greenfinch and brambling calls; cheerful rattling song is usually delivered from a perch.

FIELD MARKS. Can be told at all ages from all other birds of same size by combination of white shoulder-patch, white wing-bar and white in tail; note especially that hen house sparrows have only a whitish wing-bar and lack both shoulder-patch and white in tail; white shoulder-patch often enables chaffinches to be picked out at a distance in poor light.

FLOCKING. Very gregarious outside breeding season, sometimes in flocks of one sex only, but often in company with other seed-eaters, especially greenfinches, bramblings, yellowhammers and house sparrows.

HABITAT. Breeds almost wherever there are trees and bushes, in woods, copses, commons, parks, gardens, hedgerows; a common suburban bird; in winter mainly on ploughed fields, stubbles, rickyards, the ground under beeches, and other places favoured by seed-eaters.

RANGE AND STATUS. The commonest British land bird; resident throughout the British Isles; in winter residents pack and wander but do not migrate, while very large numbers from Continent arrive on E coast England.

WHEATEAR *Oenanthe oenanthe* Plates 5, 7 Thrush Family
Stonechat (N England); Greenland Wheatear (N America).

PLUMAGE. Upperparts are clear French grey in summer cock, speckled in juvenile and brownish-grey in all other plumages; underparts are varying shades of buff; rump and base of tail white, contrasting with black tip and central tail-feathers; prominent white eyestripe above black line through eye. In summer cock is more buffish in other plumages. Black bill and legs.

STRUCTURE. *Wing length* MS. *Ratios:* wing M; tail M; neck S; bill S; legs M.

MOVEMENT. Flitting flight; occasionally hovers; hops on ground, frequently bowing and bobbing and chasing after flies; will perch on bushes, trees, fences, etc., especially on migration; stance of Greenland race tends to be more upright.

VOICE. Call-note a rather grating 'chack, chack' or 'weet-chack-chack'; song a squeaky little warble, usually delivered from a slight eminence, a foot or two from the ground, but occasionally in flight.

Wheatear in flight, showing white rump

FIELD MARKS. The only small bird often seen on the ground in the summer that has a prominent white rump, as distinct from white sides to tail. Cocks of slightly larger Greenland race are fairly easy to identify in spring, when their very bright pinkish underparts and much browner grey upperparts are very distinct from the buff underparts and French grey upperparts of breeding cocks; hen and autumn cock *Greenlands* are much more tricky, even for experienced observers, but in some cases can be identified with reasonable certainty by their slightly larger size, more upright stance and brighter underparts.

FLOCKING. Loose parties on migration.

HABITAT. Breeds in all kinds of open, uncultivated country, downs, hills, moors, mountains, cliffs, dunes, rabbit warrens; on migration also in cultivated open country, and even on rubble in towns.

RANGE AND STATUS. Summer visitor, breeding throughout British Isles, but local in lowland England; also passage migrant, Greenland race occurring especially in northern isles and along W coast.

BLACK-EARED WHEATEAR or Black-eared Chat *Oenanthe hispanica*
Thrush family. Resembles wheatear (above) in general appearance and habits, but cock is strikingly distinct, having black on tail, wings, cheeks and sometimes throat, rest being either white or creamy buff; hen is like common wheatear, but has darker wings and less white in tail. Several other rare wheatears might occur, so that doubtful birds need to be very carefully examined in the field. Rare vagrant from S Europe.

HEDGE SPARROW *Prunella modularis* Plates 4, 5 Accentor Family
Dunnock.

PLUMAGE. Brown above, streaked darker; grey beneath, with heavily streaked flanks. Thin blackish-brown bill; flesh-brown legs.

STRUCTURE. *Wing length* S. *Ratios:* wing MS; tail M; neck S; bill S; legs M.

MOVEMENT. Flight rather less flitting than most small birds, but rarely flies far; on ground moves with hops and a kind of jerky, shuffling walk.

VOICE. Chief call-note, an insistent, shrill 'tseep', often betrays its presence where it has been overlooked (it is inconspicuous rather than skulking). Rather flat little warbling song has none of the vehemence of the wren, nor the sweetness of the robin and is usually delivered from a perch, and sometimes in short snatches in middle of night.

FIELD MARKS. The only small brown land-bird with grey underparts; these, with streaked flanks and thin bill, distinguish it from the unrelated house sparrow.

HABITAT. Any places with bushes, scrub, bramble brakes and other thickish undergrowth, e.g. gardens, shrubberies, copses, open woods, heaths, commons, hedgerows, cliffs and moorland cloughs, combes and gullies; a common suburban bird.

RANGE AND STATUS. Resident, breeding throughout British Isles; a southward movement occurs in autumn and some birds emigrate.

BARRED WOODPECKER *Dendrocopos minor* Plate 16
Lesser Spotted Woodpecker.

PLUMAGE. Black, heavily barred white above; brownish-white below; male and juvenile have red crown. Blackish-grey bill; dark grey-green legs; reddish-brown eye.

STRUCTURE. *Wing length* MS. *Ratios:* wing M; tail M/ML; neck MS; bill MS; legs S.

MOVEMENT. Flight markedly undulating; hops; climbs about trees.

VOICE. Commonest note is a rather weak, flat 'pee-pee-pee-pee-pee', not unlike the wryneck's call, but lacking its ringing quality; also a 'tchick', weaker and more sibilant than pied woodpecker, but much more rarely used; drums like pied woodpecker (p. 79), but more prolonged and without any terminal acceleration.

FIELD MARKS. Can be told by its black-and-white plumage from all other small birds that habitually climb up trees; for distinctions from much larger pied woodpecker, see that species. Often among topmost twigs of trees.

HABITAT. As green woodpecker (p. 92).

RANGE AND STATUS. Resident, breeding throughout S England, Midlands and E Wales; local in Yorkshire and W Wales, and very rare Lancashire and N England; no reliable records from Scotland or Ireland.

MEADOW PIPIT *Anthus pratensis* Plate 8 Wagtail Family

Titlark.

PLUMAGE. As tree pipit (below), but hind claw long, legs of adult brownish-flesh, and some have pinkish tinge on breast in spring.

STRUCTURE. *Wing length* s. *Ratios:* wing MS; tail M; neck s; bill MS; legs s.

MOVEMENT. Flight dipping; walks or runs; sometimes perches in trees, especially on migration.

VOICE. Call-note is 'pheet' or more often 'pheet, pheet pheet', closely resembling *rock* and quite different from tree pipit. Song, which is like *tree's* shorn of its final 'see-er's, is normally uttered in a similar song-flight, but, always starting from and returning to ground, and singing on both upward and downward flight.

Song-flight of Meadow or Tree Pipit

FIELD MARKS. Between April and September voice is only safe distinction from tree pipit (which see for close-range plumage characters); special care is necessary against confusion between *tree* and juvenile *meadow*, which has much pinker legs than adult (and may retain them until at least the spring of the following year) and is also yellowish-buff in colour, some appearing in a bright light almost as yellow as a rather dull yellow wagtail; *meadow* can be told from rather larger and darker rock pipit by its white (not smoky) outer tail-feathers.

FLOCKING. Gregarious outside breeding season, often accompanying skylarks and sometimes wagtails.

HABITAT. Breeds in all kinds of open uncultivated country, moors, bogs, rough grazings, heaths, sandhills, also on commons with bushes and trees; in winter resorts mostly to damp places, such as fresh and salt marshes, wet grassland, sewage farms, the margins of ponds and lakes, estuarine sea-walls and arable land with green crops.

RANGE AND STATUS. Resident throughout British Isles, though scarcer in S and E; most leave N and W in winter and move S, some emigrating; large numbers arrive E coast in autumn.

RED-THROATED PIPIT *Anthus cervinus* Wagtail Family

Similar to meadow pipit (above), and best told from other pipits by distinctive call-note, 'chüp'; in spring has reddish throat and breast (but beware pink flush on breasts of some *meadow* and rock pipits in spring), and in winter has streaked (not uniform) rump. Rare vagrant from N Europe.

PECHORA PIPIT *Anthus gustavi* Wagtail Family

Like a rather small tree pipit (below) with two pale streaks down the back and buffish outer tail-feathers, best distinguished by its call-note, a loud 'pwit'; rare autumn visitor to Fair Isle (Shetland).

TREE PIPIT *Anthus trivialis* Plate 8 Wagtail Family

Woodlark (N England).

PLUMAGE. Brownish, streaked darker, paler beneath; white feathers in tail. Thin brownish bill; flesh-pink legs; short hind claw.

STRUCTURE. *Wing length* S/MS. *Ratios:* wing M; tail M/ML; neck S; bill MS; legs M.

MOVEMENT. Flight rather dipping; walks or runs sedately, wagging tail slowly; habitually perches in trees.

VOICE. Call-note, a rather loud, harsh 'teez', is diagnostic. Undistinguished song, which nearly always ends with 'see-er, see-er, see-er', is delivered in special song-flight, bird flying up from song-post, usually a tree or bush, and singing on descent to perch again, or occasionally to ground; sometimes also sings from a perch, and exceptionally even on ground.

FIELD MARKS. Only safe distinctions from meadow pipit in field are call-note and song-flight; short hind claw is visible only at very close range; is also a trifle larger and has pinker legs (but see above for warning as to immature *meadow*) and fewer streaks on breast, lower breast being sometimes almost unstreaked, but these fine points can normally be used only to confirm the evidence of the voice; see p. 123 for distinctions from rock pipit.

FLOCKING. In small parties on migration.

HABITAT. Wherever scattered trees and telegraph or other poles provide song-posts, e.g. heaths, bogs, commons, hillsides, wood edges and clearings, railway cuttings, parkland; on migration in open country and coastal areas, including marine islands.

RANGE AND STATUS. Summer visitor, but thins out and does not breed in extreme W Cornwall and N Scotland; passage migrant in Scottish isles and vagrant in Ireland.

WOODLARK *Lullula arborea* Plate 8

PLUMAGE. Brownish, streaked darker and paler beneath; a noticeable crest. Thin brownish bill; flesh-brown legs.

STRUCTURE. *Wing length* MS. *Ratios:* wing ML; tail MS; neck S; bill MS; legs S.

MOVEMENT. Flight undulating, also a circular song-flight; walks.

VOICE. Flight- and call-note, 'tit-looeet'; song recognisably akin to skylark's, but much mellower and rather jerkier on a descending scale; delivered either from a perch or in flight, and not infrequently at night (hence sometimes reported as nightingale).

FIELD MARKS. In flight, even at some distance, can be told at once from adult skylark by noticeably shorter tail, which gives it a somewhat bat-like appearance (but beware juvenile skylark, which has shorter tail than adult): at closer range a distinctive dark brown and white mark shows on the leading edge of the wing; buff eyestripes meeting at back of head, and tail with white tip but no white feathers afford additional distinctions; crest not always visible in field; beware 'woodlark' as local name in N England for tree pipit, which is smaller and has no crest.

FLOCKING. In parties and small flocks after breeding.

HABITAT. Like cirl bunting (below), rather hard to define, and in W somewhat overlaps that species; in E favours heathy areas on sandy soils; presence of scattered trees is common factor in all haunts, and uncultivated ground much preferred; will also breed on chalk and limestone scarps, parkland, sites of felled woods, wood edges and in W in combes.

RANGE AND STATUS. Resident, breeding locally in S England and Wales; commonest in counties S of Thames and E Anglia; very local in all counties immediately N of Thames and in Lincs, Notts and Yorks; irregular migrant on Scottish islands, but apparently regular in autumn on Fair Isle; rare vagrant elsewhere.

BARRED WARBLER *Sylvia nisoria* Plate 17

PLUMAGE. Greyish-brown, cock greyer, hen browner; adult has barred, juvenile plain buff underparts. Thin brownish bill; legs grey-brown; eye yellow in adult.

STRUCTURE. *Wing length* S/MS. *Ratios:* wing M; tail ML; neck S; bill S; legs M.

MOVEMENT. Jerky, rather shrike-like flight; skulking; hops.

VOICE. Call-notes, a churr and a hard 'tacc', like blackcap and garden warbler.

FIELD MARKS. A large, stout, greyish warbler with a longish tail; barred underparts and yellow eye of adult together rule out confusion with any other small bird; juvenile is like long-tailed garden warbler (p. 48), but with noticeably pale tips to outer flight-feathers and a steep, whitethroat-like forehead.

HABITAT. Mostly at coastal migration stations, where likes to skulk in any available cover, from stunted bushes to oats or potatoes.

RANGE AND STATUS. Regular autumn passage migrant, usually in very small numbers; most often on E coast, Shetland, Fair Isle, Isle of May, and from Holy Island to Suffolk.

GREENLAND WHEATEAR See Wheatear, p. 58

SWALLOW, juvenile See *Land: Medium Short*, p. 73

CHAFFINCH See above, p. 57

REED-BUNTING See *Waterside: Short*, p. 121

LAPLAND BUNTING *Calcarius lapponicus* Plates 13, 15 Finch Family

Lapland Longspur (N America).

PLUMAGE. Brownish, streaked darker; summer cock with black head and breast, chestnut nape, and marked whitish stripe back from eye; white feathers in cleft tail; winter cock and summer hen are similar but duller. Winter hen and immature resemble hen reed bunting with two pale stripes down back. Stout yellow bill; dark brown legs. Edges of wing-feathers markedly chestnut.

STRUCTURE. *Wing length* MS. *Ratios:* wing M; tail M; neck S; bill S; legs S.

MOVEMENT. Flight bounding; usually runs.

VOICE. Flight-note a hard flat little rattle, 'tr-r-r-ik', also a flat toneless contact-note, 'teuk'.

FIELD MARKS. Cock can be told from cock reed bunting by lack of white on nape, which is strikingly chestnut; in other plumages much like hen reed bunting and best told by voice, yellow bill and pale stripes on back; can be told from snow bunting by lack of white in plumage and from shore lark by lack of yellow on throat.

FLOCKING. Gregarious, and often with flocks of other seed-eaters, especially snow buntings, also with sky and shore larks.

HABITAT. Rough ground near sea, sometimes also moorland.

RANGE AND STATUS. Passage migrant, mostly in autumn, but regular in spring on Fair Isle and so probably overlooked elsewhere; most often seen on Scottish isles and E and SE coasts of England, also on hills inland, e.g. Lancashire Pennines.

RED-HEADED BUNTING *Emberiza bruniceps* Drawing p. 64

Finch Family

The striking plumage of the cock, with chestnut or golden-yellow head and bright yellow underparts, makes it both easy to identify and attractive to cage-bird enthusiasts, and escapes probably account for the great majority of the numerous occurrences of cocks since about 1950. There has also been a suspicious shortage of records of the yellow-vented but otherwise sparrow-like hens, which are less frequently imported from India.

ORTOLAN *Emberiza hortulana* Plates 12, 13 Finch Family

Ortolan Bunting.

PLUMAGE. Brownish upperparts streaked darker, with greyish-olive head and breast, pinkish-brown underparts, and distinctive throat-pattern showing pale stripe under eye separated from cream throat by dark line; white feathers in cleft tail. Cock much brighter than hen, which has dark streaks on upper breast; immature much browner still. Legs and stout bill reddish-brown; a yellowish-white orbital ring or 'spectacle' round eye.

STRUCTURE. *Wing length* S/MS. *Ratios:* wing M; tail ML; neck S; bill S; legs S.

MOVEMENT. Flight bounding: hops.

VOICE. Call-note a rather weak 'zit', like cirl bunting; flight-note 'pwit'.

FIELD MARKS. White 'spectacle' marks ortolan out from all other small brownish birds at all ages, but only visible at close range; adult cocks should present no difficulty; throat pattern and bill and leg colour are best pointers in other plumages.

FLOCKING. Should be looked for in migrant flocks of seed-eaters.

HABITAT. Most often seen at coastal migration stations.

Red-headed Bunting

RANGE AND STATUS. Passage migrant in small numbers in spring and autumn on S and E coasts and Scottish isles; regular on Fair Isle and in N Norfolk, and probably often overlooked elsewhere.

CIRL BUNTING *Emberiza cirlus* Plates 12, 15 Finch Family

PLUMAGE. Cock chestnut above and yellow below, with grey crown and black throat; hen and juvenile yellowish-brown streaked darker; olive rump, white feathers in cleft tail. Stout horn-coloured bill, flesh-brown legs.

STRUCTURE. As yellowhammer (below).

MOVEMENT. Flight bounding; hops.

VOICE. Call-note, 'zit'; usual song a brief trilling rattle, somewhere between trills of lesser whitethroat and wood warbler, normally delivered quite high up in a tree and quite distinct from yellowhammer's song, though a rare variant resembles this without the 'cheese'. Alarm-note a wren-like churr.

FIELD MARKS. Cock can be told from yellowhammer by black throat, grey crown and greyish-green band across breast; all ages can be told by olive rump; white outer tail-feathers show in flight.

FLOCKING. In parties and small flocks after breeding, often with other seed-eaters, especially yellowhammer.

HABITAT. Hard to define, but trees are always and hedges usually present; often on borderland of downs and farmland, and will nest in large gardens on outskirts of villages and small towns; in winter on stubbles and other places favoured by seed-eaters.

RANGE AND STATUS. Resident, breeding locally in all counties S of Thames, and very locally in widely scattered colonies in Wales and S Midlands; elsewhere a vagrant or very exceptional breeder; in winter small flocks wander to places where they do not breed.

YELLOWHAMMER *Emberiza citrinella* Plates 12, 13 Finch Family
Yellow Bunting.

PLUMAGE. Cock predominantly yellow, with chestnut upperparts streaked darker; hen and juvenile much browner and less yellow; white feathers in cleft tail. Stout greyish-horn bill; pale flesh-brown legs.

STRUCTURE. *Wing length* S. *Ratios:* wing MS; tail M; neck S; bill S; legs S.

MOVEMENT. Flight direct or bounding; hops and occasionally runs.

VOICE. Flight-notes 'twit-up' with a rather sibilantly liquid tone; and a rather grating 'twink' and 'twit'. High-pitched song, popularly rendered 'little-bit-of-bread-and-no-cheese', or in Scotland 'deil, deil, deil, deil, tak ye', is unmistakable (but see under cirl bunting, above), though final 'cheese' is sometimes omitted.

FIELD MARKS. Cock is the only bright yellow small bird with a chestnut back; hen and juvenile can be told from cirl bunting by chestnut rump; white outer tail-feathers are prominent in flight at all ages.

FLOCKING. Very gregarious after breeding, often with other seed-eaters, especially greenfinch, chaffinch and house sparrow.

HABITAT. A typical hedgerow bird, also on well-bushed heaths and commons, but hardly ever in human settlements, except rickyards in winter, when also visits stubbles and other places favoured by seed-eaters.

RANGE AND STATUS. Resident throughout British Isles, packing and wandering in winter; some immigrants on E coast in autumn.

SNOW-BUNTING, summer See *Waterside: Short*, p. 123

CROSSBILL *Loxia curvirostra* Plates 10, 11, 12 Finch Family
Red Crossbill (N America).

PLUMAGE. Adult cock predominantly red, immature cock orange, hen yellowish-brown, juvenile brown streaked darker; all with dark brownish wings and tail. Rather deeply cleft tail; stout dark brown bill with crossed mandibles; legs dark brown.

STRUCTURE. *Wing length* MS. *Ratios:* wing M; tail M; neck S; bill M; legs S.

MOVEMENT. Flight bounding; hops.

VOICE. Flight-note a distinctive 'jip-jip'; song, delivered from perch or in air, is not unlike greenfinch (p. 54).

FIELD MARKS. At close range crossed bill precludes confusion with any other bird (but see two-barred crossbill, p. 56); distinctly larger and longer than all other finches except hawfinch; cock is only predominantly red or orange small bird, except very rare cock scarlet grosbeak (p. 56). Exclusive addiction to conifers is a good pointer.

FLOCKING. In parties after breeding, but not with other birds.

HABITAT. Open coniferous woods, and sometimes among scattered conifers on roadsides and in parks or gardens; feeds predominantly on seeds extracted from cones by dexterous use of crossed bill.

RANGE AND STATUS. Resident over a wide area of central Scottish Highlands, in breck district of E Anglia since irruption of 1910; breeds irregularly elsewhere, most often on Greensand heaths of SE England and in parts of Ireland; Continental birds periodically irrupt into Britain in summer, sometimes in huge numbers (as in 1910), and turn up almost anywhere, even on sporadic pines in suburban gardens, but less commonly in W England and Wales. The native Scottish birds are now regarded by some ornithologists as belonging to a different species, *L. pytyopsittacus*, but despite their slightly larger bills, they cannot be distinguished in the field from *L. curvirostra*.

HAWFINCH *Coccothraustes coccothraustes* Plates 14, 15, 22

PLUMAGE. Chestnut brown, with black wing-tips; white patch on wing and border to cleft tail; juvenile has barred underparts; throat black in adult, yellow in juvenile. Grotesquely stout bill is grey-blue in summer, yellow in winter adult and juvenile; legs flesh-brown.

STRUCTURE. *Wing length* MS. *Ratios:* wing M; tail M; neck S; bill M; legs M.

MOVEMENT. Flight bounding; hops.

VOICE. A clipped, robin-like 'tick', and a rather shrill, sibilant 'tsip'; feeble song is rarely heard.

FIELD MARKS. Can best be picked up by the characteristic 'tick' note, which it often utters when flying overhead, when a quick look up will reveal the dumpy form and bounding flight; white on wing and tail conspicuous when flying away; at close range the huge bill is unmistakable.

FLOCKING. Often flocks after breeding.

HABITAT. Woods and well-timbered parks, orchards and gardens.

RANGE AND STATUS. Resident, but rather local and mainly in SE England; rare or unknown in Devon, Cornwall, W Wales, Scotland (local in south) and Ireland.

WRYNECK *Jynx torquilla* Plate 17 Woodpecker Family

Cuckoo's Mate; Snake Bird.

PLUMAGE. Mottled grey-brown, with paler underparts. Bill and legs pale horn-colour.

STRUCTURE. *Wing length* S/SM. *Ratios:* wing MS; tail M; neck MS; bill S; legs S.

MOVEMENT. Flight less undulating than other woodpeckers; hops; creeps up trees.

VOICE. A loud, clear, rather musical 'kew-kew-kew-kew-kew', bearing some resemblance to calls of nuthatch, barred woodpecker and kestrel.

FIELD MARKS. From treecreeper, the only other small brown bird that creeps about trees, can be told by larger size, longer tail, straight bill and brown underparts; can be told from nuthatch and barred woodpecker by brown plumage; tail appears distinctly longish in flight, and away from trees wryneck is more like a small brown shrike or a large warbler than a woodpecker.

HABITAT. As green woodpecker (p. 92), but fonder of gardens and orchards, especially where there are old fruit-trees.

RANGE AND STATUS. Decreasing summer visitor, now almost confined to SE England, though formerly locally N to York and W to Devon; elsewhere only a rather scarce passage migrant, though fairly regular in N isles.

NIGHTINGALE *Luscinia megarhyncha* Plates 3, 5, 6 Thrush Family

PLUMAGE. Rufous brown with paler underparts; tail more rufous than mantle; juvenile speckled paler. Dark brown bill; legs vary from flesh to grey-brown.

STRUCTURE. *Wing length* S. *Ratios:* wing MS; tail M; neck S; bill S; legs M.

MOVEMENT. Normally extremely skulking, and rarely seen except diving into thick cover; flitting flight; hops.

VOICE. Chief call-notes, a leaf warbler-like 'hweet' and a chat-like 'tacc, tacc'; alarm-notes, a scolding 'krrrr' and a grating "tchaaaa'. Song, usually delivered from thick cover and just as often by day as by night, is outstandingly rich in volume and range of notes, and includes several, such as the 'jug-jug' or 'chooc-chooc' note and the crescendo based on 'pioo' that no other bird can approach, but there are many harsh, guttural and almost frog-like notes in the songs of the more indifferent performers.

FIELD MARKS. Much more rufous than other small brown birds, none of which have so reddish a tail; is more like a robin than a warbler in general appearance.

HABITAT. Thickets of all kinds, in woods, copses, commons, heaths and overgrown hedgerows.

RANGE AND STATUS. Summer visitor, commonest in S and E England, but extending W to Devon, Glamorgan, lower Wye valley and Severn valley, and N to Shrewsbury, Trent valley and extreme S Yorkshire; very local at W and N limits of range; elsewhere an uncommon passage migrant, very rare in Scotland and unknown in Ireland.

TAWNY PIPIT *Anthus campestris* Plate 8 Wagtail Family

PLUMAGE. Sandy-brown with faint darker streaks; juvenile streaked more heavily; whitish feathers in tail. Thin brownish bill; flesh-coloured legs.

STRUCTURE. *Wing length* MS. *Ratios:* wing M; tail ML; neck S; bill M; legs M.

MOVEMENT. Stance even more wagtail-like than Richard's pipit (p. 71); flight dipping; runs.

VOICE. Various 'tsip', 'tsup', 'tseep' notes, louder than other pipits and rather more like wagtails, especially yellow; quite distinct from Richard's pipit.

FIELD MARKS. Adult is less streaked than any other pipit, and looks more like a sandy-brown wagtail; buff eyestripe noticeable in field; juvenile is smaller, paler and shorter-legged than *Richard's*, and larger, paler, longer-legged and much longer-tailed than any other pipit.

HABITAT. Most often seen in coastal districts.

RANGE AND STATUS. Irregular migrant, nearly always in SE England in autumn; rare vagrant elsewhere; it breeds as near as France and Holland.

YELLOW WAGTAILS See *Waterside: Short*, p. 125

SWIFT *Apus apus* Plates 9, 66 and p. 227

Devil Bird, Devil Screamer, Deviling, and variations on this theme.

PLUMAGE. All blackish-brown, except for whitish throat, which is more prominent in juvenile. Forked tail; thin black bill; black feet.

STRUCTURE. *Wing length* ML. *Ratios:* wing L; tail ML; neck S; bill VS; legs S.

MOVEMENT. Constantly in flight, dashing through the air with vigorous wheeling, winnowing and gliding action; only accidentally on ground.

VOICE. Has a harsh scream, and a more high-pitched squeal associated with parties swooping and swerving round houses on a summer evening; also a ticking note and a more chirruping version, heard at nest.

FIELD MARKS. Can easily be told from swallows and martins (the only other small, long-winged aerial birds) by quite different outline, the tail being relatively shorter and the wings curved in scimitar fashion instead of the Maltese-cross appearance of the swallow tribe; nor do swallows and martins indulge in the excited screaming chases 'round the houses'; can also be told by uniformly dark plumage, above and below, except for pale throat, which is only visible at close range.

FLOCKING. Gregarious, both at breeding places and on migration; often flies with swallows and martins.

HABITAT. Aerial; breeds mainly in roofs of human dwellings, but also in crevices in walls, cliffs and quarries; often feeds some way away from nest, and then frequents open country, including moorlands, rivers and lakes, and even the centre of London and other large towns.

RANGE AND STATUS. Summer visitor, breeding throughout British Isles, except NW Scotland; also passage migrant.

RED-BACKED SHRIKE *Lanius cristatus* Plates 17, 31

Butcher Bird.

PLUMAGE. Rufous brown above and creamy below; cock has blue-grey head and rump and black stripe back through eye; hen has crescentic bands on underparts, and juvenile has them all over; much white at sides of base of tail. Slightly hooked bill is black in cock, brownish in others; greyish legs.

STRUCTURE. *Wing length* MS. *Ratios:* wing M; tail ML; neck S; bill S; legs M.

MOVEMENT. Flight rather undulating, occasionally hovers to catch prey; hops, but not often on ground; fond of look-out perches, but not quite such prominent ones as great grey shrike.

VOICE. Various harsh calls, including 'chack, chack', and a mimetic warbling song, somewhat like garden warbler.

FIELD MARKS. Combination of blue-grey head and rump with chestnut back of cock is superficially like fieldfare and cock kestrel, but is much smaller than either, and no other bird has these two features; black stripe through eye and

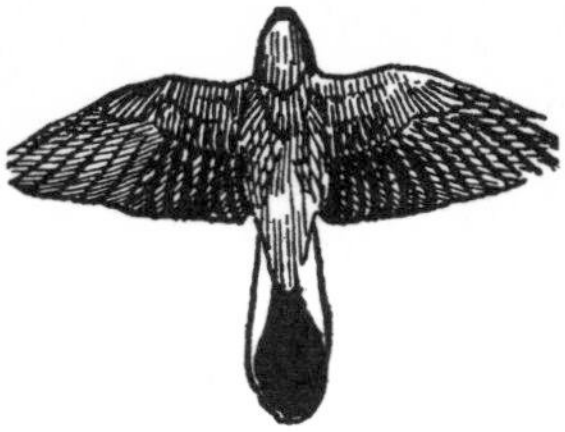

Shrikes in flight: Great Grey (top left), Red-backed (top right) and Woodchat (lower)

white at base of tail are useful additional distinctions. Can be told at all ages from all other same-sized rufous brown birds by hooked beak, longish tail, and habits of using prominent perches and moving tail either up and down or from side to side; front view can look very white or whitish.

FLOCKING. Never more than family parties.

HABITAT. Commons, heaths, overgrown hedgerows and other places with a scattered cover of thick bushes.

RANGE AND STATUS. Decreasing summer visitor, now confined to S England from Norfolk to Devon, but formerly breeding N to Mersey and Humber and occasionally beyond; elsewhere a passage migrant, very rare in Ireland.

WOODCHAT *Lanius senator* Plate 23 and p. 48 Shrike Family

PLUMAGE. Black and white, with chestnut crown and nape; whole underparts, rump, patch on scapulars, wing-bar and tip of tail are white, the rest black. Slightly hooked blackish bill; grey-black legs.

STRUCTURE. *Wing length* MS. *Ratios:* wing M; tail ML; neck S; bill S; legs M.

MOVEMENT. As red-backed shrike (above).

VOICE. A harsh chattering note.

FIELD MARKS. No other black and white bird has a chestnut crown and nape; white scapulars and rump show up in flight; longish tail; habit of perching on prominent look-outs.

HABITAT. As red-backed shrike.

RANGE AND STATUS. Very irregular spring visitor, mainly to S England; also occasionally in autumn and as far N as Fair Isle.

DUNLIN, summer See *Waterside: Medium Short*, p. 129

LAND BIRDS: Medium Short

CORN BUNTING *Emberiza calandra* Plate 13 and p. 213 Finch Family
Common Bunting.

PLUMAGE. All brown, streaked darker. Tail cleft; stout, yellowish-horn bill; legs yellow.

STRUCTURE. *Wing length* MS. *Ratios:* wing M; tail M; neck S; bill S; legs S/M.

MOVEMENT. Flight direct or bounding, sometimes with legs dangling; hops and occasionally runs.

VOICE. Flight-note 'quit' or 'quit-it-it', rather liquid in tone. High-pitched song, like jangling of bunch of keys, is usually delivered from a perch, which can be as low as a clod of earth or as high as 30-40 ft. up in a tree.

FIELD MARKS. Can be told by comparatively large and plump appearance, coupled with complete lack of distinctive features, in particular no wing-bar or white feathers in tail; hen house sparrow has a pale wing-bar and is appreciably smaller, and other nondescript small brown finches are smaller still; no other small land bird flies with dangling legs.

FLOCKING. In small parties after breeding, sometimes with other seed-eaters, especially yellowhammer.

HABITAT. Open country, especially arable and downland in chalk and limestone districts, and rough ground near the sea; in winter will visit rickyards, but otherwise, like all buntings, shuns human settlements.

RANGE AND STATUS. Resident throughout British Isles in large scattered colonies and especially local in Wales, Scotland and Ireland; a small autumn immigration on E coast.

SKYLARK *Alauda arvensis* Plate 8
Laverock (Scotland).

PLUMAGE. Brown, streaked darker and paler beneath; a noticeable crest at times; white feathers in tail. Thin horn-coloured bill; yellowish-brown legs.

STRUCTURE. *Wing length* M. *Ratios:* wing M; tail M; neck S; bill S; legs VS/S.

MOVEMENT. Flight rather undulating; walks.

VOICE. Flight- and call-note a liquid 'chirrup'; sustained, warbling song is normally delivered in the air, but sometimes on ground and even from a perch. The only bird which habitually sings while ascending almost vertically, while hovering in the air (often nearly out of sight) and again while descending almost vertically.

FIELD MARKS. Can confidently be identified by song habits alone; for distinctions from woodlark, see p. 61; can be told from all pipits by crest and much larger size.

FLOCKING. Very gregarious after breeding, especially on migration and in hard weather; often accompanied by meadow pipits.

HABITAT. Exclusively open country, rather treeless farmland, downland, estuarine marshes, moors and rough grazings, sand dunes, peat bogs and mosses; in winter especially on cultivated land, the landward fringes of estuaries, airfields, golf courses, etc.

RANGE AND STATUS. Breeds throughout the British Isles, but many emigrate in winter and are replaced by huge numbers arriving on E coast in autumn.

RICHARD'S PIPIT *Anthus novaeseelandii* Plate 8 Wagtail Family

PLUMAGE. Brownish, streaked darker; whitish stripe over eye; white outer tail-feathers. Thin dark brown bill; flesh- or yellowish-brown legs.

STRUCTURE. *Wing length* MS. *Ratios:* wing MS; tail M; neck S; bill MS; legs M.

MOVEMENT. Rather wagtail-like stance; flight dipping; runs.

VOICE. Distinctive, rather harsh call-notes, 'r-r-rüüp'.

FIELD MARKS. The largest pipit, with tail longer than larks and commoner pipits, rather like a wagtail in pipit's plumage; eyestripe conspicuous in field; larger, darker and longer-legged than immature tawny pipit.

HABITAT. Most often seen in coastal districts.

RANGE AND STATUS. A Siberian species, which normally migrates westwards and occasionally overshoots the mark to reach the British Isles, chiefly in autumn and most often on Fair Isle and the coasts of Norfolk, Kent and Sussex; rare vagrant elsewhere.

PIED and WHITE WAGTAILS *Motacilla alba* Plate 67

Water Wagtail, or Dishwasher.

PLUMAGE. Black, white and grey; adult has white forehead, cheeks and underparts, and black on rest of head and breast; juvenile has grey upperparts, whitish cheeks and underparts, and blackish bib on breast; black tail with white outer feathers. Thin black bill; black legs.

STRUCTURE. *Wing length* S/MS. *Ratios:* wing MS; tail ML; neck S; bill S; legs S/M.

MOVEMENT. Flight markedly dipping; runs and walks, frequently moving tail up and down.

VOICE. *Pied* has a high-pitched flight-note, 'tschizzick'; *white* has a very similar but softer and more sibilant note. Twittering song may be delivered in air, on ground or from perch.

FIELD MARKS. No other small black and white birds have such a long tail; adult of both forms has black crown, nape, throat and breast, but *pied* has black back and rump where *white* has grey; juveniles cannot be told apart in autumn, but in spring more immature *whites* than *pieds* still have the whole top of the head grey, and at this time the colour of the rump is the only really safe distinction, black in the *pied* and grey in the *white*. Any black and white wagtail which has completely grey upperparts, from forehead to rump, but no juvenile blackish bib on the breast, can confidently be identified as a *white*; and any such wagtail with a black rump can confidently be set down as a *pied*.

FLOCKING. Fairly gregarious after breeding, especially at roosts and on migration, when sometimes accompanied by yellow wagtails.

HABITAT. *Pied* usually breeds in or very near small human settlements, from

Wagtails in flight

a PIED *black rump;* b WHITE *grey rump;* c GREY *yellow rump;* d YELLOW *green rump*

farms to the outskirts of towns, and occasionally even in the centre of a large city, often but by no means always near water; in winter shows a rather greater preference for neighbourhood of water; migrating *whites* mostly in coastal districts or at reservoirs and sewage farms inland.

RANGE AND STATUS. *Pied* is resident almost throughout the British Isles, but there is a general southward movement in autumn, and many cross the Channel; *white* is a regular spring and autumn passage migrant in some numbers on the W coast (going to and from the Faeroes and Iceland), and to a less extent on the E coast and inland; has bred exceptionally in Fair Isle and several English counties.

WAXWING *Bombycilla garrulus* Plate 22

Bohemian Chatterer; Bohemian Waxwing (N America).

PLUMAGE. Cinnamon-brown, with distinctive crest, black chin, and grey rump; yellow tip to tail, and red, yellow and white markings on dark wings. Black bill and legs.

STRUCTURE. *Wing length* M. *Ratios:* wing M; tail M; neck S; bill S; legs S.

MOVEMENT. Flight not unlike starling, but rather wavering; rarely on ground, except at water.

VOICE. Call-note 'sirrrrr', but rather silent, despite its old name.

FIELD MARKS. The only brown bird with a crest and yellow and red markings on wing and tail; even in poor light can be told from starling, when crest partly down, by grey rump; hawfinch has large bill, white tip to tail and no crest; jay has white rump and harsh call and is much larger.

FLOCKING. Normally in small parties, and occasionally in sizable flocks.

HABITAT. Nearly always seen on berried trees or shrubs, most often hawthorn, not infrequently exotics in suburban gardens, such as cotoneaster or pyracantha.

RANGE AND STATUS. Irregular winter visitor, a few appearing in most years, less common on W side and rare Ireland; occasionally a substantial irruption, when birds are seen in almost every part of Britain.

ALPINE ACCENTOR *Prunella collaris*

A large edition of the hedge sparrow (p. 59), with more contrasty plumage, a wing-bar showing in flight. Rare vagrant from Continental mountain ranges.

QUAIL *Coturnix coturnix* Plates 25, 71 Pheasant Family

A game bird.

PLUMAGE. Brown, marked darker and paler above and in hen also on breast (cock buff below); pale streaks on flanks; throat buff (cock has dark central stripe with two bands curling back to nape); buff streak on crown, and buff eyestripe. Juvenile resembles hen. Grey bill; pale flesh-coloured legs.

STRUCTURE. *Wing length* MS/M. *Ratios:* wing M; tail S; neck S; bill S; legs S/M.

MOVEMENT. Typical whirring game-bird flight, sometimes gliding on down-curved wings; walks.

VOICE. Unmistakable 'quic-ic-ic' or 'wet-mi-lips' call, plangent and far-carrying; also at very close range a curious growling 'row-ow'; call-note when flushed 'crwee-crwee' or 'crucc-crucc'.

FIELD MARKS. Much the smallest game bird, and more often heard than seen. Adult can be told from juvenile partridges at close range by lack of chestnut tail and by buff streaks on head; cock can further be told by dark markings on throat and unstreaked underparts. Can at once be told from corncrake by legs not dangling in flight and no chestnut on wings.

FLOCKING. After breeding season goes in small parties called bevies; does not mix with partridges.

HABITAT. Fields of growing crops, clover, lucerne and young corn, also rough, tussocky grassland, young hayfields, and in autumn root-fields.

RANGE AND STATUS. Scarce and erratic summer visitor, breeding at times throughout British Isles, but more often on light chalk and limestone soils of S England than elsewhere; occasional in winter.

SWALLOW *Hirundo rustica* Plates 9, 65

Barn Swallow (English Provinces and N America).

PLUMAGE. Blue-black above and on breast-band; forehead, chin and upper throat chestnut; rest of underparts varying individually from rufous buff to cream; wing-tips blackish-brown; forked tail is spotted white. Thin black bill; black legs.

STRUCTURE. *Wing length* M. *Ratios:* wing ML; tail VL (adult), L (juvenile); neck S; bill VS; legs VS.

MOVEMENT. Constantly on wing with an easy, gliding flight; hardly ever on ground, but habitually perches on buildings and telegraph wires, rarely in trees.

Swallow's nest

VOICE. Commonest note is twittering 'tswit, tswit, tswit'; alarm note a shrill 'tsink, tsink'. Pleasant, twittering song, delivered both from perch and on wing, has been aptly rendered as 'feetafeet, feetafeetit'.

FIELD MARKS. Can be told at all ages from martins and swift (the only other small aerial birds with long wings and forked tails) by chestnut throat and forehead; long streamers of adult's tail are also distinctive, but juvenile has short fork like martins; lacks white rump and underparts of house martin, brown upperparts of sand martin and sooty brown underparts of swift.

FLOCKING. Gregarious, especially on migration and when feeding over water; often flies with martins and swift.

HABITAT. Aerial; breeds in or near human settlements, especially in farm buildings, outhouses and boat-houses, but not in centre of large cities; feeds over open country, lakes and rivers.

RANGE AND STATUS. Summer visitor, breeding throughout British Isles, but very local in NW Scotland; also passage migrant.

SCOPS OWL *Otus scops* Plate 33

PLUMAGE. Grey-brown or rufous, with darker streaks and vermiculations; ear-tufts. Rounded wings; hooked, bluish-black bill, set in flattened facial disk; feathered legs, grey feet; yellow eye.

STRUCTURE. *Wing length* M. *Ratios:* wing ML; tail MS; neck S; bill does not project; legs S.

MOVEMENT. Flight less bounding than little owl.

VOICE. A rather monotonous 'piu', not unlike single note of common redshank, repeated at short intervals; usually at night.

FIELD MARKS. Much more nocturnal than little owl, from which, and from rare Tengmalm's owl, can be told by small size, ear-tufts and unfeathered toes; is also much slimmer than dumpy little owl, and very much smaller than other owls with ear-tufts.

HABITAT. Might occur in any area with scattered trees, especially in or near towns and villages.

RANGE AND STATUS. Vagrant, most often in spring, and in S England.

RINGED PLOVER, summer See *Waterside: Medium Short*, p. 131

BUDGERIGAR *Melopsittacus undulatus*; Warbling Grass Parrot in Australia; Plate 20 Parrot Family

Various shades of green, yellow or blue, but most often a rather yellowish-green and a bright pale blue; no native bird with long tail or hooked bill is blue or green, but many less common cage birds may escape and lead to confusion; most lories and parakeets are bigger and have some other colour, e.g. red, about them as well. Rather weak flight; has a musical chirrup, a loud screech when excited or alarmed, and an inward warbling song not unlike house martin's. An escaped cage bird, most likely to be seen in or on the edge of a large town; at liberty in several places; tends to join flocks of house sparrows and to be chased by swallows.

PINE GROSBEAK *Pinicola enucleator* Finch Family

An outsize crossbill, with no crossed bill and a double white wing-bar; cock predominantly pink, hen and immature greyer. More than 2 in. longer than two-barred crossbill (p. 56). Rare vagrant from N Europe.

LESSER GREY SHRIKE *Lanius minor*

A smaller edition of the great grey shrike (p. 81), intermediate between it and the *red-backed* in size; can be told at once by broad black band across forehead (beware optical illusion of narrow black band on some *great greys*, due to rictal bristles and wishful thinking). Rare vagrant from S Europe.

Male Lesser Grey Shrike

ALPINE SWIFT *Apus melba* Plate 66

PLUMAGE. Brown above and on broad breastband and under tail-coverts; throat and rest of underparts white. Forked tail; thin blackish-brown bill; dark flesh-coloured legs.

STRUCTURE. *Wing length* ML. *Ratios:* wing L; tail ML; neck S; bill VS; legs VS.

MOVEMENT. As swift (p. 68).

VOICE. Apparently silent away from breeding places.

FIELD MARKS. Easily recognisable as an unusually large swift, but paler brown and with a white chin and belly and brown band on breast; so much bigger than sand martin, which is similarly coloured and patterned, that confusion hardly possible, even apart from difference of shape.

FLOCKING. Normally gregarious; sometimes in company with common swifts.

HABITAT. Aerial.

RANGE AND STATUS. Vagrant, chiefly to S England.

STARLING *Sturnus vulgaris* Plates 19, 69

Stare.

PLUMAGE. Adult is blackish, iridescent with green and purple, and spotted white, especially on breast; appears more iridescent in spring and summer and more spangled at other times. Juvenile is dull brown with a paler throat, but in Shetland race is as dark as adult. In late summer and autumn moulting immatures may be seen with adult bodies but still juvenile heads and necks. Bill of summer adult yellow, of winter adult and juvenile brownish; legs reddish-brown.

STRUCTURE. *Wing length* M. *Ratios:* wing M; tail MS/M; neck S; bill M; legs M.

MOVEMENT. Flight fast and direct, with frequent glides; walks with bustling gait.

VOICE. Utters a wide variety of clipped, undistinguished notes; song, usually delivered from building or tree, and often in chorus, sounds rather like an orchestra tuning up or several birds engaged in whispered conversation; hunger-cry of young birds, an insistent 'cheeerr', is ubiquitous in late May and June; will mimic any sound, natural or artificial, and where any bird call is heard at unlikely season or place it is wise to investigate possibility of starling first.

FIELD MARKS. Adult can be told from cock blackbird by shorter tail, bustling gait and sharply triangular shape of wings in flight; blackbird is jet black and has bright orange or yellow bill at all seasons. Juvenile can likewise be told from hen and young blackbirds by tail, wings and gait, and also by its duller brown plumage; from thrushes also by lack of spots on breast.

FLOCKING. Highly gregarious except in breeding season, and even then non-breeding birds flock and roost together; often feeds with flocks of other birds such as rooks, jackdaws and especially lapwings.

HABITAT. Almost universal, but not on moorland or downs except at end of breeding season; in woods only in and immediately after breeding season, when caterpillar plagues burst; often on coastal marshes in winter; breeds in cliffs regularly in N Scotland and isles, and locally elsewhere; common in towns and suburbs, pairs breeding and large flocks roosting in centre of largest cities; roosts communally in thickets, copses and reed-beds in winter.

RANGE AND STATUS. Resident, but local N Scotland, W Wales and W Ireland, though may be common here in winter. Some emigrate in winter and many others move S and W; huge numbers arrive E coast in autumn.

ROSY STARLING *Pastor roseus* Plates 19, 23

Rose-coloured Pastor.

PLUMAGE. Adult is rose-pink, with black head, wings and tail and a marked crest. Juvenile resembles rather pale young starling. Bill of summer adult and juvenile is pink, of winter adult brownish; legs pink.

STRUCTURE, MOVEMENT AND VOICE. As starling (above), but bill ratio MS.

FIELD MARKS. Adult is only medium-sized black and pink land bird, but juvenile can only be told from young starling by paler plumage and pink legs; general outline like starling.

FLOCKING. Often associates with starling flocks.

HABITAT. As starling in winter.

RANGE AND STATUS. Vagrant; one or two seen in most years and occasionally in fair numbers; a native of Russia and SE Europe, its appearances in Britain are probably largely correlated with the westward migration of locusts, a favourite food. Commonly imported from India and may well escape.

REDWING *Turdus musicus* Plates 18, 21 Thrush Family

PLUMAGE. Olive-brown above, with marked light eyestripe; paler beneath, with spotted breast and chestnut flanks and underwing. Blackish-brown bill; yellowish-brown legs.

STRUCTURE. *Wing length* M. *Ratios:* wing MS; tail M; neck S; bill S; legs S.

MOVEMENT. Direct flight like song thrush; hops or runs.

VOICE. Flight-note, a thin 'seeih', is very like, but more sibilant and lower-pitched than, song thrush and blackbird; it can often be heard from invisible migrating flocks overhead at night, but migrant redwings are identified in this way with much too great confidence by observers who have not taken sufficient care to rule out blackbirds and song thrushes. Other call-notes a soft 'chup' and a harsher 'chittick' or 'chittuck'. True song is rarely heard, but its few stilted, fluty notes sometimes occur in the warbling communal subsong in which flocks indulge in late winter and which sounds rather like a group of starlings mimicking song thrushes.

FIELD MARKS. Can easily be told from all other thrushes by its small size, white eyestripe and reddish-chestnut flanks and underwing.

FLOCKING. Highly gregarious, most often consorting with fieldfares.

HABITAT. Forages on farmland, parks, playing fields, etc., but also in fairly open woodland and in hard weather in town parks; often feeds on berry-bearing shrubs, notably hawthorns.

RANGE AND STATUS. Winter visitor and passage migrant throughout British Isles; has nested several times in N Scotland and is occasionally heard singing there in the breeding season in birch woods.

DOTTEREL *Charadrius morinellus* Plates 38, 42, 78, 82 Plover Family

PLUMAGE. Grey-brown above, with white eyestripes (meeting in V on nape), throat, breast-band and under tail-coverts, and chestnut lower breast and black belly. In winter white eyestripes and breast-band are faint, breast paler grey-brown and belly white. Juvenile as adult winter. Black bill; yellowish legs.

STRUCTURE. *Wing length* M. *Ratios:* wing ML; tail MS; neck MS; bill S/MS; legs ML.

MOVEMENT. Similar to golden plover (p. 87).

VOICE. A piping whistle, a harsh alarm note and a brief song uttered on the ground.

FIELD MARKS. A smallish plover, intermediate between *ringed* and *golden*, it has the usual short bill, but the eyestripes and yellowish legs are the best field marks. Is sometimes very tame, so that the chestnut, white and black pattern of the underparts can be clearly seen. Apart from dunlin, the only smallish wader likely to be seen on a mountain-top.

FLOCKING. Usually in small parties or 'trips'.

HABITAT. Breeds on stony or tussocky mountain-tops; on migration may halt on moors, downs or open places in lowlands, and occasionally on the coast.

RANGE AND STATUS. Summer visitor breeding in small numbers on Cairngorms and a few other high mountains in Scotland and in very small numbers in N England; elsewhere scarce passage migrant, chiefly England and S Scotland.

LITTLE OWL *Athene noctua* Plates 33, 73

PLUMAGE. Grey-brown, mottled whitish; rounded wings. Hooked, greenish-yellow bill, set in flattened facial disk; feathered legs and feet; yellow eye.

STRUCTURE. *Wing length* M. *Ratios:* wing ML; tail MS; neck S; bill does not project; legs S.

MOVEMENT. Flight conspicuously undulating; occasionally hovers; runs; often perches prominently on posts, telegraph poles, haystacks, etc.; bobs body and waggles head when curious or suspicious.

VOICE. A loud ringing 'kiew, kiew', habitually uttered by day; also song, closely resembling opening sequence of curlew's song. Juvenile has a persistent, shrill wheeze.

FIELD MARKS. Much smaller than any native owl, and can be told from other birds of same size by rather long, rounded wings, short tail and bounding flight; habitually flies by day as well as by night.

HABITAT. Mainly open country with scattered trees, especially farmland, but also rocky and treeless places, such as sand dunes and marine islands, and occasionally ruined buildings and quarries.

RANGE AND STATUS. Resident; since introduced in Northants in 1889 and Kent in 1896 has occupied whole of England and Wales except Lakeland; spreading into SE Scotland; vagrant in Ireland.

SONG THRUSH *Turdus philomelos* Plates 18, 21

Throstle; Mavis.

PLUMAGE. Warm olive-brown, with paler underparts, spotted breast and golden-buff underwing. Juvenile has mantle speckled buff. Brownish bill, flesh-coloured legs.

STRUCTURE. *Wing length* M. *Ratios:* wing MS; tail MS; neck S; bill MS; legs S/M.

MOVEMENT. Flight more direct than mistle thrush; hops or runs; frequently stands with head on one side listening for worms.

VOICE. Call-notes, a short 'sipp' is the most frequent, a thin 'seep' very similar to redwing, and a 'chook' like blackbird being both less often used. Loud, clear song can easily be told from other thrush songs by tendency to repeat each note (cf. Browning's 'That's the wise thrush; he sings each song twice over'); much less mellow than blackbird; usually delivered fairly high up in a tree, but sometimes from lower down, occasionally at night; not infrequently mimics other birds.

FIELD MARKS. Smaller and warmer brown than mistle thrush, with smaller spots on breast, golden-buff underwing and no whitish tips to tail-feathers; slightly larger than redwing, with no chestnut flanks or prominent white eyestripe; hen and young blackbirds are much more blackish on upperparts and have no contrast of dark spots on paler underparts.

FLOCKING. Flocks only on migration, but often feeds in loose association with other thrushes.

HABITAT. Wherever bushes and shrubs occur, especially in gardens, town parks, hedgerows, commons, heaths, woods and copses, and common in suburbs; rarely far from bushes except on migration.

RANGE AND STATUS. Resident, breeding throughout British Isles, but many, especially in N, move S in autumn, and some migrate, while others arrive on E coast; some migrants appear darker than native birds, but origin of these is not known.

PIED WOODPECKER *Dendrocopos major* Plates 16, 23

Great Spotted Woodpecker.

PLUMAGE. Black, with large and small white spots and blotches, and red under tail-coverts; male has red nape and juvenile has red crown. Thick grey bill; grey-green legs; adult has red eye.

STRUCTURE. *Wing length* M. *Ratios:* wing M; tail M/ML; neck MS; bill MS; legs S.

MOVEMENT. Flight conspicuously undulating, wings being completely folded against body at bottom of each bound; hops; climbs about trees.

Pied Woodpecker in flight, seen from below

VOICE. Usual call-note is 'tchick', also various trills and titters, and a harsh churring note similar to mistle thrush; 'drumming' is a mechanical sound, made by sharp taps of bill on resonant dead wood, and resembling creaking of broken branch or vibration of small metal clappers on wooden sounding board; differs from drumming of barred woodpecker by lasting only one instead of two seconds, and consisting of 8-10 or fewer blows instead of 10-30.

Cream-coloured Courser

FIELD MARKS. The only other black and white bird that creeps up trees is much smaller barred woodpecker, from which *pied* can be told by prominent white patches on wings in flight, spotted rather than barred appearance, and red vent (male also by red nape).

HABITAT. As green woodpecker (p. 92), but shows greater preference for woodland, especially conifers.

RANGE AND STATUS. Resident, breeding almost throughout England and Wales; in Scotland rather local N to Great Glen and gradually spreading farther W and N; a regular autumn immigrant on E coast, in some years in some numbers and wandering to all parts of Scotland and Ireland.

CREAM-COLOURED COURSER *Cursorius cursor* Pratincole Family

Like a small sandy golden plover, with conspicuous black wing-tips and underwing, and black and white stripes back from eye; blackish decurved bill, whitish legs. Rare vagrant from N Africa; a desert bird.

LAND BIRDS: Medium

GOLDEN ORIOLE *Oriolus oriolus* Plates 20, 21

PLUMAGE. Cock is bright yellow with black wings and tail; hen and young are yellowish-green, with paler underparts and darker wings and tail. Fairly thick dark pinkish bill; dark grey legs; eye red.

STRUCTURE. *Wing length* ML. *Ratios:* wing M; tail M; neck S; bill M; legs S.

MOVEMENT. Flight undulating on a long wave-length; hops on rare occasions when comes to ground.

VOICE. Cock has loud, mellow, fluty song, 'weela-weeo'; also a cat-like squalling cry from both sexes.

FIELD MARKS. Cock is only medium-sized black and yellow land bird, but is very retiring and often betrays presence by loud call, with perhaps a silhouette glimpse as it moves among dense foliage. Hen and young are sometimes confused with green woodpecker (whose juvenile has no red on head), which also has markedly undulating flight, but the oriole's bill is much smaller and less stout and it would never crouch on a bole or branch like a woodpecker.

HABITAT. Hardly ever seen away from trees, and favours well-timbered parks and large gardens, especially with groves of the evergreen or holm oak.

RANGE AND STATUS. Annual spring visitor in very small numbers to S and E England, occasionally remaining to breed; vagrant elsewhere.

GREAT GREY SHRIKE *Lanius excubitor* Plate 31 and p. 69

Northern Shrike (N America).

PLUMAGE. Grey, with black and white on head, wings and tail; usually has a white stripe above the eye; may have either one or two white wing-bars. Hen and immature have faint grey bars on breast. Blackish hooked bill; black legs.

STRUCTURE. *Wing length* M. *Ratios:* wing MS; tail M; neck S; bill S; legs S.

MOVEMENT. Flight very undulating, usually ending with an upward sweep on to a look-out post at the summit of a bush, tree or pole; will hover after prey.

VOICE. Has a harsh chattering cry and an alarm note, 'sheck, sheck'.

FIELD MARKS. The only medium-sized black, white and grey bird that perches on prominent look-outs; but see rare lesser grey shrike (p. 75).

HABITAT. Heaths, commons and other places with scattered trees and bushes; also overgrown hedgerows and roadside telegraph wires.

RANGE AND STATUS. Annual passage migrant and winter visitor in very small numbers; rare in Ireland.

TENGMALM'S OWL *Aegolius funereus*

Slightly larger than little owl (p. 78), but with a more scowling expression and legs and feet feathered white; no ear-tufts. Rare vagrant from Europe.

BARBARY DOVE or Domesticated Turtle Dove *Streptopelia risoria*

Plate 24

Resembles turtle dove (p. 85) in general appearance and habits, but can be distinguished by black collar round neck, unspotted mantle and grey-blue instead of black in tail. Doves of this or closely allied species are frequent aviary escapes, and are breeding ferally in N. Lancs. See also Collared Dove, p. 93.

PRATINCOLE *Glareola pratincola* Plates 38, 81

This rather specialised type of wader, with its forked tail and rapid dancing and hawking flight, resembles a cross between a huge brown swallow and a brown tern, more especially the latter. Upperparts brown, contrasting with darker wing-tips and whitish trailing edge; underparts paler, with chestnut underwing, white rump and belly, and buff chin and throat, bordered in summer by a narrow black line. (Much rarer black-winged pratincole *G. nordmanni* has uniformly darker upperparts and black underwing.) Juvenile is mottled above and lacks the black line. Bill black, red at base; legs black. Vagrant, mostly May and June, and in S and E England.

BOB-WHITE QUAIL *Colinus virginianus* Pheasant Family

An introduced game bird, resembling a small common partridge (p. 91) or a large quail (p. 73); brown with streaked flanks and dark tail, the cock easily told by the conspicuous black and white head and throat pattern, which is brown and buff in the hen; call, a loud double whistle 'bob-white'; frequently released on sporting estates in recent years, especially in East Anglia, where it is locally established.

RING OUZEL *Turdus torquatus* Plates 18, 19, 23 Thrush Family

Mountain Blackbird; Mountain Ouzel.

PLUMAGE. Summer cock is black-brown with white gorget; hen and winter cock browner with grey flecks and duller gorget. Juvenile is grey-brown with speckled breast. Dark yellowish-brown bill; dark brown legs.

STRUCTURE. *Wing length* M. *Ratios:* wing M; tail M/ML; neck S; bill S; legs S.

MOVEMENT. Flight direct and impetuous; hops or runs.

VOICE. Chief call-notes are a clear pipe and a rather harsh, grating 'tac-tac-tac', which may run into a loud chatter. Most frequent song is a rather simple elaboration of the clear, piping call-note, but early in the season it has a somewhat more complex performance.

FIELD MARKS. Adult can be told from normal blackbird by white gorget, coupled with pale appearance of wing, but partially albino blackbirds may have similar gorget. Juveniles of both species are much alike, but the spots on the underparts of the ring ouzel are more distinct. Remember that blackbirds often occur in typical ring ouzel habitats in hill country, while 'ring ouzels' seen in suburban gardens in summer or winter are much more likely to be partially albino or strongly marked juvenile blackbirds.

FLOCKING. Small loose flocks on migration.

HABITAT. Mountains and moorlands, especially wooded valleys, cloughs, combes and hillsides; on migration is partial to berry-bearing shrubs.

RANGE AND STATUS. Summer visitor to all hilly and mountainous districts except in S England and Midlands, but very local Ireland, Isle of Man and W Scotland; alleged breeding in lowlands almost invariably albinistic blackbirds; also passage migrant on E and W coasts and sporadically inland; a very few occasionally winter, especially in Ireland.

BLACKBIRD *Turdus merula* Plates 18, 19, 69 Thrush Family

Ouzel Cock.

PLUMAGE. Cock all black; hen and immature dark brown, with speckled breast and blackish wings and tail; juvenile more rufous and mottled than hen; white markings not at all uncommon. Adult cock has bright orange-yellow bill; others have brownish bills, those of immature cocks becoming yellower as season advances; dark brown legs.

STRUCTURE. *Wing length* M. *Ratios:* wing MS; tail M/ML; neck S; bill S; legs S.

MOVEMENT. Flight direct and impetuous, with a curious flicking motion of the wings; usually flirts up tail on alighting; hops or runs; will stand with head on one side listening for worms.

VOICE. Chief call-notes include, 'tchook, tchook', which develops into a loud chattering scream if bird is alarmed; a persistent 'pink, pink' used in going to roost and in mobbing owls, etc.; a robin-like anxiety note, 'tsee', and a similar but vibrant note, not at all unlike redwing and often heard from migrants. Mellow, fluty song, usually delivered from tree, sometimes from chimney stack, is not repetitive like song thrush.

FIELD MARKS. No other jet-black bird has a bright orange-yellow bill (starling has mottled, iridescent appearance, bustling gait and shorter tail); for possible confusion of white-marked birds with ring ouzel, see above; hen and young can be told from other thrushes by generally darker plumage, less distinct spotting of underparts and (in juvenile) more rufous appearance; most alleged hybrid blackbird/song thrushes are in fact perfectly ordinary hen or young blackbirds.

FLOCKING. Flocks only on migration, but often feeds in loose association with song thrushes.

HABITAT. Much as song-thrush (p. 78), but more partial to wild, uncultivated districts, such as cloughs and combes in hills.

RANGE AND STATUS. Resident throughout British Isles, but most northern birds move S and some emigrate; large influx on E coast in autumn.

FIELDFARE *Turdus pilaris* Plates 18, 21 Thrush Family

Felt; Felfer.

PLUMAGE. Blue-grey head and rump, chestnut back, blackish tail, buffish underparts with well spotted breast, whitish underwing. Yellowish bill, brown legs.

STRUCTURE. *Wing length* M. *Ratios:* wing M; tail M; neck S; bill S; legs S.

MOVEMENT. As mistle thrush (below).

VOICE. Flight-note a chuckling 'chack, chack', also some harsh call-notes resembling mistle thrush; flocks in spring will warble together.

FIELD MARKS. Blue-grey and chestnut plumage of upperparts is distinctive at close range (a combination shared only by smaller red-backed shrike and larger kestrel, both with hooked beaks); in flight at any distance closely resembles mistle thrush, and is then best told by its distinctive flight-note.

FLOCKING. Highly gregarious, and often associates with redwings.

HABITAT. Mostly on farmland, playing fields, grass marshes, etc., and in hard weather also in town parks; also feeds on berry-bearing shrubs, notably hawthorn and rowan.

RANGE AND STATUS. Winter visitor and passage migrant throughout British Isles. Bred in Orkney in 1967.

MISTLE THRUSH *Turdus viscivorus* Plate 18

Stormcock.

PLUMAGE. Greyish-brown, with paler underparts heavily spotted on breast, and whitish underwing. Juvenile spotted paler above. Horn-coloured bill, yellowish-brown legs.

STRUCTURE. *Wing length* ML. *Ratios:* wing M; tail M/ML; neck S; bill MS; legs S.

MOVEMENT. Has a very characteristic flight, shared with the fieldfare, in which the wings are closed at regular intervals for a perceptible time but without producing an undulation; as the wings open and close the white underwing appears to flash on and off, and in bright sunshine the bird may seem to show almost as much white as a jay; hops on ground.

VOICE. Flight-note a harsh, grating chatter, like sound of comb scraped against piece of wood. Loud, ringing song, normally delivered high up in a tree, can be confused with blackbird at a distance, but at close quarters has none of the fluty mellowness of the blackbird, nor any of the repetitive variety of the song thrush.

FIELD MARKS. Can be told from song thrush by larger size, greyer appearance, bigger spots on breast, whitish tips to outer tail-feathers, and in flight also by white underwing; from redwing also by lack of reddish flanks and white eyestripe; from fieldfare by uniform grey-brown upperparts and distinctive flight note. Juveniles have sometimes been mistaken for rare White's thrush (below).

FLOCKING. In family parties and small flocks after breeding, and on migration sometimes in larger flocks.

HABITAT. Varied in breeding season, but almost always has at least scattered trees; generally in cultivated country, farmland, gardens, parks, orchards, also in woods and not uncommon in suburbs; afterwards resorts to more treeless places, such as downs, moors and marshes, and is especially fond of rowans in autumn.

RANGE AND STATUS. Resident, generally distributed, but local in NW Scotland; a good many arrive on E coast in autumn, when some native birds are moving S and W.

WHITE'S THRUSH or Golden Mountain Thrush *Turdus dauma*

Resembles mistle thrush (above) in general appearance and habits, and immature *mistles* are often confused with it, but *White's* can readily be told by crescentic black marks all over both upper and underparts, and in flight also by black and white bands on underwing. Rare vagrant from Siberia.

NIGHTJAR *Caprimulgus europaeus* Plates 17, 29, 73

Goatsucker, Night Hawk, Fern Owl.

PLUMAGE. Brown, mottled darker and paler; male has white tips to outer tail-feathers and three white spots on outer wing-quills. Blackish-brown bill; flesh-brown feet.

STRUCTURE. *Wing length* ML. *Ratios:* wing ML; tail ML; neck S; bill VS; legs S/M.

MOVEMENT. Gliding and wheeling flight, with sudden darts after moths and other insects; perches along or across a branch.

VOICE. Commonest call-note is a soft but insistent 'cu-ic', also a whip-crack sound made by clapping wings together. Song is a sustained, far-carrying churr, remarkably like a distant two-stroke motor-cycle, with occasional abrupt changes of pitch; not normally heard till 45-60 minutes after sunset, and not to be confused with grasshopper warbler's much shriller reel, also often heard by night.

FIELD MARKS. Hardly ever seen by day unless stumbled upon and flushed, when it appears a long-winged, long-tailed, hawk-like bird, and can be told from birds of prey by its short, unhooked bill, and from juvenile cuckoo by lack of barring on underparts and of white patch on nape; white spots on male are also distinctive; at night outline is much sharper-winged and longer-tailed than little owl, the only owl of comparable size.

HABITAT. All kinds of gorsy and brackeny places, such as heaths, commons, woodland clearings, felled woodlands, moorland cloughs and corries, and even sand dunes.

RANGE AND STATUS. Summer visitor, breeding almost throughout British Isles, but rather local and decreasing in some areas.

CORNCRAKE *Crex crex* Plates 25, 71 Rail Family

Land Rail.

PLUMAGE. Brown, streaked darker above, with much chestnut on wings; paler below, with flanks barred darker. Bill pale flesh-brown with darker tip; legs pale flesh.

STRUCTURE. *Wing length* M. *Ratios:* wing MS; tail S; neck M; bill MS; legs M.

MOVEMENT. Except on migration, flight weak, with dangling legs; walks or runs; can swim.

VOICE. Unmistakable harsh double call, like a grated comb and aptly rendered by its scientific name, 'crex, crex', repeated incessantly in breeding season.

FIELD MARKS. A skulker, rarely seen in the open, and most often detected by craking voice, but when flushed its chestnut wings are conspicuous and separate it at once from quail and juvenile partridges, which also do not dangle legs in flight.

HABITAT. Hayfields, and occasionally rough grass on hillsides, damp sedgy meadows and hedge bottoms.

RANGE AND STATUS. Summer visitor, breeding throughout Scotland and Ireland, but mainly in the N and W, and locally in N England and N and W Wales; elsewhere very sporadic and local, but breeds regularly in a few places; also passage migrant, but always uncommon in E and S England; occasionally winters in W England and Ireland.

TURTLE DOVE *Streptopelia turtur* Plates 24, 29, 68

PLUMAGE. Crown and nape blue-grey, black and white patch on side of neck, upperparts chestnut marked black, tail black with white tip, throat and breast pink-purple, with paler belly. Juvenile has brown crown and nape, pale grey-brown chin and throat, and no shoulder patch. Blackish bill; pink legs and skin round yellow eye.

STRUCTURE. *Wing length* ML. *Ratios:* wing M; tail M; neck MS; bill MS; legs VS/S.

MOVEMENT. As woodpigeon (p. 102), but much more rapid, clipped flight, wings being brought in and out again with quick jerks; display flight has more flaps and fewer glides.

VOICE. A soothing 'turrr-turrr', with variations.

FIELD MARKS. The smallest and slimmest of the pigeons and doves, with distinctive chestnut upperparts (giving it a superficial resemblance to the otherwise very different male kestrel). Far the best field mark is the conspicuous white tip to the tail, which catches the eye as soon as the bird takes flight. See also collared dove (p. 93).

FLOCKING. Gregarious after breeding; will feed with other pigeons or doves.

HABITAT. All kinds of well timbered and hedged country, commons, heaths, open woodland, large gardens, parks; feeds on cultivated ground.

RANGE AND STATUS. Summer visitor, breeding commonly in S and E England and Midlands, locally in Wales and N and SW England; in Scotland and Ireland only scarce passage migrant.

YELLOW-BILLED CUCKOO *Coccyzus americanus*

The more frequent of the two N American cuckoos that sometimes stray to Europe, but still a rare vagrant; a slim brownish, rather dove-like bird, with a conspicuously black and white tail, rufous primaries showing up in flight, and the base of the lower mandible yellow. The still rarer Black-billed Cuckoo *C. erythrophthalamus* lacks the three distinctive features of the *yellow-billed*, but has a narrow red ring around its eye.

BEE-EATER *Merops apiaster* Plate 20

PLUMAGE. Brilliantly coloured, with chestnut head and mantle; yellow back, rump and throat; blue-green tail, wing-tips and underparts; black band on breast; central tail-feathers project. Slightly curved black bill; dark brownish legs; red eye.

STRUCTURE. *Wing length* ML. *Ratios:* wing MS; tail ML; neck S; bill L; legs VS.

MOVEMENT. Flight rather swallow-like, with long glides on level, triangular wings; often hawks for insects, showing tremendous acceleration to capture them.

VOICE. Flight-note an unmistakable, constantly uttered liquid 'quilp' or 'quirlp'; also a throaty 'kroop, kroop'.

FIELD MARKS. The only land-bird with central tail-feathers projecting, its harlequin plumage, with long, slightly curved bill, makes it unique among wild birds likely to be seen in Britain; yellow back and rump, and pale orange underwing with black trailing edge, are especially noticeable in flight.

FLOCKING. Gregarious, more often than not in small parties.

HABITAT. Mainly open country with trees or at least telegraph wires; resembles sand martin in breeding habits.

RANGE AND STATUS. Very irregular spring visitor to S and especially SW England, occasionally farther N and in autumn; bred in Sussex, 1955.

HOOPOE *Upupa epops* Plates 21, 22

PLUMAGE. Head, mantle and breast pinkish-cinnamon, with prominent crest tipped black; rump and belly white; back, scapulars, rounded wings and tail strongly barred black and white. Curved blackish bill; grey legs.

STRUCTURE. *Wing length* M. *Ratios:* wing MS; tail M; neck MS; bill ML/L legs S.

MOVEMENT. Flight direct and rather like a large butterfly; walks and runs like a dove.

VOICE. A rapid, far-carrying, clipped 'hoo-hoo-hoo', of cuckoo pitch; less drawn out and quavering than tawny owl's hoot, but beware occasional day-hooting tawny owl. Also a harsh, starling-like scolding 'errrr'.

FIELD MARKS. At rest cinnamon-pink plumage, with barred wings, long curved bill and prominent crest (which may be erected like a spread fan, or folded up) make it quite unlike any other bird in this book; in flight its resemblance to a huge, round-winged, black and white butterfly or moth is equally distinctive.

HABITAT. Parks, gardens and open country with scattered trees; fond of probing in lawns and manure heaps for larvae.

RANGE AND STATUS. Annual spring visitor in very small numbers, much scarcer in autumn, to S and E England and S Ireland, especially on coast; rare vagrant elsewhere; has occasionally bred in S England.

GREAT SNIPE See *Waterside: Medium*, p. 140

GOLDEN PLOVER *Charadrius apricarius* Plates 38, 40, 41, 78, 82

PLUMAGE. Golden-brown speckled black above; in summer has blackish (black in northern race) cheeks, throat and underparts, with white line from forehead through eye and down side of neck to flanks in northern race only. Winter adult and juvenile have breast golden and belly white. Black bill; grey-green legs.

STRUCTURE. *Wing length* ML. *Ratios:* wing M; tail MS; neck MS; bill MS; legs M.

MOVEMENT. Quick, direct flight, flocks performing aerial evolutions like dunlin; also bat-like display flight. Walks on ground, wades in water, and when feeding has usual plover trick of a short run and a pause; fond of standing on a slight eminence on breeding ground.

VOICE. Chief note a liquid piping 'tlu-i', with various elaborations; mournful song is delivered in display flight.

FIELD MARKS. In winter can be told from all shore-birds of same size except grey plover (p. 142) by short bill and mottled appearance of upperparts, and in summer black or black and white pattern of face, throat and belly is similarly distinctive. In mixed flocks on the wing easily picked out by its sharp wings from the blunt-winged lapwings. In summer extreme examples of northern race can readily be told from extremes of southern by the deeper black face and underparts bordered by a broad white stripe, but there are many intermediates, and individuals resembling the northern race may even be found breeding; in winter the two forms cannot be told apart.

FLOCKING. Highly gregarious in winter; often with lapwings inland and with other waders on the coast.

HABITAT. Breeds on moors and mosses; in winter on grassland and arable fields, and on muddy shores, especially estuaries.

RANGE AND STATUS. Southern race breeds throughout hill country of N England and Wales and also in Scottish Lowlands and Ireland, but scarce in S Wales, and only occasional in SW England; in winter generally distributed on all coasts and inland, and joined by many migrants of northern race.

MERLIN *Falco columbarius* Plates 29, 30, 31 Falcon Family

Jack Merlin (male), Stone Falcon (immature), Pigeon Hawk (N America).

PLUMAGE. Male is grey-blue above, with buff underparts streaked darker and blackish band at tip of tail. Female and juvenile are dark brown above, with white or whitish underparts streaked darker. Hooked, bluish-grey bill, with yellow cere (blue-grey in juvenile); yellow legs; bare skin round eye blue-grey.

STRUCTURE. *Wing length* ML. *Ratios:* wing ML; tail ML; neck S; bill MS; legs S/M. Female larger than male.

MOVEMENT. Flight much swifter and more dashing than kestrel, though without the vigorous aerial grace of the hobby; outflies small birds by sheer, dogged persistence; sometimes hovers. Usually flies close to ground.

VOICE. A typical shrill, chattering falcon call, 'quik-ik-ik' or 'quek-ek-ek'; alarm note, 'queeek'.

FIELD MARKS. Small size of male, not much bigger than a mistle thrush, is best field character; from male sparrowhawk can also be told by streaked underparts; from hobby by black bar on tail, and lack of moustache and white side of neck. Female is rather like female kestrel, but can be told by brown upperparts and whitish underparts; from hobby can be told by brown upperparts and lack of face pattern. Merlin is least distinctive of smaller birds of prey, and is most easily told by its flight, habitat and general habits.

HABITAT. Moors, fells, mountains, rough hilly country, sand dunes and bogs; in winter tends to desert higher ground for coastal marshes and estuaries, and less commonly rough ground inland.

RANGE AND STATUS. Resident, breeding throughout British Isles, except in S and E England and Midlands; more widely distributed in winter, especially on coasts; a small immigration on E coast in autumn.

SPARROWHAWK *Accipiter nisus* Plates 29, 30, 31 and p. 71

PLUMAGE. Male slate-grey, female grey-brown, young dark brown above; underparts whitish to rufous, barred. Broad, bluntish wings; tail barred; hooked, grey bill, with yellow cere; yellow legs and eye.

STRUCTURE. *Wing length* ML. *Ratios:* wings ML (female), M (male); tail ML; neck S; bill MS; legs M. Female larger than male.

MOVEMENT. Most characteristic flight habit is the quick dash along a hedgerow, up and over to pounce on its prey; also has a fast, low flight through undergrowth of a wood, or across open ground; so-called 'prospecting' flight is a circular glide, with intermittent spasms of three or four wing-flaps; soars, sometimes at a considerable height, and will plunge like a gannet, with folded wings.

VOICE. A harsh chatter, based on 'kek', 'kew' or 'kyow'.

FIELD MARKS. Can be told from all other smaller birds of prey by shortish, broad wings with longish tail; wings of female are much blunter than those of smaller male, which may approach the shape of a female kestrel or merlin;

especial care is needed in identifying the smaller birds of prey when soaring, as in this position the outspread wings and tail make them all look much alike; barred underparts are another useful distinction from all smaller birds of prey, but not from cuckoo (p. 92); dashing flight is best distinction from other birds of prey at any distance, but for other differences, see kestrel (p. 95), merlin (above) and hobby (below); female has whitish eyestripe, and both sexes may have a whitish patch on nape (juvenile cuckoo always has this).

HABITAT. Woods, and all kinds of well-timbered country, including the outer suburbs of large towns; exceptionally in open country.

RANGE AND STATUS. Decreasing resident, formerly breeding throughout British Isles, but very local in N Scotland; now local everywhere and absent from much of E England; some arrive E coast in autumn.

RED-FOOTED FALCON *Falco vespertinus* Plate 30

PLUMAGE. Male all dark grey, with chestnut thighs and under tail-coverts; female rufous buff on head, nape and underparts, otherwise grey above with tail barred darker. Immature is browner than female, and both have dark moustachial stripe. Hooked bill is orange in male, bluish-grey in others; cere, legs and bare skin round eye are orange-red.

STRUCTURE. *Wing length* ML. *Ratios:* wing L; tail ML; neck S; bill MS; legs S.

MOVEMENT. As kestrel (p. 95), but hovers less and flies much at dusk, feeding on moths.

VOICE. Similar to kestrel.

FIELD MARKS. Outline resembles a small, slender kestrel rather than hobby; male is only all-grey bird with reddish thighs, vent, bill and legs (hobby also has rufous thighs and vent, but is grey only above), and orange-red legs are distinctive at all ages; female and immature can be told from merlin and kestrel by moustachial stripe, from kestrel and female merlin by grey upperparts, and from hobby by rufous buff head and nape.

HABITAT. Most likely to be seen in fairly open country.

RANGE AND STATUS. Irregular migrant, chiefly in spring and in S and E England.

HOBBY *Falco subbuteo* Plates 30, 31 Falcon Family

PLUMAGE. Slate-grey above, whitish streaked darker below; black moustachial stripe, sides of neck white, thighs and under tail-coverts rusty red. Young are browner above and lack the rusty red. Hooked, grey-blue bill; cere, legs and bare skin round eye are yellow in adult, grey-blue or greenish in juvenile.

STRUCTURE. *Wing length* L. *Ratios:* wing ML; tail ML; neck S; bill MS; legs S. Female larger than male.

MOVEMENT. Fast, dashing flight recalls now a huge swift, now a small peregrine, with its winnowing wing-beats, followed by a glide; captures flying insects and small birds, especially swallows, on the wing; often rolls over in flight.

VOICE. A loud, shrill 'kiew-kiew-kiew . . .' and a high-pitched 'keek'.

FIELD MARKS. In the air closely resembles a small peregrine, with its swift-like outline of long, scythe-shaped wings and relatively short tail, and its characteristic flight; at close range adult can be told from all birds of prey, except rare red-footed falcon, by reddish thighs and vent, and at all ages can be told from all except peregrine by moustachial streak and white side of neck; kestrel has chestnut mantle and longer tail; sparrowhawk has barred underparts, rounded wings and longer tail; male merlin has black bar on tail and female is brown above; flight also distinguishes from all last three.

HABITAT. All kinds of country with scattered timber, especially downland with shelter-belts of pines, but also farmland, heaths, commons and open woodland; sometimes with migrating flocks of swallows and martins.

RANGE AND STATUS. Summer visitor, breeding mainly in S England, and occasionally in Midlands as far N as Cheshire and Yorkshire; rare vagrant elsewhere.

ROLLER *Coracias garrulus* Plate 22

PLUMAGE. Blue-green, with chestnut back; in flight wings show bright blue with black tips. Thick, slightly hooked, blackish bill; yellowish legs.

STRUCTURE. *Wing length* M. *Ratios:* wing M; tail M; neck S; bill MS; legs S

MOVEMENT. Direct flight, not unlike woodpigeon.

VOICE. A harsh, rather corvine, 'rack-kack, kacker'.

FIELD MARKS. The only blue-green bird with a chestnut back (smaller bee-eater shows much yellow on rump and throat), and the only one except the jay which has a bright blue wing patch; in flight looks not unlike a small crow.

HABITAT. Prefers open country with scattered trees; likes exposed perches.

RANGE AND STATUS. Vagrant, most often seen on S and E coasts England, spring to autumn.

GREENSHANK, summer See *Waterside: Medium*, p. 144

LAPWING *Vanellus vanellus* Plates 41, 45, 83 Plover Family

Green Plover, Peewit, Black Plover, Pyewipe.

PLUMAGE. Black (actually dark green shot with purple) above and on breast, white below and on cheeks, with prominent crest; black bar at tip of white tail. Throat is black in summer, white in winter. Juvenile is like adult winter, but has shorter crest. Black bill; flesh-brown legs.

STRUCTURE. *Wing length* ML. *Ratios:* wing ML; tail MS; neck MS; bill S/MS; legs M.

MOVEMENT. Slow, direct flight, flocks performing complicated aerial evolutions, but without the rapid twisting and turning of the dunlin type. In spring has striking aerobatic display flight, in which wings make a loud throbbing or 'lapping' sound. Runs on ground, with typical plover action of a short pause after each few patters; wades in water.

VOICE. Call-notes and song are all variations on main 'pee-wit' theme, ground call being usually 'peeet', flight call 'pee-wit' and song, delivered in flight, 'p'weet, pee-wit, pee-wit'.

FIELD MARKS. In flight the only medium-sized pied bird with rounded wings, and at rest the only one with a crest and longish legs; though it normally appears black and white, it can look a brilliant green above in bright sunshine.

FLOCKING. Highly gregarious; often with other waders and starlings, especially golden plover in winter and common redshank in summer.

HABITAT. At all times on farmland, both grass and arable; breeds also largely in damp, rushy fields and on coastal marshes and moorland; in winter also at freshwater margins and on estuarine and coastal mudflats and sands.

RANGE AND STATUS. Resident, breeding throughout the British Isles; in autumn some emigrate and many more arrive on E coast.

COMMON PARTRIDGE *Perdix perdix* Plates 25, 26, 71 Pheasant Family
Hungarian, or European Partridge (N America); a game bird.

PLUMAGE. Brown, with dark and light markings; rufous head, tail and bars on flanks; grey breast, with chestnut horseshoe on all cocks and many hens. Juvenile has no horseshoe, no rufous markings, and streaked underparts. *Montana* variety is much more rufous all over. Bill greenish-horn; legs grey (yellow in juvenile); small patch of red skin behind eye.

STRUCTURE. *Wing length* M. *Ratios:* wing MS; tail S; neck MS; bill S; legs M.

MOVEMENT. Has typical whirring game-bird flight, alternating with periods of gliding on down-curved wings; walks.

VOICE. A loud, high-pitched, grating or creaky 'keev' or 'keev-it', degenerating into a rapid cackle, 'it-it-it . . .' when flushed.

FIELD MARKS. A medium-sized game bird, with a dark horseshoe on the breast and chestnut tail, both easily seen in flight; adult must be distinguished from red-legged partridge (p. 98), and juvenile from quail (p. 73). Juvenile is like juvenile pheasant, but is smaller, has short tail, and yellower legs.

FLOCKING. After breeding season goes in small parties called coveys; does not mix with red-legged partridge or quail.

HABITAT. All kinds of cultivated farmland, both grass and arable, with some cover such as hedges, bushes or rough grass balks or ditches; also extensively on rough ground adjacent to farmland, hillsides, grass moorland, heaths, sand dunes, shingle tracts, etc.

RANGE AND STATUS. Resident, breeding almost throughout British Isles, but now very local in those parts of Scotland, Ireland and Wales where the natives have no respect for English social customs.

NUTCRACKER *Nucifroga caryocatactes* Plate 22 Crow Family

PLUMAGE. Mainly brown with white spots, but crown unspotted; wings, tail and upper tail-coverts black; tip of tail and under tail-coverts white. Thick, black bill; legs black.

STRUCTURE. *Wing length* ML. *Ratios:* wing M; tail ML; neck S; bill M; legs M.

MOVEMENT. Flight undulating; hops.

VOICE. A rather high-pitched caw; alarm note a curious nightjar-like trill.

FIELD MARKS. The only brown bird of its size with white spots; white on tail and under tail-coverts very noticeable in flight.

HABITAT. To be expected among conifers or hazels.

RANGE AND STATUS. A vagrant, chiefly in autumn and mostly in S and E England.

GREEN WOODPECKER *Picus viridis* Plates 20, 21

Yaffle; Rain Bird.

PLUMAGE. Green, with yellowish rump and red crown; male also has red and black moustachial stripe (hen black stripe only). Juvenile is speckled darker. Thick grey-black bill; olive-grey legs; white eye.

STRUCTURE. *Wing length* ML. *Ratios:* wing MS; tail MS/M; neck MS; bill M; legs S.

MOVEMENT. Flight conspicuously undulating; hops; climbs about trees.

VOICE. A loud, ringing, far-carrying 'plue-plue-plue' and various yelping cries.

FIELD MARKS. The only green bird with red on the head and, in flight, a conspicuous yellow rump; bright coloration often causes it to be reported as golden oriole or even as 'a bird like a toucan'; seen against the light may look almost black. Cf. rare and much larger great black woodpecker (p. 105).

HABITAT. All kinds of well-timbered country, from open woodlands, heaths, commons and farmland to parks and large gardens, much preferring broad-leaved trees to conifers; feeds on ground, especially at anthills, as well as in trees, and is especially fond of lawns.

RANGE AND STATUS. Resident, breeding throughout S England, Midlands and Wales, but rather local N of line joining Humber and Mersey; has recently been seen more frequently S Scotland, but rare vagrant elsewhere in Scotland, and not recorded Ireland since 1854.

MERLIN, female See p. 88

CUCKOO *Cuculus canorus* Plates 5, 29, 30, 31

Gowk (Scotland and Ireland).

PLUMAGE. Adult is uniform grey above and on throat, and barred beneath; male also has uniform grey breast; white spots and tips on tail. Juveniles are of two forms, grey and red-brown, both barred all over, with a white patch on the nape, the barring showing more heavily on the red-brown form. The rare 'hepatic' form of the adult hen is even redder than the red-brown juvenile. Horn-coloured bill; yellow legs, eye and eyelids.

STRUCTURE. *Wing length* ML. *Ratios:* wing ML; tail ML; neck MS; bill MS; legs VS/S.

MOVEMENT. Flight direct, with wings hardly raised above horizontal plane and far down below body at bottom of downstroke; hops.

VOICE. Well-known 'cooc-ooo' note has variants 'cooc-cooc-ooo', etc., also extraordinary variety of coughing and choking notes when excited. Hen has a 'water-bubbling' trill, not unlike nightingale in tone. Juvenile has a persistent and penetrating cheep, like that of young song-birds just out of the nest, with which it attracts other birds to feed it after it has left the nest.

FIELD MARKS. Sufficiently like a bird of prey, especially male sparrowhawk, to be shot by keepers and mobbed by small birds, but can be told at once by long, graduated tail, with white spots and tips, and pointed wings, which together give it a very rakish rig, as well as by characteristic low-wing flight, and at close range by non-hooked bill. Juvenile has conspicuous white patch on nape (which some sparrowhawks also have) and when just out of the nest is very round-winged.

FLOCKING. Not gregarious, but often mobbed by smaller birds; any large bird being fed by a smaller one is almost certainly a young cuckoo.

HABITAT. Extremely catholic: woods, reed-beds, farmland, sand dunes, bogs, large gardens, open moorland, almost wherever there are small birds for it to victimise; chief fosterers are meadow pipit, hedgesparrow, reed warbler, robin, pied wagtail and sedge warbler.

RANGE AND STATUS. Summer visitor, breeding almost throughout British Isles; also passage migrant.

JACKDAW *Corvus monedula* Plates 69, 70 Crow Family

Daw.

PLUMAGE. All black except for grey nape, shoulders and ear-coverts. Black bill and legs; pearl-grey eye.

STRUCTURE. *Wing length* ML. *Ratios:* wing ML; tail M; neck S; bill MS; legs M.

MOVEMENT. Both flight and gait much quicker and jerkier than those of the larger black crows.

VOICE. Typical notes are higher-pitched than the larger black crows; a clipped, metallic 'kow' or 'kyow', and a softer 'tchack', both of which may be repeated several times with an antiphonal effect, viz. 'kyow-kiew kyow-kiew-kyow' or 'tchack-tchoock-tchack-tchock-tchack'.

FIELD MARKS. The only black bird with a grey nape; can also be told from all other black crows by smaller size, voice and quicker movement, from adult rook by feathered base of bill and from chough by black bill and legs.

FLOCKING. Highly gregarious at all seasons, habitually associating with rooks; nests communally, often in rookeries.

HABITAT. In breeding season in small towns and villages, cathedrals, castles, quarries, inland and coastal cliffs, parkland with old trees; afterwards mainly on farmland.

RANGE AND STATUS. Resident, but local N and W Highlands; some move S and W in winter, and large numbers arrive E coast every autumn.

COLLARED DOVE *Streptopelia decaocto* Plate 24

Collared Turtle Dove, Eastern Collared Dove.

PLUMAGE. Ashy brown, with blackish wing-tips, pinkish tinge on breast, blue-grey belly and leading edge to wings, black base to white underside of tail, and white-edged black half-collar on neck (obscure in juvenile). Blackish bill, pink legs.

MOVEMENT. Intermediate between wood-pigeon (p. 102) and turtle dove (p. 85).

VOICE. Song a persistent and distinctive triple 'coo-cooo-cuk', with accent on middle syllable and last one somewhat truncated; anger note 'cwurr'.

FIELD MARKS. Differs from both *turtle* and Barbary doves (p. 81) in its larger size, blackish wing-tips and pattern of black and white on tail; also from *turtle* in its grey plumage and black half-collars.

FLOCKING. Gregarious, like other doves.

HABITAT. Towns, suburbs, villages and even remote hamlets, with their associated gardens, parks and farmland; especially near granaries, chicken farms and other places where grain is scattered on the ground.

RANGE AND STATUS. Resident since 1955, when first proved to breed in N Norfolk; now widespread in small colonies throughout British Isles, and will doubtless become universal in human settlements before long.

Collared Dove

STOCK DOVE *Columba oenas* Plates 24, 68

Blue rock (Provincial).

PLUMAGE. Blue-grey, with pinkish breast and paler belly; green patch at side of neck (adult only), black tips to wings and tail, and two small black bars on wing. Yellowish bill, pink legs.

STRUCTURE. *Wing length* ML. *Ratios:* wing M; tail MS; neck MS; bill S; legs VS/S.

MOVEMENT. Similar to woodpigeon (p. 102), but has different display flight, in which birds fly round in circles, sometimes gliding with raised wings.

VOICE. A coughing or grunting double coo, with accent on the second coo; much gruffer and shorter than woodpigeon.

FIELD MARKS. Very similar to rock dove and blue-rock type of domestic pigeon, but can always be told by black wing-tips and no white rump; from larger woodpigeon can be told by shorter tail and no white on wings or neck.

FLOCKING. Gregarious; often feeds with flocks of woodpigeons.

HABITAT. Remarkably catholic, favouring both woods and open country where old timber is present, and rocks, cliffs, old buildings, sand dunes and rabbit warrens; often feeds on cultivated land.

RANGE AND STATUS. Resident, breeding throughout British Isles, except N Scotland, but local in Ireland and Isle of Man.

LONDON PIGEON See *Waterside: Medium*, p. 144

MOORHEN See *Water: Medium*, p. 172

HOBBY, female See p. 89

KESTREL *Falco tinnunculus* Plates 29, 31 Falcon Family
Windhover.

PLUMAGE. Rufous chestnut. Male has blue-grey head and tail, with a black band at end of tail. Female and juvenile have barred tail, also with a black band. All have mantle spotted and underparts streaked black or blackish. Hooked, bluish-horn bill; yellow cere, legs and skin round eye.

STRUCTURE. *Wing length* ML. *Ratios:* wing ML; tail ML; neck S; bill MS; legs S.

MOVEMENT. Fairly rapid direct flight, also soars; frequently and habitually hovers, with tail fanned out and wings flapping vigorously, followed by a pounce.

Kestrel hovering (left) and soaring (middle); Sparrowhawk soaring (right), showing difference in shape of wing

VOICE. A loud shrill 'kee-kee-kee-kee', not unlike wryneck, nuthatch or barred woodpecker; also 'kik-kik-kik' and occasionally a whinnying or keening note.

FIELD MARKS. Constant hovering is far and away the best field character, though several other birds (including merlin) occasionally hover; when flying direct, long pointed wings and long tail give it a rather rakish appearance. No other bird of prey has male's combination of blue-grey head and tail, chestnut mantle and black bar on tail. Female can be told from peregrine, hobby and female merlin by bar on tail; also lacks the moustachial streak and white side of neck of the peregrine and hobby, the whitish underparts of the merlin, and the barred underparts of the sparrowhawk.

HABITAT. Almost universal, from the centre of London to the wildest and remotest mountains and coastal areas, and a not uncommon suburban bird; nests in trees, rocks or buildings.

RANGE AND STATUS. Resident, breeding throughout British Isles, but many northern birds move S in winter, while others arrive from Continent, mostly on E coast, in autumn.

JAY *Garrulus glandarius* Plates 21, 22 Crow Family

PLUMAGE. Pinkish-brown, with blue patch on wings, white on wings and rump, and black on wings and tail; black and white feathers on crown can form a crest. Thick, blackish bill; brownish legs.

STRUCTURE. *Wing length* ML. *Ratios:* wing MS; tail ML: neck S; bill MS; legs S.

MOVEMENT. Flight weak and rather undulating; hops.

VOICE. A harsh, scolding screech, 'skaaak, skaaak'.

FIELD MARKS. The only medium or large land bird (except for rare roller) with a blue wing patch: white rump very conspicuous when flying away.

FLOCKING. Usually only in parties, but larger numbers occur at ceremonial gatherings in spring and on oaks at acorn-time.

HABITAT. Woods and well-timbered open country; sometimes in large gardens and even town parks.

RANGE AND STATUS. Resident, but local in Scotland and Ireland; some arrive E coast England in autumn.

BARN OWL *Tyto alba* Plates 33, 74, 76

Screech Owl, White Owl.

PLUMAGE. Golden-buff above, more or less mottled grey; flattened white facial disk; white, sometimes speckled darker, below. Dark-breasted race, sometimes known as 'blue barn-owl', tends to be much more blue-grey above and golden-buff below. Rounded wings; hooked, whitish bill; feathered legs and feet; black eye.

STRUCTURE. *Wing length* L. *Ratios:* wing L; tail MS; neck S; bill does not project; legs M.

MOVEMENT. Flight slow and flapping, like other large owls.

VOICE. A prolonged, strangled, eldritch screech; also hisses and snores.

FIELD MARKS. The only bird which is golden-buff above and white below; even the occasional abnormal bird with almost white upperparts is so much smaller than the snowy owl that only a wishful thinker could mistake it for the rarer bird; most often seen ghost-like in the dusk, or caught in the headlights of a car, when it appears white all over, but also not uncommonly flies by day, especially in winter. The more extremely marked specimens of the dark-breasted race can be told in the field by their deep buff underparts and blue-grey upperparts, the latter also distinguishing them from the tawny owl, which has shorter wings and may also have buff underparts.

HABITAT. Usually breeds in or near farms or villages, but also in derelict buildings, old trees, cliffs, etc.; hunts over farmland and other open country.

RANGE AND STATUS. Resident, breeding throughout British Isles, but rare in NW Scotland, and not in NE Scotland or isles; dark-breasted Continental race occurs most often in S and E England, but even there very irregularly.

LONG-EARED OWL *Asio otus* Plates 33, 73

PLUMAGE. Brown, streaked darker, with prominent ear-tufts. Juvenile is barred. Rounded wings; hooked, blackish-horn bill, set in flattened facial disk; feathered legs and feet; golden-orange eye.

STRUCTURE. *Wing length* L. *Ratios:* wing L; tail M; neck S; bill does not project; legs S.

MOVEMENT. Flight rather slow and flapping, like other large owls.

VOICE. A more long-drawn-out, moaning hoot than the tawny owl, usually uttered at night. Young birds have an 'unoiled hinge' hunger-cry.

FIELD MARKS. Normally seen by day only when roosting against a tree-trunk in a somewhat attenuated posture, or when flushed from ground; ear-tufts may or may not be visible, but are noticeably longer than in short-eared owl; slimmer than short-eared and tawny owls, and from latter can also be told by longer wings, yellow eyes and ear-tufts.

FLOCKING. Small parties roost together, and sometimes occur on migration.

HABITAT. Woods, especially of conifers, and sometimes heaths, dunes and marshes; hunts over open country.

RANGE AND STATUS. Resident, breeding throughout British Isles, but local in S England and Midlands, and very local in Wales and NW Scotland; the only brown owl breeding in Ireland; also passage migrant in small numbers, E coast and N Isles.

WOODCOCK *Scolopax rusticola* Plates 25, 39, 73 Sandpiper Family

Cock.

PLUMAGE. Warm brown, streaked and marbled darker above, with blackish markings on head and neck, and barred darker below. Flesh-coloured bill, dark at tip; greyish flesh-coloured legs.

STRUCTURE. *Wing length* ML. *Ratios:* wing M; tail MS; neck S; bill L; legs M.

MOVEMENT. Flight can be strong and swift, or slow and weak, but bill is nearly always carried pointing downwards; in 'roding' display flight, male flies a circuit at dusk and dawn, with a somewhat owlish flight and curious interrupted wing-beats, uttering two distinct notes.

VOICE. When roding has a rather sibilant 'tsiwick' and a frog-like croak or grunting growl.

FIELD MARKS. Is usually seen either in unmistakable roding flight, or as a rather large rufous brown bird flushed among undergrowth and flying fast and twistingly out of sight among the trees. On ground blends remarkably well with dried vegetation, being betrayed only by large black eye set well back in head. Can be told from common snipe by larger size, dark bars across instead of along head, no pale streaks on back or face, shorter bill carried downwards in flight, and differences in voice, flight and habitat. See also great snipe (p. 140).

FLOCKING. Gregarious only on migration.

HABITAT. Woodland, feeding in marshy and boggy ground, and on rough ground with shrubs and other cover; also in autumn among heather and bracken on moors; will use any available cover on sea-shore when newly arrived.

RANGE AND STATUS. Resident, breeding commonly in the New Forest, the Weald, the Welsh Marches, N Midlands, N England and many parts of Scotland and Ireland; elsewhere breeds irregularly or in small numbers, especially in Wales, SW England, and coastal strip from N Norfolk to Thames estuary. Winter visitor in considerable numbers, arriving on E coast and many passing to Ireland.

PTARMIGAN *Lagopus mutus* Plate 26 Grouse Family

Rock Ptarmigan (N America); a game bird.

PLUMAGE. In winter all white, except for black lores (cock only) and tail. In summer pale brown (grey in brief autumn eclipse) mottled darker above and on breast, with white wing-tips and belly. Juvenile like summer adult but with dark wing-tips. Black bill; feathered legs; red wattle over eye.

STRUCTURE. *Wing length* ML. *Ratios:* wing M; tail MS; neck MS; bill S; legs S.

MOVEMENT. As common partridge (p. 91); perches on rocks.

VOICE. A hoarse croak, and a crackling note.

FIELD MARKS. Restricted habitat and partly or wholly white plumage distinguish it from all other birds. In winter no other medium-sized land-bird is so white, and in summer the white belly and wing-tips, giving it a very pied appearance in flight, easily separate it from red grouse.

FLOCKING. Flocks or packs in the autumn.

HABITAT. Barren, rocky mountain-tops, usually above 2,500 ft. and rarely below 2,000 ft.

RANGE AND STATUS. Confined to the highest Scottish mountains from Ben Lomond northwards and in some Inner Hebrides.

RED GROUSE *Lagopus lagopus* Plates 26, 71

A game bird.

PLUMAGE. Dark red-brown, with darker mottlings, and blackish tail and wing-tips. Blackish bill; whitish feathered legs; cock has prominent red wattle over eye.

STRUCTURE. *Wing length* ML. *Ratios:* wing M; tail MS; neck MS; bill S; legs S.

MOVEMENT. As common partridge (p. 91); occasionally perches in trees and on walls.

VOICE. Typical calls are a loud 'kok-kok-kok' and 'gobak, gobak'; various other notes associated with courtship.

FIELD MARKS. Smaller than black grouse (p. 103), though can look almost black at a distance in poor light and always separable in flight by lack of white wing-bar. Rarely occurs in same type of country as partridges, but when it does can be told by larger size, no distinct barring on flanks, tail not rufous, and no dark horseshoe on breast (common partridge) or black and white chin and throat (red-legged partridge).

FLOCKING. Flocks or packs in the autumn.

HABITAT. Moors, bogs or mosses with heather or crowberry (not grass); occasionally on stubble near moorland in autumn.

RANGE AND STATUS. Resident on all suitable moorlands in Scotland, England S to Cannock Chase (also introduced on Exmoor), and Wales (except Glamorgan and Pembroke); scarce in Ireland.

RED-LEGGED PARTRIDGE *Alectoris rufa* Plates 25, 26, 71

French Partridge; Frenchman; Red-leg; a game bird. Pheasant Family

PLUMAGE. Brown, with grey crown; white chin, cheeks and stripe over eye; black stripe through eye and down neck, widening out to black bib on lower neck, with black spotting below it on grey breast; flanks strongly barred blue-grey, chestnut, black and buff; tail chestnut. Juvenile resembles juvenile common partridge (p. 91). Bill and legs red (juvenile's bill brown and legs paler).

STRUCTURE. *Wing length* M. *Ratios:* wing S; tail S; neck MS; bill MS; legs S.

MOVEMENT. As common partridge, but often perches on posts, fences, corn-stacks, etc., and even in trees.

VOICE. A loud, challenging 'chucka, chucka' or 'chik-chik-chikar', also a sound like the whetting of a scythe, or a decrepit steam locomotive.

FIELD MARKS. At a distance looks like common partridge, but can easily be told by white and black eyestripes, white chin and throat, black bib, grey crown, red bill and legs, and especially by conspicuous barring on flanks, which stand out much more clearly than on *common*; also lacks dark horseshoe on breast. Note, however, that both have chestnut tail, so that hard to separate when flying away; at rest *red-legged* appears a slightly longer, more pheasant-like bird than *common*, stands higher and more erectly, and often perches at a small elevation, which *common* hardly ever does. Juveniles are very similar, and best separated by leg colour if no parent is present; see also quail (p. 73). See also chukor partridge (below).

FLOCKING. As common partridge.

HABITAT. Similar to common partridge, but rather less catholic, preferring on the whole arable fields, stony and sandy heaths and wastes, extensive shingle and chalk downs.

RANGE AND STATUS. Resident, having been introduced in 18th century; now breeds commonly in E and SE England, gradually thinning out through the Midlands, N to Yorkshire and N Wales, and W to Somerset; occasional elsewhere. Outnumbers *common* in parts of E England.

CHUKOR PARTRIDGE *Alectoris graeca* Plate 26 Pheasant Family

Resembles red-legged partridge (above) in general appearance and habits, but is rather larger and much greyer on mantle and breast, with buff throat and lores and no black spots on breast below bib. A race of the European rock partridge occasionally introduced for ornamental and sporting purposes.

BLACK-HEADED GULL See *Water: Medium*, p. 175

SHORT-EARED OWL *Asio flammeus* Plates 33, 74

Woodcock Owl.

PLUMAGE. Buff, mottled dark brown, with short ear-tuft. Juvenile is barred. Rounded wings; hooked, dark horn-coloured bill, set in flattened facial disk; feathered legs and feet; golden-yellow eye.

STRUCTURE. *Wing length* L. *Ratios:* wing ML; tail MS; neck S; bill not does project; legs S.

MOVEMENT. Has typical slow, flapping flight of larger owls, but also soars, wheels and glides like a buzzard; carriage less upright than other owls.

VOICE. Has a harsh barking flight-note.

FIELD MARKS. Length of wing is one of salient characters, though this varies individually; a buff and black patch at the 'elbow' of the wing, and a blackish mark at the corresponding place underneath. Name is misleading, as ear-tufts can rarely be seen in the field. Much the most likely large brown owl to be seen by day; *long-eared* is slimmer and has noticeable ear-tufts; *tawny* has shorter wings, black eyes and no ear-tufts.

FLOCKING. Small parties occur on migration, and several pairs may inhabit quite a small area during a vole plague.

HABITAT. All kinds of open country, especially where the field vole is abundant, moors, downs, rough hillsides, heaths, bogs, fens, marshes, sand dunes, sea-walls and very young plantations; also in winter on farmland.

RANGE AND STATUS. Resident, breeding locally in Scotland, N England, E Anglia and W Wales, and sporadically elsewhere in England and Wales, according to the abundance of voles; more generally distributed in winter, especially on coast.

LAND BIRDS: Medium Long

TAWNY OWL *Strix aluco* Plates 33, 73
Brown Owl; Wood Owl.

PLUMAGE. Very variable, ranging from rich chestnut tawny through various shades of buff, brown and grey-brown to greyish-white; grey birds commoner in N England and especially Scotland. Juvenile is barred. Rounded wings; hooked, pale greenish-yellow bill, set in flattened facial disk; feathered legs and feet; black eye.

STRUCTURE. *Wing length* L. *Ratios:* wing ML; tail M; neck S; bill does not project; legs S.

MOVEMENT. Flight slow and flapping like other large owls.

VOICE. Most familiar note is the hoot, 'hooo, hooo, hoo-oo-oo-oo-oo-oo', the final phase with a quavering effect; also 'ke-wick', especially in autumn (these two comprise the traditional 'tu-whit, tu-whoo', but in fact are rarely uttered together); calls mostly by night, but occasionally by day.

FIELD MARKS. Most often discovered in daytime by following up noisy mobbing parties of small birds, especially jays, blackbirds and chaffinches, at its roost; on infrequent occasions when it flies by day, can be told from *barn* and the two eared owls by shorter wings, from *long-eared* also by larger size and stouter build; at rest can be told from *barn* by brown underparts, and from the two eared owls by black eyes and no ear-tufts.

HABITAT. Woods, copses and well-timbered parks, gardens and farmland; not uncommon in suburbs; occasionally in open country.

RANGE AND STATUS. Resident, breeding almost throughout Great Britain, but absent from Ireland and Isle of Man.

CHOUGH *Pyrrhocorax pyrrhocorax* Plates 23, 69, 70 Crow Family

Cornish Chough.

PLUMAGE. All black, glossed bluish. Curved red bill; red legs.

STRUCTURE. *Wing length* L. *Ratios:* wing ML; tail M; neck S; bill MS; legs S/M.

MOVEMENT. Flight buoyant; will indulge in aerobatics like raven; walks and hops.

VOICE. One common note is very like a young jackdaw's 'kyow', another is more gull-like than corvine, a third, 'k'chuf', has given the bird its name.

FIELD MARKS. The only black bird with red bill and legs; can also be told from jackdaw by lack of grey on nape; in flight more like rook than jackdaw.

FLOCKING. Gregarious, in parties and where sufficiently numerous in small flocks.

HABITAT. Cliffs and quarries, both coastal and inland; feeds on grassy slopes and fields near cliff-top rather than on shore.

RANGE AND STATUS. Resident; almost extinct in N Cornwall; local on coasts of Pembroke, Cardigan and Caernarvon, and inland in N and Central Wales; Isle of Man; local in Inner Hebrides; not uncommon on N, S and W coasts of Ireland and in a few places inland.

SPARROWHAWK, female See *Land: Medium*, p. 88

PEREGRINE *Falco peregrinus* Plates 29, 30, 31 Falcon Family

Duck Hawk (N America).

PLUMAGE. Slate-grey above buff barred darker below; juvenile is dark brown above, streaked below; thick, dark moustachial streak, side of neck white. Hooked, blue-grey bill; cere, legs and bare skin round eye are yellow in adult, blue-grey in juvenile.

STRUCTURE. *Wing length* L. *Ratios:* wing ML; tail M; neck S; bill MS; legs S/M. Female larger than male.

MOVEMENT. Characteristic flight has swift, winnowing wing-beats, followed by a glide; also soars, and much given to aerobatics; fond of watching for prey from look-out on cliff or crag, and normally kills by 'stooping', a kind of avian power-dive.

VOICE. Usual notes are shrill, chattering 'kek-kek-kek-kek' and a hoarser 'kwaahk-kwaahk-kwaahk'.

FIELD MARKS. In flight is best identified by distinctive, anchor-like outline of long wings and relatively short tail, and large size (a small male peregrine is nearly as small as a large female hobby, kestrel or sparrowhawk, but a large female peregrine is nearly as large as a small male buzzard or marsh harrier). Moustache distinguishes from all birds of prey except hobby, which has orange thighs and vent; kestrel has longer tail and rufous mantle; sparrowhawk has longer tail and rounded wings.

HABITAT. Breeds chiefly on sea-cliffs and on crags in hilly districts, but occasionally in wooded lowlands; in winter also frequents estuaries and flat shores; exceptionally preys on pigeons in towns; may be seen passing over almost anywhere.

RANGE AND STATUS. Resident, breeding throughout British Isles, except inland in S and E England and Midlands, but much decreased in recent years due to pesticide residues: also passage migrant.

RED GROUSE, cock See *Land: Medium*, p. 98

WHIMBREL See *Waterside: Medium Long*, p. 149

STONE CURLEW *Burhinus oedicnemus* Plates 25, 73

Norfolk Plover; Thick-knee.

PLUMAGE. Sandy brown, streaked darker, with black and white marks on wings. Bill black at tip, yellow at base; legs and eye yellow.

STRUCTURE. *Wing length* ML. *Ratios:* wing M; tail MS; neck MS; bill MS; legs ML/L.

MOVEMENT. Rather slow, direct flight, with legs trailing behind; walks or runs.

VOICE. A wild, shrill, curlew-like wail, often heard at night, 'coo-leee'.

FIELD MARKS. Not unlike a curlew in general appearance, but can be told at once by short bill, and in flight by black and white marks on wings. At close quarters conspicuous yellow eye makes it unmistakable.

FLOCKING. Often in parties in autumn, and sometimes in large flocks.

HABITAT. Breeds on sandy heaths and warrens, open stony fields and downland on the chalk, and extensive shingle; on migration sometimes in other types of open country.

RANGE AND STATUS. Summer visitor, breeding now only on the brecklands and coastal heaths of E. Anglia, at Dungeness, very locally on the Chilterns and South Downs, and more widely and commonly on the main mass of the southern chalk in Wessex. Elsewhere scarce passage migrant; occasional in winter, mostly in SW England.

WOODPIGEON *Columba palumbus* Plates 24, 68 Dove Family

Ring Dove, Cushat, Cushie Doo.

PLUMAGE. Head, neck and black-tipped tail blue-grey, with green, purple and prominent white patches at side of neck; mantle and wings grey-brown, with conspicuous white wing patch; breast purplish-brown, much paler on belly. Juvenile lacks neck patches. Pinkish bill; pink legs; pale yellow eye.

STRUCTURE. *Wing length* ML. *Ratios:* wing M; tail M; neck MS; bill S; legs VS/S.

MOVEMENT. Normal flight fast and direct; with a noisy clatter when flushed from tree-tops; in display flaps upwards at a steep angle and then glides down with wings scarcely upraised, often repeating the movement several times; walks.

VOICE. Well-known cooing note, 'coo-cooo-coo, coo-coo'.

FIELD MARKS. Any large greyish bird with a prominent white patch on the neck and/or wing is most likely to be a woodpigeon; other pigeons and doves are smaller and have no white on wing or neck, while some have white on rump or tail. Juvenile woodpigeons are darker and have no white on the neck.

FLOCKING. Highly gregarious; sometimes feeding together with stock doves.

HABITAT. All kinds of wooded country, feeding both in the trees and in adjacent open country, especially cultivated fields; regular in town parks and large gardens.

RANGE AND STATUS. Resident, breeding almost throughout British Isles, but local and uncommon in N Scotland; some arrive on E coast in autumn.

COMMON GULL See *Water: Medium Long*, p. 180

BLACK GROUSE *Lyrurus tetrix* Plates 26, 27, 28, 72

Blackcock (male); greyhen (female); blackgame (collective); a game bird.

PLUMAGE. Cock is black glossed dark blue (black-brown during brief autumnal eclipse), with white wing-bar and under tail-coverts, and lyrate tail. Hen and juvenile are brown, mottled blackish above and barred below with white wing-bar and forked tail. Blackish-brown bill; feathered legs; bright red wattle above eye.

STRUCTURE. *Wing length* ML (hen), L (cock). *Ratios:* wing MS; tail S (hen), M (cock); neck MS; bill S/MS; legs S. Cock larger than hen.

MOVEMENT. As common partridge (p. 91), but flight intermediate between capercaillie and red grouse, and less noisy than caper in leaving trees, where it habitually perches and feeds; flies higher than red grouse.

VOICE. Cock has a cooing, bubbling or crowing song, also various notes heard only at communal display at lek. Hen has a pheasant-like 'kok, kok'.

FIELD MARKS. Intermediate in size between capercaillie and red grouse. Cock is only large black land bird with white wing-bar and lyre-shaped tail. Hen is like small hen caper with forked tail and no rufous patch on breast, or like large grey red grouse with wing-bar, forked tail and darker legs. Beware occasional hybrids with common pheasant.

FLOCKING. More gregarious than capercaillie; in spring and to lesser extent in autumn large gatherings occur at communal display ground called 'lek'.

HABITAT. Borders of moorland and woodland, or moorland with scattered trees, especially birches and pines.

RANGE AND STATUS. Resident, breeding on Exmoor, Central and N Wales, locally in Pennines N from Staffordshire, and scattered over most of Scotland, but local and decreasing almost everywhere except mid-Wales, Staffordshire and a few places in Scotland.

MONTAGU'S HARRIER *Circus pygargus* Plates 32, 74, 76 Hawk Family

Ring-tail (female).

PLUMAGE. Male is all grey, with black wing-tips and bar on wing, rump paler than mantle, and rufous streaks on whitish flanks. Female is brown, streaked darker below, with barred tail and white rump. Young are like female, but have unstreaked chestnut underparts and creamy chin. A dark melanic form occurs. Pointed wings; hooked, black bill, with yellow cere; yellow legs; male has yellow eye.

STRUCTURE. *Wing length* L. *Ratios:* wing L; tail L; neck S; bill MS; legs M.

MOVEMENT. Buoyant and graceful flight, quartering low over reed-beds or heathland with typical harrier way of gliding with wings slightly canted up.

VOICE. A chattering 'yick, yick, yick'.

FIELD MARKS. Graceful flight and extremely rakish appearance due to long, slender wings and tail make *Montagu's* look like a large kestrel; at a distance male can be taken for a gull or heron, but at close range resembles only the male hen-harrier, from which can be told by generally smaller size (though the two overlap), more pointed wings, black bar on the mid-wing (not always easy to see even at quite close range), less conspicuous pale rump, and rufous streaks on flanks; female *Montagu's* cannot be separated from female and young *hen* in the field, the two species in this plumage being lumped together as 'ring-tails' from the barring on the tail; the ring-tail *Montagu's* is in fact more slenderly built than the ring-tail *hen*, and has a rather less conspicuous white rump, but identification in the field on these characters is hardly possible even for experts unless the two are seen together (an unlikely event, as they only overlap in Britain in April and October); young *Montagu's*, however, can easily be told from all other ring-tails by their unstreaked deep chestnut-buff under-parts; see also marsh harrier (p. 153).

FLOCKING. Tends to nest in small colonies, though in Britain these rarely exceed two or three pairs.

HABITAT. A wide variety of open, rough ground, such as heaths, commons, downs, moors, sand dunes, salt and fresh marshes, reed-beds, fens, young plantations and even cornfields.

RANGE AND STATUS. Summer visitor, now very rare, though formerly breeding in most coastal counties in S England and Wales, also in N Wales and occasionally in N England; vagrant only in Scotland and Ireland.

HEN-HARRIER *Circus cyaneus* Plates 32, 74, 76 Hawk Family

Ring-tail (female and young); Marsh Hawk or Harrier (N America).

PLUMAGE. Male is all grey, with black wing-tips and a prominent white rump. Female and young resemble female Montagu's harrier (above). Bluntly pointed wings; hooked, black bill, with yellow cere (greenish in young); yellow legs; adult has yellow eye.

STRUCTURE. *Wing length* L. *Ratios:* wing ML; tail ML; neck S; bill MS; legs S. Female larger than male.

MOVEMENT. As Montagu's harrier, but more inclined to hover.

VOICE. A chattering 'ke-ke-ke' or 'kek-kek-kek'.

FIELD MARKS. Closely resembles *Montagu's*; see also marsh harrier (p. 153).

HABITAT. Now breeds chiefly on moors, but might occur in any of the habitats of Montagu's harrier; in winter both on moors and in coastal areas, especially marshes, reed-beds, estuaries and sand dunes, and in other types of open country.

RANGE AND STATUS. Resident in Orkney and locally in Hebrides, Highlands and Ireland; has increasingly bred elsewhere in recent years; also winter visitor, not uncommon on E and S coasts and occasional elsewhere.

GREAT BLACK WOODPECKER *Dryocopus martius* Plate 23

PLUMAGE. Male all black, with red crown and crest. Hen is browner, with red on nape only. Thick bluish- or yellowish-white bill with dark tip; dark grey legs; yellow eye.

STRUCTURE. *Wing length* ML. *Ratios:* wing MS; tail M; neck M; bill M; legs VS/S.

MOVEMENT. Flight has even more marked undulations than green woodpecker; hops; climbs about trees.

VOICE. A far-carrying, loud, clear, vibrant, fluty string of double notes, quite distinct from green woodpecker; also a single, repeated musical yelp, and another note more like *green*; has a loud, hollow 'drum', longer and louder than *barred* and much longer than *pied*.

FIELD MARKS. The only medium or large black bird with red on head; also has a merganser-like mane, and a remarkably angular way of holding its neck; but beware green woodpecker (which, however, is markedly smaller) seen against the light, and possibility of an aberrant black specimen. Tails of all woodpeckers may appear forked when pressed against tree-trunk.

HABITAT. Might be seen in any well-wooded district.

RANGE AND STATUS. Has been reported from various parts of England some 80 times; some of these records have been due to fraud, confusion with other woodpeckers, and introduced specimens, but the rest can only be explained by the occasional wandering to Britain of birds from the Continent; it is not, however, admitted to the official 'British List'.

LITTLE BUSTARD *Otis tetrax* Plate 25

PLUMAGE. Sandy brown, with white wings and belly and white in tail; male in summer has cheeks and throat grey-blue, neck black and white and rest of underparts white. Blackish bill; yellow legs and eye.

STRUCTURE. *Wing length* ML. *Ratios:* wing M; tail S; neck M; bill MS; legs M.

MOVEMENT. Strong, whirring flight like red grouse, with wings all the time below the level of the body; runs or walks.

VOICE. Flight-note, 'dahg'.

FIELD MARKS. Resembles a large, long-legged game bird; though mainly brown at rest, shows striking contrast on taking wing, when looks fully as white as a shelduck and might perhaps be mistaken for a large ptarmigan. No other bird has male's striking pattern of grey-blue, black and white on head and neck.

HABITAT. Similar to stone curlew, but more tolerant of scattered trees and bushes.

RANGE AND STATUS. Vagrant, most often recorded winter, and in Yorkshire, E Anglia, Sussex and Cornwall.

OYSTERCATCHER See *Waterside: Medium Long*, p. 152

ARCTIC SKUA See *Water: Medium Long*, p. 186

MAGPIE *Pica pica* Plates 23, 70 Crow Family

PLUMAGE. Strikingly pied; actually black with prominent white patches on sides of mantle and white belly. Long graduated tail is glossed dark green; thick, black bill; black legs.

STRUCTURE. *Wing length* ML. *Ratios:* wing S; tail L; neck S; bill M; legs S.

MOVEMENT. Flight weak for its size; walks and will hop sideways.

VOICE. A harsh chattering or chuckling note.

FIELD MARKS. The only large black and white land bird with a long tail.

FLOCKING. Normally singly or in small parties, but larger numbers occur at roosts and at ceremonial gatherings in early spring.

HABITAT. Open country with trees, or at least substantial bushes; sometimes in suburbs.

RANGE AND STATUS. Resident, but local in Scotland.

ROOK *Corvus frugilegus* Plates 69, 70 Crow Family

PLUMAGE. All black, with a purplish gloss; adult has bare greyish-white skin round base of bill. Thick bill is blackish at tip, greyish at base; legs black.

STRUCTURE. *Wing length* L. *Ratios:* wing ML; tail M; neck S; bill ML; legs S.

MOVEMENT. Rather heavy flight; walks sedately.

VOICE. Harsh 'caw' and 'caah' notes are more deliberate and prolonged than carrion crow; also has extensive repertoire of other calls, including a misleading raven-like croak and a 'ki-ook', not unlike a herring gull.

FIELD MARKS. Adult is the only all black bird with a bare face patch; all ages can be told from carrion crow by purplish gloss and baggy 'plus-four' appearance of thigh-feathers; from jackdaw by larger size and no grey on nape; from raven by smaller size and less stout bill; and from all these by voice.

FLOCKING. Intensely gregarious throughout the year, frequently consorting with jackdaws; nests communally in trees, though odd pairs sometimes nest in isolated trees, and may then be confused with carrion crows.

HABITAT. Mainly farmland, but feeds in uncultivated country in summer and will also feed on shore; rookeries usually near human settlements, but rarely in large towns.

RANGE AND STATUS. Resident, but local N and W Highlands; some move S and W in winter, large numbers arrive E coast in autumn.

CARRION CROW *Corvus corone* Plates 69, 70

Corbie (Scotland).

PLUMAGE. All black, with a greenish gloss. Thick black bill; black legs.

STRUCTURE. *Wing length* L. *Ratios:* wing ML; tail M; neck S; bill M; legs S.

MOVEMENT. Rather heavy flight; walks, and sidles with ungainly hops.

VOICE. Chief call-notes are usually repeated three times; an abrupt jerky, rasping 'keerghr' and 'kaaah', and a similar but more high-pitched 'keerk', not unlike certain types of motor-horn.

FIELD MARKS. Can be told from raven by smaller size and less stout bill; from rook by greenish gloss and tight-fitting appearance of thigh-feathers; from adult rook also by feathered base of bill; from jackdaw by larger size and no grey on nape; from chough by black bill and legs; and from all these by voice.

FLOCKING. Normally goes singly, or in pairs or family parties, but where common will flock, especially to roost, though never in such numbers as are habitual with the rook.

HABITAT. Almost any kind of country, including sea-cliffs, town parks and suburbs; often feeds on shores, both salt and freshwater.

RANGE AND STATUS. Resident in England, Wales and S and E Scotland, where it overlaps and may interbreed with hooded crow (below) in a narrow band from Galloway to Morayshire; in Ireland and Isle of Man rare but increasing; also winter visitor in small numbers on E coast.

HOODED CROW *Corvus cornix* Plates 69, 70

Hoodie, Grey Crow or Royston Crow; Corbie (Scotland).

PLUMAGE. Black, with grey shoulders, mantle, rump and underparts. Thick black bill; black legs.

STRUCTURE, MOVEMENT AND VOICE. Similar to carrion crow (above).

FIELD MARKS. The only large black bird with a grey body, but beware the light shining on a rook or carrion crow on a bright day.

FLOCKING. Normally unsociable, but will flock on migration and to roost.

HABITAT. In breeding season mainly in mountainous or hilly country and on sea-cliffs; in winter also over a wide range of open country, but especially near the shore.

RANGE AND STATUS. Resident in Ireland, Isle of Man and N and W Scotland, where it overlaps with carrion crow; winter visitor to E and SE, especially on coast; less common in W and SW England, and scarce Wales.

CURLEW See *Waterside: Long*, p. 157

PEREGRINE, female See p. 101

HEN-HARRIER, female See p. 104

GOSHAWK *Accipiter gentilis* Plate 75

PLUMAGE. Brown above, whitish barred darker below; juvenile buff spotted darker below; barred tail; whitish eyestripe. Blunt wings; hooked, blue-black bill, with greenish-yellow cere; yellow legs; orange-yellow eye.

STRUCTURE. *Wing length* L. *Ratios:* wing M; tail ML; neck S; bill MS; legs M. Female larger than male.

MOVEMENT. Similar to sparrowhawk (p. 88); tail appears very broad when soaring.

VOICE. 'Hi-aa, hi-aa'.

FIELD MARKS. Essentially a huge sparrowhawk, with the same relatively short, rounded wings, and rather long tail; of the other large birds of prey, the buzzards have longer wings and shorter tail, the harriers both wings and tail longer, the peregrine narrower and pointed wings. Beware 'goshawk' as a local name for peregrine.

HABITAT. Woods and wooded districts.

RANGE AND STATUS. Rare vagrant, mostly immatures arriving on E coast from Continent, but has occasionally bred, especially in S England.

COMMON BUZZARD *Buteo buteo* Plates 34, 75 Hawk Family

PLUMAGE. Brown, with rather paler underparts, but a very variable bird and may have substantial areas of pale whitish brown. Broad, rounded wings; hooked, dark horn-coloured bill, with yellow cere (greenish in juvenile); yellow legs.

STRUCTURE. *Wing length* L. *Ratios:* wing ML; tail M; neck S; bill MS; legs M. Female larger than male.

MOVEMENT. Soaring with splayed wing-tips is most characteristic flight-habit, eye-like devices on underside of wing making bird look like gigantic moth; usually holds wings straight but sometimes in crooked-wing attitude favoured by kite; when taking off, has a markedly slow, flapping flight; when hunting in a high wind leans on air currents with angled wings and partly lowered legs; also carries out aerobatics, closing wings and plummeting down like a peregrine; occasionally hovers.

VOICE. A loud mewing 'peeioo', sometimes recalling the cry of the herring gull.

FIELD MARKS. Buzzards are large, broad-winged and relatively short-tailed birds, substantially smaller than eagles and overlapping with the mostly smaller harriers; they are not easy to separate on the wing, and being variable, plumage characters are of little value, though *common* tends to be less whitish underneath and to have a less well-marked dark patch at the carpal joint than *rough-legged.* Tail is best field character, being distinctly whitish with a single dark bar at the end in *rough-legged,* and barred in both *common* and *honey*; *common* has whole tail narrowly barred, while *honey* has several broader bands interspersed with the narrow ones (this is a good point if you get a fair view of a bird soaring overhead). *Honey* also has tail slightly longer and wings rather more pointed than *common,* as well as a distinctive call-note; at close range *rough-legged* can also be told from *common* by its feathered legs.

Tails of Buzzards: Common (left), Rough-legged (centre) and Honey (right), showing the differences in barring

From the kite, buzzards can be told at once by unforked tail, and at a distance the kite's preference for soaring with its wings slightly crooked is a useful clue; from harriers they can be told by their blunter wings, shorter tails and more burly appearance, as well as by plumage differences; from eagles smaller size is the best distinction.

FLOCKING. Not strictly gregarious, but up to a dozen may be seen soaring over one wood or in one valley in favoured places.

HABITAT. Hilly and mountainous districts, sea-cliffs and marine islands, and in S also woods and wooded valleys and combes.

RANGE AND STATUS. Resident, breeding mainly in SW England, Wales and parts of N England, more locally in Welsh Marches and Scotland, and very locally in S England and in Ireland; also autumn immigrant on E coast in small numbers.

ROUGH-LEGGED BUZZARD *Buteo lagopus* Plates 34, 75 Hawk Family
Rough-legged Hawk (N America).

PLUMAGE. Mainly brown above and whitish below, but very variable. Broad, rounded wings; hooked, dark horn-coloured bill, with yellow cere; feathered legs, yellow feet.

STRUCTURE. As common buzzard (above), but wing length VL; legs S. Female larger than male.

MOVEMENT. Similar to common buzzard, but frequently hovers.

VOICE. Similar to common buzzard, but wilder and more strident.

FIELD MARKS. For distinctions from closely similar common buzzard, and from other large birds of prey, see above; frequent hovering in a buzzard would point to this species, though both *common* and *honey* will occasionally hover.

HABITAT. Mostly in the wilder coastal districts, with extensive tracts of marsh, dune or shingle, but also inland on hills, moors, downs and other open country.

RANGE AND STATUS. Irregular winter visitor to E coast and Pennines, most regularly in N Isles and E Scotland; vagrant elsewhere.

HONEY BUZZARD *Pernis apivorus* Plates 34, 75 Hawk Family

PLUMAGE. Mainly brown above, with very variable amounts of white and brown below. Hooked, black bill, with black and yellow cere; legs and eye yellow.

STRUCTURE. *Wing length* L/VL. *Ratios:* wing ML; tail ML; neck S; bill MS; legs S.

MOVEMENT. Similar to common buzzard (above), but less given to soaring; occasionally hovers; walks and runs freely on ground.

VOICE. Quite distinct from and shriller than common buzzard, though less often heard; commonest notes are 'puihu' and 'piha'.

FIELD MARKS. For distinctions from common buzzard, see above; any large brown bird found feeding on a nest of wasps or wild bees is more likely to be a honey buzzard than anything else.

HABITAT. Extensive woods.

RANGE AND STATUS. Scarce passage migrant, most often E coast; occasionally breeds in the larger woodlands of S England and Midlands.

BLACK GROUSE, cock See p. 103

SILVER PHEASANT or Silver Kalij Pheasant *Gennaeus nycthemerus* Plates 27, 28

Resembles common pheasant (p. 111) in general appearance and habits, but sharply contrasted plumage of cock (crown, crest and underparts black, upperparts white marked black, long black and white tail) could hardly be mistaken for anything except another species of kalij pheasant (but see Reeves's and Lady Amherst's pheasants (pp. 115 and 112)). Hen can be told from other hen pheasants by blackish-brown crest and black and white markings of outer tail-feathers. Introduced for ornamental and sporting purposes; most likely to be seen near Woburn (Bedfordshire).

LAND BIRDS: Long

SNOWY OWL *Nyctea scandiaca* Plate 76

PLUMAGE. White; male may have a few, female has many black-brown bars, but not on facial disk, throat or breast. Rounded wings; hooked, blackish-horn bill; feathered legs and feet; golden-yellow eye.

STRUCTURE. *Wing length* VL. *Ratios:* wing ML; tail M; neck S; bill does not project; legs S. Female larger than male.

MOVEMENT. Flight more like buzzard than typical owl; alights on ground as often as on a perch.

VOICE. Usually silent, but has two loud calls, 'krow-ow' and 'rick, rick, rick'.

FIELD MARKS. Can be told at once from barn owl by huge size and white upperparts, but beware exceptional barn owls with much white on normal golden-buff upperparts. Greenland falcon has smaller head, no facial disk, shorter and pointed wings and much faster flight. All other large white birds have long necks.

HABITAT. Open country, especially moors, sand dunes and coastal marshes; flies largely by day.

RANGE AND STATUS. Rare winter visitor, most often to N and NW Scotland and N and NW Ireland. A pair bred in Shetland in 1967.

LESSER BLACK-BACK See *Water: Long*, p. 195

HERRING GULL See *Water: Long*, p. 196

BLACK GROUSE, cock See *Land: Medium Long*, p. 103

COMMON BUZZARD, female See *Land: Medium Long*, p. 108

HONEY BUZZARD See *Land: Medium Long*, p. 109

ROUGH-LEGGED BUZZARD, female See *Land: Medium Long*, p. 109

GOSHAWK, female See *above*, p. 107

SNOWY OWL, female See *above*, p. 110

MALLARD See *Water: Long*, p. 201

LESSER WHITE-FRONT See *Waterside: Long*, p. 158

COMMON PHEASANT *Phasianus colchicus* Plates 25, 27, 28, 71, 72
Long-tail (poachers' slang); Ring-necked Pheasant (N America); a game bird.

PLUMAGE. Cock has head and neck dark green, with small ear-tufts; chin, throat and cheeks glossed purple; sometimes a white collar or half-collar at the base of the neck; rest of body varies from fiery copper-red to golden-orange, variously marked with black, but rump uniform and sometimes blue, and wing-coverts sometimes white; tail strongly barred black. Two not uncommon variants are the wrongly named 'melanistic mutant' (var. *tenebrosus*), which is mainly blackish or dark green, and the 'Bohemian pheasant', a buff or cream-coloured variety with dark head and blackish mottlings. Hens and juveniles of all forms are brown marked darker, 'melanistic mutants' being the darkest and Bohemians and *principalis* type the palest. Pale greenish bill; greyish legs; cock has prominent red wattle round eye.

STRUCTURE. *Wing length* ML. *Ratios:* wing S; tail ML; neck M; bill S/MS; legs S.

MOVEMENT. As common partridge (p. 91), but often runs, and will rocket upwards with remarkable acceleration when startled.

VOICE. Cock crows with a loud, hard 'korr-kok'.

FIELD MARKS. Long tail distinguishes pheasants in all plumages, and gaudy plumage marks out cock from all birds except other pheasants, most of which are highly distinctive, but 'melanistic mutant' needs to be distinguished from Japanese pheasant (below). There are no pure-bred pheasants in Britain, but broadly speaking cocks with white collars can be counted as Chinese (*torquatus*), and those without collars as Caucasian (*colchicus*), often erroneously called the 'Old English pheasant'. Hen pheasants are hard to tell apart, but their long tails differentiate them from all other game birds. Juvenile pheasants while still growing their long tails need to be distinguished from partridges (pp. 91 and 98), unless accompanied by adults. Beware occasional hybrids with black grouse and with other species of pheasant.

FLOCKING. Family parties only, though in heavily preserved areas substantial aggregations of birds, giving the appearance of loose flocks, may be seen feeding in the open.

HABITAT. Mainly woodland, also in copses, low scrub, well-bushed and timbered commons and heaths, reed- and sedge-beds, and exceptionally in large gardens; habitually feeds on growing crops and stubbles.

RANGE AND STATUS. Resident, birds of *colchicus* race having been introduced over 900 years ago, with substantial further introductions of *torquatus*, *principalis*, *mongolicus* and other races during the past 300 years. Now breeds almost throughout British Isles, but scarce Ireland; in S England and Midlands cannot truly be regarded as a wild bird (except on outskirts of towns), as it is artificially preserved, food being put down and many young birds reared and released annually; elsewhere, however, it has proved able to survive in small numbers even when quite unprotected. Bohemian pheasant most often seen in NE Norfolk.

JAPANESE PHEASANT *Phasianus versicolor*

Closely resembles common pheasant (above) in general appearance and habits, and both sexes are very similar to melanistic form, the issue being made more complex by the presence of *common* × *Japanese* hybrids, which can hardly be identified in the field. Typical *Japanese* cocks, however, differ from typical melanistic *common* cocks in having dark green rather than blackish-brown underparts, pale rather than dark rump, and blue wing-coverts. Hens cannot be separated in the field. Introduced for sporting purposes.

GOLDEN PHEASANT *Chrysolophus pictus* Plates 27, 28

Cock is quite distinctive with its brilliant red and yellow plumage and yellow cape over nape and back of neck. Hen closely resembles hen *Lady Amherst's* (below), but has greenish bill and legs and red bare skin round eye; is paler and has longer and more strongly barred tail than hen *common*. Introduced for ornamental and sporting purposes; most likely to be seen in the Breckland of Norfolk and Suffolk.

LADY AMHERST'S PHEASANT *Chrysolophus amherstiae* Plates 27, 28

Cock is a black (actually dark green) and white edition of the *golden* (above), with its nuchal cape white barred black, and differs from cocks of *silver* and *Reeves's* (p. 115) in having this cape and a red crest. Hen closely resembles hen *golden*, but has yellow eye, blue-green bare skin round it, horn-coloured bill and blue-grey legs. Introduced for ornamental and sporting purposes; most likely to be seen in W Bedfordshire (Woburn area) and the New Forest.

GREAT SKUA See *Water: Long*, p. 204

CAPERCAILLIE *Tetrao urogallus* Plates 27, 28, 72 Grouse Family

Caper (sportsman's slang); a game bird.

PLUMAGE. Cock is blackish-grey, with green throat and upper breast, brown wing-coverts and white on flanks. Hen and juvenile are brown mottled darker, with chestnut patch on breast and white on flanks. Pale horn-coloured bill; feathered legs; red skin round eye, brightest in cock.

STRUCTURE. *Wing length* ML (hen), L (cock). *Ratios:* wing S; tail S (hen), MS (cock); neck MS; bill MS; legs S. Cock larger than hen.

MOVEMENT. A common partridge (p. 91), but much heavier; makes a great clatter when leaving trees, where habitually perches and feeds.

VOICE. Cock has a raucous cry, and an almost indescribable song that starts with a resonant rattle and ends with a sound like drawing a cork and pouring liquid out of a narrow-necked bottle, followed by a crashing sound made by scraping wing-feathers on the ground. Hen has a pheasant-like 'kok, kok'.

FIELD MARKS. Cock is much the largest bird likely to be met with in a pinewood, and could only be mistaken for an escaped and unexpectedly airborne turkey; immature cock is smaller and can be told from blackcock by no wing-bar. Hen is same size as blackcock, but is brown and has no wing-bar; can also be told from smaller greyhen by rufous breast and rounded tail. Both sexes may erect hackles on neck when alarmed, to form prominent whiskers.

FLOCKING. Small parties only.

HABITAT. Breeds in coniferous woods only, but in autumn may visit other woods, heather moor or even farmland.

RANGE AND STATUS. Resident (reintroduced 1837, having become extinct *c.* 1760), breeding in most of Scotland S and E of a line from Brora to Oykell Bridge (Sutherland) and then S to Stirlingshire; also locally or sporadically in Argyll and Tweed valley.

KITE *Milvus milvus* Plates 34, 75 Hawk Family

Red Kite.

PLUMAGE. Brownish, streaked darker, with rufous forked tail, head more or less whitish, and prominent whitish patch towards tip of underwing. Hooked, black bill, with yellow cere; yellow legs, eye and skin round eye.

STRUCTURE. *Wing length* VL. *Ratios:* wing ML; tail L; neck S; bill MS; legs S.

MOVEMENT. Resembles buzzards (pp. 108-9), and is equally given to soaring; especially with wings held slightly crooked.

VOICE. A shrill mew, not unlike common buzzard.

FIELD MARKS. Can be told at once from all other large birds of prey by deeply forked tail; the pale patch on the underwing is a useful point, but buzzards have a similar one; general aspect is perhaps more reminiscent of the harriers than of the buzzards. Birds seen away from breeding area need to be distinguished from very rare black kite *Milvus migrans*, which is more buzzard-like, and has a much less deeply forked tail. Beware loose country use of 'kite' for any large bird of prey.

HABITAT. Wooded valleys in hill districts.

RANGE AND STATUS. Resident, breeding only in central Wales, where fewer than 20 pairs survive; a rare vagrant elsewhere.

RAVEN *Corvus corax* Plates 69, 70 Crow Family

Corbie (Scotland).

PLUMAGE. All black; very stout black bill; black legs.

STRUCTURE. *Wing length* VL. *Ratios:* wing M; tail M; neck S; bill L; legs S.

MOVEMENT. Flies rather heavily, but often soars and in spring performs aerobatics, 'tumbling', flying upside down and nose-diving; walks.

VOICE. A deep croak, 'pruk, pruk'.

FIELD MARKS. The largest all-black bird; adult can be told from other crows by large size, stouter bill and voice, though rook sometimes has similar but less deep note. Even juvenile shows the greater length of head, bill and neck projecting in front, which can give adult an almost Maltese-cross appearance on the wing.

FLOCKING. Will flock where common, especially to roost.

HABITAT. Mainly in mountainous or hilly country and on sea-cliffs; will feed on shore and roost on ledges.

RANGE AND STATUS. Resident, except on E coast from Moray to Sussex, and in inland counties E of a line from Portland Bill to the mouth of the Tyne.

CURLEW See *Waterside: Long*, p. 157

PINK-FOOTED GOOSE See *Waterside: Long*, p. 159

WHITE-FRONTED GOOSE See *Waterside: Long*, p. 159

LAND BIRDS: Very Long

MUSCOVY DUCK See *Water: Very Long*, p. 210

EGYPTIAN GOOSE See *Water: Very Long*, p. 210

PINK-FOOTED GOOSE See *Waterside: Very Long*, p. 159

WHITE-FRONTED GOOSE See *Waterside: Very Long*, p. 159

GREY-LAG GOOSE See *Waterside: Very Long*, p. 161

BEAN GOOSE *See Waterside: Very Long*, p. 162

SEA EAGLE See *Waterside: Very Long*, p. 162

GOLDEN EAGLE *Aquila chrysaëtus* Plates 34, 77 Hawk Family

Black Eagle (young).

PLUMAGE. Dark tawny brown, sometimes with a pale head. Young have white tail with black bar at end. Hooked, blackish bill, with yellow cere; feathered legs, yellow feet.

STRUCTURE. *Wing length* H. *Ratios:* wing ML; tail M; neck S; bill M; legs S/M. Female larger than male.

MOVEMENT. Majestic flight, with much soaring and gliding, when wing-tips are splayed out and upturned.

VOICE. Rather silent, but has a buzzard-like 'twee-o' and a barking call.

FIELD MARKS. Immense size, with relatively short neck and tail, distinguishes from all brown birds except sea eagle, from which can best be told by square, not wedge-shaped, tail, and at close range also by fully feathered legs. Adult *sea* also differs from young *golden* by lacking black bar at end of tail, while young *sea* resembles adult *golden* in having brown tail. At long range general outline of eagles resembles buzzards, but has a more Maltese-cross effect, with head projecting farther forward and tail relatively longer.

HABITAT. Mountainous districts.

RANGE AND STATUS. Resident, confined to Highlands of Scotland and Hebrides, but has recently been spreading S to Galloway, Co. Antrim and elsewhere; rare vagrant elsewhere.

JAPANESE PHEASANT, cock See *Land: Long*, p. 112

COMMON PHEASANT, cock See *Land: Long*, p. 111

REEVES'S PHEASANT *Syrmaticus reevesi* Plates 27, 28

Can be told from other pheasants by large size and immense length of tail (over 6 ft. in fully grown cocks); cock's head is obverse of silver pheasant's (white, with black collar), and other plumage (upperparts cinnamon marked black, underparts chestnut, wings white marked black) is quite distinct from other cock pheasants. Hen is as large as cock common pheasant, and can also be told from other hens by chestnut crown with rest of head buff. Call-note a high-pitched musical pipe, like a passerine. Does not rocket when flushed. Usually drives away common pheasants. Likes high ground. Introduced for ornamental and sporting purposes; most likely to be seen in Bedfordshire or Inverness-shire.

CAPERCAILLIE, cock See *Land: Long*, p. 112

GREAT BUSTARD *Otis tarda*

More than twice the size of the little bustard, like which it shows much more white in flight than at rest. Grey head and neck, with moustachial whiskers, warm brown barred black above, white below and on wings and tip of tail. Male larger than female. Rare vagrant from Europe, most likely to be seen on open downs or heaths. Very turkey-like at a distance.

DEMOISELLE CRANE See *Waterside: Very Long*, p. 164

CHINESE GOOSE See *Water: Very Long*, p. 213

LAND BIRDS: Huge

BLACK STORK *Ciconia nigra*

Resembles white stork (below) in general appearance and habits, but is all black except for white underparts from lower breast downwards. Bill and legs red or reddish-brown. Rare vagrant from Europe.

WHITE STORK *Ciconia ciconia* Plates 45, 86

PLUMAGE. All white, but wings are black (blackish-brown in immature) with a white patch. Bill and legs red; bare skin on lores and round eyes black.

STRUCTURE. *Wing length* H. *Ratios:* wing M; tail S; neck L; bill L; legs VL.

MOVEMENT. Slow, deliberate flight, with neck outstretched and legs trailing slightly downwards; sometimes soars; walks sedately.

VOICE. Normally silent, but will hiss if annoyed.

FIELD MARKS. Can be told from all other large white birds by combination of long red bill and legs, long neck, short tail and black wings with white patch. Heron and common crane appear grey at rest and grey or grey and black in flight; cranes also have much shorter bill. Can be told from herons by outstretched neck in flight, and from herons and spoonbill by legs trailing slightly downwards.

HABITAT. Open marshes, pastures and arable land.

RANGE AND STATUS. Very scarce passage migrant, chiefly in S and E England.

SARUS CRANE See *Waterside: Huge*, p. 165

COMMON CRANE See *Waterside: Huge*, p. 165

GREAT BUSTARD, male See *Land: Very Long*, p. 115

SILVER PHEASANT, cock See *Land: Medium Long*, p. 110

GOLDEN PHEASANT, cock See *Land: Long*, p. 112

LADY AMHERST'S PHEASANT, cock See *Land: Long*, p. 112

REEVES'S PHEASANT, cock See *Land: Very Long*, p. 115

WATERSIDE BIRDS: Very Short

SAND MARTIN *Riparia riparia* Plates 9, 65 Swallow Family

Bank Martin; Bank Swallow (English Provinces and N America).

PLUMAGE. Earthy brown above, and white below with brown breast-band. Forked tail; black-brown bill and legs.

STRUCTURE. *Wing length* MS. *Ratios:* wing L; tail VL; neck S; bill VS; legs S.

MOVEMENT. As swallow (p. 73).

VOICE. Reedy double call-note and song are like swallow and house martin, but song less developed and usually delivered in the air.

FIELD MARKS. Can be told from other small, long-winged, aerial birds (swallow, adult house martin, swift) by brown upperparts and brown band across otherwise white underparts; from all house martins also by lack of white rump; from adult swallow also by shorter tail.

FLOCKING. As house martin (p. 44).

HABITAT. Aerial; breeds in holes in natural or artificial sandy banks, such as cliffs, river banks, sand- and gravel-pits, and railway cuttings; feeds over open country, lakes and rivers.

RANGE AND STATUS. Summer visitor, breeding almost throughout British Isles, but scarce and local in N Scotland and in chalk and limestone districts of S and E England.

GRASSHOPPER WARBLER See *Land: Very Short* (p. 42)

REED WARBLER *Acrocephalus scirpaceus* Plate 3

PLUMAGE. Brown, with a rusty tinge, especially in juvenile; underparts paler, with whitish throat and in juvenile a cinnamon tinge. Thin brownish bill; legs of adult dark brown, of juvenile pale flesh-colour.

STRUCTURE. *Wing length* VS/S. *Ratios:* wing MS; tail M; neck S; bill MS; legs M.

MOVEMENT. Flitting action in flight, but rarely flies far; skulks about in reeds, but will sidle to top of a stem while singing.

VOICE. Call- and alarm-notes consist of a variety of churrs. Song needs to be carefully distinguished from *sedge* and marsh warblers; much less varied than *sedge*; with general pattern, 'churr-churr-churr . . . chirruc-chirruc-chirruc' and sounding not unlike a pair of pebbles being rubbed together in a rather leisurely way, interspersed with frequent mimicry of other birds, and normally lacking the harsh interjections of the *sedge*. For distinctions from *marsh*, see below; beware possibility of mimicry of *reed* by *marsh* or *sedge*.

FIELD MARKS. Can be told at once from *sedge* by lack of prominent eyestripe and by unstreaked upperparts; from *marsh* can only safely be separated in the field by song.

FLOCKING. Nests in colonies, often with sedge warblers nearby.

HABITAT. Breeds predominantly in clumps and beds of the reed *Phragmites communis*, but occasionally also among osiers and other coarse vegetation near water, and exceptionally right away from water, among bamboos, lilacs and other bushes in parks and gardens.

RANGE AND STATUS. Summer visitor, fairly common S and E of a line from the Humber to the Mersey and thence S to Lyme Regis; local in N and SW England and S Wales; vagrant in Scotland and Ireland.

MARSH WARBLER *Acrocephalus palustris* Plate 3

PLUMAGE. Brown, with an olivaceous tinge, but juvenile inclines to rufous; underparts paler with whitish throat. Thin brownish bill, legs flesh-brown.

STRUCTURE. *Wing length* S. *Ratios:* wing MS; tail M/ML; neck S; bill MS; legs M.

MOVEMENT. Similar to reed warbler (above), but is rather less skulking and more prone to sing from exposed perches.

VOICE. Call-note a harsh, scolding churr, very similar to, but higher-pitched than, sedge warbler. Strongly mimetic song is much louder, more musical and less uniform than *reed* or *sedge*, and in typical form can hardly be mistaken for either; a secondary type of song, less often heard, is however much harder to tell from the other two warblers.

FIELD MARKS. Adult can only be told from somewhat slimmer *reed* in the field by sight by those very familiar with the latter's range of coloration; juvenile not separable at all. Can be told at once from *sedge* by lack of prominent eye-stripe and by unstreaked upperparts; *garden* is slightly larger and has greyish legs and no whitish throat.

FLOCKING. Nests in small colonies, often with sedge warblers nearby.

HABITAT. Seems to prefer lush and coarse vegetation growing up among smallish groups of trees, and hence most often breeds in osier-beds, small copses and other places overgrown with meadow-sweet and hairy willow-herb, but also occurs away from water in growing crops, orchards, etc.

RANGE AND STATUS. Unusually local summer visitor, breeding only in S England, perhaps now regularly only in lower Severn valley; vagrant elsewhere.

SEDGE WARBLER *Acrocephalus schoenobaenus* Plate 3

PLUMAGE. Brown, streaked darker above, paler below; rump unstreaked and washed rufous; marked buff eyestripe. Thin blackish bill; greyish legs.

STRUCTURE. *Wing length* S. *Ratios:* wing MS; tail M; neck S; bill S; legs M.

MOVEMENT. As reed warbler (above), but has special song-flight.

VOICE. Has a harsh churring note and a scolding 'tucc'. Song consists of a jumble of many contrasting notes, some sweet, some harsh and unpleasing, all mixed up together with the mimicked songs and notes of other birds in 'a loud, hurried, varied, vigorous medley'; contains comparatively little of the even 'pebble-rubbing' of the *reed* or the canary-like liquid notes of the *marsh*; delivered from concealed or open perch or in aerial song-flight; beware possibility of *reed* or *marsh* mimicking *sedge*.

FIELD MARKS. Can be told by broad buff eyestripe from all warblers except rare *aquatic* (below); streaked upperparts, with unstreaked rufous rump, also distinguish *sedge* from all other breeding warblers except *grasshopper* (p. 42), which has graduated tail.

FLOCKING. Nests in colonies, often with reed warblers nearby.

HABITAT. Any place where coarse, rank vegetation grows up over bushes and hedgerows fairly near water, e.g. osier- and reed-beds, the margins of lakes, ponds, rivers and streams, bramble brakes on marshy ground; exceptionally in copses, etc., away from water.

RANGE AND STATUS. Summer visitor, breeding almost throughout the British Isles; passage migrant on both E and W coasts.

Aquatic Warbler (left) and Sedge Warbler

AQUATIC WARBLER *Acrocephalus paludicola*

Like a yellowish sedge warbler (above), but has buff stripe down centre of crown (more distinct than on juvenile *sedge*), and streaked (not uniform) rump. Vagrant from W Europe.

HOUSE MARTIN See *Land: Very Short*, p. 44.

WATERSIDE BIRDS: Short

BLUETHROAT *Luscinia svecica* Plate 5 Thrush Family

PLUMAGE. Dark brown above, buff below, with base of tail rufous. Cock has bright blue chin and throat, with red or white spot, and red and black bands on breast. Hen has underparts all buff except for black band (a few hens show traces of blue). Dark brown bill; yellowish-brown legs.

STRUCTURE. *Wing length* S. *Ratios:* wing MS; tail M; neck S; bill S; legs M.

MOVEMENT. Very skulking; flitting flight; hops.

VOICE. Chief call-notes are nightingale-like 'hweet' and 'tacc, tacc'.

FIELD MARKS. Adult showing blue on throat can be told at once from all other birds, the red- and white-spotted races being easily separated by their respective spots. The two races cannot be told apart in the field in other plumages, but combination of distinct eyestripe, black band on breast, rufous base of tail, and in good light steely striations on head and nape, should serve to differentiate them from other birds.

HABITAT. Most often seen at coastal migration stations, skulking in whatever cover is available.

RANGE AND STATUS. Passage migrant on E coast, mainly in autumn, but probably also regular in spring, especially Fair Isle, Isle of May, and E coast England, Northumberland to Norfolk; great majority of adult cocks are of Scandinavian red-spotted race.

BLACK REDSTART See *Land: Short*, p. 51

TEMMINCK'S STINT *Calidris temminckii* Plates 37, 79 Sandpiper Family

PLUMAGE AND STRUCTURE. As little stint (below), but wing-ratio ML, is less warm brown in summer and has white outer tail-feathers. Blackish-brown bill; legs various shades of green and yellow.

MOVEMENT. As dunlin (p. 129), but characteristically towers when flushed.

VOICE. A shrill, spluttering 'pt-r-r-r-r'.

FIELD MARKS. Very similar to little stint (see below for distinctions), which does not tower in the same way when flushed; resembles a small common sandpiper, but does not have its curious spasmodic wing-action.

FLOCKING. Occasionally in small parties.

HABITAT. Much more partial to inland marshes than little stint; likes plenty of cover, and on coast prefers grassy pools and gutters on salt-marsh to the mud-flats.

RANGE AND STATUS. Scarce passage migrant, chiefly Trent valley and E and S coasts England; has attempted to breed Scottish Highlands and Yorkshire.

LITTLE STINT *Calidris minuta* Plates 37, 79 Sandpiper Family

PLUMAGE. In summer warm brown spotted darker above and on breast, with faint pale wing-bar and dark wing-tips, and white below. In winter grey-brown on warm-brown parts, except breast, which is white in centre. Juvenile like adult winter, but has buffish breast. Black bill and legs.

STRUCTURE. *Wing length* MS. *Ratios:* wing M; tail MS; neck MS; bill M; legs M.

MOVEMENT. As dunlin (p. 129), and has restless feeding action of sanderling.

VOICE. Flight-note, 'chik', or a soft trilling 'chik-chik-chik'.

FIELD MARKS. The two stints are much the smallest shore birds, being approached only by the smaller specimens of the dunlin, from which *little* can be told by no white in tail, straight bill, and in summer white belly and in winter white breast. *Little* can be told from rarer *Temminck's* by no white in tail, black legs and less grey appearance, especially on breast, as well as voice and habitat; a common comparison is that *little* is like a small dunlin, while *Temminck's* resembles a small common sandpiper. Beware wildfowlers' general name of 'stint' for dunlin and various other shore birds.

FLOCKING. In small parties; often with other shore birds, especially dunlins, curlew-sandpipers and ringed plovers.

HABITAT. As dunlin in autumn and winter.

RANGE AND STATUS. Passage migrant, commoner in some years than others; chiefly in E and S England, and in autumn. Occasional in winter.

REED BUNTING *Emberiza schoeniclus* Plates 13, 15 Finch Family

Reed Sparrow, Pit Sparrow.

PLUMAGE. Brown streaked darker; white outer feathers in cleft tail. Cock in summer has black head and throat and white collar, but these markings are somewhat obscured in winter. Hen and juvenile have brown head with buff throat and buff lines above and below eye. Legs and stout bill dark brown.

STRUCTURE. *Wing length* S. *Ratios:* wing MS; tail ML; neck S; bill S; legs S.

MOVEMENT. Jerkily bounding flight; hops, walks or runs; constantly flicks tail.

VOICE. Chief call-note, 'tseep', is rather like yellow wagtail's; also 'ching' and 'chit'. Squeaky, staccato song has 'tweek, tweek, tweek, tititick' pattern.

FIELD MARKS. Black and white head pattern of cock distinguishes it from all other small birds except cock stonechat, which is smaller and has no white in tail. Hen and juvenile are more difficult, but are markedly larger than all other small thick-billed 'brown-streaked' birds, except noticeably bigger corn bunting which has no white in tail; beware young males moulting into adult plumage, for at one stage a triangular brown patch appears on the breast. Doubtful, solitary, brown, finch-like birds often turn out to be hen reed buntings.

FLOCKING. Gregarious after breeding, often with other finches and buntings; also with pied wagtails and meadow pipits on spring migration.

HABITAT. Breeds in almost any kind of marshy place, fens, reed-beds, rushy fields, river banks, osier-beds, etc., but in winter will resort to stubbles, kale and root fields, and other places favoured by seed-eaters.

RANGE AND STATUS. Resident throughout British Isles; native birds move S, some emigrating, and many others arrive on E coast in autumn.

LITTLE RINGED PLOVER *Charadrius dubius* Plates 38, 79

PLUMAGE. As ringed plover (p. 131), but has no white wing-bar, yellow on bill only at base of lower mandible, legs flesh to yellowish-green, and orbital ring yellow.

STRUCTURE. *Wing length* MS/M. *Ratios:* wing ML; tail MS; neck MS; bill S/MS; legs ML.

MOVEMENT. As ringed plover.

VOICE. Flight- and alarm-notes 'pee-oo' and 'pip-pip . . .', also a reedy call like little tern. Song, delivered in bat-like display flight, is a trilling elaboration of the call-notes.

FIELD MARKS. Closely resembles ringed plover, but can easily be told in flight by lack of wing-bar, and by distinct call-note; at rest may not be separable, unless at close enough range to see colour of bill, legs and orbital ring, and to appreciate smaller size.

FLOCKING. Family parties only.

HABITAT. Breeds mainly at gravel pits, sewage farms and other places with extensive areas of sand or gravel; on passage at inland and coastal marsh pools and freshwater margins.

RANGE AND STATUS. Summer visitor, having colonised SE England since 1938; now breeds thinly over an area extending N to Yorkshire and Cheshire, and W to Hants and Glos., especially in the Home Counties; is also becoming rather more widespread on passage to and from breeding areas.

KENTISH PLOVER *Charadrius alexandrinus* Plates 38, 79

Snowy Plover (N America).

PLUMAGE. Sandy-brown above, with white wing-bar, white below. Male has black patches on crown, cheeks and sides of breast; female has these dark brown, juvenile not at all. Bill black; legs blackish-grey.

STRUCTURE. *Wing length* MS. *Ratios:* wing M; tail MS; neck MS; bill MS; legs M/ML.

MOVEMENT. Similar to ringed plover (p. 131); runs very fast.

VOICE. Principal notes are 'wit' or 'wee-it' and 'prr-ip'; trilling song is delivered in bat-like display flight.

FIELD MARKS. Distinctly smaller, slimmer and paler than *ringed,* lacking its striking black and white head and breast; can also be told by its voice, black bill and dark legs (but beware *ringed* with legs coated with dark mud, especially juveniles, which lack the black of the adults). Can also be told from *little ringed* by wing-bar, and from dunlin, sanderling and similar small waders by short bill. May look dumpy and almost robin-like.

FLOCKING. Family parties only; goes with other waders.

HABITAT. Breeds only on extensive coastal shingle banks and sand dunes; on passage at fresh- and salt-water margins.

RANGE AND STATUS. May still occasionally breed in Romney Marsh area, and perhaps elsewhere on E and SE coasts England; otherwise scarce passage migrant, mainly in S and E England, occasionally in winter, vagrant only in Scotland and Ireland.

MEADOW PIPIT See *Land: Short*, p. 60

ROCK and WATER PIPITS *Anthus spinoletta* Plates 8, 37 Wagtail Family
Alpine Pipit (water pipit).

PLUMAGE. *Rock* is dark olive-brown with a slight greyish tinge and darker streaks above, and paler beneath with breast streaked darker; grey outer tail-feathers. *Water* is similar in winter, but lacks greyish tinge and has white outer tail-feathers, and in summer has an almost unstreaked breast with a pinkish tinge, and a marked whitish eyestripe. Both have thin blackish-brown bill; legs flesh-brown, darker in *water* than in *rock*.

STRUCTURE. *Wing length* S/SM. *Ratios:* wing M; tail ML; neck S; bill S; legs M.

MOVEMENT. Dipping flight; walks or runs.

VOICE. Call-note 'phist' is rather less shrill than meadow pipit's 'pheet' and rarely uttered in triplicate as latter often is. Song very like *meadow*,and delivered in similar song-flight, rising from and descending to the ground or a rock.

FIELD MARKS. *Rock* differs from all other pipits by grey (not white) feathers in tail. Winter *water* differs from *meadow* and *tree* only by slightly larger size, darker legs, less streaked upperparts and paler breast. Summer *water*, with its conspicuous eyestripe and unstreaked breast, could only be mistaken for rare tawny pipit, which has much longer tail.

FLOCKING. *Rock* goes in small parties out of breeding season.

HABITAT. *Rock* occurs almost exclusively on rocky coasts, but in winter also on sandy and muddy shores and salt-marshes, and exceptionally inland by margins of reservoirs, etc. *Water* occurs in typical winter habitats of both *meadow* and *rock*, but prefers freshwater margins.

RANGE AND STATUS. *Rock* breeds on practically all rocky shores of British Isles, but more thinly in S and E; in winter on all coasts and estuaries; some arrive E coast in autumn. A small number of *water* may winter every year, though few have been reliably identified, the majority in mid and S England; it is really a mountain-breeding race, whose connections with water occur only on its winter wanderings.

SWALLOW, juvenile See *Land: Medium Short*, p. 73

SNOW BUNTING *Plectrophenax nivalis* Plates 14, 16 Finch Family
Snow bird, Snowflake.

PLUMAGE. Black and white in summer cock, with increasing admixtures of brown in winter cock, hen, immature and juvenile in that order. Much white on wing in all plumages (except immature hen) and underparts always white or whitish. Tail cleft; stout bill is black in summer, yellowish-brown in winter; legs black.

STRUCTURE. *Wing length* MS. *Ratios:* wing M; tail M; neck S; bill S; legs M.

MOVEMENT. Flight bounding; runs and hops.

VOICE. Flight-notes a silvery, rippling 'tirrirrirrip', mostly from flocks; contact-note a clear sad unbunting-like 'tüü'; alarm-note a buzzy 'jeet'. Loud and fairly musical song is uttered from rock or boulder or on wing.

FIELD MARKS. Longish wings, gregarious habits, white underparts, and large amounts of white on wings are distinctive at all times; solitary immatures, which look very brown at rest, are hard to identify until flushed, when dunlin-like whitish bar on wing can be seen.

Snow Buntings in winter plumage in flight: male (left) and female

FLOCKING. Highly gregarious in winter, but rarely with other birds, except sometimes Lapland buntings and shore larks.

HABITAT. Breeds on barren, stony mountain tops; in winter on shingle, dunes, stubbles and other rough open ground near sea, also sometimes on upland moors.

RANGE AND STATUS. Breeds sparingly on the Cairngorms and other high mountains in Scottish Highlands; in winter on all coasts, but most often E England, also sometimes on hills inland, e.g. Lancashire Pennines.

SHORE LARK *Eremophila alpestris* Plate 35

Horned Lark (N America).

PLUMAGE. Brown with a pinkish tinge and faint darker streaks above; underparts paler, unstreaked. Striking black and yellow pattern on face and throat; cock also has black 'horns'. Some white in tail. Thin horn-coloured bill; black legs.

STRUCTURE. *Wing length* MS. *Ratios:* wing M; tail M; neck S; bill S; legs M.

MOVEMENT. Flight more undulating than skylark (p. 70); walks, or runs very fast.

VOICE. Commonest note is 'tsip' or 'tseep', quite different from other larks, and more like rock pipit or yellow wagtail; also a thin, falling 'si-di-wi'.

FIELD MARKS. Can be told at once by black and yellow on head, and 'horns' if present, but at any distance appears very similar to skylark, though much less streaky. In flight tail looks black, especially from below.

FLOCKING. Usually in parties or small flocks, often together with snow or Lapland buntings.

HABITAT. On or very close to sea-shore, not straying farther inland than nearby stubbles.

RANGE AND STATUS. Winter visitor, mainly E coast from Fife to Kent (only really regular in N Norfolk), occasionally S coast; regular passage migrant in small numbers, Fair Isle; vagrant elsewhere.

YELLOW WAGTAILS *Motacilla flava* Plate 35 and p. 51

PLUMAGE. All forms are greenish-brown above and yellow below, differing only in head colour (see below); white outer tail-feathers. Juveniles have a blackish band on the breast. Thin, greyish-black bill; black legs.

STRUCTURE. *Wing length* S. *Ratios:* wing MS; tail M/ML; neck S; bill S; legs M.

MOVEMENT. Flight markedly dipping; runs and walks, frequently moving tail up and down.

VOICE. Flight-note, 'tsweep', quite distinct from other wagtails; brief, trilling song, not often heard, is somewhat robin-like, and may be delivered in a bounding song-flight or from a perch.

FIELD MARKS. Yellow and grey wagtails (see p. 127 for distinctions) are the only small, predominantly yellow birds with longish tails. Several races of *yellow* occur on migration, and breeding cocks are easiest to distinguish; typical *yellow* has top of head and ear-coverts greenish yellow and eyestripe, chin, throat and sides of neck brilliant yellow; *blue-headed* has top of head and ear-coverts blue-grey, eyestripe and chin white, and throat yellow; *grey-headed* has more slate-grey head, darker ear-coverts, no eyestripe and white of chin extending less far down on to throat. In addition a number of variants have been met with, especially in E and SE England during the past fifty years, in which the head is pale blue-grey with or without a white eyestripe (for further details of these variants, see Stuart Smith, *The Yellow Wagtail*, Collins, 1950, pp. 109-12). Winter cocks have roughly the same but much duller head patterns, and on autumn passage cock *blue-headed* can be told by the white eyestripe and chin, and cock *grey-headed* by the lack of any eyestripe and the ear-coverts being much darker than the head. Breeding hens resemble winter cocks (hen *yellows* are darker and less yellow on the head than cocks), but winter hens and juveniles cannot be told apart in the field.

FLOCKING. *Yellow* usually breeds in small colonies, and afterwards goes in small parties, sometimes roosting with *pied*; all forms flock on migration, often with *pied* or white wagtails.

HABITAT. *Yellow* breeds in two distinct types of country, most often in damp river-valleys, water-meadows, sewage farms and fresh and salt-marshes, but also on dry heaths and commons, moorland and arable land under crops; on passage in all kinds of open country, especially near the coast; fond of feeding among cattle.

RANGE AND STATUS. *Yellow* is a rather local summer visitor, but common in E, SE and NW England, almost absent from SW England and N and W Wales; in Scotland only in the Clyde valley, and now only erratically in Ireland. *Blue-headed* breeds sporadically in E and SE England, especially in S Kent and

SE Sussex, and variants (see above) also occasionally breed in this area. On migration all forms occur in many places where they do not breed, *blue-headed* most often in E and SE England, and *grey-headed* most often on the Scottish isles.

BEARDED TIT *Panurus biarmicus* Plate 17

Reedling or Reed Pheasant.

PLUMAGE. Predominantly rufous or tawny. Cock has grey head and black moustachial stripes, black and white bars on wings and very rufous tail; hen lacks all distinctive markings except on wings. Juvenile is brown, with a whitish throat and black on the back. Yellow bill, black legs, yellowish eye.

STRUCTURE. *Wing length* VS. *Ratios:* wing S; tail ML; neck S; bill VS; legs S.

MOVEMENT. Flight rather weak and undulating; almost never comes to ground, its life being spent among the reed-stems.

VOICE. Call-note a rather metallic 'ching', also 'dzü-dzü', and a kissing note.

FIELD MARKS. The only small reed-bed bird with a longish tail; cock's striking head pattern and juvenile's whitish throat and black on back are also distinctive.

FLOCKING. Collects into parties or small flocks after breeding.

HABITAT. Confined to sedge- and reed-beds.

RANGE AND STATUS. Resident, breeding mainly on the Norfolk Broads and on some coastal marshes in E Anglia, with a tendency to migrate to reed-beds farther W and S in winters after good breeding years.

SWIFT See *Land: Short*, p. 68

KINGFISHER *Alcedo atthis* Plate 20

PLUMAGE. Brilliant blue-green above, reddish-chestnut below; broad chestnut stripe through eye; whitish throat and patch on side of neck. Thick black bill, female's with reddish base; red legs.

STRUCTURE. *Wing length* S. *Ratios:* wing MS; tail MS; neck S; bill M; legs VS.

MOVEMENT. Direct, swift, whirring flight; sometimes hovers, dives from perch or air; habitually perches on vantage point overlooking water.

VOICE. Shrill and penetrating 'chee' or 'chi-kee', also a tittering call, associated with courtship. Song is a whistling trill.

FIELD MARKS. The only bird which is all blue-green above and all rich chestnut below. Can look either a blue, a green or a red bird, according to light and angle of view, and is perhaps most often seen as a spot of sapphire streaking away downstream or making a wide detour over a meadow to avoid the observer, who has only been attracted to it by hearing the shrill call. Long and rather stout bill and short tail are useful points in poor light.

HABITAT. Breeds in holes on rivers, streams, canals and lakes, and occasionally in sand pits some distance from water; in winter some go down to coast and frequent both estuaries and open shores.

RANGE AND STATUS. Resident, breeding throughout lowlands in England, Wales, Ireland and S Scotland; rare vagrant in N Scotland, often severely decreased after hard winters.

BROAD-BILLED SANDPIPER *Limicola falcinellus*

Resembles a winter dunlin (p. 129) in general habits and appearance, but can be told in summer by dark snipe-like appearance of mantle and in winter by white chin and throat and more marked eyestripe. In size rather closer to a small dunlin than to little stint. Sometimes reminiscent of jack snipe. Has marked downward kink near tip of bill. Vagrant from N Europe.

Broad-billed Sandpiper

WHITE-RUMPED SANDPIPER or Bonaparte's Sandpiper *Calidris fuscicollis*

A small N American sandpiper, like a diminutive curlew-sandpiper (p. 130), sharing its white rump, but with a shorter, slenderer, usually quite straight bill; now annual in autumn in very small numbers, mainly in the S. Call, a mouse-like 'jit' or 'jeet'.

DUNLIN See *Waterside: Medium Short*, p. 129

WATERSIDE BIRDS: Medium Short

GREY WAGTAIL *Motacilla cinerea* Plate 35 and p. 51

PLUMAGE. Blue-grey above with yellow-green rump, and yellow beneath; white outer tail-feathers. Breeding cock has black gorget, juvenile a slightly speckled breast. Thin greyish-black bill; flesh-brown legs.

STRUCTURE. *Wing length* S. *Ratios:* wing MS; tail L; neck S; bill S; legs S/M.

MOVEMENT. Flight very dipping; runs and walks, constantly moving tail up and down; often perches on rocks in streams.

VOICE. Call-note closely resembles pied wagtail, (p. 71) but more metallic and staccato and sometimes only a single 'tit'. Rather infrequent song, delivered from a perch, is a shrill treble or quadruple 'tsee-tee-tee', reminding various observers of pied wagtail, blue tit and spotted flycatcher; a more trilling version is uttered in flight, and a low rippling subsong is also recorded.

FIELD MARKS. Only likely to be confused with yellow wagtails (and is in fact all too often so confused, even in winter), but can at once be told from these by call-note, longer tail and colour of upperparts. Black gorget of breeding cock also marks it out from all yellow wagtails; white eyestripe is much less conspicuous than in *blue-headed*. Juvenile can always be told from juvenile *pied* by longer tail and yellow under tail-coverts.

FLOCKING. Rather solitary, but will congregate at roosts.

HABITAT. Breeds mainly on swift, rocky, hill streams and occasionally at lakes or tarns, but also in lowlands, especially at or near waterfalls, weirs, lashers, etc.; in winter frequents all kinds of water margins, mostly inland but sometimes on coast, even puddles and pools in cities, also cress-beds.

RANGE AND STATUS. Resident, common in all hill districts, but very local in N Scotland and S and E of line joining Humber and Lyme Regis; a southward movement occurs in autumn, when birds are seen regularly in places where they do not breed, including Central London.

PIED WAGTAIL See *Land: Medium Short*, p. 71

DIPPER *Cinclus cinclus* Plate 39

Water Blackbird, Water Crow, Water Pyet and many other local names.

PLUMAGE. Blackish-brown on upperparts, flanks and belly; white throat and breast. Chestnut gorget in breeding birds, but not in black-bellied race. Juvenile is grey-brown above and whitish speckled darker below. Blackish-brown bill and legs.

STRUCTURE. *Wing length* S/MS. *Ratios:* wing MS; tail MS; neck S; bill S; legs M.

MOVEMENT. Straight, fast flight; runs or walks on land, but most often seen standing on rock in stream, bobbing and dipping. Can swim both on and under surface; enters water by wading in, or diving from water or air, habitually walks under water on stream-bed.

VOICE. Commonest note is 'zit, zit, zit', also a metallic 'clink, clink'. Loud, rather wren-like warbling song is usually delivered from a rock or other perch.

FIELD MARKS. Conspicuous white throat and constant habit of bobbing or dipping on rock in stream make dipper almost unmistakable, but some reports of dippers on lowland streams appear to be due to imperfect views of common sandpipers. The chestnut band is only visible at fairly close quarters; its absence indicates the black-bellied race.

HABITAT. Almost confined to fast-running streams in hilly districts, but sometimes on shores of hill-lochs, occasionally on lowland streams, and in winter on shores of sea-lochs.

RANGE AND STATUS. Resident, breeding in almost all hill districts W and N of a line drawn from Lyme Regis through the Cotswolds to the Peak District, and thence to the Humber; breeds sporadically in the Midlands immediately to the E of this line, and is very local on the E fringe of the breeding area. Vagrant in S and E England, where birds more likely to belong to wintering Continental black-bellied form.

NORTHERN WILLOW-WARBLER
brown type
WOOD-WARBLER
WILLOW-WARBLER
WILLOW-WARBLER
juv
SIBERIAN
CHIFFCHAFF
CHIFFCHAFF
YELLOW-BROWED
WARBLER
juv
♂ GOLDCREST
♀
♂
FIRECREST
♀

NUTHATCH
CRESTED TI
juv
GREAT TIT
adult
juv
adult
BLUE TIT
adult
juv
COAL-TIT
MARSH-TIT
LONG-TAILED
TIT
WILLOW-TIT

NIGHTINGALE
BLACKCAP ♀
♀
WHITETHROAT
♂
GARDEN-
WARBLER
MARSH-
WARBLER
SEDGE-
WARBLER
REED-WARBLER
WREN
GRASSHOPPER-WARBLER

♂ winter
PIED FLYCATCHER
♀
SPOTTED FLYCATCHER
adult
BLACKCAP
♂
♀
RED-BREASTED FLYCATCHER
LESSER WHITETHROAT
DARTFORD WARBLER
TREE-CREEPER
HEDGE-SPARROW

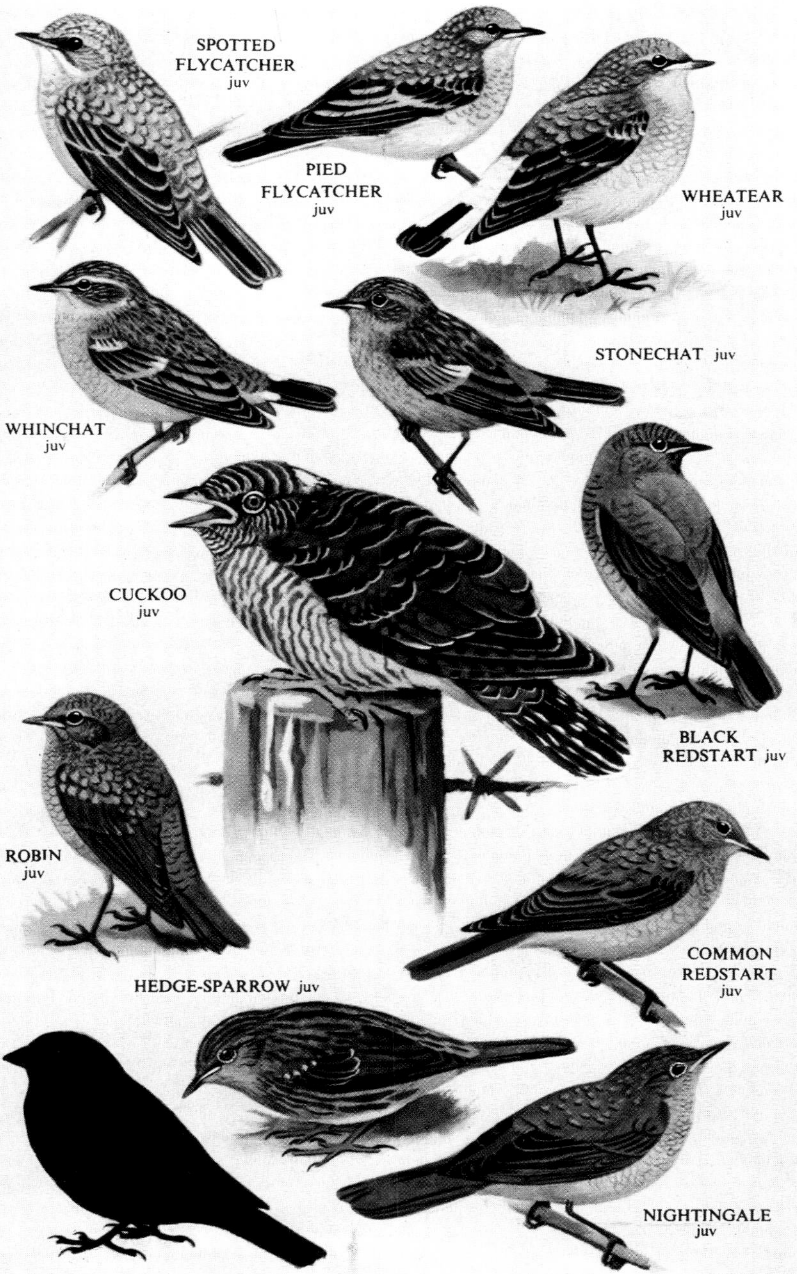
SPOTTED FLYCATCHER juv
PIED FLYCATCHER juv
WHEATEAR juv
STONECHAT juv
WHINCHAT juv
CUCKOO juv
BLACK REDSTART juv
ROBIN juv
COMMON REDSTART juv
HEDGE-SPARROW juv
NIGHTINGALE juv

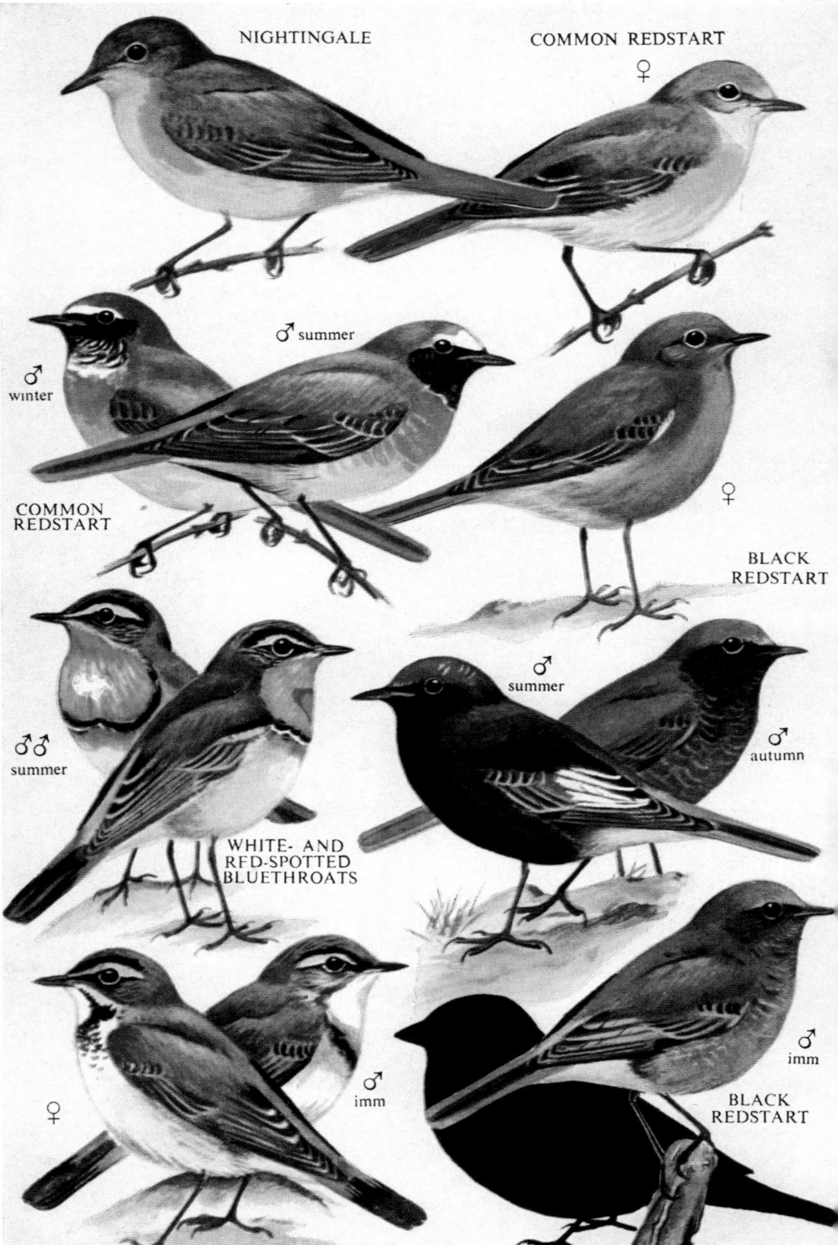
NIGHTINGALE
COMMON REDSTART
♀
♂ summer
♂
winter
COMMON
REDSTART
♀
BLACK
REDSTART
♂
summer
♂♂
summer
♂
autumn
WHITE- AND
RED-SPOTTED
BLUETHROATS
♂
imm
♀
♂
imm
BLACK
REDSTART
RED-SPOTTED BLUETHROAT

GREENLAND WHEATEAR
♂ winter
♂ summer
WHEATEAR
♂ summer
WHEATEAR
♀
RED-BREASTED FLYCATCHER
♂ summer
WHINCHAT
♂
WHINCHAT
♀
♀
♂
STONECHAT

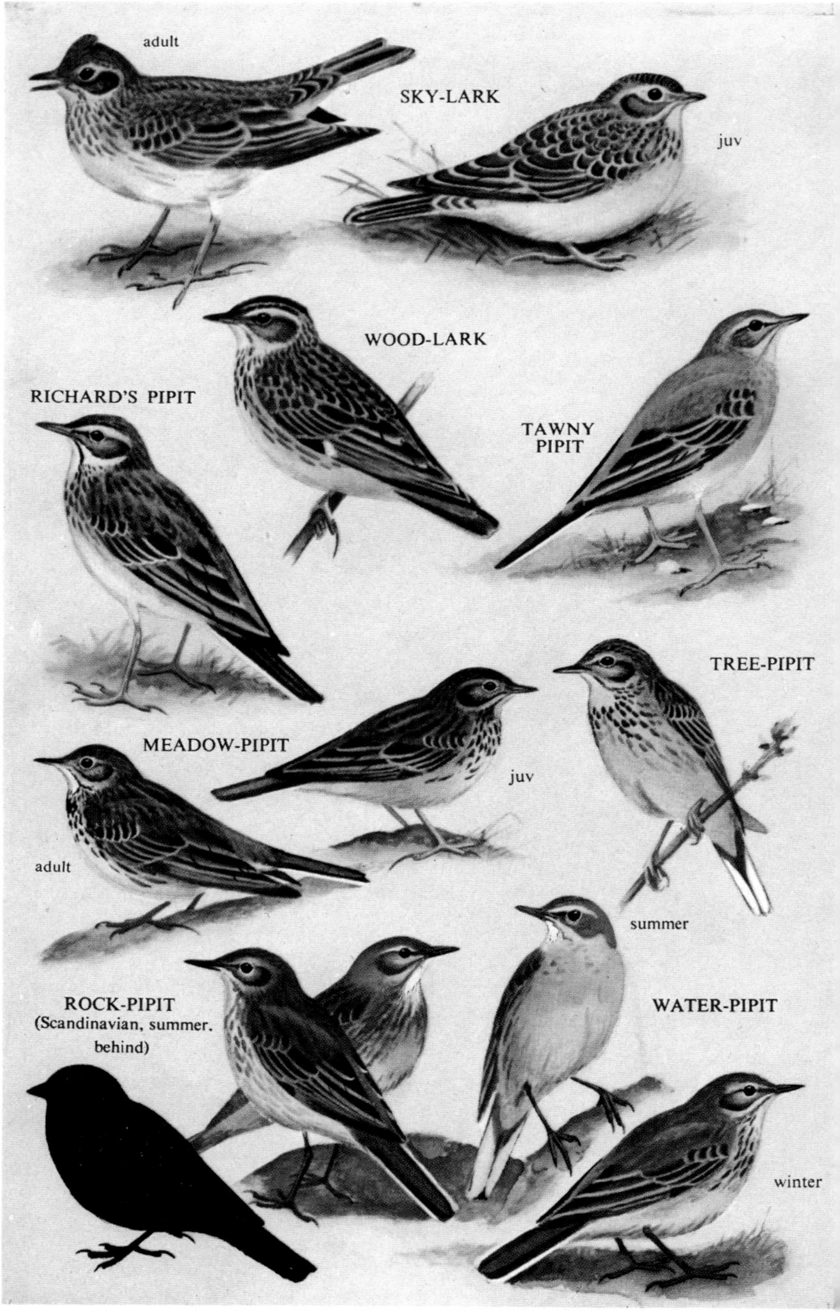
adult
SKY-LARK
juv
WOOD-LARK
RICHARD'S PIPIT
TAWNY PIPIT
TREE-PIPIT
MEADOW-PIPIT
juv
adult
summer
ROCK-PIPIT (Scandinavian, summer, behind)
WATER-PIPIT
winter

SWIFT
adult
SAND-
MARTIN
HOUSE-
MARTIN
adult
HOUSE-
MARTIN
juv
adults
SWALLOW
SWALLOW
juv

LESSER
REDPOLL
♂
MEALY
REDPOLL
♂ winter
LINNET
♂ summer
BULLFINCH ♂
CROSSBILL
adult ♂
WHINCHAT
♂
CHAFFINCH
♂ summer
ROBIN
adult
RED-BREASTED
FLYCATCHER
adult ♂
STONECHAT
♂ summer
COMMON
REDSTART
♂ summer

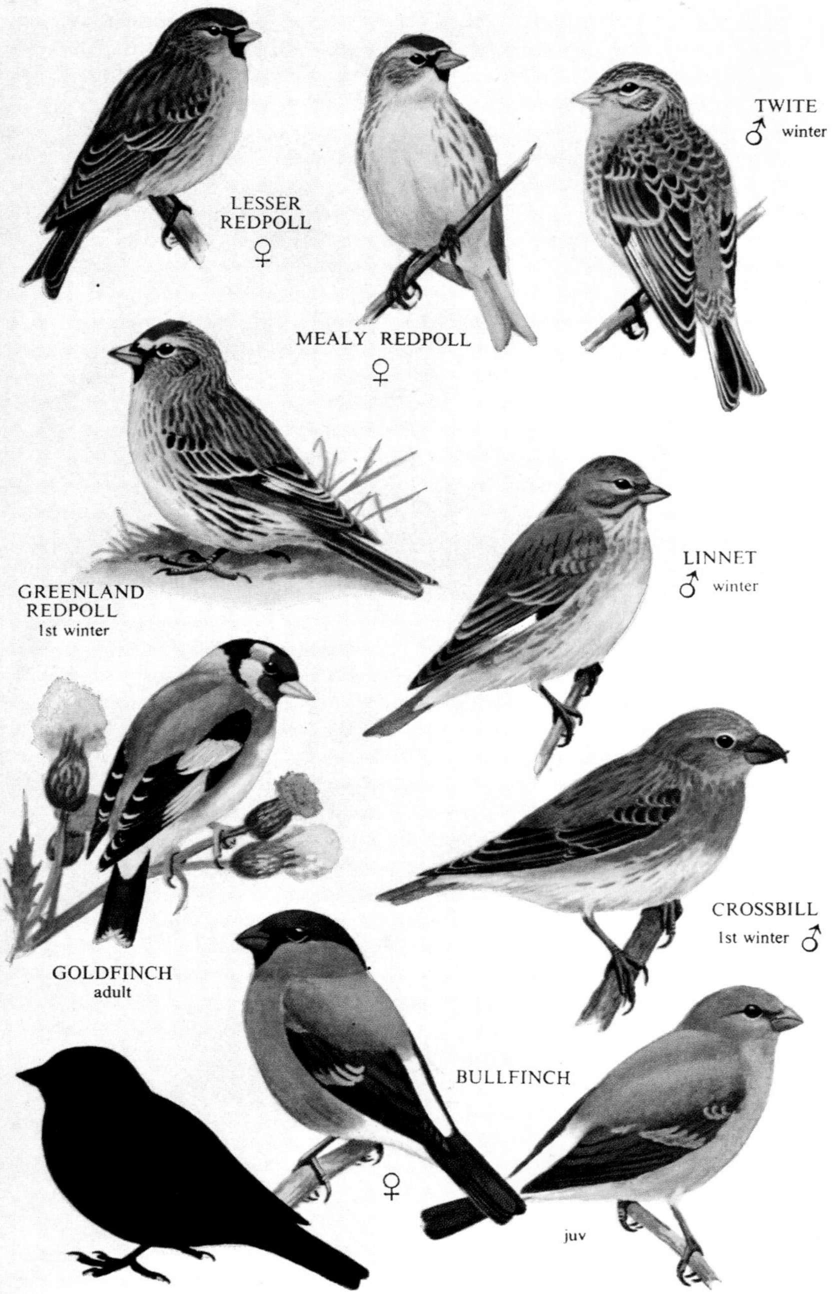
LESSER
REDPOLL
♀
MEALY REDPOLL
♀
TWITE
♂ winter
GREENLAND
REDPOLL
1st winter
LINNET
♂ winter
GOLDFINCH
adult
CROSSBILL
1st winter ♂
BULLFINCH
♀
juv

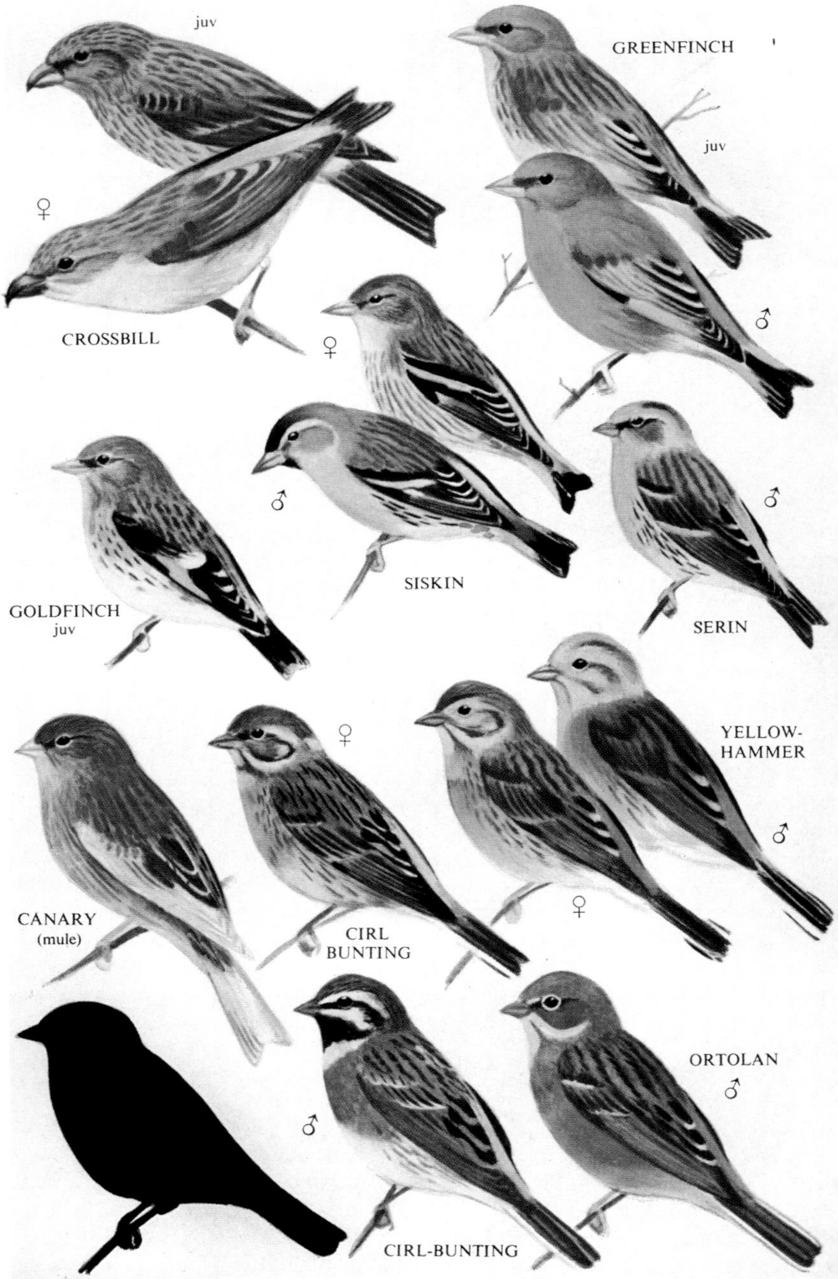
juv
GREENFINCH
juv
♀
CROSSBILL
♀
♂
♂
♂
GOLDFINCH
juv
SISKIN
SERIN
YELLOW-
HAMMER
♀
♂
CANARY
(mule)
CIRL
BUNTING
♀
ORTOLAN
♂
♂
CIRL-BUNTING

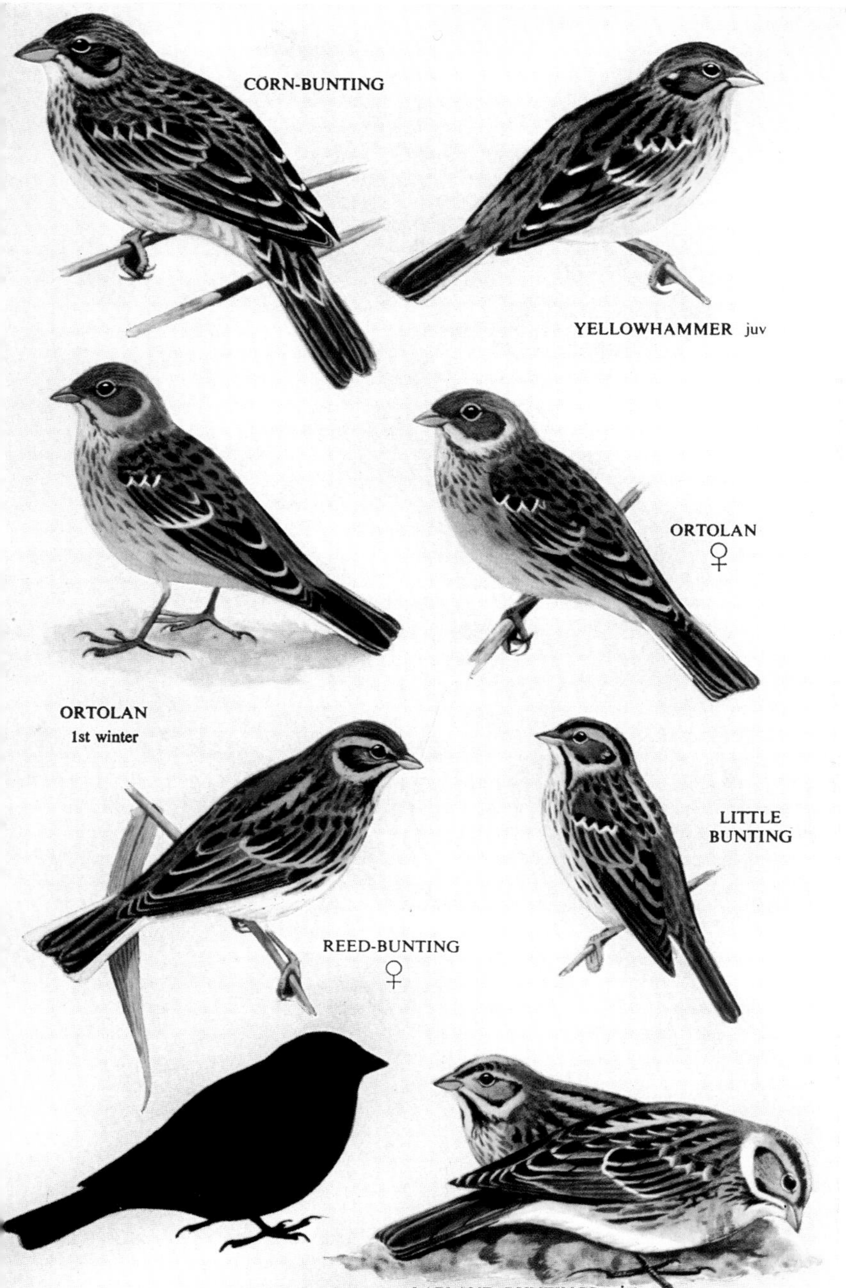
CORN-BUNTING
YELLOWHAMMER juv
ORTOLAN
♀
ORTOLAN
1st winter
LITTLE
BUNTING
REED-BUNTING
♀
LAPLAND BUNTINGS winter

HAWFINCH juv
SNOW-BUNTING
1st winter ♀
SCARLET GROSBEAK
1st winter
HOUSE-SPARROW ♀
TWITE
♀ summer
CHAFFINCH
♀
BRAMBLING ♀
LINNET
♀

HAWFINCH
♂
♂
summer
♂
winter
BRAMBLING
♂ summer
♂ winter
LAPLAND BUNTING
♂ summer
REED-BUNTING
TREE-SPARROW
CIRL BUNTING
♂
♂
winter
♂
summer
HOUSE-SPARROW

♂
♀
♂
♀
BARRED
WOODPECKER
PIED
WOODPECKER
juv
juv
SNOW-BUNTING
♀
PIED
FLYCATCHER
♂ summer
♂
♀
♂
SNOW-BUNTING
winter

♂
♀
BEARDED TIT
♂
RED-BACKED
SHRIKE
♀
LONG-TAILED
TIT
juv
1st winter
BARRED
WARBLER
adult
WRYNECK
NIGHTJAR

FIELDFARE
adult
MISTLE-THRUSH
REDWING
juv
SONG-THRUSH
adult
BLACKBIRD
♀
juv
SONG-THRUSH
juv
RING-OUZEL
juv

♂ adult
♂ 1st winter
BLACKBIRD
RING OUZEL
♂
STARLING
♀ winter
RING-OUZEL ♀
(pale-breasted ♀ blackbird behind)
♂ summer
STARLING juv
with juv moulting into first
winter behind
ROSY STARLING juv

GOLDEN ORIOLE
♀
♂
NUTHATCH
juv
♂
GREEN WOODPECKER
BEE-EATER
KINGFISHER
BUDGERIGARS

JAY
GREEN WOODPECKER
GOLDEN ORIOLE ♂
SONG THRUSH
REDWING
FIELDFARE
HOOPOE

NUTCRACKER
JAY
HOOPOE
ROLLER
WAXWING
♀ winter
♂
summer
HAWFINCH

MAGPIE
CHOUGH
PIED WOODPECKER
adult ♂
adult ♂
GREAT BLACK WOODPECKER
WOODCHAT
BLACK REDSTART
adult ♂ summer
RING-OUZEL
♂
ROSY STARLING
♂ summer

WOODPIGEON
juv
adult
STOCK DOVE
ROCK DOVE
LONDON PIGEON
"red chequer"
"blue chequer"
"mealy"
BARBARY DO
adult
TURTLE DOVE
juv
COLLARED
DOVE
adult
adult

♀
WOODCOCK
LITTLE
BUSTARD
♂ summer
STONE-
CURLEW
CORNCRAKE
RED-LEGGED
PARTRIDGE
juv
QUAIL
COMMON
PARTRIDGE
juv
COMMON PHEASANT
juv

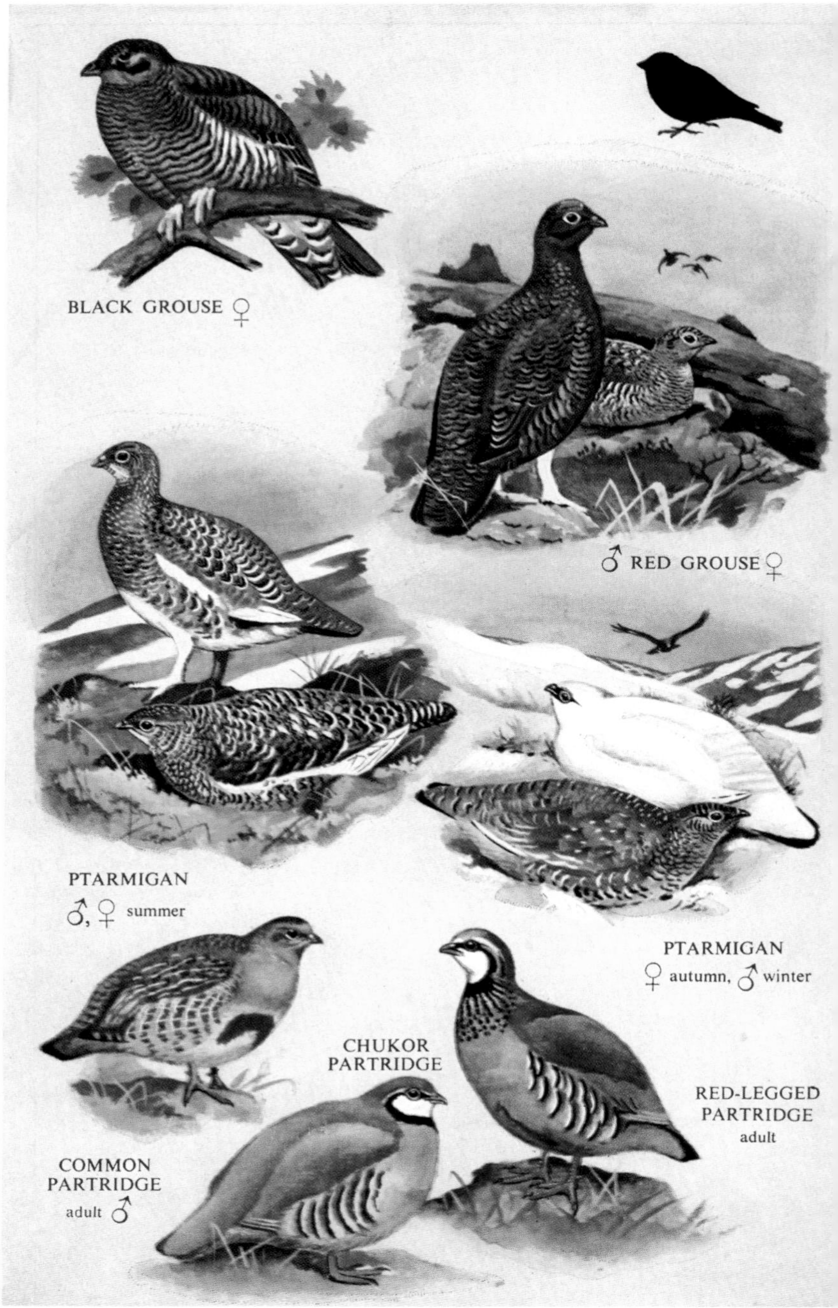

BLACK GROUSE ♀
♂ RED GROUSE ♀
PTARMIGAN
♂, ♀ summer
PTARMIGAN
♀ autumn, ♂ winter
CHUKOR
PARTRIDGE
RED-LEGGED
PARTRIDGE
adult
COMMON
PARTRIDGE
adult ♂

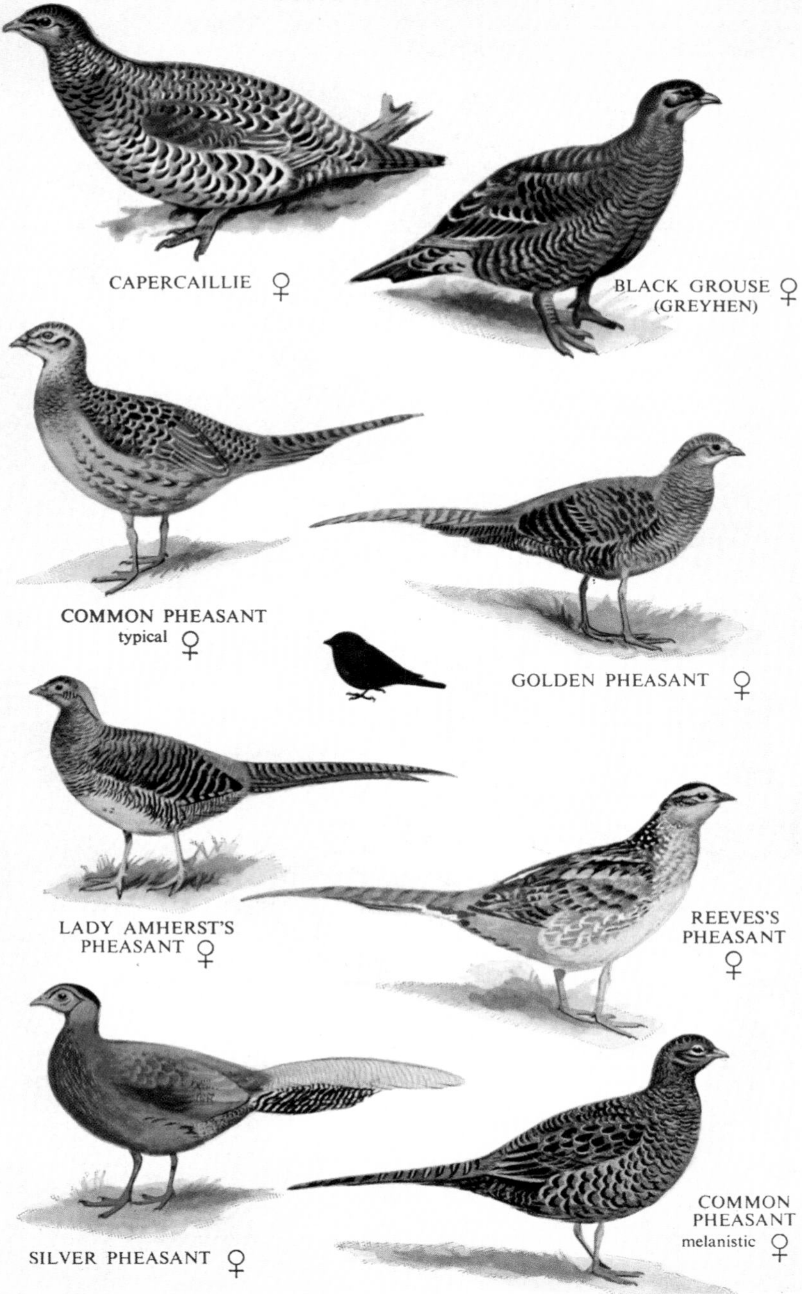

CAPERCAILLIE ♀

BLACK GROUSE ♀
(GREYHEN)

COMMON PHEASANT
typical ♀

GOLDEN PHEASANT ♀

LADY AMHERST'S
PHEASANT ♀

REEVES'S
PHEASANT
♀

SILVER PHEASANT ♀

COMMON
PHEASANT
melanistic ♀

CAPERCAILLIE
♂
♂
Ring-necked type
♂
" Old-English " type
BLACK GROUSE
♂
COMMON PHEASANT
GOLDEN PHEASANT
♂
LADY AMHERST'S PHEASANT
♂
REEVES'S PHEASANT
♂
♂ SILVER PHEASANT
♂ COMMON PHEASANT
Melanistic type

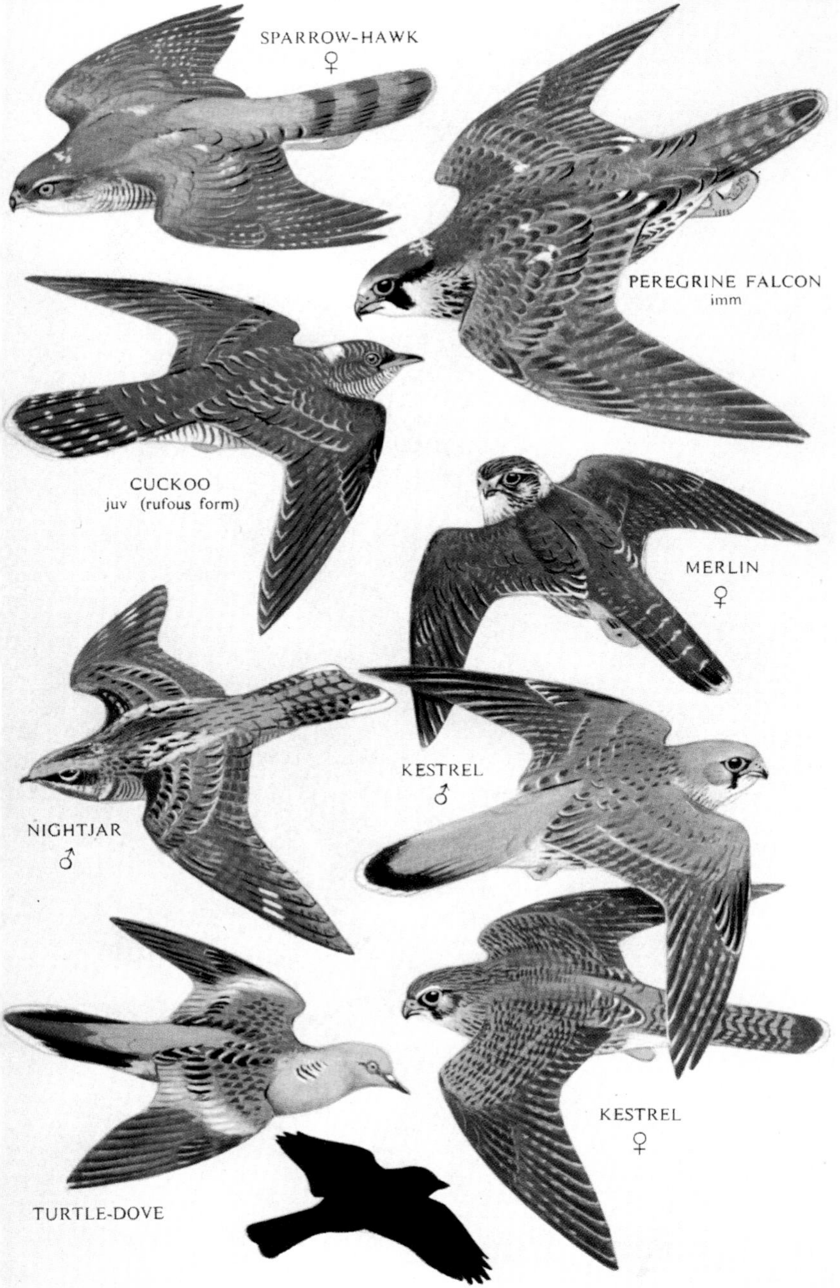
SPARROW-HAWK
♀
PEREGRINE FALCON
imm
CUCKOO
juv (rufous form)
MERLIN
♀
KESTREL
♂
NIGHTJAR
♂
KESTREL
♀
TURTLE-DOVE

PEREGRINE FALCON
adult ♀
juv
grey-brown type
CUCKOO
adult
MERLIN
♂
SPARROW-HAWK
♂
HOBBY
RED-FOOTED FALCON
♂

HOBBY
PEREGRINE
FALCON
♂
CUCKOO
MERLIN
♂
♂
KESTREL
♂
SPARROW-
HAWK
♂
RED-BACKED AND GREAT GREY SHRIKES

OSPREY
♀
MARSH-HARRIER
HEN-HARRIER
♀
♂
MONTAGU'S HARRIER
♀
juv

grey type
TAWNY OWL
LONG-EARED OWL
BARN OWL
LITTLE OWL
SCOPS OWL
SHORT-EARED OWL

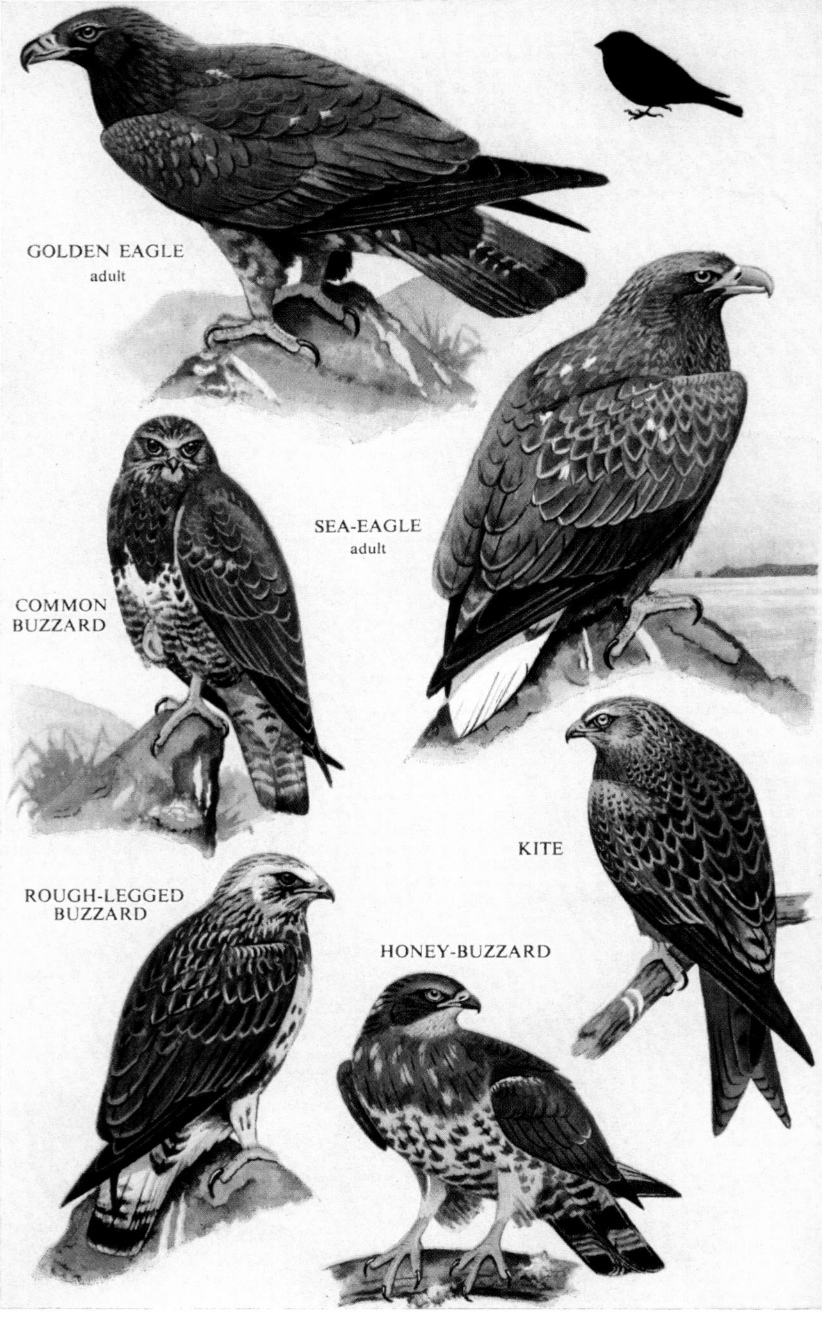
GOLDEN EAGLE
adult
SEA-EAGLE
adult
COMMON
BUZZARD
KITE
ROUGH-LEGGED
BUZZARD
HONEY-BUZZARD

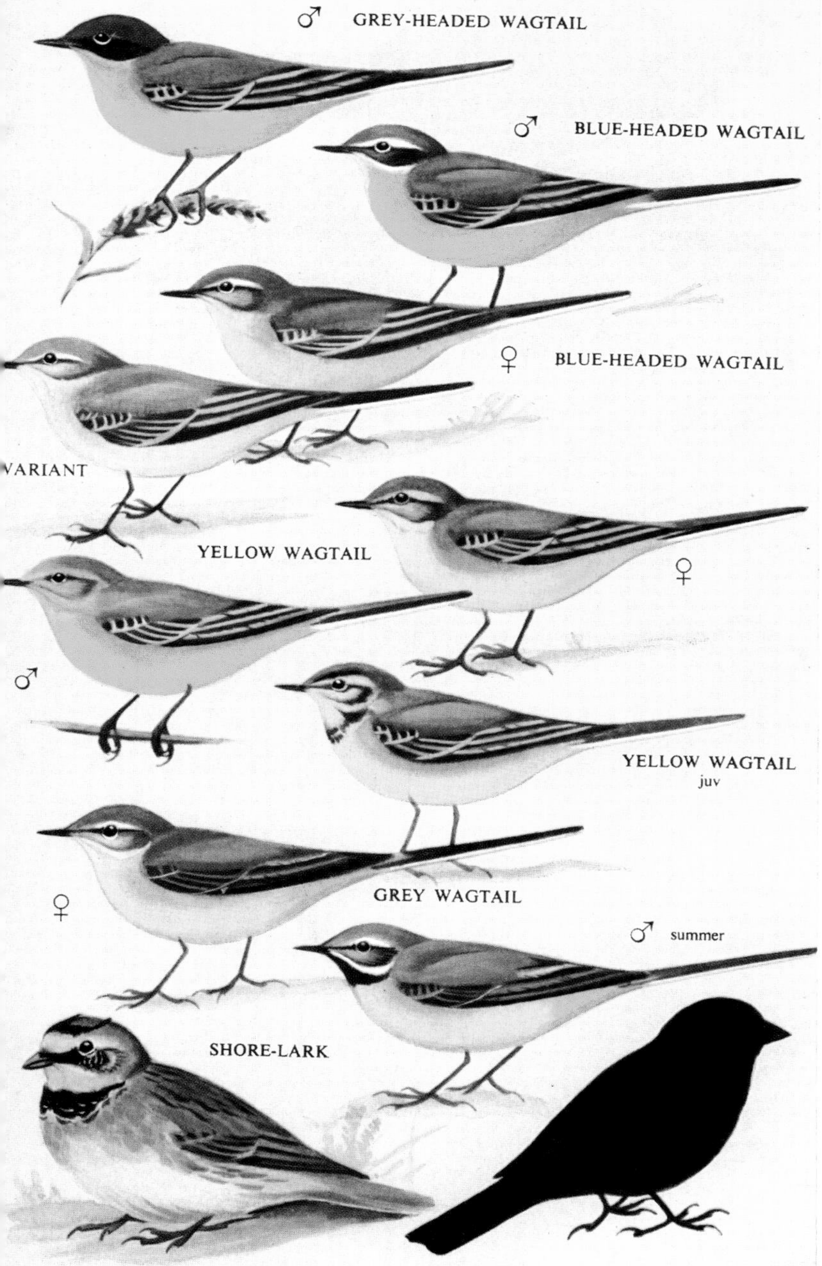

♂ GREY-HEADED WAGTAIL
♂ BLUE-HEADED WAGTAIL
♀ BLUE-HEADED WAGTAIL
VARIANT
YELLOW WAGTAIL
♀
♂
YELLOW WAGTAIL
juv
♀
GREY WAGTAIL
♂ summer
SHORE-LARK

COOT
adult and chick
COOT
juv
juv
adult and
chick
MOORHEN
BAILLON'S
CRAKE
WATER-RAI
♂
♀
SPOTTED
CRAKE
LITTLE CRAKE

DUNLIN
ROCK-PIPIT
northern race
winter
southern race
winter
CURLEW-
SANDPIPER
juv
DUNLIN juv
PECTORAL SANDPIPER
PURPLE
SANDPIPER
LITTLE STINT
juv
TEMMINCK'S STINT
juv
summer
SANDERLING
winter

GREY PLOVER winter
GOLDEN PLOVER winter
PRATINCOLE adult
DOTTEREL winter
TURNSTONE winter
adult
juv
RINGED PLOVER
♀
KENTISH PLOVER
♂
adult
juv
LITTLE RINGED PLOVER

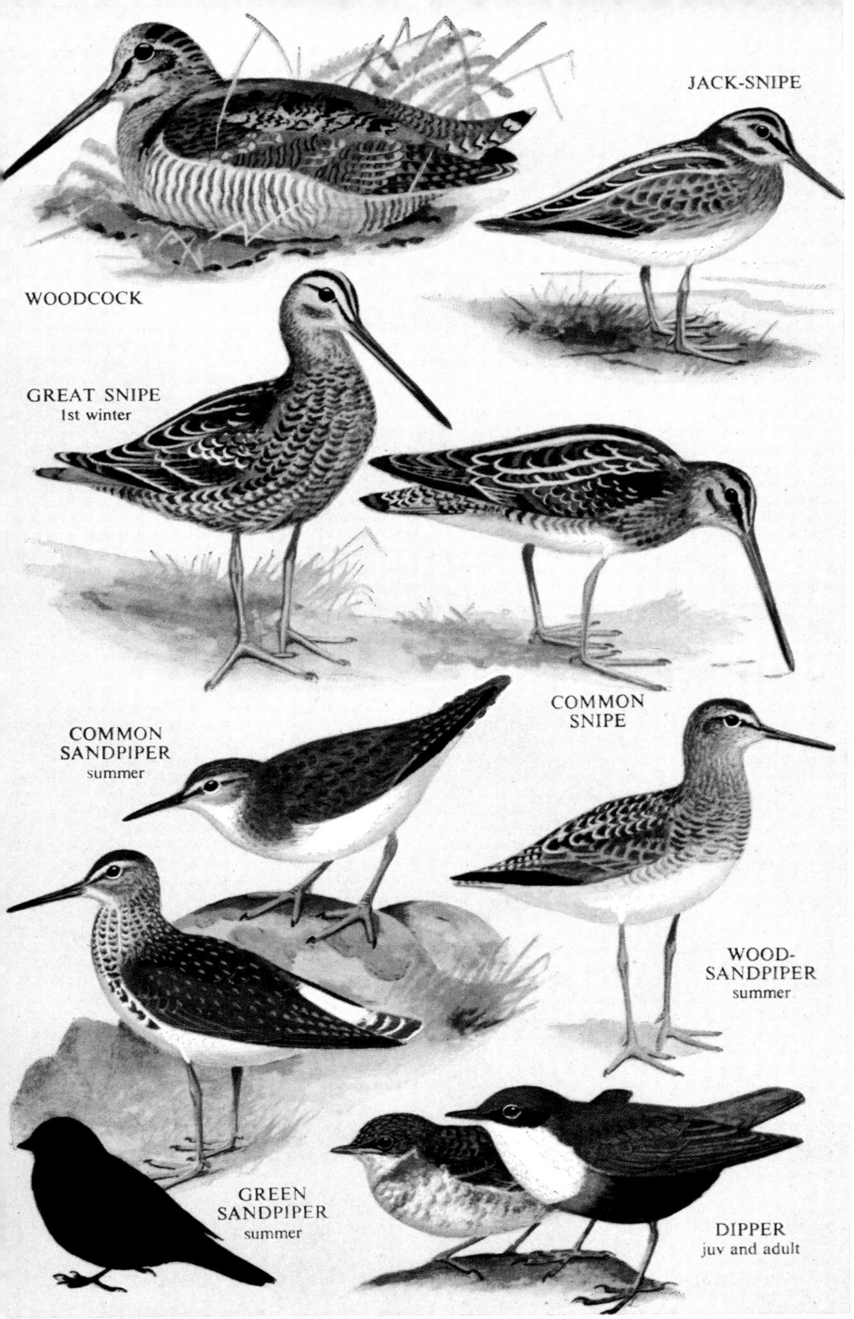

JACK-SNIPE
WOODCOCK
GREAT SNIPE
1st winter
COMMON
SNIPE
COMMON
SANDPIPER
summer
WOOD-
SANDPIPER
summer
GREEN
SANDPIPER
summer
DIPPER
juv and adult

GREY PLOVER
winter
GOLDEN
PLOVER
winter
KNOT
winter
REEVE
RUFF
winter
COMMON
REDSHANK
adult
SPOTTED
REDSHANK
winter
COMMON
REDSHANK
juv
GREEN-
SHANK
GREEN
SANDPIPER

LAPWING – summer
juv
SOUTHERN
GOLDEN PLOVER
summer
NORTHERN
GOLDEN PLOVER
summer
REY PLOVER
summer
DUNLIN
summer
TURNSTONE
summer
SPOTTED REDSHANK
summer

BLACK-TAILED GODWIT
adult summer
BAR-TAILED GODWIT
♂ summer
RUFF
♂ summer
DOTTEREL
♀ summer
CURLEW-
SANDPIPER
summer
KNOT
summer

GLOSSY IBIS
CURLEW
WHIMBREL
GREENSHANK
BAR-TAILED GODWIT
winter
BLACK-TAILED GODWIT winter

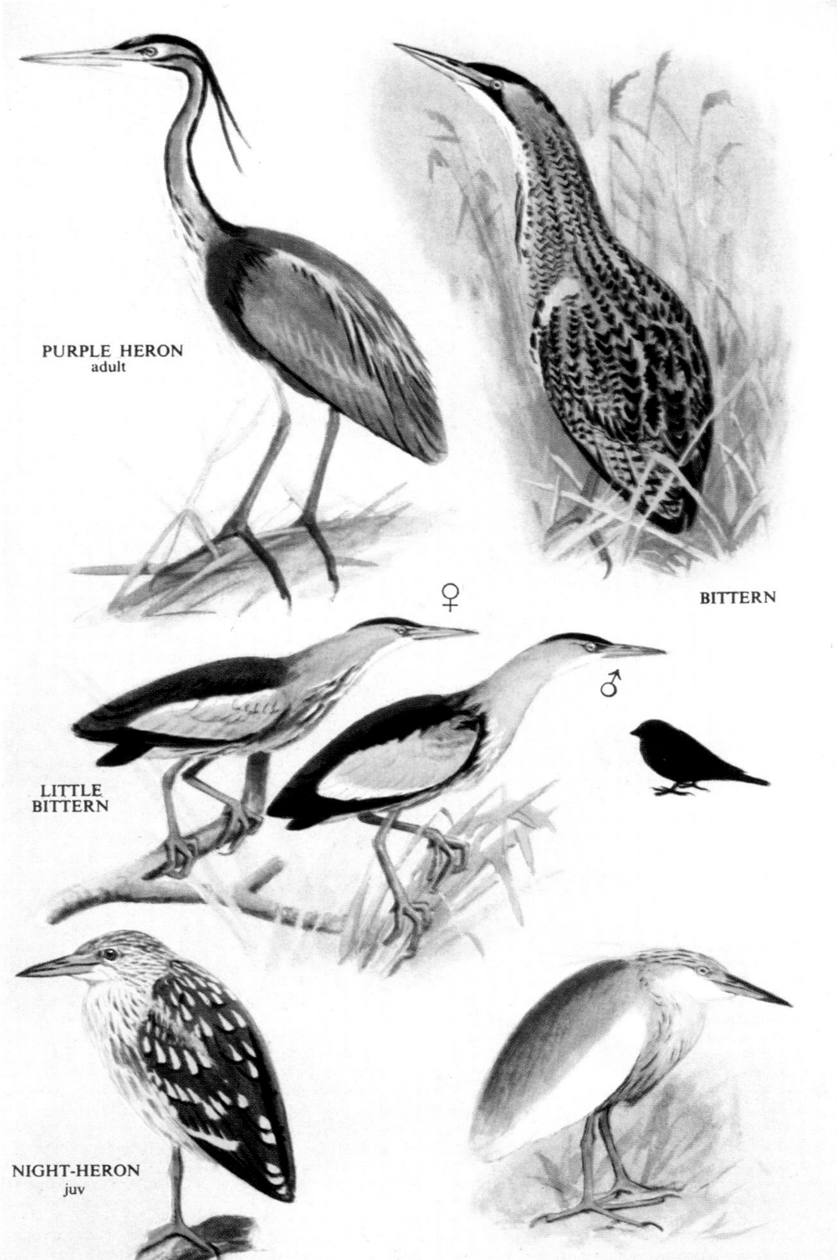
PURPLE HERON
adult
BITTERN
♀
♂
LITTLE
BITTERN
NIGHT-HERON
juv
SQUACCO HERON adult

WHITE STORK
SPOONBILL
adult
♂ summer
STILT
♀
AVOCET
LAPWING
♂ summer
OYSTERCATCHER
summer

RED-THROATED DIVER
summer
RED-BREASTED
MERGANSER
♂
RED-NECKED GREBE
summer
BLACK-NECKED
GREBE
summer
SLAVONIAN GREBE
summer
DAB-CHICK
summer
GREY PHALAROPE
summer
RED-NECKED
PHALAROPE
summer

GREEN-WINGED TEAL ♂
TEAL ♂
BLUE-WINGED TEAL ♂
GARGANEY ♂
GOLDENEYE ♀
SMEW ♀
GREAT CRESTED GREBE
adult summer
DABCHICK
adult summer

WIGEON ♂
COMMON POCHARD ♂
AMERICAN WIGEON ♂
FERRUGINOUS DUCK ♂
RED-CRESTED POCHARD ♂
GOOSANDER ♀
♀ RED-BREASTED MERGANSER

CHILEAN or
BROWN PINTAIL
BAHAMA PINTAIL
YELLOW-BILLED TEAL
GARGANEY ♀
TEAL ♀
DABCHICK
winter

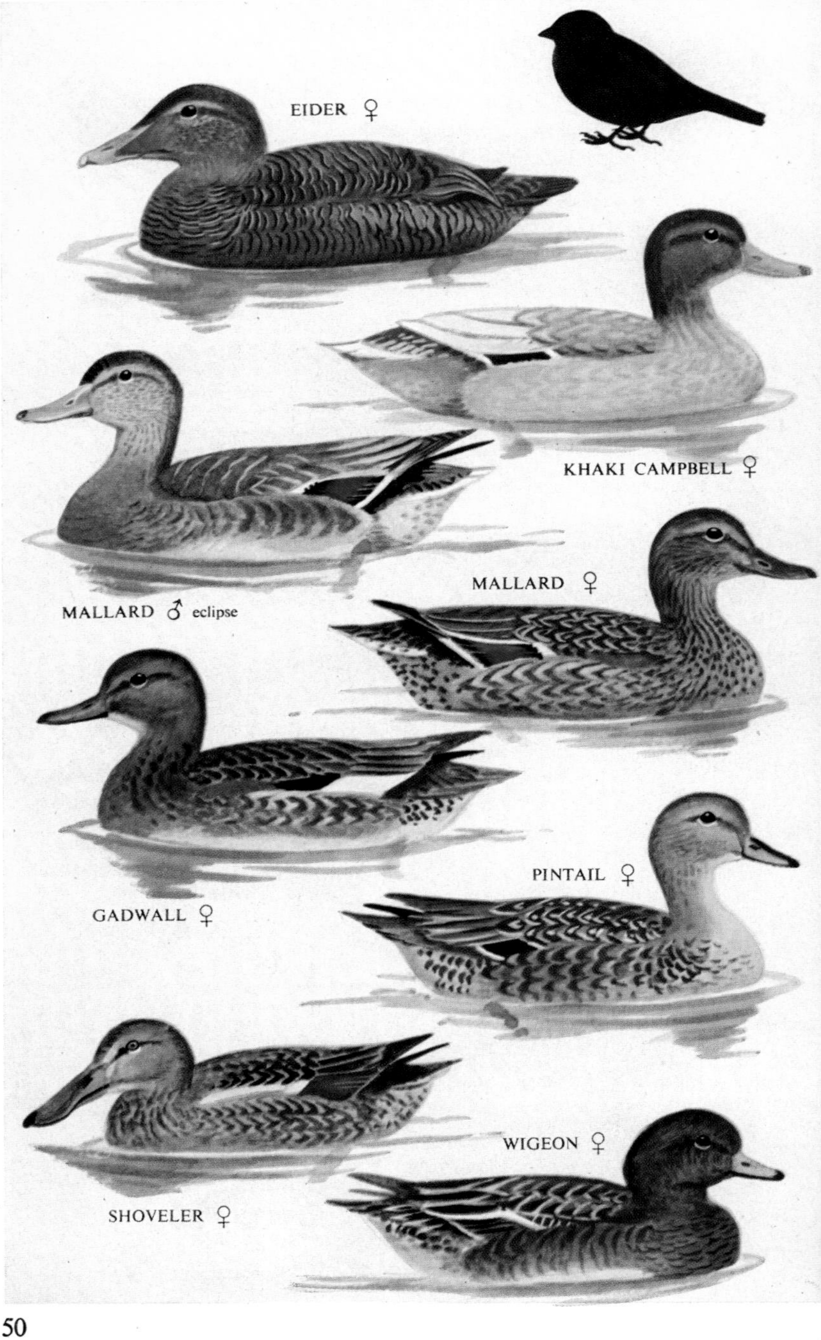
EIDER ♀
KHAKI CAMPBELL ♀
MALLARD ♂ eclipse
MALLARD ♀
GADWALL ♀
PINTAIL ♀
SHOVELER ♀
WIGEON ♀

VELVET SCOTER ♀
♀ COMMON SCOTER
SCAUP ♀
TUFTED
DUCK
♀ with white blaze
TUFTED DUCK ♀
GOLDENEYE ♀
EIDER 1st winter ♂

GADWALL ♂
PINTAIL ♂
MANDARIN ♀
DUCK
CAROLINA DUCK ♀
COMMON POCHARD ♀
RED-CRESTED POCHARD ♀
ROSY-BILL ♀

GOOSANDER ♂
RED-BREASTED MERGANSER ♂
MALLARD ♂
KHAKI CAMPBELL ♂
SHOVELER ♂
CHILOE WIGEON
sexes similar

MUSCOVY DUCK
domesticated, farmyard type
MAGELLAN GOOSE ♂
MAGELLAN GOOSE ♀
ASHY-HEADED GOOSE
sexes similar
BLUE-WINGED GOOSE
sexes similar
CAROLINA DUCK ♂
MANDARIN DUCK ♂

EGYPTIAN GOOSE
RUDDY SHELD-DUCK
SOUTH-AFRICAN SHELD-DUCK
PARADISE SHELD-DUCK
ROSY-BILLED DUCK
COMMON SHELD-DUCK

SHELD-DUCK
CANADA GOOSE
BARNACLE-GOOSE
PALE-BREASTED BRENT-GOOSE
DARK-BREASTED BRENT-GOOSE
BLUE SNOW-GOOSE
PARADISE SHELD-DUCK ♂
BAR-HEADED GOOSE

GREY-LAG GOOSE
CHINESE GOOSE
PINK-FOOTED GOOSE
segetum type
arvensis type
BEAN GOOSE
adult, with Greenland dult behind
juv
adult
WHITE-FRONTED GOOSE
juv
LESSER WHITE-FRONT

imm
adult
WHOOPER SWAN
imm
adult
BEWICK'S SWAN
imm
adult with
rusty-stained
head
MUTE SWAN
adult
SNOW-GOOSE
adult
BLACK SWAN
GANNET adult

PUFFIN
juv and adult
summer
RAZORBILL
adult summer
BLACK
GUILLEMOT
adult summer
adult summer
COMMON
GUILLEMOT
Southern race
bridled form
adult
summer
COMMON
GUILLEMOT
Northern race

BLACK-HEADED GULL
summer
LITTLE GULL
summer
COMMON TERN
summer
ARCTIC TERN
summer
ROSEATE TERN
summer
LITTLE TERN
summer
SANDWICH TERN
summer

GLAUCOUS GULL
adult winter
ICELAND GULL
adult winter
HERRING-GULL
adult winter
COMMON GULL
adult winter
FULMAR
KITTIWAKE
adult
LITTLE GULL
adult winter
BLACK-HEADED GULL adult winter

GLAUCOUS GULL
3rd winter
ICELAND GULL
3rd winter
HERRING-GULL
2nd winter
COMMON GULL
1st winter
COMMON
GULL
juv
juv
1st winter
BLACK-HEADED GULL

2nd winter
juv
GREAT BLACK-BACK
GLAUCOUS GULL 1st winter
GREAT SKUA
ICELAND GULL 1st winter
ARCTIC SKUA adult, dark phase
LESSER BLACK-BACK 2nd winter
HERRING-GULL juv

CORMORANT
typical race
adult summer
SHAG
adults summer
CORMORANT
Continental or
Southern race,
adult summer
LESSER
BLACK-BACK
Scandinavian race
adult winter
LESSER
BLACK-BACK
British race
adult summer
3rd winter
adult summer
GREAT BLACK-BACK

SWALLOW, adult See *Land: Medium Short*, p. 73

BAILLON'S CRAKE *Porzana pusilla* Plate 36 Rail Family

PLUMAGE. Brown above, marked black, with white streaks on wing-coverts; grey below and on cheeks, with flanks, belly and under tail-coverts barred black and white. Bill green; legs greyish-pink; eye red.

STRUCTURE. *Wing length* S/MS. *Ratios:* wing MS; tail MS; neck M; bill M; legs M/ML.

MOVEMENT. As water rail (p. 141)

VOICE. Call has a turkey-like rhythm, 'te-te-te-terrerrer' or 'uck-uck-uck-errr'.

FIELD MARKS. Both sexes closely resemble male little crake (below).

HABITAT. As water rail.

RANGE AND STATUS. Vagrant, mainly spring and autumn, and most often Norfolk; has bred.

LITTLE CRAKE *Porzana parva* Plate 36 Rail Family

PLUMAGE. Brown streaked black above, male with grey, female with buff face and underparts; under tail-coverts barred black and white. Bill pale green with red base; legs green; eye and orbital ring red.

STRUCTURE. *Wing length* MS/M. *Ratios:* wing M; tail MS; neck M; bill MS; legs ML.

MOVEMENT. As water rail (p. 141).

VOICE. A low 'ück-ück-ück-tirre' or 'tjip-tjip-tjip-rreeo'.

FIELD MARKS. The two small crakes, *little* and *Baillon's*, are like miniature water rails with short bills, except that female *little* differs from all the rest in buff face and underparts. Both are smaller than *spotted* and can also be told from it by no white spots above, barred under tail-coverts, and green bill. Male *little* can be told from both sexes of *Baillon's* by no white streaks on wing-coverts, unbarred flanks, red at base of bill and green legs. It is unusual, however, for a small crake to stay long enough in the field of view for adequate plumage details to be seen.

HABITAT. As water rail.

RANGE AND STATUS. Vagrant, or very rare passage migrant, chiefly in spring, and most often in Norfolk and Sussex.

GREAT REED WARBLER *Acrocephalus arundinaceus*

An almost thrush-sized reed warbler (p. 117), otherwise differing from the common species only in a prominent pale stripe through its eye, its stouter bill, and its loud croaking and grating voice; an increasing but still rare visitor to reed beds in the SE, which may have bred in Kent.

DUNLIN *Calidris alpina* Plates 37, 41, 79, 82 Sandpiper Family

Ox-bird, Ploverspage, Sea-snipe, Stint; Red-backed Sandpiper (N America).

PLUMAGE. In summer chestnut streaked black above, except grey-brown wings with light bar and dark tips, and white sides to rump and tail; breast white streaked darker, belly black, under tail-coverts white. In winter chestnut parts are grey-brown and belly white. Juvenile is similar but with buff instead of grey tinge. Blackish bill is sometimes perceptibly decurved; legs dark olive.

STRUCTURE. *Wing length* M. *Ratios:* wing M; tail MS; neck MS; bill M/ML; legs M/ML.

MOVEMENT. Fast direct flight; flocks perform remarkable evolutions, like wisps of smoke blown by the wind; has a special display flight; walks or runs.

VOICE. Flight note is a rather weak 'treep' or 'teerp'; flocks have a conversational twitter. Trilling song is delivered in air or from ground with wings upstretched.

FIELD MARKS. The commonest small wader of the shore, it is easy to identify in summer, as it is the only one with a black belly. In winter can be told from sanderling by less strongly contrasting grey and white plumage and no blackish shoulder spot, from knot by smaller size, browner upperparts and white sides to rump and tail; from common sandpiper by quite different voice and wing-action, and from ringed plover by longer bill and no black and white on head. For distinctions from curlew- and purple sandpipers, see below, and from little stint, see p. 121. The northern and southern races of dunlin are identical in plumage, but the smaller individuals of the southern (nearly as small as little stints) and the larger individuals of the northern (nearly as large as curlew-sandpipers) may be told apart with a fair degree of confidence by experienced observers. Juveniles have a smudgy speckling on the sides of the lower breast, which is often mistaken for an adult's moulting black patch.

FLOCKING. Highly gregarious; often with other shore birds, especially ringed plover and sanderling; on moors with golden plover.

HABITAT. Breeds on grassy and peaty moorlands up to high altitudes, lowland peat-mosses and coastal marshes; in winter on muddy and sandy coasts and estuaries and adjacent marshes; on passage regularly at freshwater margins, especially sewage farms.

RANGE AND STATUS. Southern race breeds on moors from Brecon and Derbyshire northwards, and on coast in S Lancashire and many parts of Scotland and Ireland; has exceptionally bred in E and SW England; also widespread passage migrant, but very few appear to stay the winter. Northern race is abundant passage migrant on all coasts and inland, and winter visitor on all coasts, while a few non-breeders appear to summer.

CURLEW-SANDPIPER *Calidris testacea* Plates 37, 42, 80

Pigmy Curlew.

PLUMAGE. In summer all pinkish-cinnamon, except white rump and under tail-coverts, black streaks on mantle, and wings grey-brown with a pale bar and dark tips. In winter pinkish parts are grey-brown above and on breast-band, white below. Juvenile is similar but with buff instead of grey tinge, and scaly markings on upperparts. Blackish, slightly decurved bill; olive-brown legs.

STRUCTURE. *Wing length* M. *Ratios:* wing ML; tail MS; neck MS; bill ML; legs L.

MOVEMENT. Similar to dunlin (above).

VOICE. Flight note a soft 'chirrip'.

FIELD MARKS. White rump, recalling house martin, distinguishes curlew-sandpiper in flight at once from all small waders, except green and wood sandpipers, which have shorter, straight bills, and quite different voice and flight, and are rarely seen on shore. At rest in summer curlew-sandpiper can be told by ruddy plumage from all waders except knot (which is larger) and sanderling (which has white belly), neither of which have a curved bill. In winter can easily be confused with the larger specimens of the dunlin at rest, as its longer legs are not always apparent, and some dunlin have just as long and curved bills as some curlew-sandpipers. Distinctions from other grey-brown waders at rest are same as for dunlin. Note that many curlew-sandpipers in autumn are in the buffish juvenile plumage, and very like juvenile dunlins except for their rump, but rather greyer above and cleaner beneath.

FLOCKING. Gregarious, in small flocks; often with other waders, especially dunlins and little stints.

HABITAT. As dunlin in winter.

RANGE AND STATUS. Passage migrant, commoner in some years than others; chiefly in E and S England.

PECTORAL SANDPIPER *Calidris melanotos* Plate 37

American Pectoral Sandpiper.

PLUMAGE. Brown streaked darker, with snipe-like pale streaks down the back, and white belly and under tail-coverts. Greenish-black bill; yellowish legs.

STRUCTURE. *Wing length* M. *Ratios:* wing ML; tail MS; neck MS; bill M; legs ML.

MOVEMENT. Similar to dunlin (above), but may zigzag when flushed.

VOICE. Flight note 'trrit, trrit' has resemblances to both dunlin and curlew-sandpiper.

FIELD MARKS. Superficially like a rather large, plump juvenile dunlin, but its stance and 'jizz' are quite distinct; can be told from dunlin by yellow legs, shorter, straight and rather sandpiper-like bill, and sharp division between streaked breast and white belly (not usually visible in front view) which gives effect of a bib. Bib effect also distinguishes from very rare Siberian pectoral sandpiper *C. acuminata*; for differences from other small shore birds, see dunlin. Somewhat resembles a small, rather rufous reeve (p. 142).

HABITAT. Prefers inland and coastal pools and marshes with some vegetation cover to open shore.

RANGE AND STATUS. Very scarce annual autumn visitor from Arctic America, most likely to be seen after strong westerly gales.

BUFF-BREASTED SANDPIPER *Tryngites subruficollis* Drawing p. 132

A North American wader, somewhat like a small reeve (p. 142), with a longish neck, small head and shortish bill; the head and neck are warm yellowish-buff, the whole underparts uniformly buffish, and the underwing white; no wing-bars or white on rump; vagrant, now almost annual, mainly in the S in autumn.

RINGED PLOVER *Charadrius hiaticula* Plates 38, 79

Ring Dotterel; Sea-Lark; Stonehatch; Semipalmated Plover (N America).

PLUMAGE. Sandy-brown above, with a white wing-bar; white below. Male has black crown, cheeks and breast-band, and white collar and forehead; female is browner and juvenile greyer on the black parts. Bill of male and summer female is orange with black tip, of immature and winter female horn-coloured with dark tip, of juvenile blackish with yellowish base; legs orange-yellow, paler in winter female and young.

STRUCTURE. *Wing length* M. *Ratios:* wing ML; tail MS; neck MS; bill MS; legs M.

MOVEMENT. Swift, direct flight, flocks performing aerial evolutions similar to dunlin; also a special bat-like display flight. Walks or runs on ground, and wades in water; like other plovers, will run a little way and then stop, and perhaps bob its head; feeds usually with head up as if listening, not with head down like dunlin and knot.

Buff-breasted Sandpiper

VOICE. Characteristic note when disturbed is a liquid, musical 'too-i', also 'queep' or 'queeo'. Song, delivered in display flight, is a plangent elaboration of the latter note.

FIELD MARKS. Can be told from other common small shore birds, especially dunlin, by short bill, also by striking black and white head pattern, yellow legs, liquid note, and in flight more prominent white wing-bar. For distinctions from little ringed and Kentish plovers, see p. 122.

FLOCKING. Highly gregarious; frequently with dunlin and other shore birds.

HABITAT. Breeds mainly on sandy and pebbly beaches, also in other flat places near coast, and exceptionally on sandy warrens far inland and on inland loch and river margins and islands; in winter on sandy and muddy shores and estuaries, and on passage at sewage farms and other freshwater margins.

RANGE AND STATUS. Resident, breeding on all suitable coasts, and inland in E Anglia (Breckland) and parts of N England, Scotland and Ireland; otherwise common winter visitor to all coasts and widespread passage migrant inland.

JACK SNIPE *Lymnocryptes minimus* Plates 39, 78 Sandpiper Family

PLUMAGE. Warm brown, streaked darker, with green and purple glossing on mantle, and two prominent light stripes on either side of back; white belly and under tail-coverts. Yellow-flesh bill, dark at tip; greyish legs.

STRUCTURE. *Wing length* MS/M. *Ratios:* wing M; tail MS; neck MS; bill L; legs M/ML.

MOVEMENT. Slower and less erratic flight than common snipe, and when flushed usually alights again fairly soon; walks on ground, wades in water.

VOICE. Flushed birds occasionally give a low, weak call.

FIELD MARKS. Resembles a small common snipe with a much shorter bill; can also be told from the other two snipes by different mode of flight and head pattern (two narrow pale streaks in centre of crown instead of one broad one), and relative silence when flushed; and from adult great snipe by no white at all in tail.

FLOCKING. Occasionally in small wisps.

HABITAT. As common snipe (p. 139), but sometimes in dry places.

RANGE AND STATUS. Winter visitor and passage migrant, local but generally distributed; has summered, but never been proved to breed.

COMMON SANDPIPER *Actitis hypoleucos* Plates 39, 79

Summer Snipe; Willy Wicket.

PLUMAGE. Grey-brown above, with white wing-bar, sides to rump and sides and tip of tail; white below. Dark brown bill; greenish-grey legs.

STRUCTURE. *Wing length* M. *Ratios:* wing M; tail MS; neck MS; bill ML; legs M.

MOVEMENT. Typically flies low over water, with shrill call and flickering wings, held momentarily at the downward stroke, when they appear distinctly bowed; also a circular display flight; does not tower when flushed. Walks or runs on ground, wades in water, and will perch on low objects, bobbing head and tail.

VOICE. Flight note a shrill 'twee-wee-wee'; song, uttered in flight, on ground or from low perch, is mainly an elaboration of this.

FIELD MARKS. Most easily identified by characteristic flight and call-note; at rest appears slimmer than winter dunlin, which has longer bill and does not constantly bob head and tail. See below for distinctions from wood and green sandpipers, and see dunlin (p. 129) for distinctions from other small brown waders.

FLOCKING. Occasionally in small parties, but mostly solitary.

HABITAT. Breeds beside streams, lochs (including sea-lochs) and other waters in hilly districts, and sporadically by lowland waters; on passage at all kinds of freshwater margins, but not so much on marshy pools; sometimes also on salt-marshes and rocky coasts, but rarely on mudflats or sandy beaches.

RANGE AND STATUS. Summer visitor to hill districts of Scotland, Wales, N and W England, and Ireland (except SE); breeds very sporadically in S and E England; otherwise common passage migrant, occasionally wintering in S.

WOOD SANDPIPER *Tringa glareola* Plates 39, 80

PLUMAGE. Grey-brown with dark and light markings (looking much more spotted in summer), belly and upper tail-coverts white, and tail white barred darker. Blackish bill; greenish legs.

STRUCTURE. *Wing length* M. *Ratios:* wing M; tail MS; neck MS; bill M/ML; legs L.

MOVEMENT. As green sandpiper (below), but less often towers when flushed, and flight generally more uncertain.

VOICE. Usual flight note a rather flat triple 'wee-wee-wee' or 'wit-wit-wit', sometimes only 'wee-wee'; also a more musical, greenshank-like 'chew-ew', and a shrill 'chip-chip-chip' uttered both on ground and in the air. Snatches of bubbling, redshank-like or woodlark-like song may occasionally be heard from migrants.

FIELD MARKS. Intermediate between *common* and green sandpipers, it can be told from *common* by white rump and quite different flight and voice, from *green* by barred tail, longer legs, voice, greyish (not blackish) underwing, and much less strongly contrasted black and white appearance and from both by legs projecting beyond tail in flight.

FLOCKING. Sometimes in small parties.

HABITAT. Marshy places of all kinds, freshwater margins, salt-marshes, but rarely on the open shore.

RANGE AND STATUS. Passage migrant, commoner in autumn than spring, exceptional in summer; most often from Wash to Dorset, rare on W coast, very rare Ireland; has bred occasionally in the N, especially extreme N Scotland.

SANDERLING *Crocethia alba* Plates 37, 79 Sandpiper Family

PLUMAGE. In summer warm brown streaked darker, except for white wing-bar, sides of rump, belly and under tail-coverts, and dark wing-tips. In winter warm brown parts are pale grey above and white below, with a blackish shoulder spot. Black bill and legs.

STRUCTURE. *Wing length* M. *Ratios:* wing M; tail S/SM; neck MS; bill M; legs M.

MOVEMENT. Similar to dunlin (p. 129), but patters remarkably fast and restlessly about the edge of the tide, and prefers to run away rather than fly when approached.

VOICE. Flight note 'twick, twick'; flocks twitter conversationally.

FIELD MARKS. In winter easily told by whiteness and blackish shoulder spot, being much paler than any other small shore bird; can also be told from dunlin by more conspicuous wing-bar, different note, and in summer by no black on belly. At all times extremely restless feeding behaviour and preference for sandy shores are useful pointers. For differences from other small shore birds, see dunlin.

FLOCKING. Highly gregarious; often with other shore birds.

HABITAT. Mainly sandy sea-shores; occasional on coastal mud and at freshwater margins.

RANGE AND STATUS. Winter visitor and passage migrant to all suitable coasts; occasional inland, mainly on spring passage; non-breeders frequently summer, especially on northern coasts.

DUNLIN See *Waterside: Medium Short*, p. 129.

PURPLE SANDPIPER *Calidris maritima* Plates 37, 79

PLUMAGE. Blackish-brown with mantle glossed purple, but summer adult and juvenile are speckled paler; whitish wing-bar; white belly. Blackish-brown bill with yellow base; yellow legs.

STRUCTURE. *Wing length* M. *Ratios:* wing M; tail MS; neck MS; bill M; legs M.

MOVEMENT. Similar to dunlin (p. 129), occasionally swims.

VOICE. A low 'weet-wit', also a piping note somewhat reminiscent of snow-bunting.

FIELD MARKS. The only small dark wader with yellow legs likely to be met with on rocky shores; white wing-bar, round-shouldered appearance, and frequent association with turnstones are also useful pointers. Size just larger than the biggest dunlins.

FLOCKING. In small parties; habitually goes with turnstones.

HABITAT. Rocky shores, reefs, patches of stones below high-water mark, groynes and breakwaters (even on sea-fronts of holiday resorts), especially when covered with seaweed; exceptionally on muddy or sandy shores with stony or weedy patches, and at freshwater margins.

RANGE AND STATUS. Winter visitor to all suitable coasts, a few non-breeders occasionally summering in the north.

DOTTEREL See *Land: Medium Short*, p. 78

RUFF, female See *Waterside: Medium*, p. 142

GREEN SANDPIPER *Tringa ochropus* Plates 39, 40, 80

Martin Snipe.

PLUMAGE. Dark grey-brown above, with white rump and tail, except tip; white below, but breast speckled. Blackish bill with green base; greenish legs.

STRUCTURE. *Wing length* M. *Ratios:* wing M; tail MS; neck MS; bill ML; legs M/ML.

MOVEMENT. When flushed, starts up high into the air with shrill call, and towers before flying off with a rather snipe-like flight; will also fly low over water, but never with the extreme flickering flight of the common sandpiper. Walks or runs on the ground, bobs like a *common*, wades in the water.

VOICE. On being flushed almost always utters a shrill 'weet-a-weet' or 'kit-a-wake', with many variations, such as 'too-eet-a-too-et', but none of them resembling typical wood-sandpiper calls. Snatches of liquid, musical song occasionally heard on passage.

FIELD MARKS. The only smallish bird which dashes up from water's edge with shrill cries and has a conspicuous white rump contrasting strongly with darker upperparts, making it look like a large house martin. Can be told from *common* by white rump, voice and mode of flight; for distinctions from *wood*, see above. Of other waders with white rumps, greenshank is much larger and paler, curlew-sandpiper has curved bill and is paler, and both have different voice and mode of flight.

FLOCKING. Sometimes in small parties.

HABITAT. Marshes, and freshwater margins of all kinds down to small pools and even puddles of flood water; more often along rivers and streams than most waders; in salt-marshes, but rarely on the open shore.

RANGE AND STATUS. Passage migrant throughout British Isles, occasional in summer and winter; has bred occasionally in the N. (N.B.—Uses old nest of another bird in a tree.)

TURNSTONE *Arenaria interpres* Plates 38, 41, 79, 82 Sandpiper Family
Ruddy Turnstone (N America).

PLUMAGE. In winter blackish-brown, with white underparts except for black breast-band; in summer more white on head and much chestnut on upperparts. Black bill; orange legs.

STRUCTURE. *Wing length* M. *Ratios:* wing ML; tail MS; neck MS; bill M; legs M.

MOVEMENT. Swift, direct flight on long distances, but slower and more uncertain on short ones; runs and walks on ground and will lift small stones and weed in search of food; perches on rocks, and occasionally on objects in the water.

VOICE. A twittering 'kitititit', a clear 'keeoo, keeoo' and a rather grunting note.

FIELD MARKS. The only small wader with a short bill and a pied appearance, both at rest and in flight, the black and white pattern of the spread wings being in striking contrast to other small waders. At close range the short orange legs are a useful field mark, and in summer the tortoiseshell appearance of the upperparts is distinctive.

FLOCKING. Usually in small parties, but sometimes in large flocks on passage; often with dunlins and other small waders and accompanied by purple sandpipers.

HABITAT. Chiefly rocky shores, feeding on weed-covered rocks, reefs, mussel-scaups, etc.; also on other types of shore and even at freshwater margins.

RANGE AND STATUS. Common winter visitor and passage migrant on all coasts; regular on passage inland in small numbers; a few non-breeders habitually summer, but never proved to have bred.

SPOTTED CRAKE *Porzana porzana* Plate 36 Rail Family

PLUMAGE. Brown, streaked black and speckled white above, barred white below; under tail-coverts buff. Bill brown at tip, shading into green, yellow and finally red at base; legs pale olive-green.

STRUCTURE. *Wing length* M. *Ratios:* wing MS; tail S; neck M; bill M; legs M/ML.

MOVEMENT. As water rail (p. 141).

VOICE. A loud 'h'wit, h'wit, h'wit' like the crack of a whip, and a rhythmical 'tic-toc'.

FIELD MARKS. Extremely skulking, but in the open looks like a small dark corncrake with whitish spots, or perhaps a small brown moorhen if swimming a marsh pool; appreciably larger than little and Baillon's crakes (p. 129). Can be told from water rail and moorhen by white-spotted upperparts and buff under tail-coverts. Most likely to be seen towards dusk feeding on mud at edge of thick swampy cover. In flight shows large pale wing-patches.

HABITAT. As water rail, but particularly fond of swamps that are almost inaccessible owing to spongy nature of ground.

RANGE AND STATUS. Summer visitor and passage migrant; range obscure, but has bred during past forty years in Brecon, Cheshire, Dorset, Flint, E Anglia, Somerset and probably Northumberland; otherwise scarce passage migrant (regular in Norfolk at least) and occasional in winter.

WATERSIDE BIRDS: Medium

WHITE-WINGED BLACK TERN *Chlidonias leucopterus* Plates 102, 103

A marsh tern. Gull Family

PLUMAGE. In summer black head, mantle, underwing and underparts, grey wings with white forewing, and white rump, tail and tail-coverts; in winter similar to black tern, but has no dark spot on side of breast; slightly forked tail. Black bill, tinged red; vermilion legs.

STRUCTURE AND MOVEMENT. As black tern (below), but bill-ratio MS.

VOICE. Call-note based on 'kweek' or 'kwek'.

FIELD MARKS. In summer can easily be told from black tern by white forewing, rump and tail and black underwing, but in winter, unless traces of summer plumage remain, can be separated in field only if absence of dark spot on side of breast can be established or brighter red legs seen. This dark spot is a variable character in the black tern, and not always easy to detect; by its definite absence the *white-winged* can also be told from the sea terns, but not from the little gull. For other distinctions from sea terns, see black tern, and from little gull, see p. 170.

FLOCKING. Occasionally in small flocks; often with black terns.

HABITAT. Mostly over inland waters, less often on estuaries or coast.

RANGE AND STATUS. Scarce passage migrant, mainly in E and S England, and most often E Anglia; more often spring than autumn, when, however, probably often overlooked.

BLACK TERN *Chlidonias niger* Plates 102, 103 Gull Family

A marsh tern.

PLUMAGE. In summer black head and underparts, dark grey upperparts and underwing, white under tail-coverts; in winter black crown and nape, grey upperparts, white forehead, shoulder and underparts; tail slightly forked. Juvenile similar to winter adult, but browner above. Black bill (yellow base to lower mandible in juvenile); dark red-brown legs (yellow in juvenile).

STRUCTURE. *Wing length* ML. *Ratios:* wing L; tail MS; neck S; bill M; legs S.

MOVEMENT. Graceful, dipping flight, often stooping to surface of water, but rarely touching it. Rarely walks, but perches on posts, etc., in water.

VOICE. Large flocks have a collective reedy cry; otherwise rather silent, but occasionally calls 'kik, kik', 'keek', or 'krew'.

FIELD MARKS. No other bird that hawks over water has a black head and body, with grey upperparts showing no white (though white vent is often conspicuous). In winter can be told from *little* and all larger terns by less deeply forked tail, more sharply defined white shoulder-patch, black bill, and dipping flight; for distinctions from *white-winged black*, see above, and from little gull, see p. 170.

FLOCKING. Gregarious, mostly in small parties; sometimes goes with sea terns, especially in autumn.

HABITAT. Mostly over inland waters, but sometimes on estuaries and coast; breeds in marshy places inland.

RANGE AND STATUS. Spring and autumn passage migrant, much commoner in some years than others, mainly E and S England, where it formerly bred.

WHISKERED TERN *Chlidonias hybrida* Gull Family

A marsh tern; grey below, whiter above, with a black cap in breeding plumage, when it is quite distinct from the two other marsh terns; in winter cannot be separated from white-winged black tern in the field. Double flight note alternates a shrill cheep like a domestic chick with a rasping note like a corncrake. Rare vagrant from S Europe.

Whiskered Tern

LITTLE TERN *Sterna albifrons*

Plates 60, 102 Gull Family

Lesser Tern; Least Tern (N America); a sea tern.

PLUMAGE. As common tern (p. 146), but has white forehead in summer. Bill yellow with black tip (brown in juvenile); legs orange (brownish-yellow in juvenile).

STRUCTURE. *Wing length* L. *Ratios:* wing ML; tail M; neck S; bill M; legs VS.

MOVEMENT. As common tern, but flight rather quicker.

VOICE. Chief calls are 'kik-kik', 'pee-e-eer', and various trilling elaborations on these; other notes at breeding colonies.

FIELD MARKS. Much the smallest sea tern, and the only one with forehead white and bill yellow in breeding season. For distinctions from marsh terns, see black tern (above).

FLOCKING. Gregarious at all times, but less often with other terns; breeds in small colonies.

HABITAT. Breeds on shingly and sandy coasts and marine islands only, never inland; on passage in coastal waters, rather uncommon on fresh water.

RANGE AND STATUS. Decreasing summer visitor, breeding in small scattered colonies on all coasts, but absent or very local S Wales, N Scotland, S Ireland; elsewhere passage migrant, mainly on coast, rare inland.

KNOT *Calidris canutus* Plates 40, 42, 78 Sandpiper Family

PLUMAGE. In summer all reddish-chestnut, except for grey wings with light bar and dark tips, and white under tail-coverts; in winter reddish parts are grey above and white below. Black bill; olive-green legs.

STRUCTURE. *Wing length* ML. *Ratios:* wing ML; tail S; neck MS; bill ML; legs M.

MOVEMENT. As dunlin (p. 129), but generally rather less brisk, and has characteristic head-down attitude when feeding.

VOICE. A low 'knut'; flocks have a collective chatter, like jackdaws.

FIELD MARKS. Intermediate in size between common redshank and dunlin, it has the dumpy appearance of the latter, but can be told from it by uniform grey tail, also in winter by greyer upperparts and in summer by reddish plumage. Can also be told from sanderling by larger size and uniform grey tail, and in summer by reddish belly. For distinctions from curlew-sandpiper, see p. 130. In winter grey plover is superficially similar, but it is appreciably larger with a shorter bill, has black patch under wing and white patch at base of tail, and rarely goes in flocks of as many as fifty. Flocks of knot can be told at a distance by their closely packed appearance when feeding.

FLOCKING. Highly gregarious; often with other shore birds.

HABITAT. Sandy and muddy shores and estuaries; occasionally at freshwater margins.

RANGE AND STATUS. Winter visitor and passage migrant to all coasts, but commonest E coast, and W coast from Solway to Dee; uncommon W coast Scotland; small numbers summer on more northern coasts; occasional inland on passage.

LESSER YELLOWLEGS or Yellowshank *Tringa flavipes*
Sandpiper Family

A North American wader, rare but increasing as an autumn visitor, looking like a large wood sandpiper (p. 133) with conspicuous yellow legs. The much rarer Greater Yellowlegs *T. melanoleuca* is appreciably larger, the size of a greenshank (p. 144).

COMMON SNIPE *Gallinago gallinago* Plates 39, 73, 78 Sandpiper Family

Bleater; Heather Bleater; Wilson's Snipe (N America).

PLUMAGE. Warm brown, with darker and lighter streaks, including dark bars along the head, a pale eyestripe and several conspicuous pale streaks running down the back; white belly and under tail-coverts. Sabine's snipe is a melanistic variant, which has no pale stripes down the back and is much darker, almost blackish-brown, all over. Reddish-brown bill with dark tip; pale greenish legs.

STRUCTURE. *Wing length* M. *Ratios:* wing MS; tail MS; neck MS; bill VL; legs M.

MOVEMENT. When flushed, dashes up with a loud cry and rapid flight, zigzag at first, but later direct; flocks will perform compact manoeuvres like shore birds.

In remarkable display flight, bird dives at an angle of 45° while 'drumming'. Walks on ground, wades in shallow water, and will perch on low objects.

VOICE. Flight note when disturbed is a loud, harsh 'creech'; in spring has an insistent 'chip-per, chip-per', delivered on ground or in air. 'Drumming', caused by vibration of two protruding outer tail-feathers when diving, is a quavering, bleating or humming sound.

Common Snipe 'drumming' in display flight

FIELD MARKS. Very long bill, zigzag flight, loud harsh note when flushed and 'drumming' are all hallmarks of the common snipe, which is much the most likely wader to be found at marshy inland pools with plenty of cover. For distinctions from woodcock, see p. 97; also great snipe (below) and jack snipe (p. 132).

FLOCKING. Often in small parties or 'wisps'.

HABITAT. All kinds of damp, marshy and boggy places inland, including sewage farms, and sometimes at considerable elevations; uncommon on the shore.

RANGE AND STATUS. Resident, breeding throughout British Isles, but local in S England; also widespread winter visitor and passage migrant.

GREAT SNIPE *Gallinago media* Plates 39, 73 Sandpiper Family

PLUMAGE. Closely resembles common snipe (above), but is more heavily marked below, and adult has conspicuous white feathers at sides and tip of tail. Dark brown bill with yellowish base; greyish legs.

STRUCTURE. *Wing length* M. *Ratios:* wing MS; tail S; neck MS; bill L; legs M/ML.

MOVEMENT. Flight slower and more direct than *common*; tends to shuffle rather than walk on ground.

VOICE. Will croak on being flushed.

FIELD MARKS. Appears larger, heavier and darker on the wing than *common*, but can be safely identified (by white feathers in tail) only by those familiar with much smaller extent of white in latter's tail. Other useful points are drier habitat, different flight and voice, less white on underparts, and slightly shorter bill, but these can only be relied on to support decision when tail has been well seen. Juvenile cannot be separated from *common* in field.

HABITAT. In addition to the marshy places favoured by *common*, occurs in quite dry open country, such as farmland and brackeny commons.

RANGE AND STATUS. Scarce and decreasing autumn passage migrant, exceptional in winter and spring; most often in S and E England.

LONG-BILLED DOWITCHER *Limnodromus scolopaceus* Sandpiper Family

One of two North American waders formerly lumped together as the red-breasted snipe or red-breasted sandpiper, resembling a cross between a large snipe and a small godwit, with the shape and bill-length of a common snipe (below) and the general plumage pattern (both summer and winter) of a knot or a bar-tailed godwit (p. 149), but showing more white on the rump. Most British records, however, are of the buffish immatures. A scarce but apparently increasing vagrant in autumn, differing from the very similar but smaller and still scarcer Short-billed Dowitcher *L. griseus* in having usually longer bill wings falling short of tail tip instead of projecting just beyond it, and call-note a shrill 'keeek' or 'keeek-keeek-keeek' instead of 'chü-chüchü' like a greenshank but weaker.

Long-billed Dowitcher

WATER RAIL *Rallus aquaticus* Plate 36

PLUMAGE. Brown streaked black above, grey on cheeks and breast, flanks and belly barred black and white, under tail-coverts white. Young have all underparts slightly barred. Bill red with brown tip; legs flesh-brown; eye red.

STRUCTURE. *Wing length* M. *Ratios:* wing S; tail S; neck M; bill ML; legs ML.

MOVEMENT. Except on migration, flight weak, with dangling legs; walks and runs, and may flirt under tail-coverts like moorhen; swims, and dives from water.

VOICE. Various clucking, grunting and miaouing notes, and a loud harsh call beginning as a grunt and ending as a squeal.

FIELD MARKS. Like a small moorhen with a long red bill, which also distinguishes it from all smaller crakes; most frequent view is from rear as it rushes back into cover (it is extremely skulking), and then barred flanks and under tail- coverts separate it from moorhen in all plumages; looks mainly grey in flight. Most often seen in hard weather, when forced into the open to feed.

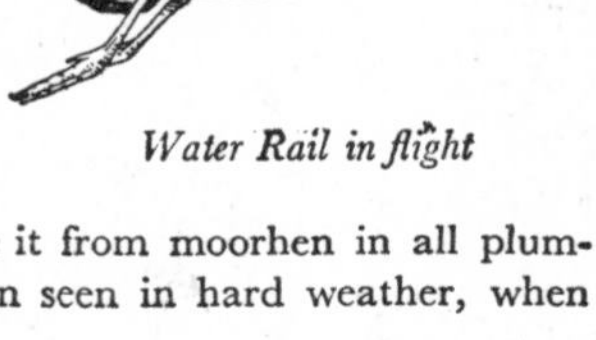

Water Rail in flight

HABITAT. Swamps, fens, bogs and mosses; also, especially on migration, reed-beds, margins of lakes, ditches, and other damp places with thick cover.

RANGE AND STATUS. Breeds in most parts of British Isles except W Scotland, but not known whether as resident or summer visitor; occurs on passage and in winter in many places where does not breed, but relative proportions of native birds and Continental immigrants unknown.

MERLIN, male See *Land: Medium*, p. 88

GOLDEN PLOVER See *Land: Medium*, p. 87

GREY PLOVER *Charadrius squatarola* Plates 38, 40, 41, 80, 82
Black-bellied Plover (N America).

PLUMAGE. Grey speckled black above, with black patch under wing and whitish rump and wing-bar; in summer cheeks, throat and underparts are black, with forehead, sides of neck and breast, flanks and under tail-coverts white. Winter adult and juvenile are all white below. Black bill; grey legs.

STRUCTURE. *Wing length* ML. *Ratios:* wing ML; tail S; neck MS; bill M; legs ML.

MOVEMENT. Similar to golden plover (p. 87).

VOICE. Call-note, 'tee-oo-ee', is less musical than *golden*, and more like a boy whistling, with middle syllable lower than other two.

FIELD MARKS. Generally similar to *golden*, but can always be told by black mark under wing, and whitish rump and wing-bar. In winter adult has more uniform grey-brown upperparts than *golden*, but juvenile appears spangled and has yellowish tinge. In summer can be told from *golden* by silver-grey ground-colour of upperparts and white under tail-coverts, also from southern race of *golden* by white line bordering face and underparts. See p. 139 for distinctions from knot.

FLOCKING. Gregarious, but in loose parties rather than close flocks, usually scattered widely over the shore; often with other waders.

HABITAT. Muddy shores, especially estuaries; uncommon at freshwater margins.

RANGE AND STATUS. Winter visitor and passage migrant to all coasts, but especially E and S England; a few non-breeders stay the summer.

RUFF *Philomachus pugnax* Plates 40, 42, 79, 82 Sandpiper Family
Reeve (female).

PLUMAGE. Summer male has remarkable outgrowth of ruff and ear-tufts, which may be black, brown, buff or white, and either plain, streaked or barred; ruff usually different from ear-tufts. Rest of upperparts equally variable, but belly and sides to rump and tail white, and narrow pale wing-bar. Winter male, female and juvenile have no head adornments, and are brown streaked darker above, with buffish breast. Bill of summer male brown, red or yellow, or others blackish-brown; legs may be green, yellow, orange or flesh.

STRUCTURE. *Wing length* ML. *Ratios:* wing M; tail S; neck MS; bill M/ML; legs ML. Ruff larger than reeve.

MOVEMENT. Fast, direct flight; walks on ground, wades in water.

VOICE. Rather silent, but has flight note 'too-i' and in spring a single deep 'uk'.

FIELD MARKS. Male in breeding plumage with ruff and ear-tufts can hardly be mistaken for any other bird. Winter males resemble common redshank, but can be told by thicker neck, no white on hind-wing, rump dark in centre, and sometimes by bill- and leg-colour; reeve and juvenile are similar but markedly smaller, without the thick neck, and with a distinctive pattern like a hen pheasant on the back. Winter males look round-shouldered.

FLOCKING. Small parties are most usual.

HABITAT. Breeds in grass marshes and damp fields; otherwise at sewage farms and other freshwater margins; less commonly on estuaries, salt-marshes and the open shore.

RANGE AND STATUS. Regular passage migrant, occasionally staying winter; most frequent E side Great Britain, Forth to Dorset; uncommon in Ireland; once bred regularly; non-breeding birds still not infrequently summer, especially in E Anglia.

COMMON REDSHANK *Tringa totanus* Plates 40, 80, 81

Red-leg, Teuk. Sandpiper Family

PLUMAGE. Grey-brown, darker above, with white rump and hind-wing. Bill orange-red at base, blackish at tip; legs of adult orange-red, of juvenile orange-yellow.

STRUCTURE. *Wing length* ML. *Ratios:* wing M; tail MS; neck MS; bill ML; legs ML/L.

MOVEMENT. Fast, direct flight, with quick, clipped wing-beats giving a rather jerky effect; also a special display flight. Walks or runs on ground, perching on low objects, and bobbing head when suspicious. Wades in water, and occasionally swims.

VOICE. Various loud, yelping, but fairly musical calls, mainly elaborations of a 'tu' note; also a loud clamorous cry when flushed or startled, and a scolding 'teuk-teuk-teuk' or 'chip-chip-chip' when alarmed. Yodelling song, based on the more musical call-notes, may be delivered in air or on ground or perch.

FIELD MARKS. The only wader, indeed the only medium-sized bird, with a conspicuous broad white hind-wing, which with the equally prominent white rump gives it a very chiaroscuro appearance in flight, in contrast to its uniform appearance at rest. At rest, however, the orange-red bill and legs are useful pointers; but see ruff (above) and spotted redshank (below).

FLOCKING. Gregarious, sometimes in substantial flocks; often with other waders on shore, and breeds in same fields as lapwings.

HABITAT. Breeds in all kinds of damp grassland, marshes, meadows and pastures, often near rivers or lakes, also on salt-marshes; otherwise frequents inland marshes and freshwater margins, but in winter mostly on coast, especially estuaries and muddy open shores.

RANGE AND STATUS. Resident, breeding throughout British Isles, except Cornwall, Pembroke and parts of S Ireland; in autumn some emigrate, but many more arrive on N and E coasts from Continent and Iceland.

SPOTTED REDSHANK *Tringa erythropus* Plates 40, 41, 80, 82

Dusky Redshank. Sandpiper Family

PLUMAGE. In summer grey-black, spotted white above, with white rump. In winter grey-brown above except white rump, white below except grey breast juvenile like winter. Bill red at base, blackish at tip; legs blood-red.

STRUCTURE. *Wing length* ML. *Ratios:* wing M; tail S; neck MS; bill L; legs L.

MOVEMENT. Similar to common redshank (above).

VOICE. A clear 'too-it' or 'tchu-eet', quite distinct from both *common* and greenshank.

FIELD MARKS. In summer is the only all-dark wader with a white rump; in winter can at once be told in flight from *common* by dark wings, and at rest by rather larger size, longer bill and legs (latter trailing well behind in flight), and whiter underparts. In winter can also be told from greenshank by darker plumage, longer bill with red base, and red legs.

FLOCKING. Sometimes in small parties.

HABITAT. Mainly inland marsh pools and freshwater margins; less commonly on salt-marshes and coastal mud.

RANGE AND STATUS. Scarce passage migrant, most frequent SE England from Wash to Sussex, and NW England from Solway to Dee.

GREENSHANK *Tringa nebularia* Plates 40, 43, 81 Sandpiper Family

PLUMAGE. Grey-brown head, mantle and wings; white rump, tail and underparts, with throat and breast marked darker in summer. Grey-blue bill, very slightly upcurved; pale olive-green legs.

STRUCTURE. *Wing length* ML. *Ratios:* wing M; tail MS; neck MS; bill ML/L; legs L.

MOVEMENT. Similar to common redshank (above), but less inclined to bob head.

VOICE. Flight note, nearly always uttered when flushed, a loud, clear 'chu-chu-chu'; also an insistent 'chip' note like common redshank and occasionally a 'tchu-it' not unlike spotted redshank. Song, a fluty, repeated 'ru-tu' may be delivered in air or from ground or perch, sometimes heard on migration.

FIELD MARKS. Resembles a large pale common redshank, with no white on wings, whiter tail and underparts, and no red on bill or legs; for distinctions from spotted redshank, see above, and from green sandpiper, see p. 135. White rump extends in long wedge up back.

FLOCKING. Parties occasional on coast, but very rare inland.

HABITAT. Breeds on moorland, with or without trees, visiting loch shores to feed; on passage at all kinds of marsh pools and water margins, especially sewage farms and estuaries, less often on sandy and rocky shores.

RANGE AND STATUS. Summer visitor, breeding in many parts of northern Scottish Highlands and Skye, but only irregularly in other isles; elsewhere widespread passage migrant, also winters in small numbers, especially in Ireland.

LAPWING See *Land: Medium*, p. 90

ROCK DOVE and LONDON PIGEON *Columba livia* Plates 24, 68

Rock Pigeon (Rock Dove); Feral Domestic, or Semi-Domestic, Pigeon (London Pigeon).

PLUMAGE. *Rock* is similar to stock dove (p. 94), but has more prominent black bars on wing, no black wing-tips, and a prominent white rump; grey bill, red legs and eye. *London* occurs in several plumage types, with much intergrading between them; blue rock type is identical with *rock*; blue chequer has whole upperparts except tail and white rump mottled grey-blue and black; red rock is cinnamon-red with white wing-tips and no black bars; red chequer is similar but has wings and mantle mottled white; black forms occur, and others are white or much splashed with white.

STRUCTURE. *Wing length* ML. *Ratios:* wing M; tail MS; neck MS; bill MS; legs S.

MOVEMENT. Similar to stock dove.

VOICE. The familiar coo of the dovecot pigeon.

FIELD MARKS. *Rock* can be told from all other pigeons and doves by white rump, also from stock dove by no black wing-tips, and from woodpigeon by shorter tail and no white on neck or wings; beware of mistaking stock doves on sea-cliffs for *rock*. The blue-chequer plumage of *London* occurs as a genuine wild variant in some colonies of *rock* and does not necessarily indicate an admixture of semi-domesticated birds. Blue rock type of *London* cannot be distinguished from wild *rock*, but *London* nearly always occurs in extremely mixed flocks, so there is likely to be little doubt about identity of any individual plumage pattern. White pigeons in flight can be told from gulls by lack of black wing-tips.

FLOCKING. Gregarious, and breeds in colonies.

HABITAT. *Rock* is confined to maritime cliffs, but will feed on cultivated ground a mile or more inland. *London* occurs mainly in fully built-up areas in towns, rarely in suburbs after gardens begin; also on sea-cliffs and occasionally on cliffs inland; feeds in streets, on shores (including tidal rivers in cities), and particularly in docks and on grain-barges and grain-wharves.

RANGE AND STATUS. *Rock* is resident, breeding on most parts of Scottish and Irish coasts, especially in N and NW and on isles, and locally in Isle of Man. Most colonies of wild pigeons on coasts of England and Wales consist of *London*, but in some, e.g. Pembrokeshire, Flamborough Head, there appears to be a substantial element surviving from the original wild stock, and even in Scotland and Ireland there is a good deal of semi-domesticated blood in the wild colonies. Feral London pigeons, originating from escaped domestic stock, occur in all large and many small cities and towns, especially ports; in the smaller towns it becomes harder to separate them from birds still inhabiting dovecots, and by the time inland rural districts are reached, any pigeon of *London* type plumage can be confidently put down as domesticated, unless there are large cliffs or quarries near. Most racing pigeons wear a special numbered ring, and if captured or found dead the inscription should be sent with details to the National Homing Union, 22 Clarence Street, Gloucester.

MERLIN, female See *Land: Medium*, p. 88

KESTREL See *Land: Medium*, p. 95

LITTLE BITTERN *Ixobrychus minutus* Plate 44 Heron Family

PLUMAGE. Male is black above and buff-brown below, with a prominent white patch on the wing. Female is dark brown above and buff-brown streaked darker below, with black crown and nape and no wing patch. Yellow bill, green legs, yellow eye.

STRUCTURE. *Wing length* ML. *Ratios:* wing S; tail S; neck VL; bill M/ML; legs M.

MOVEMENT. Flight as other herons, but with faster wing-beats; fond of climbing about reeds, like a giant reed warbler; will freeze in upright position like common bittern. Neck is usually retracted at rest, held withdrawn in flight.

VOICE. Various short notes, including a flight note, 'quer', and a toad-like 'gonk, gonk' from cover.

FIELD MARKS. Much smaller than any other heron-like bird, none of which in any case have male's white patch on wing, which is very prominent in flight, nor have any other brown heron-like birds got black upperparts; however, is very skulking and hard to get in view unless actually flushed.

HABITAT. Reed-beds and reeds fringing rivers and lakes.

RANGE AND STATUS. Very irregular passage migrant, most frequently S and E coasts; has bred E Anglia.

COMMON TERN *Sterna hirundo* Plates 60, 102, 103 Gull Family

Sea Swallow; a sea tern.

PLUMAGE. French grey above, with darker wing-tips, white forked tail and black crown and nape (forehead white in winter); very pale grey below (faintly tinged mauve in summer), with breast much whiter. Juvenile is like winter adult, with black shoulders and brown mottling on mantle and wings. Bill is vermilion-red with dark tip in summer, blackish sometimes with red base in winter and juvenile; legs vermilion in summer, brownish-red in winter, orange-yellow in juvenile.

STRUCTURE. *Wing length* L. *Ratios:* wing ML; tail M; neck S; bill M; legs VS.

MOVEMENT. Light, buoyant, rather bobbing flight, with measured up-and-down wing-beats; dives from air, sometimes submerging, but does not normally dip down to surface like marsh terns. Can swim; walks awkwardly on land.

VOICE. Main calls are flight notes, 'kik-kik-kik . . .' and 'keerree', also alarm note, 'keeeyah'; other notes at breeding colonies.

FIELD MARKS. Terns may be told from gulls by their more buoyant flight, habit of fishing by diving from the air, forked tail (but see little and Sabine's gulls (pp. 170 and 173), and kittiwake (p. 180), and black crown and nape. Common tern very closely resembles *Arctic*, and beginners cannot expect to be able to separate the two until they have become familiar with at least one of them. Two of the safest field marks are the colour of the bill (vermilion in *common*, blood-red in *Arctic*) and the length of the leg (much shorter in *Arctic*, which may almost appear to have no legs at rest), but bill colour can only be differentiated at close range in good light, and leg-length when the bird is perching. In full breeding plumage *common* normally has a dark tip to the bill and *Arctic* does not, but *Arctics* may not infrequently be seen with dark bill-tips (especially on spring passage and in the early autumn), while a few *commons* at the height of the summer may have all-red bills. All *Arctic's* primaries, when seen against the sun, appear silvery and semi-transparent, but in *common* only the innermost four primaries on each wing appear like this. *Arctic* tends to have longer tail-streamers than *common*, but this again is a fine point and only of much value if tail is seen to extend well beyond wings at rest. The majority of *commons* have much whiter breasts and underparts than the majority of *Arctics*, contrasting strongly with their mantles; this is not a good point in flight, but at rest often enables a small group of birds of one species to be picked out in a colony of the other. In particular, the grey on some *Arctics'* faces is so dark that a white streak shows between it and the black crown; this is never so with the *common*. For distinctions from other terns and gulls, see little, black and white-winged black terns (pp. 137-8), Sandwich tern (p. 150), roseate tern (below) and little gull (p. 170).

FLOCKING. Gregarious at all times; breeds in colonies; often with other terns.

HABITAT. Breeds mainly on sandy and shingly shores, also on rocky islands in both sea and freshwater lochs, and exceptionally elsewhere inland; at other times on both fresh and salt waters.

RANGE AND STATUS. Summer visitor, breeding on almost all suitable coasts, also inland in Ireland and exceptionally in England and Scotland; otherwise passage migrant to coastal and inland waters.

ARCTIC TERN *Sterna macrura* Plates 60, 103 Gull Family

Sea Swallow; a sea tern.

PLUMAGE. As common tern (above), but in summer most birds have underparts so much darker grey that there is little or no contrast with upperparts, and cheek shows as white streak between black crown and grey neck. Bill blood-red or coral-red in summer, blackish in winter (and juvenile) with intermediate stages when tip is dark and base red; legs coral-red in summer, blackish in winter, orange in juvenile.

STRUCTURE, MOVEMENT AND VOICE. As common tern, but tail ML/L, and alarm note shriller and more whistling and monosyllabic.

FIELD MARKS. See common tern.

FLOCKING AND HABITAT. As common tern, but breeds less commonly inland; the two often breed together.

RANGE AND STATUS. Summer visitor, breeding widely on coasts and inland in Scotland and Ireland (commoner in W); in England breeds in numbers only on Farne Is. and NW England, but odd pairs fairly regularly in Norfolk and Isle of Man; three colonies off Anglesey. Otherwise widespread passage migrant, inland and on coast.

ROSEATE TERN *Sterna dougallii* Plates 60, 103 Gull Family

A sea tern.

PLUMAGE. As common tern (above), but with a pink flush on the breast in spring. Bill black, base becoming red in summer; legs red.

STRUCTURE. *Wing length* ML. *Ratios:* wing M; tail VL; neck S; bill ML; legs VS.

MOVEMENT. As common tern, but flight rather more buoyant.

VOICE. Call-note a harsh, grating 'aach, aach', also a softer 'tchu-ick' or 'chik-ik' other notes at breeding colonies.

FIELD MARKS. Very like *common* and Arctic terns, from which can best be told by black bill (in winter and until midsummer) and distinctive call-note. Other field marks are more tricky owing to overlapping with the other two, e.g. longer tail-streamers (overlap with *Arctic*, but a good point against *common*, especially if can be seen projecting well beyond wings at rest, *common's* wings being usually longer than tail); pinkish flush on breast (breast of *Sandwich* may be pinkish, of *common* very pale mauve); red base to bill in summer and early autumn (bills of *common* and *Arctic* may both be like this in autumn); and generally whiter appearance. In flight at a distance looks very white, like *Sandwich*. Also stands higher, like *Sandwich*.

FLOCKING AND HABITAT. As common tern, but very rare on fresh water.

RANGE AND STATUS. Summer visitor; in England odd pairs breed from time to time among other terns in Norfolk, Dorset, Farne Is., NW England and Scilly Is.; two or three colonies in Anglesey; Ayrshire and a few places on E coast Scotland; in Ireland about ten colonies, in Donegal, Down, Dublin and Wexford. Elsewhere a very scarce passage migrant, particularly uncommon inland.

GULL-BILLED TERN *Gelochelidon nilotica* Plate 103 Gull Family

PLUMAGE. As Sandwich tern, (p. 150) but bill is all black, and juvenile has whitish forehead and red-brown legs.

STRUCTURE. *Wing length* L. *Ratios:* wing L; tail MS; neck S; bill M; legs S.

MOVEMENT. As common tern (above), but flight even heavier and more gull-like than *Sandwich*.

VOICE. Flight notes, 'chi-chi-chi-chik' and 'quac-quac-quac', also 'cher-wuc'.

FIELD MARKS. Closely resembles the somewhat larger *Sandwich*, but can be told by its shorter, stouter bill with no yellow tip, different flight note, and at rest by longer legs. Juvenile can be told from juvenile *Sandwich* by white forehead and reddish legs. Head of winter adult is whiter than that of other terns.

FLOCKING. Occasionally in small parties.

HABITAT. Inland and coastal waters, both in and out of breeding season.

RANGE AND STATUS. Scarce passage migrant, now annual on S coast England; bred in Essex in 1949-50.

BAR-TAILED GODWIT See *Waterside: Medium Long*, p. 149

SHORT-EARED OWL See *Land: Medium*, p. 99

WATERSIDE BIRDS: Medium Long

CHOUGH See *Land: Medium Long*, p. 101

PEREGRINE, male; See *Land: Medium Long*, p. 101

STILT *Himantopus himantopus* Plates 45, 83 Avocet Family
Black-winged Stilt.

PLUMAGE. Black and white; male is white with black mantle and wings, and in summer black crown and nape. Female is like male winter but with brownish mantle; immature is like female, but greyish about head and neck. Bill black; legs pink to red.

STRUCTURE. *Wing length* ML. *Ratios:* wing M; tail S; neck MS; bill VL; legs VL.

MOVEMENT. Direct flight of moderate speed, with legs normally trailing out behind and neck only slightly extended. Walks on ground, wades in water.

VOICE. Usual note, 'kik-kik-kik', is rather coot-like.

FIELD MARKS. No other bird has such fantastically long legs, which with black and white plumage and long straight bill at once settle identity; length of leg, however, can be concealed when bird is wading in deep water. Long legs trailing behind make bird look much longer than its overall length suggests.

FLOCKING. Usually in small parties.

HABITAT. Mostly freshwater marshes and pools; exceptionally on sea shore.

RANGE AND STATUS. Vagrant, more frequent in recent years; two pairs bred in 1945.

BAR-TAILED GODWIT *Limosa lapponica* Plates 42, 43, 81
Red Godwit (summer). Sandpiper Family

PLUMAGE. Male summer has reddish head, neck and underparts, and is brown streaked black above, with white rump and dark wing-tips. Female summer and juvenile are browner on red parts. Adult winter has paler brown head and neck, and is greyer above and white below. Flesh-coloured bill, with slightly upcurved darker tip; grey-green legs.

STRUCTURE. *Wing length* ML. *Ratios:* wing M; tail S; neck MS; bill VL; legs L. Females larger than males.

MOVEMENT. Fast, direct flight, flocks sometimes performing aerobatics; walks or runs on ground, wades in water.

VOICE. Flight notes, 'kirruc, kirruc', and 'wik-wik-wik-wik-wik'.

FIELD MARKS. Generally like a small curlew with a straight bill, and in winter can also be told from curlew and whimbrel by shorter legs; in summer reddish plumage precludes any confusion. Can most easily be told from slightly larger black-tailed godwit in flight, when lack of white marks on wings and tail becomes apparent, and feet scarcely project beyond tail; at rest can be told by shorter legs, upcurved bill-tip, and in summer reddish vent. Very variable in size, large birds overlapping with both whimbrel and *black-tailed*.

FLOCKING. Gregarious; often with other waders on shore.

HABITAT. Estuaries, mudflats and sandy shores; rarely at freshwater margins.

RANGE AND STATUS. Winter visitor and passage migrant to all coasts; rare inland.

WHIMBREL *Numenius phaeopus* Plates 43, 81 Sandpiper Family
May-bird, Titterel, Seven Whistler; Hudsonian Curlew (N America).

PLUMAGE. Similar to curlew (p. 157), but with a whitish eyestripe and streak on crown, separated by a dark streak.

STRUCTURE. *Wing length* ML. *Ratios:* wing M; tail S; neck MS; bill L; legs ML.

MOVEMENT. Similar to curlew, but noticeably faster wing-beats give it a less lumbering, gull-like flight.

VOICE. A tittering trill, quite different from curlew's normal calls, but curlew has a rarely heard call that is similar. Song, closely resembling curlew, is delivered in air.

FIELD MARKS. A smaller edition of the curlew, from which it can be told by markedly quicker flight, distinctive call, and at close range by the two dark and one pale streaks on head. Can be told from both godwits by down-curved bill (see above and below).

FLOCKING. Gregarious; often with other waders, especially curlew.

HABITAT. Breeds on moorland; on passage occurs on all coasts, on both shore and nearby fields, but rarely far inland.

RANGE AND STATUS. Spring and autumn passage migrant on all coasts, and inland in Ireland; breeds in Shetland.

BLACK-TAILED GODWIT *Limosa limosa* Plates 42, 43, 81, 83
Red Godwit (summer). Sandpiper Family

PLUMAGE. Summer adult has pink-cinnamon head, neck and breast; brown upperparts streaked black, with white wing-bar and dark wing-tips, and white tail with black bar at tip; white belly marked black. Winter adult has pink parts greyish, upperparts greyer, belly unstreaked. Juvenile is similar, but has pink parts paler than summer adult. Straight, flesh-coloured bill with dark tip, greyish legs.

STRUCTURE. *Wing length* ML. *Ratios:* wing MS; tail S; neck MS; bill L; legs L. Female larger than male.

MOVEMENT. As bar-tailed godwit (above), but does not indulge in such wild aerobatics; has a special display flight.

VOICE. Flight call, 'wicka-wicka-wicka'; also on breeding grounds a lapwing-like 'pee-oo-eee' and a greenshank-like 'wik-ik-ik'. Song, delivered in flight, a repetition of 'crweetüü'.

FIELD MARKS. Can easily be told from all other large brown waders in flight by conspicuous white bar on wing and black and white tail, also by completely straight bill; for additional distinctions, see *bar-tailed*; is just as variable in size as *bar-tailed*.

FLOCKING. Gregarious; often with other waders.

HABITAT. Estuaries, mudflats, sandy shores and freshwater margins; breeds in damp grassy and marshy places.

RANGE AND STATUS. Increasingly common passage migrant, mainly on E and S coasts England showing a marked tendency to stay both winter and summer in certain areas; has bred irregularly in several places since 1940 and regularly in one locality in England since 1952.

SANDWICH TERN *Sterna sandvicensis* Plates 60, 102, 103 and p. 213
Cabot's Tern (N America); a sea tern. Gull Family

PLUMAGE. French grey above with blackish wing-tips and white forked tail; white, sometimes tinged pink, below. In summer forehead, crown and nape black; in winter forehead white, crown and nape grey. Juvenile is speckled blackish-brown on mantle and wings, brown on forehead, crown and nape, white elsewhere. Black bill with yellow tip; black legs, yellow soles to feet.

STRUCTURE. *Wing length* L. *Ratios:* wing ML; tail M; neck S; bill ML; legs VS/S.

MOVEMENT. As common tern (p. 146), but flight rather heavier and more gull-like.

VOICE. Call-note a rather harsh 'kirrick' or 'kirr-whit', with a large vocabulary based on this at breeding colonies.

FIELD MARKS. Our largest breeding tern, it can also be told from the others by its heavier flight, less deeply forked tail, distinctive call-note, yellow-tipped black bill, and crested appearance of elongated nape feathers in a wind. White foreheads are often assumed before end of breeding season. For distinctions from rare gull-billed tern, see p. 148.

FLOCKING. Gregarious at all times; breeds in colonies; often with other terns.

HABITAT. Mainly shingly and sandy coasts and sand dunes, also breeds on islands (marine and on freshwater loughs) and frequents other coasts; unusual on freshwater on passage.

RANGE AND STATUS. Summer visitor, with six main colonies in England (E Anglia, Farne Is., NW England), in Wales on Anglesey, in Scotland on coasts and islands (Galloway, Fife, Moray Firth, Orkney), and sporadically elsewhere; in Ireland on many loughs and islands, mainly in N and W; elsewhere a passage migrant.

MONTAGU'S HARRIER See *Land: Medium Long*, p. 103

HEN-HARRIER, male See *Land: Medium Long*, p. 104

AVOCET *Recurvirostra avosetta* Plates 45, 83

Awl-bird; Yelper; Clinker.

PLUMAGE. White, with black crown, nape and stripes on back and wings. Juvenile's black is browner. Black bill curved upwards; grey-blue legs.

STRUCTURE. *Wing length* ML. *Ratios:* wing MS; tail S; neck MS/M; bill L; legs VL.

MOVEMENT. Fairly fast, direct flight, with legs trailing behind but neck only slightly stretched forward. Walks on ground, wades in water, swims readily.

VOICE. Main note, 'klooit', also a curious soft, grunting flight note, and loud yelping cries when an intruder approaches nest or young.

FIELD MARKS. No other bird has such a strikingly upcurved bill, but when this cannot be seen a single avocet may be quite hard to pick out among a crowd of gulls, especially as long legs may also be hidden if bird is in deep water. Can also be told from stilt and oystercatcher by blue-grey legs.

FLOCKING. Usually in small parties.

HABITAT. Breeds on salt-marshes and grassy and sandy flats near coast; otherwise at pools and tide-lines on shore, salt-marsh and estuary, and exceptionally at freshwater margins.

RANGE AND STATUS. Scarce passage migrant, mainly in E and S England, becoming more regular since it resumed breeding in E Anglia in 1946; now breeds regularly on Suffolk coast, and has also bred in Ireland, Essex and Norfolk since 1938; some winter in SW England.

OYSTERCATCHER *Haematopus ostralegus* Plates 45, 83

Sea-pie.

PLUMAGE. Black above, except for white rump, base of tail and wing-bar; white below, except for black breast; throat also black in breeding birds. Orange bill, with dark tip in young; legs pink, whitish in juvenile.

STRUCTURE. *Wing length* ML. *Ratios:* wing M; tail MS; neck MS; bill ML; legs M.

MOVEMENT. Direct flight, at moderate speed; walks or runs on ground; wades and occasionally swims in water.

VOICE. A shrill and penetrating 'kleeep', a shorter 'pic, pic', and a series of loud piping notes during display.

FIELD MARKS. Can be told from all other large black and white shore birds by long orange bill and longish pink legs. Shrill cry often draws attention to two or three flying low over the waves inshore.

FLOCKING. Highly gregarious; often with other shore birds.

HABITAT. Breeds on flat shingly, sandy or grassy places near shore, also on cliff-tops, marine islands, and in the north inland on shingly and grassy places near water, on moorland and even in arable fields; in winter mainly a shore bird, as often on rocky as on sandy or muddy coasts and estuaries, but exceptional at freshwater margins.

RANGE AND STATUS. Resident, breeding on all coasts of Scotland, Wales and Ireland, but in England sparingly on E and S coasts though more commonly on W coast; also breeds inland in many parts of Scotland, less commonly N England, and sporadically Ireland; more generally distributed on coasts in winter, but uncommon on migration inland; a few non-breeders summer away from breeding haunts.

SQUACCO HERON *Ardeola ralloides* Plate 44

PLUMAGE. Mainly buff, with long crest streaked darker, and rounded wings and tail white. Adult winter and immature are browner above, with neck streaked darker. Greenish bill, yellowish-green legs, yellow eye.

STRUCTURE. *Wing length* ML. *Ratios:* wing MS; tail S; neck L; bill ML; legs ML.

MOVEMENT. Flight and gait typically heron-like; fond of skulking and standing with head hunched up like a bittern.

VOICE. A shrill harsh 'karr'.

FIELD MARKS. White wings and tail, largely concealed at rest, make it appear predominantly white on the wing. Can be told from other heron-like birds by buff and white plumage, but note that adult summer of very rare buff-backed heron or cattle egret *Ardeola ibis* is all white except for buff on crown, mantle and lower throat, has a yellow bill, and habitually associates with cattle in fields. In flight squacco needs to be separated from winter or immature buff-back and from rare little egret (p. 156), both of which appear completely white in the field, and have yellow and black bills respectively.

HABITAT. As purple heron (p. 163).

RANGE AND STATUS. Vagrant, most often in E Anglia, Sussex and SW England; usually in spring.

CARRION and HOODED CROWS See *Land: Medium Long*, pp. 106-7

CURLEW See *Waterside: Long*, p. 157

CASPIAN TERN *Hydroprogne caspia* Gull Family

An immense tern, really like a black-capped herring gull with a stout, pointed red bill and a forked tail; flight gull-like rather than tern-like. Increasing vagrant, now almost annual.

Caspian Tern

PEREGRINE, female See *Land: Medium Long*, p. 101

HEN-HARRIER, female See *Land: Medium Long*, p. 104

MARSH HARRIER *Circus aeruginosus* Plate 32, 74 Hawk Family

PLUMAGE. Variable, but predominantly dark brown, with creamy-buff throat; a partial owl-like facial disk. Male has grey on wings and grey tail, black wing-tips, and streaked crown and breast. Female and young have creamy crown; female has pale shoulders. Hooked, black bill, with yellow cere; yellow legs; yellowish eye.

STRUCTURE. *Wing length* L/VL. *Ratios:* wing ML; tail M; neck S; bill MS; legs M.

MOVEMENT. Heavier flight than other harriers, and more like a buzzard, but has characteristic harrier trick of flying for a few strokes and then gliding with wings canted up at an angle.

VOICE. A variable, shrill disyllabic note.

FIELD MARKS. The largest and most buzzard-like of the harriers, and the easiest to identify, for the male can be told from male *Hen* and *Montagu's* by the brown on its mantle, wings and underparts, while in all other plumages *marsh* can be told from the other two by its pale head (osprey, which also has a whitish head, has white underparts and very different habits). Can be told from buzzards by longer and slenderer wings and tail, as well as by grey on upperparts of male and pale head of female and young birds.

HABITAT. Almost confined to extensive tracts of reeds and marshland; sometimes other types of open country on migration.

RANGE AND STATUS. Summer visitor, now very rare, breeding in E Anglia and one or two other parts of England; otherwise a vagrant.

GREENLAND and ICELAND FALCONS *Falco rusticolus* Plate 76

Two races of the Gyr Falcon.

PLUMAGE. *Greenland* is very variable, ranging from almost white with sparse black streaks and spots to such heavy marking that upperparts appear grey and underparts streaked. *Iceland* resembles darker forms of *Greenland*. Hooked, bluish-horn bill, with yellow cere; yellow legs.

STRUCTURE. *Wing length* L. *Ratios:* wing M; tail MS/M; neck S; bill MS; legs S. Female larger than male.

MOVEMENT. Flight as peregrine, but with slower wing-beats.

VOICE. Typical high-pitched falcon notes, 'gyak' and 'ke-a, ke-a, ke-a'.

FIELD MARKS. The gyr falcons are like large, pale peregrines, with the same outline, but having rather shorter wings and no moustachial streak. The two races are usually very hard to separate in the field; *Iceland* is the darker, with *Greenland* shading off to almost completely white. These extreme white *Greenlands* can be identified with some confidence (see p. 110 for distinctions from snowy owl), but the darker birds cannot safely be separated in the field.

HABITAT. The wilder coasts and islands.

RANGE AND STATUS. *Greenland* is irregular winter visitor to Scottish isles and N and W Ireland, occasional in Scotland, rest of Ireland and N England, vagrant elsewhere; *Iceland* similar but much rarer.

OSPREY *Pandion haliaetus* Plates 32, 74

Fish Hawk; Fishing Eagle.

PLUMAGE. Brown above, white below; white head, with brown at sides of neck and streaked breast-band. Hooked, black bill, with pale blue cere; greenish legs; yellow eye.

STRUCTURE. *Wing length* L. *Ratios:* wing VL; tail M; neck MS; bill MS; legs S. Female larger than male.

MOVEMENT. A rather slow flapping and gliding flight when hunting over water, not unlike one of the larger gulls; also soars, hovers, and dives from air; fond of perching on a dead tree or post in the water.

VOICE. A shrill cheeping sound, like a young bird calling.

FIELD MARKS. Large size, long wings, white head and underparts, together with fondness for fishing, make osprey one of the most distinctive birds of prey. Much larger sea eagle and somewhat smaller marsh harrier, both of which may have a pale head and be seen over water, have dark underparts.

HABITAT. Large expanses of salt and fresh water, lakes, broads, estuaries, etc.; in breeding season, woodland or moorland with lochs.

RANGE AND STATUS. Scarce passage migrant, mostly on E side Great Britain, and especially Norfolk and Scottish Highlands; bred in Scotland till 1916 and one pair has done so again in Spey valley since 1956, with a second pair since 1963.

WATERSIDE BIRDS: Long

SNOWY OWL, male See *Land: Long*, p. 110

GREENLAND FALCON, female See *Waterside: Medium Long*, p. 154

MARSH HARRIER See *Waterside: Medium Long*, p. 153

OSPREY See *Waterside: Medium Long*, p. 154

SNOWY OWL, female See *Land: Long*, p. 110

RED-BREASTED GOOSE *Branta ruficollis* Duck Family

Our smallest and most strikingly coloured goose, with very short bill, and reddish cheeks, throat and breast, rest of plumage black and white. Very rare vagrant from Arctic Asia among flocks of grey geese; also ornamental waterfowl, full-winged at New Grounds (Glos.).

Red-breasted Goose

GLOSSY IBIS *Plegadis falcinellus* Plate 43 Spoonbill Family

Black Curlew; Eastern Glossy Ibis (N America).

PLUMAGE. Purplish-brown, with rounded wings and tail darker and glossed green; in winter head and neck are streaked white. Curved, dark greyish-brown bill; greenish-brown legs.

STRUCTURE. *Wing length* L. *Ratios:* wing MS; tail S; neck M; bill VL; legs L.

MOVEMENT. Slow, heavy flight like herons, but with rather faster wing-beats and legs and neck outstretched; sometimes glides; stalks.

VOICE. A harsh, grating croak.

FIELD MARKS. The only large blackish bird with rounded wings and a curved bill, but beware large curlews, which may actually be bigger, seen against the light on a dull day. In flight rounded wings separate it at once from much paler brown curlew and whimbrel, and all whimbrels are markedly smaller than any glossy ibis.

Glossy Ibis in flight

FLOCKING. Fairly often in small parties.

HABITAT. Estuaries and muddy shores; occasionally marshy places inland.

RANGE AND STATUS. Irregular passage migrant, mostly in autumn, and most often in S, SW and E England; vagrant elsewhere.

LITTLE EGRET *Egretta garzetta* Heron Family

A small pure white heron with black bill and legs and yellow feet, which show up in flight; an increasing but still rare visitor, mainly to coastal marshes in the S. Needs to be distinguished from the even rarer squacco heron (p. 152) and cattle egret *Ardeola ibis,* which has yellow bill and dark feet and appears all white only in flight.

Little Egret

CURLEW *Numenius arquata* Plates 43, 81, 107 Sandpiper Family

Whaup (N England, Scotland).

PLUMAGE. Pale brown with darker streaks; dark wing-tips, white rump, white belly with dark bars. Curved, horn-coloured bill; greyish legs.

STRUCTURE. *Wing length* L. *Ratios:* wing MS; tail S; neck MS; bill VL; legs ML.

MOVEMENT. Fast, direct flight, but with slower wing-beats than godwits and more resembling gulls; will fly in V formation; walks on ground, wades in water.

VOICE. Very varied vocabulary includes characteristic loud 'quee, quee, quee, quee' and 'cooorwee, cooorwee' notes, and a rare whimbrel-like titter. Loud, musical bubbling song, delivered in air, opens with plangent version of 'quee' note.

FIELD MARKS. Is much the largest of the brown waders with white rumps (for distinctions from whimbrel and godwits, see pp. 149-50.) Momentary tendency to confuse it with immature gulls in flight can at once be checked by a sight of the long curved bill and feet projecting beyond tail. Extremely variable in size.

FLOCKING. Gregarious; often with other waders.

HABITAT. Breeds on a wide range of more or less damp open country, moors, bogs, swampy lowland heaths, sand dunes and even farmland; in winter mainly on estuaries and mudflats, but also on sandy and rocky shores, in grassy fields, and occasionally at freshwater margins.

RANGE AND STATUS. Resident, breeding almost throughout British Isles, but very local in S and E England and Midlands; many arrive on E coast in autumn, when becomes more generally distributed; non-breeding birds occur on S and E coasts in summer.

NIGHT HERON *Nycticorax nycticorax* Plates 44, 84, 85

Black-crowned Night Heron (N America).

PLUMAGE. Mainly grey above, pale grey and white below; black crown and mantle with elongated crest feathers. Immature has 'nutcracker plumage', brown with white streaks above, and whitish with dark streaks below. Rounded wings; greenish bill, yellow or pink legs, red eye.

STRUCTURE. *Wing length* L. *Ratios:* wing MS; tail S; neck VL; bill M; legs M.

MOVEMENT. Flight typical of other herons, though wing-beats faster than common heron; flies mainly at dusk; always carries neck retracted.

VOICE. A hoarse croak.

FIELD MARKS. Habitual retraction of neck, both at rest and in flight, make it look a shorter and bulkier bird than its measurements suggest; is smaller than common heron and lacks its black wing-tips and grey mantle, and no other heron-like birds, except much larger cranes, are black and grey above. Immature can be told from other brown heron-like birds by pale streaks on upperparts.

FLOCKING. Usually solitary, but small parties have occurred.

HABITAT. As purple heron (p. 163).

RANGE AND STATUS. Vagrant, most often in spring and in S and E England; birds seen in S Scotland are likely to be from free-flying colony at Edinburgh Zoo.

RAVEN See *Land: Long*, p. 113

LESSER WHITE-FRONT *Anser erythropus* Plate 57 Duck Family

Lesser White-fronted Goose; a grey goose.

PLUMAGE. As white-fronted goose (below), but is darker, and adult has white forehead narrower and often extending farther up crown, also a yellow orbital ring round eye.

STRUCTURE. *Wing length* L. *Ratios:* wing M; tail S; neck L; bill M; legs S.

MOVEMENT. As *greylag* (p. 161), but flies and feeds still faster than *white-front* and can be picked out of a large flock of them by its faster feeding-rate as well as by its more forward-looking stance.

VOICE. Much shriller than *white-front*, 'kü-yü' or 'kü-yü-yü'.

FIELD MARKS. See *greylag* for general note on grey geese. Is a smaller edition of *white-front*, bearing much the same relationship to it as *pink-foot* does to *bean*; at all ages can be told from *white-front* by quicker feeding, stance, call-note and smaller bill. Adult can also be told by white on forehead usually extending higher up towards crown, and narrow yellow ring round eye; these relatively fine points cannot of course be used by an observer in his first glance at his first flock of geese, but with experience and practice the problem of picking out lesser white-fronts in flocks of 2,000-3,000 other geese becomes more that of finding a needle in a haystack than the actual separation of the bird from its neighbours. For distinctions from other grey geese, see *white-front*.

FLOCKING. As *greylag*; almost invariably found consorting with substantial flock of *white-fronts*.

HABITAT. As white-fronted goose.

RANGE AND STATUS. Winter visitor in very small numbers to the New Grounds on the Severn Estuary, where up to six birds have occurred in one winter; elsewhere very rare vagrant, but careful scrutiny of flocks of *white-fronts* would probably lead to the detection of lesser white-fronts in the approximate ratio of one per thousand.

BARNACLE GOOSE *Branta leucopsis* Plates 56, 95 Duck Family

A black goose.

PLUMAGE. Crown, lores, neck, rump and tail black; forehead, cheeks, throat and underparts white; rest grey, more or less barred black and white. Immature is more brownish on wing. Bill and legs black.

STRUCTURE. *Wing length* L. *Ratios:* wing M; tail S; neck M; bill M; legs S.

MOVEMENT. As *greylag* (p. 161), but flight and gait less heavy.

VOICE. Resembles gruff yapping of a small terrier.

FIELD MARKS. Black and white head and neck are distinctive, and enable it to be picked out fairly easily from flocks of grey geese, which have much browner grey plumage. Rather smaller *brent* (sometimes called 'barnacle' by fowlers)

has head all black and no barring on body. Much larger *Canada* is a browner grey and has less white on face.

FLOCKING. Very gregarious; small numbers sometimes consort with grey geese.

HABITAT. As *white-front* (below), but much less often seen inland; particularly fond of the short turf behind the Hebridean sandhills, known as 'machair'.

RANGE AND STATUS. Winter visitor; very local, being confined as a regular visitor to the Hebrides, especially Islay, the Solway, and Ireland, mainly in the W; elsewhere either passage migrant (N Isles, Northumberland) or vagrant; especially infrequent in S England, except on Severn estuary, where an odd bird or two turns up most winters in flocks of grey geese, and as an escape from wildfowl collections.

BLUE GOOSE See *Snow and Blue Snow Geese* (*Waterside: Very Long*, p. 160)

PINK-FOOTED GOOSE *Anser brachyrhynchus* Plates 57, 95

A grey goose. Duck Family

PLUMAGE. Dark grey-brown, with dark centre to white tail and white under tail-coverts; head and neck much darker than body, which has conspicuous grey forewing and pale rump. Occasionally a narrow white line at base of bill. Bill black with varying amount of pink (exceptionally all pink), and black nail; legs pink.

STRUCTURE. *Wing length* VL. *Ratios:* wing MS; tail VS/S; neck L; bill M; legs S.

MOVEMENT. As *greylag* (p. 161), but flight and gait quicker, resembling *white-front*.

VOICE. Flocks are very vocal, with a medley of rather shrill 'wink-wink' and 'ung-ung' notes, sometimes hard to distinguish from *white-front*.

FIELD MARKS. See *greylag* for general note on grey geese. At any distance dark head and neck are best distinction from all grey geese except *bean*, from which can be told by smaller size, much smaller and partly pink bill, pink legs, pale rump and grey forewing. Pale forewing is, however, much less prominent than in *greylag*. No other grey goose has both legs and bill pink. For distinctions from immature *white-front*, see below.

FLOCKING. As *greylag*; may associate with *white-fronts*.

HABITAT. As *white-front*, but much more often in arable fields, stubbles, potatoes, young wheat, etc.

RANGE AND STATUS. Winter visitor, especially on E side Great Britain, S to Fens; much more local on W coast; occurs in S England mainly during or after hard weather; rare in Ireland.

WHITE-FRONTED GOOSE *Anser albifrons* Plates 57, 95

A grey goose. Duck Family

PLUMAGE. Grey-brown; white tail with dark centre, white under tail-coverts. Adult has white forehead and may be heavily barred black on underparts. Bill pink (yellow or orange in Greenland race) with white nail; legs orange.

STRUCTURE. *Wing length* L, VL. *Ratios:* wing M; tail S; neck L; bill M; legs S.

MOVEMENT. As *greylag* (p. 161), but flight and gait less heavy.

VOICE. Flight note a babble of 'kow-yow', 'kow-lyow' sounds, more high-pitched than *greylag*, sometimes hard to distinguish from *pink-foot*.

FIELD MARKS. See *greylag* for general note on grey geese. Combination of white forehead and black-barred underparts (seen most readily at rest and in flight respectively) distinguishes adult from all grey geese except *lesser white-front* (above) and occasional strongly marked specimens of *greylag*. At close range combinations of pink bill with orange legs and of Greenland race's white-nailed orange bill with orange legs are neither found in other grey geese. Can be told from *greylag* and *pink-foot* by uniformly grey-brown plumage with no grey forewing. Immature *white-front* is more difficult, except when in family party with adults, but can still be told from *pink-foot* by lack of black band on bill, orange legs, and head, neck, and forewing uniform with rest of upperparts. Greenland race can be identified in field by orange bill, and is darker.

FLOCKING. As *greylag*; most often consorts with *pink-feet*.

HABITAT. Marshes, floods, bogs, mosses, estuaries, etc., sometimes feeding in cultivated fields.

RANGE AND STATUS. Winter visitor; the most widespread grey goose, especially common in Ireland and Hebrides, also found all down W coast Great Britain and locally in SE half of England; elsewhere mainly a passage migrant, but appears all over S England during and after hard weather. Greenland race mainly in Ireland and W Scotland.

AMERICAN BITTERN *Botaurus lentiginosus* Heron Family

Similar to common bittern (p. 163), but a little smaller, and can be told by brown (not black) crown, wing-tips not barred and less distinct dark markings on upperparts. Rare vagrant from N America.

WATERSIDE BIRDS: Very Long

BARNACLE GOOSE See *Waterside: Long*, p. 158

PINK-FOOTED GOOSE See *Waterside: Long*, p. 159

WHITE-FRONTED GOOSE See *Waterside: Long*, p. 159

SNOW and BLUE SNOW GEESE *Anser caerulescens* Plates 56, 58

Greater and Lesser Snow Geese; Blue Goose. Duck Family

PLUMAGE. *Snow* is all white except for black wing-tips; immature much mottled ash-brown. *Blue* is grey-brown above, and usually also below, with head, neck, tail-coverts and sometimes whole or part of underparts white; blackish wing-tips; immature may have most of adult's white parts grey-brown and head spotted. Both have bill pink or red, and legs dull purplish pink.

STRUCTURE. *Wing length* VL. *Ratios:* wing M; tail S; neck M/L; bill M; legs S.

SAND-MARTIN
HOUSE-MARTIN
SWALLOW
adults
SWALLOW
juveniles

ALPINE SWIFT
SWIFT

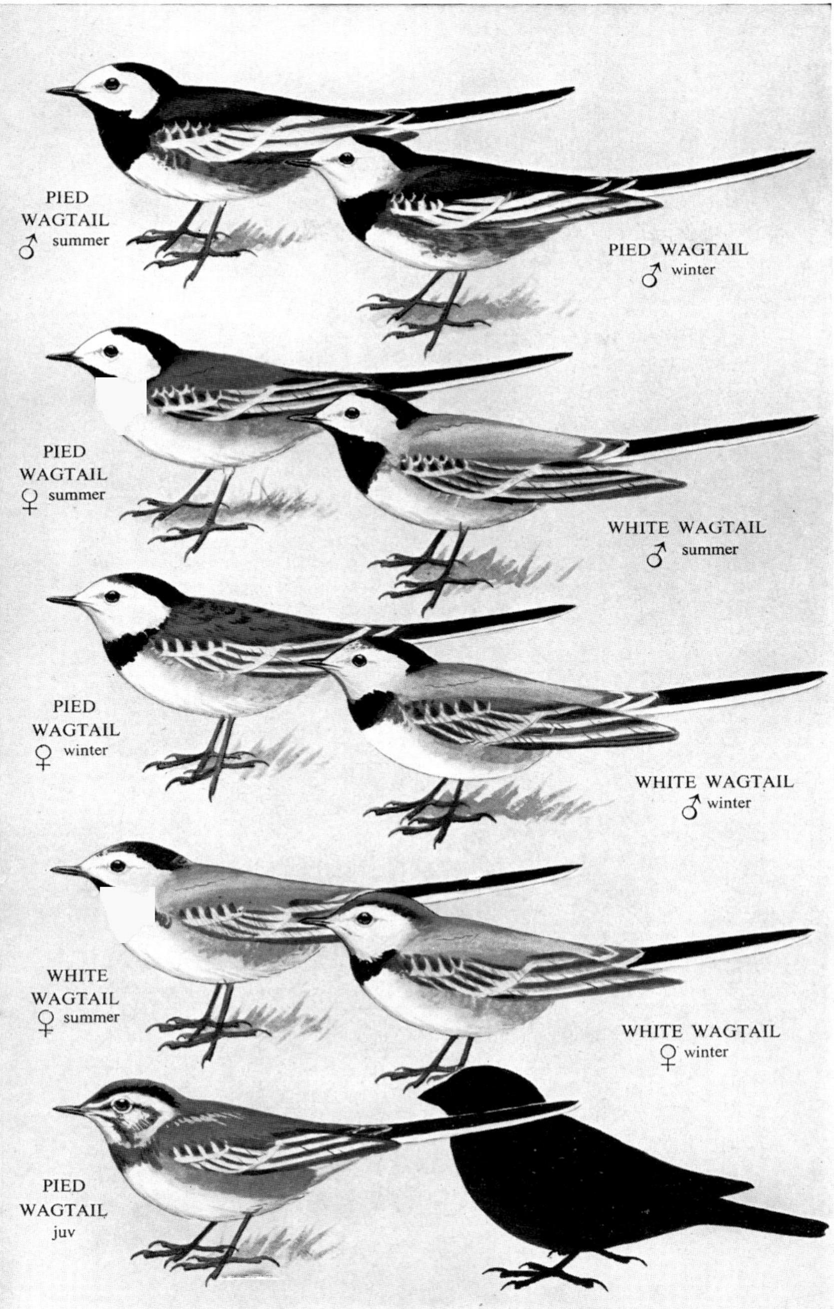
PIED WAGTAIL ♂ summer
PIED WAGTAIL ♂ winter
PIED WAGTAIL ♀ summer
WHITE WAGTAIL ♂ summer
PIED WAGTAIL ♀ winter
WHITE WAGTAIL ♂ winter
WHITE WAGTAIL ♀ summer
WHITE WAGTAIL ♀ winter
PIED WAGTAIL juv

WOOD-PIGEON
juv
adults
ROCK-DOVE
STOCK-DOVE
LONDON PIGEON
blue chequer type
LONDON PIGEON
black type
TURTLE-DOVE

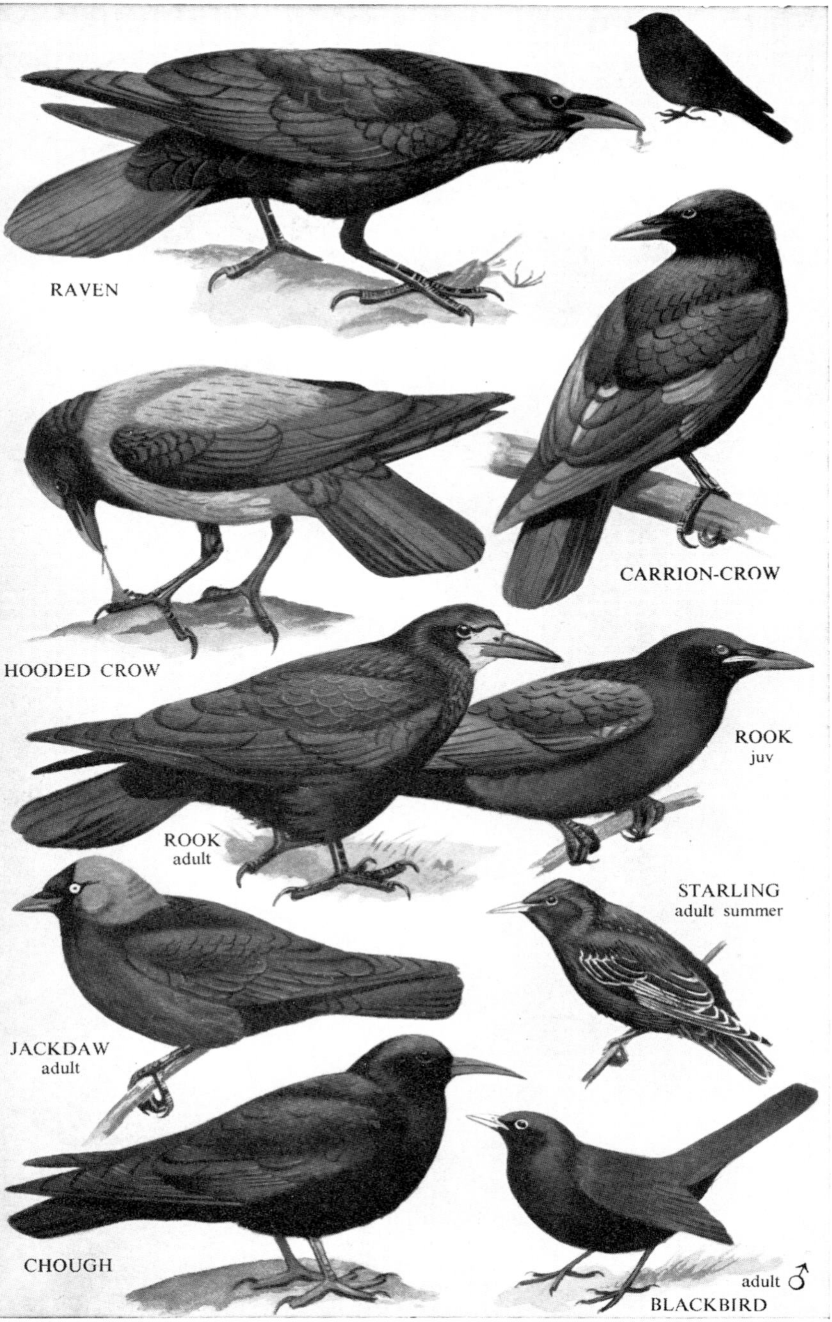
RAVEN
CARRION-CROW
HOODED CROW
ROOK
juv
ROOK
adult
STARLING
adult summer
JACKDAW
adult
CHOUGH
adult ♂
BLACKBIRD

JACKDAW
RAVEN
normal flight
RAVEN
"rolling"
RAVEN
soaring
ROOK
adult
CARRION-
CROW
HOODED
CROW
MAGPIE
CHOUGH

RED GROUSE

RED-LEGGED PARTRIDGE

COMMON PARTRIDGE

COMMON PHEASANT juv

CORNCRAKE

QUAIL

CAPERCAILLIE ♂
BLACK GROUSE ♂
COMMON PHEASANT ring-necked form ♂
BLACK GROUSE ♀
COMMON PHEASANT ♀
CAPERCAILLIE ♀

STONE-CURLEW
WOODCOCK
COMMON SNIPE
GREAT SNIPE
NIGHTJAR ♀
LITTLE OWL
TAWNY OWL
LONG-EARED OWL

OSPREY
MARSH-HARRIER
adult ♀
MARSH-HARRIER
adult ♂
"RING-TAIL" HARRIER
BITTERN
SHORT-EARED
OWLS
BARN-OWL
dark-breasted form

COMMON BUZZARD
ROUGH-LEGGED BUZZARD
KITE
GOSHAWK
adult
HONEY-
BUZZARD
GOSHAWK
juv

HERON
adult
HEN
HARRIER
♂♂
MONTAGU'S
HARRIER
♂
GREENLAND FALCON
SNOWY OWL
♀
BARN-OWL

GOLDEN EAGLE
adult
GOLDEN EAGLE
1st winter
SEA-EAGLE
adult
SEA-EAGLE
1st winter

GOLDEN PLOVER
winter
GOLDEN PLOVER
winter
DOTTEREL
winter
KNOT
winter
COMMON SNIPE
JACK-SNIPE

RUFF ♀
(REEVE)
TEMMINCK'S
STINT
COMMON
SANDPIPER
PURPLE SANDPIPER
LITTLE
STINT
DUNLIN
winter
SANDERLING
summer
GREY
PHALAROPE
winter
RED-NECKED
PHALAROPE
winter
SANDERLING
winter
KENTISH
PLOVER
♂
LITTLE
RINGED
PLOVER
TURNSTONE
winter
RINGED
PLOVER

SPOTTED, or DUSKY REDSHANK
winter
COMMON REDSHANK
GREY PLOVER
winter
CURLEW-SANDPIPER
WOOD-SANDPIPER
GREEN SANDPIPER

CURLEW
WHIMBREL
BAR-TAILED
GODWIT
winter
BLACK-TAILED
GODWIT
winter
COMMON
REDSHANK
GREENSHANK
PRATINCOLE

GREY PLOVER
summer
DUNLIN
summer
GOLDEN
PLOVER
summer
DOTTEREL
summer
TURNSTONE
summer
SPOTTED, or DUSKY
REDSHANK
summer
RUFF
black-breasted form
♂ summer

STILT
LAPWING
LAPWING
AVOCET
OYSTER-CATCHER
BLACK-TAILED
GODWIT
adult summer

COMMON CRANE
SARUS CRANE
DEMOISELLE CRANE
HERON
adult
HERON
juv
NIGHT HERON
adult

COMMON
CRANE
HERON
PURPLE HERON
NIGHT
HERON
adult
BITTERN

GANNET
adult
WHITE STORK
SPOONBILL
adult
SPOONBILL
imm
MUTE SWAN
adult
WHOOPER SWAN
adult

EIDER
♂ in eclipse
VELVET SCOTER ♂
SURF-SCOTER ♂
COMMON SCOTER ♂
BLACK GUILLEMOT
summer
COOT adult
MOORHEN adult

1st winter ♂
adult ♂
EIDER
♂ summer
♂ winter
LONG-TAILED DUCK
♀ winter
GOLDENEYE ♂
SCAUP ♂
SMEW ♂
TUFTED DUCK ♂

DABCHICK
winter
EIDER
♀
♂
♀
COMMON SCOTER
COMMON
POCHARD
♀

MALLARD
♀
PINTAIL
♀
SHOVELER
♀
WIGEON
♀
♀
♂
TEAL
GARGANEY
♀
TUFTED DUCK
♀

GOOSANDER
♀
RED-BREASTED
MERGANSER
♀
SMEW
♀
♂
GOLDENEYE
1st winter
VELVET SCOTER
♀
WIGEON
♂
GADWALL
♂

EIDER
♂
SCAUP
♀
LONG-TAILED DUCK
♀ winter
LONG-TAILED DUCK
♂ winter
SMEW
♂
GARGANEY
♂
COOT

GOLDENEYE
♂
GOLDENEYE
♀
TUFTED DUCK
♂
COMMON
POCHARD
♂
SCAUP
♂

SHELD-DUCK
adult
GOOSANDER
♂
RED-BREASTED
MERGANSER
♂
MALLARD
♂
PINTAIL
♂
SHOVELER
♂

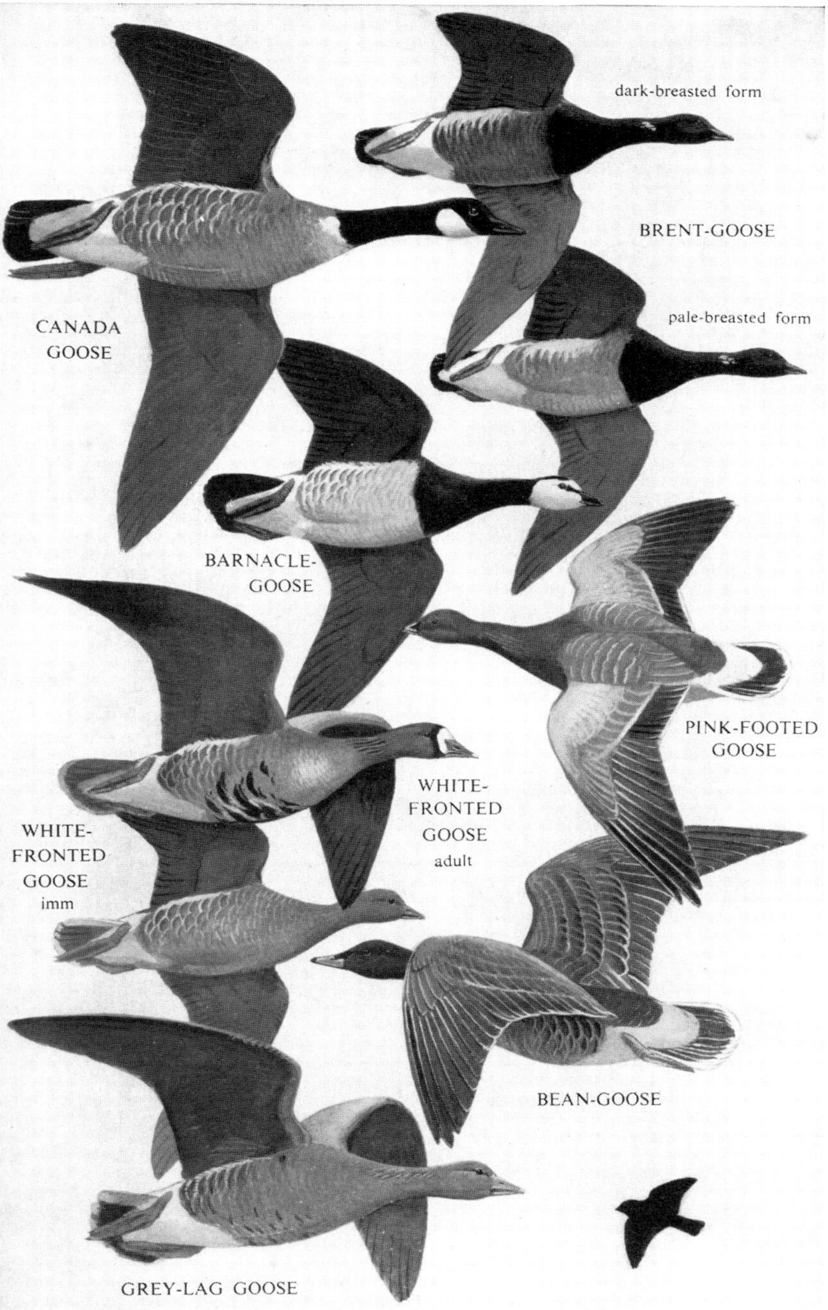
dark-breasted form
BRENT-GOOSE
pale-breasted form
CANADA GOOSE
BARNACLE-GOOSE
PINK-FOOTED GOOSE
WHITE-FRONTED GOOSE adult
WHITE-FRONTED GOOSE imm
BEAN-GOOSE
GREY-LAG GOOSE

CORMORANT
adult winter
SHAG
adult winter
GREAT NORTHERN DIVER
summer
BLACK-THROATED
DIVER
summer
CANADA GOOSE
BRENT GOOSE
SHELD-DUCK
GREAT
BLACK-BACK
adult summer

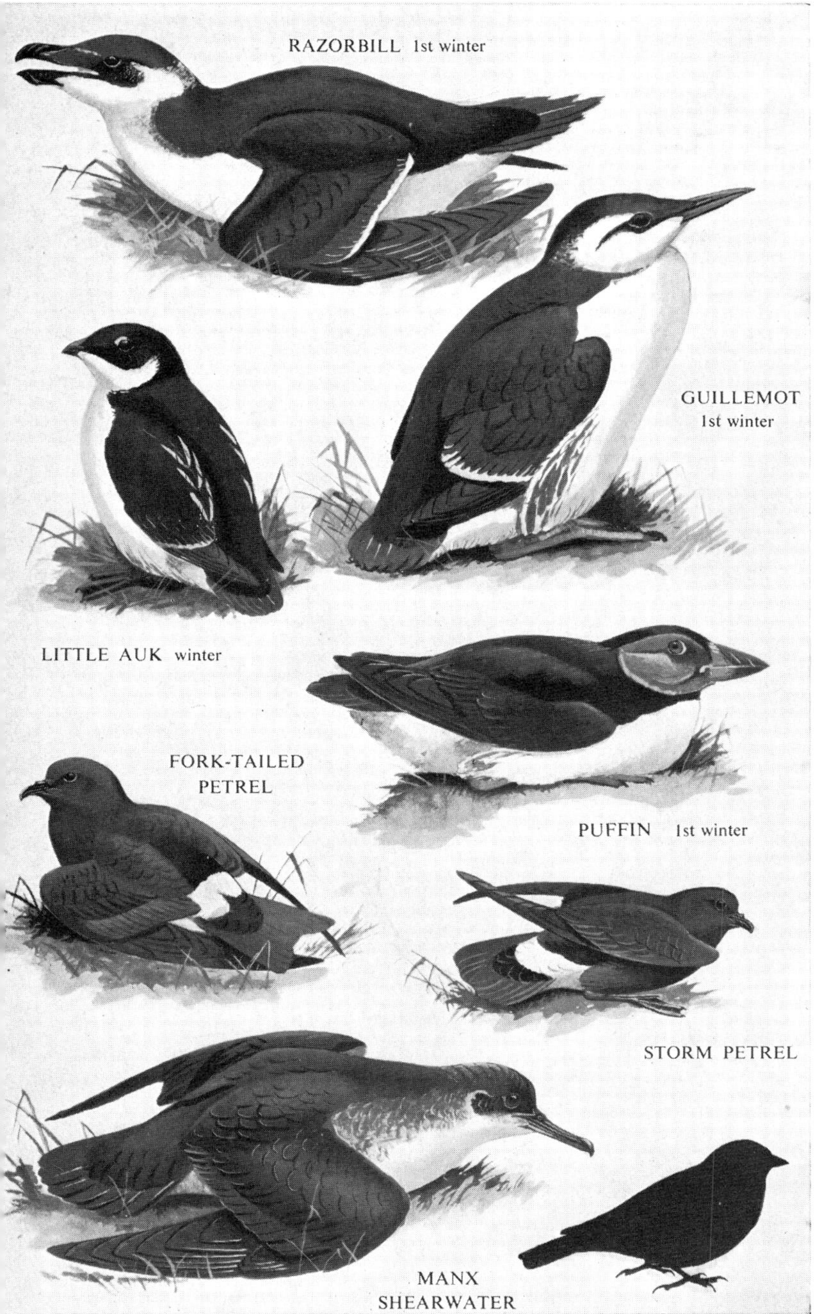
RAZORBILL 1st winter
GUILLEMOT
1st winter
LITTLE AUK winter
FORK-TAILED
PETREL
PUFFIN 1st winter
STORM PETREL
MANX
SHEARWATER

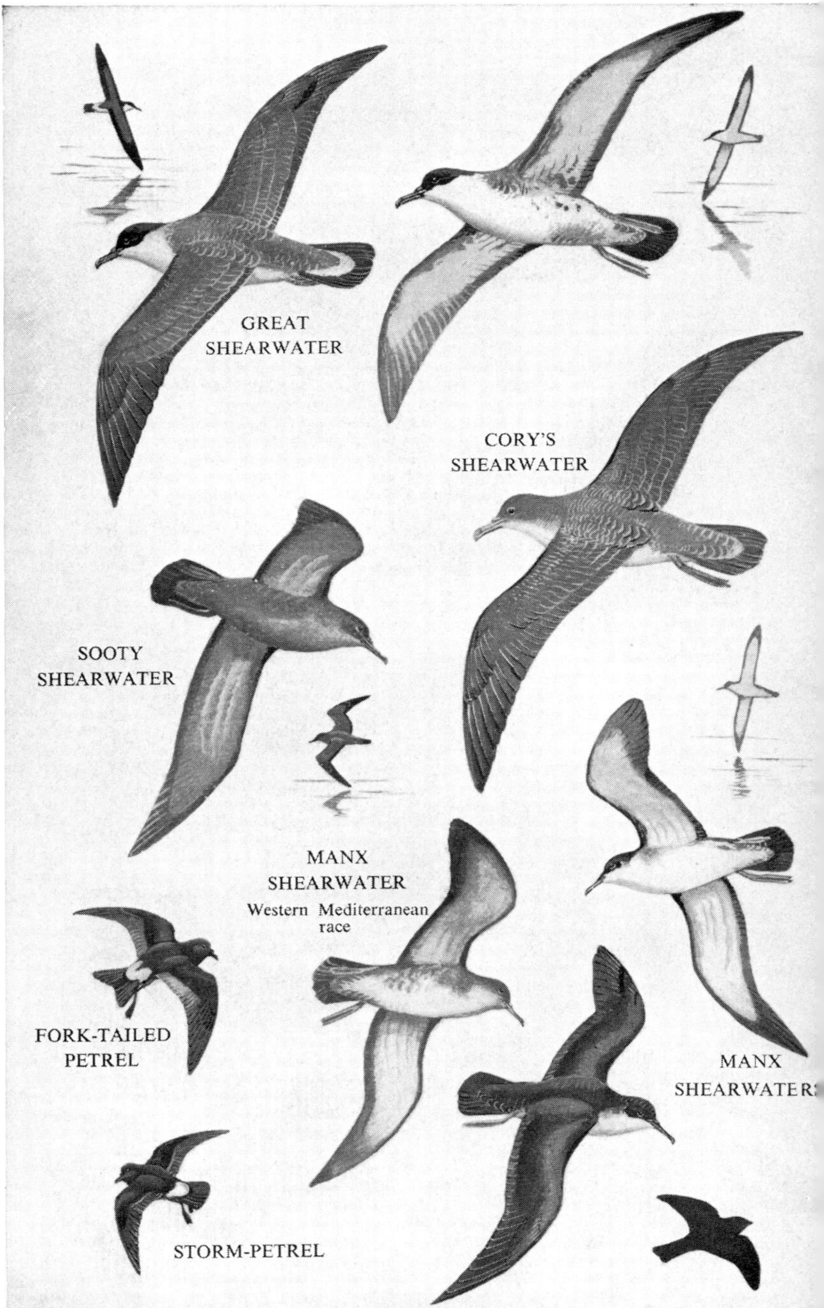
GREAT
SHEARWATER
CORY'S
SHEARWATER
SOOTY
SHEARWATER
MANX
SHEARWATER
Western Mediterranean
race
FORK-TAILED
PETREL
MANX
SHEARWATERS
STORM-PETREL

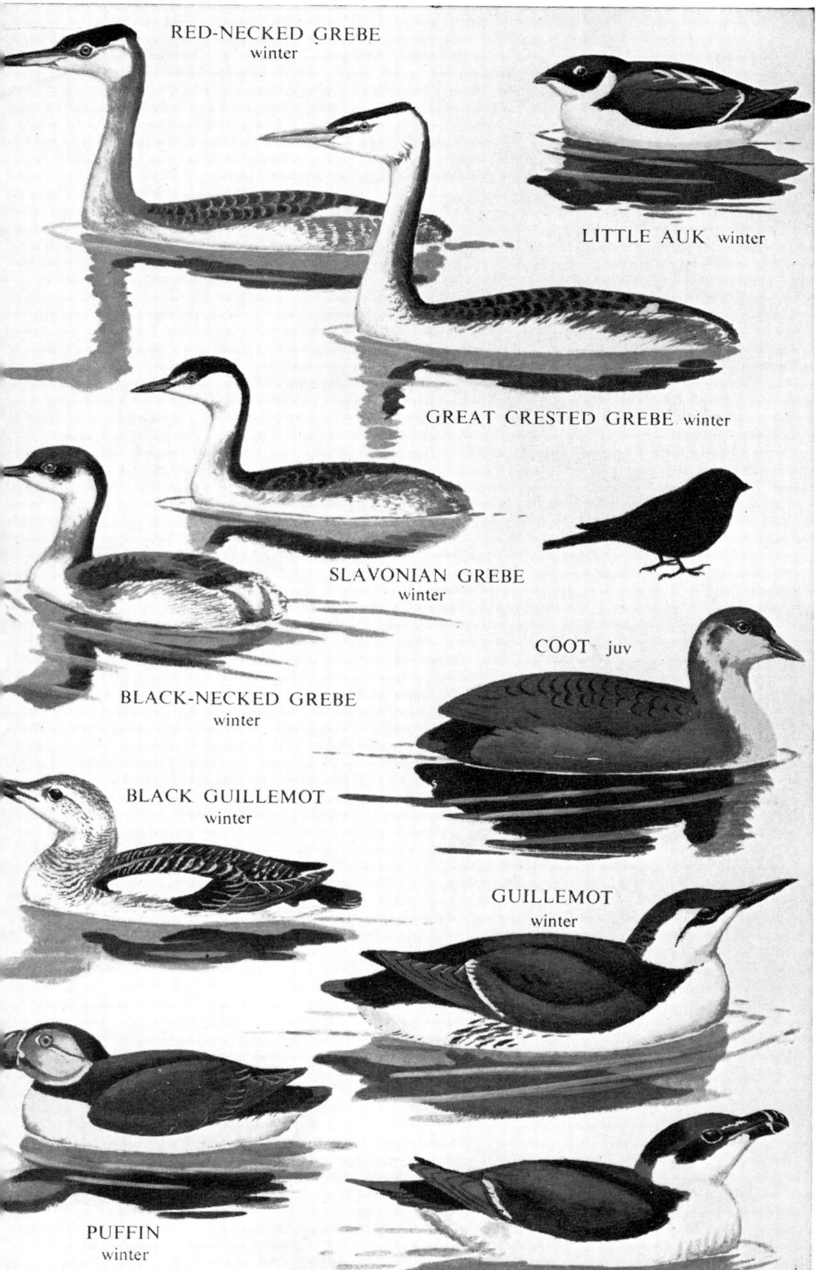
RED-NECKED GREBE
winter
LITTLE AUK winter
GREAT CRESTED GREBE winter
SLAVONIAN GREBE
winter
COOT juv
BLACK-NECKED GREBE
winter
BLACK GUILLEMOT
winter
GUILLEMOT
winter
PUFFIN
winter
RAZORBILL winter

GUILLEMOT
summer
winter
RAZORBILL
summer
winter
BLACK GUILLEMOT
summer
winter
PUFFIN
summer
winter
LITTLE AUK
winter
summer

HERRING-GULL adult winter
FULMAR
COMMON GULL
adult winter
KITTIWAKE
adult winter
BLACK-HEADED GULL
adult winter
RED-NECKED
PHALAROPE
winter
GREY
PHALAROPE
winter

SANDWICH TERN
winter plumage
as from July
juv
COMMON TERN
winter adult
LITTLE
TERN
adult
BLACK TERN
winter
WHITE-WINGED
BLACK TERN
winter

adult spring
SANDWICH TERN
juv
COMMON
TERN
adult summer
GULL-BILLED
TERN
adult summer
ARCTIC TERN
adult summer
ROSEATE TERN
adult summer
BLACK TERN
adult summer
WHITE-WINGED
BLACK TERN
adult summer

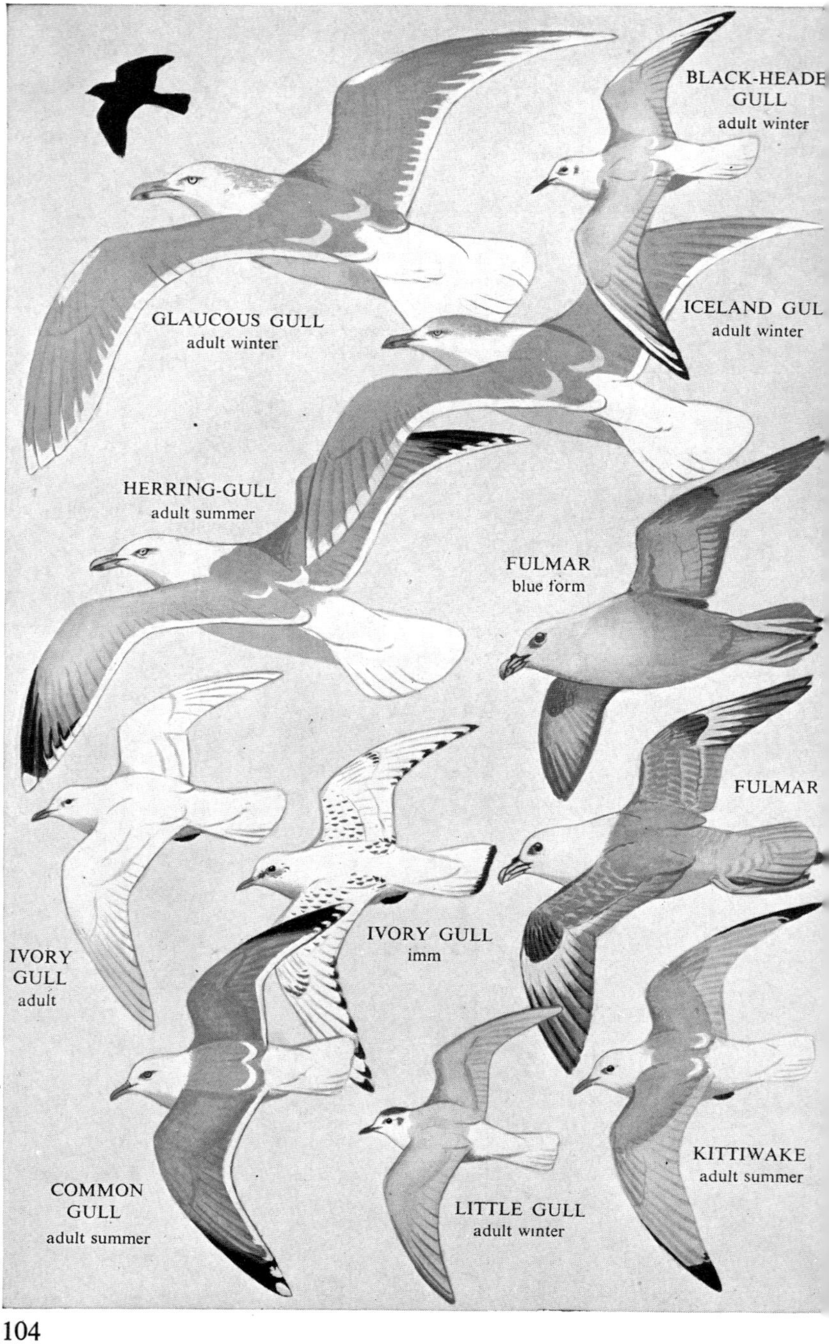
BLACK-HEADE
GULL
adult winter
GLAUCOUS GULL
adult winter
ICELAND GUL
adult winter
HERRING-GULL
adult summer
FULMAR
blue form
FULMAR
IVORY GULL
imm
IVORY
GULL
adult
KITTIWAKE
adult summer
COMMON
GULL
adult summer
LITTLE GULL
adult winter

KITTIWAKE
1st winter
juv
BLACK-HEADED
GULL
SABINE'S
GULL
1st winter
1st winter
LITTLE GULL
1st winter
SABINE'S
GULL
adult summer
adult summer
LITTLE GULL
1st summer
BLACK-HEADED GULL
summer
LITTLE GULL
adult summer
MEDITERRANEAN BLACK-HEADED GULL

GREAT SKUA
dark phase
POMARINE SKUA
pale phase
ARCTIC SKUA juv
intermediate phase
dark phase
ARCTIC SKUA
LONG-TAILED SKUA adult
ARCTIC SKUA pale phase

BLACK-HEADED GULL 1st winter
GLAUCOUS GULL 2nd winter
ICELAND GULL 3rd winter
HERRING-GULL 2nd winter
FULMAR worn plumage
COMMON GULL juv
COMMON GULL 1st winter
CURLEW

GREAT BLACK-BACK
juv
GREAT BLACK-BACK
2nd winter
GLAUCOUS GULL
1st winter
ICELAND
GULL
1st winter
LESSER BLACK-BACKED
GULL
2nd winter
HERRING-GULL
juv

GANNET
1st summer
GREAT
BLACK-BACK
adults winter
GREAT BLACK-BACK
3rd winter
Scandinavian race
LESSER BLACK-BACK
adults winter
British race

CORMORANT
1st winter
GANNET juv
SHAG 1st winter
BLACK-THROATED DIVER
winter
GREAT NORTHERN
DIVER
winter
RED-NECKED GREBE winter
GREAT CRESTED
GREBE
winter
RED-THROATED DIVER
winter

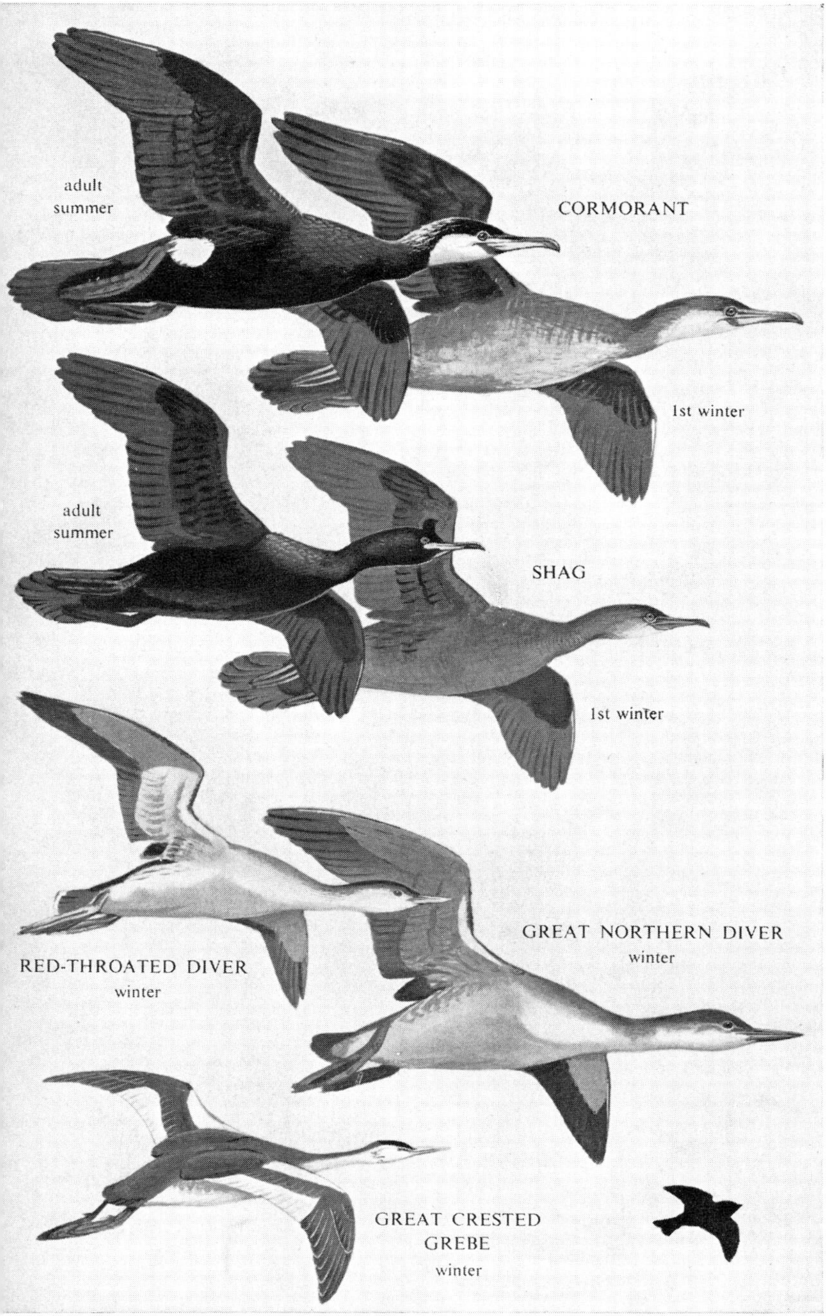
adult
summer
CORMORANT
1st winter
adult
summer
SHAG
1st winter
RED-THROATED DIVER
winter
GREAT NORTHERN DIVER
winter
GREAT CRESTED
GREBE
winter

GANNET
juv
GANNET
1st summer
GANNET
2nd summer
GANNET
adult

MOVEMENT. Much as *greylag* (below).

VOICE. A single, rather harsh note, 'kahk' or 'kaah', also 'ung-ung-ung-ung' when in flocks.

FIELD MARKS. Adult *snow* is the only substantially white goose, but beware occasional albinos of other geese, especially *pink-foot*, which, however (as also all three swans and males of ornamental kelp-goose *Chloëphaga hybrida*), lack the black wing-tips. From other large white birds with black wing-tips can be told by quite different shape of bill; in flight also has much more black on wings than immature spoonbill, and much less than white stork (both of which have legs trailing behind), while gannet has short-necked and cigar-shaped body and Coscoroba swan has longer neck and less stout bill.

Adult *blue* can be told by white head and neck from all geese except *emperor* and female paradise shelduck (p. 205); some other shelducks also have pale heads, but these are all smaller than *blue* and have mainly buff and chestnut body plumage, with green patch on wings.

FLOCKING. Consorts with flocks of grey geese.

HABITAT. As *white-front* (p. 159).

RANGE AND STATUS. Vagrant from Arctic America, and escape from waterfowl collections; wild *snow* have most often turned up on the Solway, and wild *blue* on Wexford Slob (Ireland).

GREYLAG GOOSE *Anser anser* Plates 57, 95 Duck Family

A grey goose.

PLUMAGE. Grey-brown, with mantle and rump greyer; white tail with dark centre, white under tail-coverts, pearl-grey forewing. Some adults have a thin white line at base of bill; others are sparsely (occasionally heavily) spotted black on underparts. Orange bill with white nail; pink legs and eyelids.

STRUCTURE. *Wing length* VL. *Ratios:* wing MS; tail VS/S; neck L; bill M/ML; legs S.

MOVEMENT. All the grey geese have a fast direct flight, but often with rather laboured wing-beats; on migration will fly in V formation; when descending from a height wild geese will often plummet wildly down in so-called 'whiffling' movement. All grey geese can and do swim; gait sedate like farmyard goose, especially *greylag* and *bean* which can also be picked out among flocks of *white-fronts* and *pink-feet* by slower rate of feeding.

VOICE. Flight note 'aahng-ung-ung' is much like clamour of farmyard geese; will also hiss when annoyed.

FIELD MARKS. The grey geese present one of the hardest problems of field identification for beginners, and indeed for all who have not made a close study of them. There is so much individual variation, not to mention the complications of immature birds, and they are often so hard to approach that one may well see grey geese half a dozen times before being able to identify them more exactly. Far the best way to become acquainted with them is to visit the New Grounds sanctuary of the Wildfowl Trust at Slimbridge, Glos., where there are unrivalled facilities to study wild geese at close range and a very reasonable chance of being able to see three or four species together on the same day.

The distinctive features of the *greylag* are its relatively heavy, farmyard-goose-like build, gait and flight, pale grey forewing coupled with greyish mantle and rump, and combination of orange bill and pink legs which is shared by no other grey goose. Beware confusion with *white-front* of occasional birds with white on forehead and unusually heavy black spotting beneath.

FLOCKING. Gregarious, often consorting with other grey geese; note that with all grey geese the family party is the basic unit even within the flock.

HABITAT. Breeds on moorland, especially where there are scattered lochs, and on marine islands; in winter as *white-front* (p. 159).

RANGE AND STATUS. Breeds in N Scotland and some Hebrides, but decreasing; winter visitor, mainly to Scotland, especially Angus, Fife and S Perth, with smaller numbers in Ireland and NW England; passage migrant on E coast England; elsewhere a sporadic winter visitor, most likely to be seen in or after hard weather, but beware full-winged birds wandering from private collections, especially in Norfolk, Essex, Gloucestershire, Caithness, W Ross and Co. Fermanagh.

BEAN GOOSE *Anser fabalis* Plates 57, 95 — Duck Family

A grey goose.

PLUMAGE. Dark grey-brown, with dark centre to white tail, white under tail-coverts, and head and neck darker than body; sometimes a narrow white line at base of bill. Bill has very variable amounts of orange or yellow and black, with a black nail; legs orange.

STRUCTURE. *Wing length* VL. *Ratios:* wing M; tail VS/S; neck L; bill M; legs S.

MOVEMENT. Flight and gait resemble *greylag* (above).

VOICE. Less vocal than other grey geese, its calls are like a tenor version of *pink-foot*.

FIELD MARKS. See *greylag* for general note on grey geese; at any distance dark head and neck are best distinction from other grey geese except *pink-foot*, for distinctions from which, see p. 159. Some *bean* are very dark, looking almost black in the field in poor light. No other grey geese, except *Greenland white-fronts*, have yellow or orange bill combined with orange legs.

FLOCKING. As *greylag*.

HABITAT. As *white-front* (p. 159).

RANGE AND STATUS. Winter visitor; very local, and regular only in three localities, in Norfolk, Northumberland and SW Scotland; occasional individuals with flocks of *white-fronts* in England.

SEA EAGLE *Haliæetus albicilla* Plates 34, 77 — Hawk Family

Erne; White-tailed Eagle; Grey Sea Eagle (N America).

PLUMAGE. Brown, with paler, sometimes almost white, head; wedge-shaped tail, white in adult. Large, hooked, yellow bill (horn-coloured in juvenile) with yellow cere (greenish in juvenile); legs half feathered, rest yellow; eye yellow in adult.

STRUCTURE. *Wing length* H. *Ratios:* wing L; tail M; neck S; bill M; legs M. Female larger than male.

MOVEMENT. Ponderous, heron-like or vulturine flapping flight, low over water or reed-beds when hunting; also soars and dives from air.

VOICE. Usually silent, but has a low chattering note.

FIELD MARKS. Immense bulk and wide span of very broad wings mark out sea eagle from all other large brown birds except golden eagle, for distinctions from which see p. 114. Osprey, which also has whitish head and is known locally as 'fishing eagle', is substantially smaller and has white underparts.

HABITAT. Most often on coast, also occasionally inland at lakes, broads and other large sheets of water.

RANGE AND STATUS. Rare and irregular winter visitor, most often E coast England; formerly bred, but not since at least 1910.

BITTERN *Botaurus stellaris* Plates 44, 74, 85 Heron Family

Boomer.

PLUMAGE. Warm buffish brown, heavily mottled and marked with black; crown black. Rounded wings; greenish-yellow bill, pale green legs, yellow eye.

STRUCTURE. *Wing length* L. *Ratios:* wing S; tail VS; neck VL; bill ML; legs M.

MOVEMENT. Flight typical of herons, with neck retracted and legs trailing straight behind, hind-toe touching tip of tail. Remarkable habit of freezing in upright posture gives it excellent camouflage in dried reed-stems; stalking gait.

VOICE. When flighting at dusk has a harsh call, 'kwow' or 'kwah', also clucks not unlike a domestic hen when flushed from nest; most characteristic call is the spring 'booming' note, resembling a cross between a lowing cow and a distant foghorn.

FIELD MARKS. Being a skulker, is most often detected by booming note. When seen in open or at nest, appearance depends on whether long neck is drawn in or stretched out; if neck retracted and feathers ruffled looks not unlike a large domestic hen. In flight at a distance can be told from short-eared owl by long bill and trailing legs. Unlikely to be mistaken for any other heron-like bird (except rare immature night-heron, which has pale mottlings), but away from breeding haunts needs to be differentiated from rare American bittern (p. 160).

HABITAT. Extensive reed-beds, swamps and fens.

RANGE AND STATUS. Resident, breeding in E Anglia, Lincolnshire and perhaps elsewhere in England; may occur in winter in many other parts of British Isles.

PURPLE HERON *Ardea purpurea* Plates 44, 85

PLUMAGE. Mainly dark grey, with black crown and belly, striped rufous neck and chestnut breast. Immature is brown and lacks most of black on crown and stripes on neck. Broad, rounded wings; yellowish bill; brown and yellow legs; yellow eye.

STRUCTURE. *Wing length* L. *Ratios:* wing MS; tail VS/S; neck VL; bill L; legs ML.

MOVEMENT AND VOICE. Similar to common heron (below).

FIELD MARKS. Smaller, darker and more rakish than common heron, and at close range easily distinguished from it by striped rufous neck and chestnut breast. In flight whole wing appears nearly uniform and legs project further.

HABITAT. Marshes with plenty of cover, such as reed-beds and thickets of sallow and alder; more prone to skulk in cover than common heron.

RANGE AND STATUS. Vagrant from Continent, especially E coast England.

DEMOISELLE CRANE *Anthropoides virgo* Plate 84

Resembles common crane (below) in general appearance and habits, but has black forehead, cheeks, throat, sides of neck, upper breast and wing-tips, and long white ear-tufts. Ear-tufts (not to be confused with white stripe on common crane's neck) and no red on head distinguish from common and sarus cranes. Escape from zoos and private collections; possibly also as genuine vagrant from Balkans.

SPOONBILL *Platalea leucorodia* Plates 45, 86

PLUMAGE. All white, but adult has a yellowish breast-band and in summer a yellowish crest. Immature has extreme tips of wings blackish and no crest. Spoon-shaped, black bill, with yellow tip; black legs; yellow skin round red eye.

STRUCTURE. *Wing length* L. *Ratios:* wing S; tail VS; neck VL; bill VL; legs ML.

MOVEMENT. Slow, heavy flight, with neck and legs both straight out, rather more like a swan than a heron; will glide, soar, perch on trees and occasionally swim. Stalks on ground; has characteristic side-to-side motion of bill when feeding in shallows.

VOICE. Normally silent, but occasionally grunts.

FIELD MARKS. At close range can be told from all other large white birds by spoon-shaped bill. In flight can be told from herons and egrets by neck outstretched, and from white stork by legs *straight* out behind (as well as by white wings). Adult can be told from swans, and immature from gannet, by legs out behind.

FLOCKING. Sometimes in small parties.

HABITAT. Estuaries and marsh pools near the sea.

RANGE AND STATUS. Passage migrant, especially on S and E coasts, regular in E Anglia; occasionally summers, and tends increasingly to winter in SW England; vagrant elsewhere.

HERON *Ardea cinerea* Plates 76, 84, 85

Common Heron; Grey Heron; Crane (common misnomer).

PLUMAGE. Grey, with whole outer half of broad, rounded wings black; white head and neck, with black crest (grey in juvenile). Bill yellowish (occasionally orange or pink in spring), blackish-brown in juvenile; brown legs; greenish skin round yellow eye.

STRUCTURE. *Wing-length* VL. *Ratios:* wing MS; tail VS/S; neck VL; bill ML; legs ML.

MOVEMENT. Slow, heavy, flapping flight, with neck drawn in and legs straight out behind. Stalks on ground; perches both on ground and in trees, in several typical attitudes, viz. hunched up with neck drawn in, alert with neck craned forward to full extent, and half crouched with neck forward looking for prey.

VOICE. Commonest note a harsh 'kraaank', but has a wide and raucous vocabulary at the nest.

FIELD MARKS. The only large, grey, long-legged, long-necked native bird, but see above and below for distinctions from various cranes, all rare, and beware 'crane' as vernacular name for heron in many parts of England. A large, grey bird flying with broad, rounded wings and legs straight out behind it is almost certain to be a heron, particularly if its neck is drawn in.

FLOCKING. Nests in colonies, and often feeds in small, loose parties; gatherings of non-breeding birds also take place.

HABITAT. Breeds mostly in trees, occasionally in reed-beds or on cliffs, and feeds at edge of all kinds of fresh and salt water, especially rivers, lakes and estuaries, also occasionally away from water, as when it visits rickyards for rats.

RANGE AND STATUS. Resident, breeding almost throughout British Isles; total population about 4,000 pairs; many arrive E coast in autumn.

WATERSIDE BIRDS: Huge

BLACK STORK See *Land: Huge*, p. 116

WHITE STORK See *Land: Huge*, p. 116

SARUS CRANE *Grus antigone* Plate 84

Resembles common crane (below) in general appearance and habits, but differs in having bare red skin on head and upper neck, with grey patch on ears, white ring round neck and throat and rest of neck black, also white tips to plumes and reddish legs. Red on head and no white ear-tufts also distinguish from demoiselle crane. Occasional escape from zoos and private collections.

COMMON CRANE *Grus grus* Plates 84, 85

PLUMAGE. Grey, with black head, white streak on neck and red patch on crown; black wing-tips, with elongated secondaries forming a tuft or plume of feathers obscuring the tail. Juvenile has brownish head and neck and no plumes. Greenish bill with reddish base; black legs; red eye.

STRUCTURE. *Wing length* H. *Ratios:* wing MS; tail VS/S; neck VL; bill ML; legs L.

MOVEMENT. Slow, direct flight, with neck and legs both stretched straight out; migrating flocks travel in V formation. Walks, and occasionally runs, on ground; exceptionally swims and perches.

VOICE. A harsh, clanging 'krooh' or 'krr'.

FIELD MARKS. Superficially similar to heron, but differs in flight by neck stretched out and at rest by shorter black bill, plumes, and black-white-red pattern on head. Can be told from white stork by mainly grey plumage; for distinctions from sarus and demoiselle cranes, see above. Beware local name of 'crane' for heron.

FLOCKING. Normally highly gregarious out of breeding season.
HABITAT. Marshy places, and open arable fields.
RANGE AND STATUS. Rare vagrant, mainly in the S.

FLAMINGO *Phoenicopterus ruber*
The only long-legged, long-necked bird that has a bill like an accentuated Roman nose and is generally pink but shows a brilliant contrast of black and red in its wings on taking flight. Escape from zoos and private collections, and rare vagrant from S Europe; in recent years most have been of the Chilean race with red tarsal joints and feet.

WATER BIRDS: Short

STORM PETREL *Hydrobates pelagicus* Plates 97, 98
Mother Carey's Chicken.
PLUMAGE. Black-brown, with white rump and under tail-coverts, faint white line on wing and whitish patch on underwing. Slightly hooked black bill with tubular nostrils; legs black.
STRUCTURE. *Wing length* M. *Ratios:* wing ML; tail M; neck MS; bill S; legs M.
MOVEMENT. Fast, direct flight low down across the surface of the sea, also a more fluttering flight when feeding; habitually follows in the wake of vessels; swims readily. Cannot walk on land, but flutters along on full length of leg.
VOICE. Penetrating purr, ending in a hiccup-like 'chikka', is not unlike the nightjar's churr, and is heard only at the nest.
FIELD MARKS. Looks not unlike a rather large square-tailed house martin, but shape of tail is hard to see from a tossing ship. Can be told from larger fork-tailed petrel (the only other small black, white-rumped bird at all likely to be seen at sea) by direct flight and square tail, from rare Wilson's petrel *Oceanites oceanicus* by short black legs (*Wilson's* has yellow feet extending well beyond tail in flight), and from other possible small black, white-rumped petrels by whitish underwing. Nesting birds readily located by smelling crannies in rocks, walls, etc., for characteristic pungent odour.
FLOCKING. Breeds in loose colonies; not otherwise gregarious.
HABITAT. The open sea, coming to land only at night to nest on marine islands; hardly ever in inshore waters, and inland only as a storm-blown waif.
RANGE AND STATUS. Resident, breeding Scilly Isles and many islands off coast of Wales (Skokholm, Skomer), Ireland and W and N Scotland.

RED-NECKED PHALAROPE *Phalaropus lobatus* Plates 46, 79, 101
Northern Phalarope (N America).
PLUMAGE. In winter grey above, with wing-bar and most of head white, and white below. In summer head grey-brown, with white chin and face patch and orange patch on sides of neck and throat. Juvenile is like winter adult, but browner above. Blackish bill; blue-grey legs. Feet lobed.

STRUCTURE. *Wing length* MS. *Ratios:* wing M; tail MS; neck MS; bill ML; legs M. Female larger than male.

MOVEMENT. Similar to grey phalarope (below), but fast flight more like common sandpiper, and on breeding grounds has graceful and rather swallow-like flight, and a special display flight.

VOICE. Call-notes, 'twit' and 'tirric, tirric', and a curious little grunting note prior to flight.

FIELD MARKS. See grey phalarope; *red-necked's* clear-cut white throat in summer is conspicuous and unique among waders.

FLOCKING. Breeds in small colonies.

HABITAT. Breeds in coastal or loch-side areas with scattered pools and boggy ground; otherwise as grey phalarope.

RANGE AND STATUS. Summer visitor, breeding very locally in northern and western isles of Scotland, and in one or two spots in NW Ireland; otherwise scarce passage migrant, most often in early June and autumn on S and E coasts England.

WATER BIRDS: Medium Short

FORK-TAILED PETREL *Oceanodroma leucorrhoa* Plates 97, 98

Leach's Fork-tailed Petrel; Leach's Petrel (N America). Storm-Petrel Family

PLUMAGE. Black-brown with white rump (showing dark centre at close range) and under tail-coverts; forked tail; basal part of wing appearing paler than wing-tips. Slightly hooked black bill with tubular nostrils; black legs.

STRUCTURE. *Wing length* M. *Ratios:* wing ML; tail M; neck MS; bill MS/S; legs M.

MOVEMENT. Has a very characteristic darting, zigzag, buoyant flight, and does not follow ships; otherwise resembles storm petrel (above).

VOICE. Various guttural and churring noises at the nest.

FIELD MARKS. Can be told from all other likely small petrels except very rare Madeiran fork-tailed petrel *O. castro* (which has no dark centre to rump) by its forked tail, which is, however, hard to see in the field, so that darting flight is the safest field character; for other distinctions from storm and Wilson's petrels, see p. 166.

FLOCKING. Breeds in loose colonies; not otherwise gregarious.

HABITAT. As storm petrel.

RANGE AND STATUS. Resident, breeding on St. Kilda, N Rona, Sula Sgeir and Flannan Isles (Outer Hebrides); otherwise only likely to be seen in open Atlantic or as storm-blown waif inland.

GREY PHALAROPE *Phalaropus fulicarius* Plates 46, 79, 101

Red Phalarope (N America).

PLUMAGE. In winter grey above, with wing-bar and most of head white, and white below. In summer head brown with white cheek, brown streaked darker above with white wing-bar, reddish-chestnut below. Male has black bill with yellow base, female yellow bill with black tip; horn-coloured legs. Feet lobed.

STRUCTURE. *Wing length* M. *Ratios:* wing ML; tail S; neck MS; bill M; legs M. Female larger than male.

MOVEMENT. Flight weak over short distances, but stronger and like ringed plover over longer distances; swims buoyantly, with bobbing movements of head, picking insects off surface of water, often spinning round, or with carriage of miniature gull. Walks or runs on land.

VOICE. A low 'twit'.

FIELD MARKS. Phalaropes are much the smallest birds likely to be seen swimming (except for the small petrels, which are almost all-black), and are usually so tame that they can be approached near enough to be distinguished from each other. In winter they look like tiny gulls, and have also aptly been described as 'sanderlings of the sea', but can both be told from sanderling (which very rarely swims) by a dark patch running through the eye. *Grey* can best be told from smaller *red-necked* in winter by having shorter and rather stouter bill with yellow on it instead of thin, almost needle-like blackish bill; *grey* also has rather more uniform blue-grey back. *Grey* is very rare in summer, but can be told at once by its reddish throat and underparts, as *red-necked* has white underparts and is red only on throat and sides of neck. Rare Wilson's Phalarope *P. tricolor* is larger, with white rump and no wing-bar.

HABITAT. The open sea, well offshore; when blown inland by gales may turn up on any piece of salt or fresh water down to a duckpond.

RANGE AND STATUS. Autumn passage migrant, usually scarce, but sometimes in numbers after a heavy gale; occasional in winter and spring; most frequent S England, very rare Scotland.

LITTLE AUK *Plautus alle* Plates 97, 99, 100

Rotche, Sea Dove; Dovekie (N America).

PLUMAGE. In summer all black, except for white lower breast, belly, wing-bar and streaks on scapulars. In winter white also on throat and cheeks (extending well back on to sides of nape), leaving a dark breast-band. Black bill; brown or grey legs.

STRUCTURE. *Wing length* M. *Ratios:* wing M; tail S; neck MS; bill S/MS; legs S.

MOVEMENT. As guillemot (p. 181).

VOICE. Generally silent away from breeding colonies.

FIELD MARKS. Much the smallest auk, and the smallest diving sea bird. The small bill is also distinctive, but beware juveniles of other auks, all of which have much smaller bills than their adults, though only juvenile puffin (which has grey cheeks and no wing-bar) comes anywhere near the tiny size of the little auk; none of them have the white of the cheeks extending back almost across the nape, and only puffin has the dark breast-band. All these distinctions apply also to the winter black-necked grebe (p. 171), which likewise dives before a proper view can be obtained. See guillemot for general note on auks. Beware especially juvenile razorbills, which swim S with parents from July to September, when still only half grown and unable to fly.

FLOCKING. Unlikely to be seen in flocks inshore.

HABITAT. The open sea, but driven inshore and occasionally inland by storms.

RANGE AND STATUS. Winter visitor, most frequent on E coast, Shetland to Suffolk; periodically 'wrecks' occur after gales, when birds are driven inland over a wide area and may even be caught up in flocks of immigrant starlings.

WATER BIRDS: Medium

MANX SHEARWATER *Puffinus puffinus* Plates 97, 98

Balearic or Mauretanian Shearwater (western Mediterranean race).

PLUMAGE. Blackish above, white below. Western Mediterranean race has brown back contrasting with darker crown, nape and wing-tips, shading gradually to more or less brownish-white below, but is very variable. Slightly hooked, blackish bill, with tubular nostrils; legs pale pink.

STRUCTURE. *Wing length* ML. *Ratios:* wing M; tail S; neck MS; bill M; legs (does not stand).

MOVEMENT. Shearwaters typically fly with wings held straight out, progressing by a series of glides, first on one wing then on the other, often 'shearing' the water with the wing-tips, and with occasional series of wing-beats between the glides; do not follow ships. *Manx* swims readily, and exceptionally dives from the air; gait on land a fluttering shuffle, never standing upright.

VOICE. Normally silent at sea, but vociferous at night in breeding places, with a unique range of strangled cooing noises, including one aptly rendered, 'it-i-corka'.

FIELD MARKS. Shearwaters can at once be told by their characteristic flight, and *Manx* (the only medium-sized one) shows first dark and then light, as its upper and under sides are exposed in alternate glides. The western Mediterranean race is much browner both above and below; dark specimens might be confused with sooty shearwater (p. 179), and light ones with Cory's shearwater (p. 185), both, however, usually distinctly larger.

FLOCKING. Breeds in colonies, assembling in huge flocks off breeding places at dusk; also in small parties at sea.

HABITAT. The open sea; comparatively rarely seen from shore, except in breeding season, when resorts (on cloudy nights only) to marine islands and headlands to nest; inland as storm-blown waif only.

RANGE AND STATUS. Resident, breeding on islands off W coast Great Britain (Scillies, Lundy, Skokholm, Skomer, St. Tudwal's, Bardsey and several of the Hebrides), also visits many mainland cliffs, but only occasionally breeds on them; also breeds on several islands and headlands on W coast Ireland, but not in Isle of Man. Occurs fairly widely in offshore zone all round coast at all seasons, but less commonly in winter. Western Mediterranean race is an annual autumn visitor to English Channel and North Sea.

DABCHICK *Podiceps ruficollis* Plates 46, 47, 49, 89 Grebe Family
Little Grebe; Didapper.

PLUMAGE. Brown, with paler underparts, and in summer chestnut cheeks and throat and whitish patch at base of bill. Juvenile is striped and mottled black and brown, with white markings on head. Bill black; legs greenish; eye red-brown.

STRUCTURE. *Wing length* MS. *Ratios:* wing S; tail VS; neck L; bill MS; legs (does not stand).

MOVEMENT. As great crested grebe (p. 190), but flies more freely.

VOICE. In breeding season a whinnying trill; alarm note, 'whit, whit'.

FIELD MARKS. The smallest freshwater waterfowl, markedly smaller than black-necked grebe (below). Juveniles moulting into adult plumage in autumn can be puzzling, as they have a good deal of white on the face which may be mistaken for the white on the cheek and chin of the *black-necked*. The white face patch is a good field mark in summer, and is in quite a different position from that of most ducks with white face patches, except for drake goldeneye, which is much larger and has a dark green head. The long neck is often retracted.

FLOCKING. In autumn and winter in parties or small flocks.

HABITAT. Breeds on all kinds of fresh waters, ponds, lakes and slow rivers, sometimes in town parks; in winter many resort to reservoirs and estuaries.

RANGE AND STATUS. Resident, breeding almost throughout British Isles; also winter visitor from Continent.

LITTLE GULL *Larus minutus* Plates 60, 61, 104, 105

PLUMAGE. White, with silver-grey wings and tail, and smoky grey underwing; head and upper neck black in summer, in winter white with blackish patch on back of head and nape. Immature in first winter is like adult winter, but has dark wing-tip continuous with a dark bar diagonally across wing to base of hindwing, also dark bar at tip of cleft tail, and paler underwing; in first summer also has adult head and neck, but with white forehead. Bill blackish (red-brown in summer); legs of adult red, of immature shell-pink.

STRUCTURE. *Wing length* L. *Ratios:* wing ML; tail MS; neck MS; bill MS; legs S.

MOVEMENT. Flight hesitant, graceful and wavering, much daintier than black-headed gull and recalling black tern, like which it stoops to pick up insects from surface of water. Swims, and will dart after insects like a phalarope; walks or runs.

VOICE. Sharp and rather harsh, 'kek-kek-kek' and 'ka-ka-ka'.

FIELD MARKS. Intermediate between the black-headed gull and black tern in size, appearance and habits, it can be told from *black-headed* in summer by black (not chocolate) hood extending over nape on to upper neck, in winter by black bill, and at all times by no black on wing-tips and smoky grey underwing. In winter can be told from black tern by unforked white tail, smoky underwing, and absence of sharply defined white shoulder and dark spot at side of breast. Immature can be told from all other gulls except juvenile kittiwake (which has dark patch on back of neck and dark legs, and is much larger) by cleft tail and distinctive wing pattern, but see p. 173 for possible confusion with Sabine's gull.

FLOCKING. Sometimes in small parties and with black-headed gull.

HABITAT. Mainly coastal waters, also occasionally on freshwater.

RANGE AND STATUS. Uncommon autumn and winter visitor and scarce spring passage migrant; mostly on E and S coasts England, rare in Ireland.

PUFFIN *Fratercula arctica* Plates 59, 97, 99, 100 Auk Family

Sea Parrot; Atlantic Puffin (N. America).

PLUMAGE. Black crown, band across throat, and upperparts; white below, with grey cheeks. Enormous broad and vertically flattened bill is brightly coloured with red and yellow in summer, yellow with a little red in winter when it is not so big; juvenile's bill is brownish and much smaller. Legs vermilion in summer, yellow in winter, flesh-coloured in juvenile; orbital ring red, with blue-grey appendages in summer.

STRUCTURE. *Wing length* ML. *Ratios:* wing M; tail VS; neck MS; bill ML (juvenile), L (adults); legs S.

MOVEMENT. As guillemot (p. 181).

VOICE. A growling 'arr'; juvenile call, 'chip-chip-chip'.

FIELD MARKS. At close quarters fantastic-looking bill and solemn, clown-like appearance are quite unlike any other bird. Is smaller than razorbill and guillemot and larger than little auk, and can be told from all three by lack of wing-bar in flight, and in winter also from the two larger auks by its grey cheeks and throat-band. See guillemot for general note on auks.

FLOCKING. As guillemot, but in larger breeding colonies.

HABITAT. Breeds in turf on cliffs and marine islands; otherwise the open sea, except when storm-blown inshore or inland.

RANGE AND STATUS. As guillemot, but fewer colonies; on E coast England only at Flamborough (Yorks) and Farne Is. (Northumberland).

BLACK-NECKED GREBE *Podiceps nigricollis* Plates 46, 99

Eared Grebe (N America).

PLUMAGE. Black above with white wing-bar, white below; in summer has golden-chestnut ear-tufts (pointing downwards), also black cheeks and neck, and chestnut flanks (all of which are white in winter). Juvenile has striped head and neck. Tip-tilted blue-grey bill; greyish legs; pinkish eye.

STRUCTURE. *Wing length* M. *Ratios:* wing S; tail VS; neck L; bill MS; legs (does not stand).

MOVEMENT. Similar to great crested grebe (p. 190).

VOICE. Main call is a soft 'pee-eep'.

FIELD MARKS. Slightly uptilted bill is hall-mark of *black-necked* at all times; is intermediate in size between *Slavonian* (see below for distinctions) and dabchick, which is always browner, has much less white on chin and throat in winter, and in summer has whole head and neck chestnut and a white face patch. Beware also young coots in the white-throated stage, though they always have sooty flanks and a stouter, straight bill.

FLOCKING. Sometimes breeds in colonies.

HABITAT. As *Slavonian*, but fairly regular inland on passage.

RANGE AND STATUS. Breeds irregularly in various parts of British Isles, but colonies rarely last long; mainly a winter visitor on E and S coasts England, and passage migrant inland from Cheshire S to Somerset and Thames valley; scarce elsewhere.

SLAVONIAN GREBE *Podiceps auritus* Plates 46, 99

Horned Grebe in N America.

PLUMAGE. Black above with white wing-bar, white below. In summer has neck, breast and flanks chestnut, and cheeks black (all of which are white in winter), also upward-pointing chestnut ear-tufts. Juvenile has striped head and neck. Blue-grey bill; greyish legs; pink eye.

STRUCTURE. *Wing length* M. *Ratios:* wing S; tail VS; neck L; bill MS; legs (does not stand).

MOVEMENT. Similar to great crested grebe (p. 190), but more inclined to fly than to dive when disturbed.

VOICE. A low rippling trill and other notes in breeding season; hunger cry of young resembles *great crested.*

FIELD MARKS. Is the middle of the five grebes, intermediate in size between the *red-necked* and the *black-necked*, from both of which it can be told in winter by black of crown contrasting sharply with white of cheek at eye level instead of merging into it below the eye; also has shorter bill than less dumpy *red-necked* and straight instead of tip-tilted bill of *black-necked.* In summer can be told from *red-necked* by black cheeks and ear-tufts, and from *black-necked* by chestnut neck and ear-tufts pointing up, not down. Dabchick is always both smaller and browner. The best way of identifying odd small and medium-sized grebes in winter (rather short bills distinguish them from ducks and auks, which also frequently dive) is to concentrate on the shape of the bill and the dividing line of black and white on the face. Grebe moults may last quite late into the autumn, and in-between plumages can be very puzzling.

FLOCKING. Breeds in colonies.

HABITAT. Breeds on lochs with some vegetation growing in the water at the edge; in winter mostly on inshore waters and estuaries, but sometimes (especially in hard weather) on fresh water.

RANGE AND STATUS. Resident in small numbers in Inverness and Sutherland; winter visitor to all coasts.

MOORHEN *Gallinula chloropus* Plates 36, 87 Rail Family

Waterhen; Florida Gallinule (N America).

PLUMAGE. Blackish-brown above, grey below, with white line on flank and white under tail-coverts. Young are mostly olive-brown, with whitish throat and belly, and white under tail-coverts. Bill red with yellow tip and red frontal shield (all greenish-brown in young); legs green with reddish 'garter'; eye red.

STRUCTURE. *Wing length* ML. *Ratios:* wing MS; tail S; neck M; bill M; legs M.

Moorhen taking flight

MOVEMENT. Normal flight is weak, with legs trailing behind at first, and take-off from water usually laboured and pattering. Swims with jerky forward movement, often showing white under tail-coverts; dives if alarmed. Walks or runs; less quarrelsome than coot.

VOICE. Chief notes are loud but rather liquid croaks, 'curruc', 'kittic', and a harsh 'kaak'; young are shriller.

FIELD MARKS. The only waterfowl with both red frontal shield and habit of constantly flirting its white under tail-coverts; these two features with the white line on the flank and no wing-bar showing in flight distinguish it in particular from the larger coot. Juvenile can be told from juvenile coot by white under tail-coverts and much less white on throat, and from winter dabchick by white under tail-coverts and less frequent diving.

FLOCKING. Not really gregarious, but aggregations of fifty or more will collect together to feed in winter.

HABITAT. All kinds of fresh water with plenty of thick herbage for cover, especially ponds, rivers, marshes and sewage farms, but not much on large lakes or concrete-banked reservoirs; plentiful in town parks; feeds freely on grassland, usually near water.

RANGE AND STATUS. Resident, breeding throughout British Isles; winter visitor, some arriving E coast in autumn.

SABINE'S GULL *Xema sabini* Plate 105

PLUMAGE. White, with silver-grey mantle and forewing and black wing-tip; head and upper neck are dark grey in summer, speckled brown and white in winter; slightly forked tail. Immature is similar, but has head white except for grey crown and whole nape, mantle brownish and dark band at tip of tail. Bill blackish (with yellow tip in adult); legs dark grey; orbital ring vermilion.

STRUCTURE. *Wing length* L. *Ratios:* wing L; tail MS; neck MS; bill MS; legs M.

MOVEMENT. Similar to little gull (above) or a tern.

VOICE. Harsh, grating flight note, not unlike Arctic tern.

FIELD MARKS. A small, tern-like gull, the only one with a forked tail (but juveniles of kittiwake and little gull have tail cleft). Can be told in all plumages by striking wing-pattern (forewing grey, hindwing white, wing-tip black), not to be confused with superficially similar pattern in juveniles of kittiwake and little gull, where the black bar crosses the wing diagonally from the base of the hindwing to the junction of the wing-tip and forewing. Beware especially kittiwake moulting into first summer plumage, which has almost identical wing-pattern. Adult summer is only gull with a grey hood; hood always covers whole nape like summer *little* not summer *black-headed*. Grey nape of immature is a useful additional distinction.

FLOCKING. Sometimes with flocks of terns or black-headed gulls.

HABITAT. Coastal waters; exceptionally on fresh water.

RANGE AND STATUS. Scarce autumn and winter visitor from Arctic; mainly on E coast England. Adults very rare.

BLACK GUILLEMOT *Cepphus grylle* Plates 59, 87, 99, 100 Auk Family

Dovekie; Tystie (Shetland).

PLUMAGE. In summer all black except for a large white wing patch; in winter barred black and white on head and above, white below. Young similar to adult winter. Bill black; legs red.

STRUCTURE. *Wing length* ML. *Ratios:* wing MS; tail VS; neck MS; bill MS/M; legs S.

MOVEMENT. As guillemot (p. 181), but can walk better on land.

VOICE. A rather feeble, high-pitched whistle or whine.

FIELD MARKS. The only sea bird in summer which is all black with a large white wing patch (much larger velvet scoter has much smaller wing patch), and in winter the only one with barred black and white upperparts, but plumages during moults can be very confusing. Red inside of mouth shows when bird calls, sometimes giving impression that it has a red bill. See guillemot for general note on auks.

FLOCKING. The least sociable auk, breeding in very loose colonies and occurring at other times only in small parties; does not associate much with other auks.

HABITAT. As guillemot, but breeds in crevices, not on ledges, and also on islets in sea lochs.

RANGE AND STATUS. Resident, breeding on N and W coasts and isles of Scotland, all coasts Ireland (most commonly in N and W), Isle of Man, and St. Bees Head (Cumberland); in winter at sea offshore from breeding places; rare vagrant elsewhere.

TEAL *Anas crecca* Plates 47, 49, 90 Duck Family

European Teal (N America); a surface-feeding duck; Green-winged Teal is N American race.

PLUMAGE. Drake has chestnut head, with broad green stripe from eye back to nape bordered with cream, vermiculated grey upperparts and flanks with horizontal white line on back above wing (drake green-winged teal has a vertical white mark at side of breast in front of wing instead of this line), speckled breast, and buff patches next to black under tail-coverts. Duck, eclipse drake and juveniles are brown streaked darker. All have a green and black speculum, and all except juvenile a whitish belly. Bill of adult grey, of juvenile pinkish; legs greyish.

STRUCTURE. *Wing length* ML. *Ratios:* wing MS; tail S; neck M; bill MS; legs VS.

MOVEMENT. Similar to mallard (p. 201), but has much quicker flight, especially in flocks, which perform fast collective manoeuvres similar to waders.

VOICE. Call-note of drake a whistling 'crrick, crrick', of duck, a short, high-pitched quack; in spring parties will utter a remarkable series of tinkling bell-like notes.

FIELD MARKS. The smallest native duck, its size distinguishing it at once from all except garganey (p. 177), but leading to possible confusion with medium-sized waders such as redshank when bill and legs cannot be seen in thick cover. Both sexes can be told by their speculum (when visible), and no other duck has drake's green and chestnut head pattern. Drake can also be picked out at a distance by white line above wing and buff patch behind tail-coverts. Drake green-winged teal can best be separated by difference indicated above, also by less prominent cream surround to green eyestripe, but ducks not separable at all.

FLOCKING. Very gregarious, and often flies in compact flocks at high speed; consorts regularly with other surface-feeding ducks, especially mallard.

HABITAT. Mainly inland waters, but will breed at some distance away from them on heaths, woods, etc.; in winter also on estuaries and mudflats; fonder than other ducks of resting in cover at water's edge.

RANGE AND STATUS. Resident, breeding throughout British Isles, but local in S England; many arrive E coast in autumn, some remaining for winter, when common in S England. American green-winged teal is a rare vagrant, but is liable to stray from collections.

BLACK-HEADED GULL *Larus ridibundus* Plates 60, 61, 62, 101, 104, 105, 107 Peewit Gull.

PLUMAGE. White, with silver-grey mantle and wings; wing-tip black, with prominent white streak along forewing. Head (but not nape or neck) is chocolate-brown in summer, white with a few dark smudges in winter. Juvenile has mantle and wings brown speckled darker, with black wing-tips, dark bar at end of white tail, brown patch on crown and white underparts. Immature is more like adult winter, but retains some juvenile features (tail-bar, speckled wings) into first summer, when has brown hood. Bill crimson (orange with black tip in juvenile); legs crimson (yellowish in juvenile); white eyelids.

STRUCTURE. *Wing length* L. *Ratios:* wing L; tail MS; neck MS; bill M; legs M.

MOVEMENT. Flight strong and buoyant over long distances, more wavering and almost tern-like at other times. Swims, and occasionally dives from air; walks, and perches readily on posts, etc.

VOICE. Main note is a harsh 'kwarr' or 'kraah', also 'kwurp' and other harsh cries, which can be deafening at a gullery.

FIELD MARKS. The only gull with red bill and legs (except little gull, above; terns have forked tails); in summer the only white bird with a brown hood not extending on to nape (but see little and Sabine's gulls, above). In winter can also be told at once from both common gull and kittiwake by conspicuous white forewing, white head with darker smudges (not streaks), smaller size and more pointed wings, and from *common* also by no white spots on black wing-tips. For distinctions from winter little gull, see above. Juvenile is browner, and immature has more silver-grey on upperparts than corresponding stages of *common*; see also juveniles of *Sabine's*, *little* and kittiwake (p. 173).

FLOCKING. Highly gregarious, breeding in large gulleries; often in flocks with other gulls. Flocks going to roost often fly in formation.

HABITAT. Breeds on moors, bogs and islands in lochs, also on coastal sandhills, shingle-banks, marshes and sewage farms; otherwise extremely catholic, feeding on farmland, playing fields, parks, railway sidings, and other open spaces and waste ground in towns, as well as on coasts, estuaries and tidal rivers. Roosts on freshwater lakes and reservoirs. Has become a typical urban bird in winter.

RANGE AND STATUS. Resident, breeding commonly over most of Scotland, Ireland, N and Mid-Wales, and N England, more sparingly on E and S coasts England and shores of Bristol Channel, with a few inland colonies, e.g. in Cambridge, Middlesex, Norfolk and Northants. More widespread in winter, both inland and on coast, large numbers arriving E coast every autumn; many non-breeders summer away from breeding colonies.

LONG-TAILED SKUA, immature See *Water: Medium Long*, p. 195

WATER BIRDS: Medium Long

COOT *Fulica atra* Plates 36, 87, 92, 99 Rail Family
Bald Coot.

PLUMAGE. Blackish-grey, with black head and whitish wing-bar. Juvenile is browner, with whitish face, throat and belly. Nestlings have reddish-orange head and neck. Bill white (adult also has white frontal shield); legs greenish, eye red.

STRUCTURE. *Wing length* ML. *Ratios:* wing MS; tail VS; neck M; bill M; legs M.

MOVEMENT. Heavy, laboured flight, low over water, with legs trailing behind; pattering take-off. Much given to quarrelsome swims and chases; bobbing gait on water less noticeable than in moorhen; dives; walks.

VOICE. Loud and rather high-pitched note, 'kowk', 'kewk' or even 'coot' (pronounced with the 'oo' short).

FIELD MARKS. Adult is the only all-black waterfowl with a conspicuous white forehead; more rounded in appearance than ducks. Juvenile is the only waterfowl with all-dark upperparts, all-pale underparts, and no other distinctive features; this plumage is usually moulted before it can overlap with the superficially similar grebes' winter plumage. For distinctions from moorhen, see p. 173.

FLOCKING. Quite large flocks in winter; often alongside ducks.

HABITAT. Breeds on rather larger inland waters than moorhen, and less on rivers, but also needs thick herbage for cover; will breed in town parks. At other times resorts much more than moorhen to large reservoirs and lakes without cover, also regularly on estuaries, in Ireland on inlets of the sea, and occasionally on the sea.

RANGE AND STATUS. Resident, breeding throughout British Isles; also winter visitor, some moving S from N Scotland, others arriving on E coast in autumn.

ARCTIC SKUA, immature See *below*, p. 186

GARGANEY *Anas querquedula* Plates 47, 49, 90, 92 Duck Family

Summer Teal; Cricket Teal; a surface-feeding duck.

PLUMAGE. Drake has dark brown head with broad white streak from above eye down side of neck, blue-grey forewing with long curved scapulars overhanging the wing, brown speckled breast, and grey vermiculated flanks. Duck and juvenile are brown mottled darker, and eclipse drake resembles them but still has blue-grey forewing. All have green speculum. Bill blackish in drake, greyish in duck and juvenile; legs grey.

STRUCTURE. *Wing length* ML. *Ratios:* wing MS; tail S; neck M; bill M; legs VS.

MOVEMENT. Similar to teal (p. 174), but rarely in such large flocks.

VOICE. Spring note of drake is a curious crackling sound, like a match being rattled in a match-box; duck has a low quack.

FIELD MARKS. Our smallest duck except for teal. Drake can be told from all other ducks by white streak on brown head, and in flight also by blue-grey forewing from all except shoveler (which is bluer). Duck can be told from duck teal by white throat, pale spot at base of longer and wider bill and more distinct eyestripe (fine points, only discernible at close range). In flight at a distance can be told in outline from teal at all ages by slenderer appearance, by those thoroughly familiar with teal.

FLOCKING. Occurs in small parties and consorts with other surface-feeding ducks, especially teal.

HABITAT. All kinds of inland and coastal fresh waters, preferring those with good cover during breeding season.

RANGE AND STATUS. Summer visitor, breeding in variable numbers Cambridgeshire and coastal counties from Norfolk to Dorset, and occasionally elsewhere in England, mainly in S; elsewhere a scarce passage migrant.

BLUE-WINGED TEAL *Anas discors* Plate 47 Duck Family

Generally similar to teal (p. 174), but both sexes can be told in flight by bright blue forewing from all likely ducks except shoveler and ornamental cinnamon teal *Anas cyanoptera*, and from drakes of these two drake *blue-wing* is easily told by conspicuous white crescentic mark in front of eye. Duck *blue-wing* cannot be told from duck *cinnamon*, but from duck shoveler can be told by smaller size and bill, and from duck teal by blue forewing. Note that garganey's forewing is blue-grey, which is main distinction of ducks in flight, but drakes can also be told by different pattern of white on head and ducks by *blue-wing's* lack of pale eyestripe. On water drake can be told from drake teal by white crescent on head instead of white line on wing. Rare vagrant from N America, and escape from waterfowl collections.

YELLOW-BILLED, or CHILEAN, TEAL *Anas flavirostris* Plate 49
Duck Family

Resembles duck teal (p. 174), but can be told by vermiculated head and yellow bill; the African yellow-bills *A. undulata* are larger, mallard-type ducks. See also Brown or Chilean Pintail (p. 194). Escape from watcrfowl collections.

MEDITERRANEAN GULL *Larus melanocephalus*

Immature is more like a small common gull (p. 180) than a large *black-headed* (p. 175), with heavy bill and rather jerky flight. Adults have no black on wing-tips, red bill and legs and in summer black not brown hood; immatures have no white on leading edge of wing and larger blackish smudge on face than immature *black-headed*. Has become much more frequent in winter on E, and especially S, coasts of England since about 1950, latterly averaging over a score of occurrences a year.

Mediterranean Gull

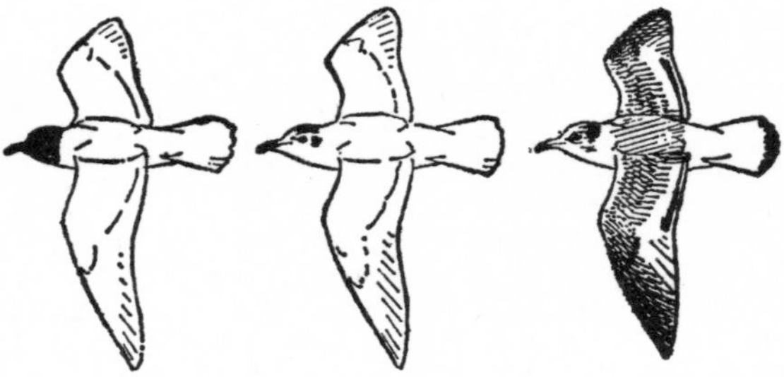

Adult summer **Adult winter** **First summer ("Common Gull" plumage)**

RUDDY DUCK *Oxyura jamaicensis*

A dumpy little white-faced American duck, with a fan-shaped tail cocked upright during display; drakes are rusty red above with black cap and nape and bright blue-grey bill, but ducks are duller and browner; an escape from wildfowl collections, especially on reservoirs in Somerset and the Midlands, sometimes breeding.

FERRUGINOUS DUCK *Aythya nyroca* Plate 48

White-eyed Pochard; a diving duck.

PLUMAGE. Drake is warm chestnut brown, with darker brown back, white belly, wing-bar and under tail-coverts. Duck and eclipse drake are duller. Blackish bill; legs grey; drake's eye white; duck's brown.

STRUCTURE. As scaup (p. 190).

MOVEMENT. Similar to tufted duck (p. 182).

VOICE. Similar to common pochard (p. 188).

FIELD MARKS. Resembles ducks of common pochard and tufted duck, but can normally be told from both by white under tail-coverts; these coverts are very occasionally white in *tufted*, but never so sharply contrasted as in *ferruginous*. Drake further distinguishable by white eye, and richer brown head, neck and breast. Can also be told from common pochard by white wing-bar.

FLOCKING. A small party might occur.

HABITAT. Most likely to occur on inland waters and estuaries.

RANGE AND STATUS. Vagrant from S and Central Europe, most often in E Anglia in autumn and winter and becoming more frequent in recent years; in the past has often escaped from waterfowl collections.

SMEW *Mergus albellus* Plates 47, 88, 91, 92 Duck Family

White Nun (drake); a saw-bill.

PLUMAGE. Drake is mainly white, with black patches on lores and nape, pendent black crest, two black streaks from shoulders to breast, black mantle and wing-tips, grey rump and tail and vermiculated flanks. Duck and immature have chestnut head and nape with white cheeks, grey upperparts and flanks and white wing-bar and underparts. Slightly hooked and serrated grey bill; grey legs; red eye.

STRUCTURE. *Wing length* ML. *Ratios:* wing MS; tail S; neck M; bill MS; legs VS/S. Drake larger than duck.

MOVEMENT. Similar to goosander (p. 206), but wings do not whistle.

VOICE. Duck has a harsh 'karr'.

FIELD MARKS. Drake can be told from all other waterfowl, except albinos, by strikingly white plumage relieved at rest by only a few black markings; in flight it appears much more pied, but even then nothing is at all like it except the much larger shelduck. 'Red-heads' (duck and immature) can be told at once by the conspicuous white cheek beneath the chestnut crown (quite different from the pale cheeks of common scoter, etc., and summer dabchick's small white face patch), and this distinguishes them in particular from any of the smaller grebes with which they might otherwise be confused, owing to their constant diving.

FLOCKING. Gregarious, usually in quite small parties.

HABITAT. All kinds of inland and estuarine waters.

RANGE AND STATUS. Scarce winter visitor, most frequent in S England, especially in Thames valley and Essex, where regular on certain reservoirs.

SOOTY SHEARWATER *Puffinus griseus* Plate 98

Black Shearwater (Yorkshire); Mutton Bird (Australia, New Zealand).

PLUMAGE. All blackish-brown, except for greyish-white underwing. Slightly hooked blackish bill, with tubular nostrils; blackish legs.

STRUCTURE. *Wing length* L. *Ratios:* wing ML; tail S; neck MS; bill ML; legs (does not stand).

MOVEMENT. As great shearwater (p. 185).

FIELD MARKS. One of the three larger shearwaters, its dark underparts distinguish it at once from the other two, and its typical shearwater flight from the larger immature gulls and skuas; can usually be told from the variable western Mediterranean race of the *Manx* (p. 169) by larger size, uniform upperparts and darker underparts.

FLOCKING. Sometimes in very small parties, and with other shearwaters.

HABITAT. The open sea, rarely close enough inshore to be seen from land.

RANGE AND STATUS. Regular autumn visitor from the S Pacific in small numbers, mostly in Atlantic and North Sea (S to Yorks), but sometimes also in the Minch and the English Channel and off Pembrokeshire.

COMMON GULL *Larus canus* Plates 61, 62, 101, 104, 107

Mew Gull; Cobb; Sea Cobb.

PLUMAGE. As herring gull (p. 196), but juvenile has more white on underparts. Bill yellow-green (blackish with pinkish base in juvenile and first winter, grey with dark subterminal band and yellow tip in second winter); legs yellow-green (yellow-flesh in juvenile, grey in second winter); eye whitish or yellowish; orbital ring vermilion in adult.

STRUCTURE. *Wing length* L. *Ratios:* wing L; tail MS; neck MS; bill M; legs S.

MOVEMENT. Flight intermediate between *black-headed* and *herring*; swims, walks and often perches on objects.

VOICE. Main note a high-pitched 'keee-ya', like a rather feeble herring gull; also a gobbling 'kak-kak-kak'.

FIELD MARKS. No other gull has yellow-green bill and legs (but see kittiwake, below). See p. 175 for distinctions from *black-headed*, and p. 196 for *herring*.

FLOCKING AND HABITAT. As black-headed gull, but does not breed on sandhills or sewage farms, and is less typically an urban bird.

RANGE AND STATUS. Resident, breeding commonly in Scotland (except SE), W coast Ireland (Donegal to Kerry), and in England at Dungeness; otherwise common winter visitor from Continent, especially on E and SE coasts England, habitually feeding some distance inland in some districts.

KITTIWAKE *Rissa tridactyla* Plates 61, 101, 104, 105 Gull Family

Tarrock (young).

PLUMAGE. White, with silver-grey mantle and wings and black wing-tips; crown and nape grey in winter. Young have black bar on back of neck, black line from wing-tip to carpal joint and thence diagonally across to base of hindwing, also black bar at tip of slightly cleft tail. Bill greenish-yellow (black in juvenile, greenish with dark tip in immature); legs blackish; orbital ring orange.

STRUCTURE. *Wing length* L. *Ratios:* wing ML; tail MS; neck MS; bill MS; legs S.

MOVEMENT. Graceful, buoyant flight, more like *black-headed* than common gull; habitually follows ships. Swims, dives from air or water, walks.

VOICE. At breeding colonies air is filled with deafening cries of 'kitt-ee-wayke', also a low 'uk-uk-uk' and a wailing note not unlike a baby crying; otherwise rather silent.

FIELD MARKS. The only adult gull with black wing-tips without white spots, except for *black-headed*, which also has a broad white blaze on forewing, and the only one with uniform grey head and nape in winter. Blackish legs are additional distinction from *common*, and together with larger size and yellowish bill from winter *black-headed*. Tarrocks can be told from all other sea birds by the dark bar on the neck, from all except the much smaller *little* by the striking wing-pattern, and from all except *little* and *Sabine's* by the cleft tail.

FLOCKING. Gregarious at all times, breeding in colonies alongside auks, but not flocking much with other gulls.

HABITAT. Breeds on cliffs and on ledges in sea caves, also exceptionally on buildings by the sea and on shingle; otherwise mainly in offshore zone, though flocks occasionally visit coast and breeding birds will even bathe in freshwater lochs near sea; very occasional inland on passage and after storms.

RANGE AND STATUS. Resident, breeding very locally on coast of E, SW and NW England and in Wales and Isle of Man, locally round Scottish and more commonly round Irish coasts; common offshore in winter; accidental inland.

RAZORBILL *Alca torda* Plates 59, 97, 99, 100 Auk Family

Razor-billed Auk (N America).

PLUMAGE. Brown-black on head and above with white wing-bar; white below. Adult winter and juvenile have white cheeks and throat; summer adult has white line from bill to eye. Bill of adult is stout, flattened in vertical plane, slightly hooked, and blackish with curved white line at base at right angles to line on face; bill of young is much less stout and Roman-nosed; legs black.

STRUCTURE. *Wing length* ML. *Ratios:* wing MS; tail S; neck MS; bill MS (juvenile), M (adult); legs S.

MOVEMENT. As guillemot (below).

VOICE. A harsh, growling 'karrrr' at nest; juvenile has a plaintive whistle.

FIELD MARKS. At close range can easily be told from all other seabirds by remarkably shaped bill and white lines on bill and face. For general note on auks and distinctions from guillemot, see below; for distinctions from puffin, see p. 171 and of juvenile from little auk, see p. 168.

FLOCKING AND HABITAT. As guillemot, but in looser colonies.

RANGE AND STATUS. As guillemot.

GUILLEMOT *Uria aalge* Plates 59, 97, 99, 100 Auk Family

Scout; Willock; Bridled Guillemot (variety); Atlantic, or Common, Murre (N America).

PLUMAGE. Dark brown head and above, with white wing-bar; white below. Northern race is darker and may be black on back. Adult winter and juvenile have white cheeks and throat, with black stripe back from eye. Bridled variety has white ring round eye. Bill black; legs yellowish.

STRUCTURE. *Wing length* ML. *Ratios:* wing S; tail VS; neck MS; bill M; legs S/M.

MOVEMENT. Fast, direct flight, low over water, with whirring wing-beats and sometimes legs outstretched like a flying squirrel; swims, and dives from water. On land has an upright posture, but shuffles awkwardly.

VOICE. A growling 'arrr'; juvenile has a shrill whistle.

FIELD MARKS. Auks can be told from other sea birds by their whirring flight, frequent diving, short tails and black and white appearance. Guillemot can be told from razorbill at all times by long straight bill, in summer also by lack of white lines on face and bill, and in winter also by presence of black line on face. In good light paler brown plumage should also be evident, but some birds of northern race (breeding in northern isles, wintering farther S) have back as black as razorbill, though head is still browner. At close range bridled variety can at once be told by narrow white ring round eye. For distinctions from other auks, see black guillemot (p. 174) and puffin (p. 171) and little auk (p. 168).

FLOCKING. Breeds in colonies; at other times in loose flocks and parties, often with other auks.

HABITAT. Breeds on cliffs with ledges, and marine islands; in winter on the open sea, but occasionally inshore; inland only as a storm-blown waif.

RANGE AND STATUS. Resident, breeding on many suitable cliffs, but not between Flamborough Head (Yorks) and Needles (Isle of Wight); northern race replaces southern N from St. Abb's Head (Berwickshire) on E coast and from Inner Hebrides on W coast. In winter at sea off all coasts.

TUFTED DUCK *Aythya fuligula* Plates 51, 88, 90, 93

A diving duck.

PLUMAGE. Drake is black, with white flanks, belly and wing-bar, and black crest. Duck, eclipse drake and young are mainly brown, usually with whitish flanks and belly and always with white wing-bar. Ducks have a short, rather obscure crest, and some have a small white patch at base of bill. Grey-blue bill and legs; yellow eye.

STRUCTURE. *Wing length* ML. *Ratios:* wing MS; tail VS; neck M; bill M; legs S.

MOVEMENT. Diving ducks have more rapid and whirring flight than surface-feeders, with feet sticking out beyond tail; when taking off they patter over the surface like a coot instead of jumping up like a mallard. Gait on land clumsy, legs being set fairly far back on the body; swims readily and habitually dives, sometimes with a preliminary jump; occasionally up-ends.

VOICE. Drake has a bubbling note in breeding season, and duck a growling 'kurrr'.

FIELD MARKS. Drake is the only duck with a pendent black crest, and can be picked out at a considerable distance by its strongly contrasted black upper-parts and white flanks, the black back serving to distinguish it from the larger drake scaup. Duck is rather variable, and may show hardly any white on underparts in summer, but can always be told from duck common pochard by slenderer build, yellow eye and white wing-bar; for distinctions from duck scaup, see p. 190. Beware wildfowlers' name of 'goldeneye' for tufted duck; true goldeneye is larger and has characteristic 'buffle-shaped' head, white neck and a white spot on face of drake. White face patch, when present in duck, is always smaller than duck scaup's. Hybrids with common pochard can be very confusing, somewhat resembling a small scaup.

FLOCKING. Highly gregarious, often consorts with common pochard and coot.

HABITAT. All kinds of inland waters, preferring those with plenty of cover in the breeding season; regularly on quite small lakes in town parks; rarely on estuaries or sea except in hard weather.

RANGE AND STATUS. Resident, breeding locally throughout British Isles, though only sporadically on W coast Great Britain and in SE Ireland; otherwise widespread passage migrant and winter visitor.

MANDARIN DUCK *Aix galericulata* Plates 52, 54

A perching duck.

PLUMAGE. Drake is highly variegated: forehead green, crown purple, crest copper-red becoming green and purple, white on sides of crown and crest, orange-chestnut side-whiskers, upperparts olive, tail black, black and white shoulder-plumes fronting orange-chestnut wing-fans, whitish wing-quills, blue hindwing, pale rufous chin and throat with throat striped white, breast purple with two white lines down the side, flanks yellow, underparts white, bill reddish-pink; legs reddish-yellow. Duck is grey-brown, with crest, white line at base of bill, narrow white ring round eye, grey crown and hind-neck, white line on back, blue hindwing and wing-tips, white underparts (except breast), black bill, dull yellow legs. Eclipse and immature drakes resemble duck, but can be told by deep reddish bill.

STRUCTURE. *Wing length* ML. *Ratios:* wing M; tail S; neck M; bill MS; legs S.

MOVEMENT. Swift, direct flight; swims readily; feeds mainly on land, but up-ends when in water and dives when wounded.

VOICE. Various squeaking, clucking, squealing and whistling notes.

FIELD MARKS. Strikingly variegated plumage of drake is only likely to be confused with Carolina duck, harlequin duck or red-breasted goose, all of which are either very rare vagrants or also escapes; its general colour is more predominantly orange-brown than the other three. None of these have the side-whiskers or the fan-like wing-feathers of the *mandarin*, and only the *Carolina* also has a crest; *Carolina* also has white chin and fore-neck, as against *mandarin's* white sides to crown and crest; both *harlequin* and *red-breasted* have prominent white patches at base of bill, and latter is larger and has only black, white and red in its colour pattern. Duck *mandarin* closely resembles duck *Carolina*, and can only be told from it by more extensive white round eye; both can be told from all other grey-brown ducks by whitish spotting on breast and substantial amount of blue on wing-tips and hindwing.

FLOCKING. Small parties might occur.

HABITAT. Most likely to be seen on inland waters, especially pools surrounded by woodland.

RANGE AND STATUS. Escape from waterfowl collections, but easily establishes itself; breeds regularly in Berkshire and Surrey, and also breeds or has bred in recent years in Cumberland, Bedfordshire, Shropshire and Kent.

LONG-TAILED DUCK *Clangula hyemalis* Plates 88, 92

Calloo (Scotland); Old Squaw (N America); a diving sea duck.

PLUMAGE. Summer drake is all brown except for white face patch, belly, flanks and under tail-coverts; eclipse drake similar but no long tail; winter drake also has white forehead, crown, nape, shoulders, upper mantle, scapulars, chin, throat and upper breast. Summer duck is brown above and whitish on face and underparts; winter duck is much whiter about head. Young similar to winter duck. Bill, black with red tip in drake, blackish in duck; legs greyish.

STRUCTURE. *Wing length* ML. *Ratios:* wing S (drake), MS (duck); tail MS (drake), VS (duck); neck M; bill MS; legs VS/S.

MOVEMENT. Has a characteristic swinging flight, in which wings are not raised much above level of body; swims buoyantly, habitually dives; upright carriage on land.

VOICE. Drake constantly utters loud call best rendered as 'ardelow-ar-ardelow'.

FIELD MARKS. Drake can be told at all times by long pointed tail from all other waterfowl except pintail drake, which has longer bill and neck and no white on head (but beware confusion of names by wildfowlers, who will call *long-tailed* 'pintail' and both 'sea pheasant'). Short bill is distinctive character at all ages and sexes, and lack of any wing-bar in flight is also important. Except for summer drakes, *long-tailed* always has a rather pied appearance; the only other ducks with pale cheeks are ducks of red-crested pochard (p. 199), common scoter (p. 191) and smew (p. 179).

FLOCKING. Gregarious, but not going much with other ducks.

HABITAT. In winter usually fairly well out at sea, but quite often offshore on open coasts; uncommon in estuaries and even more so on fresh water; very occasional on lochs and lochans in summer, more frequent at sea.

RANGE AND STATUS. Winter visitor, mainly to E coast and Scottish isles; has bred at least once and probably more often, N isles.

RED-NECKED GREBE *Podiceps griseigena* Plates 46, 99, 110

Holboell's Grebe (N America).

PLUMAGE. In winter grey-brown above and white cheeks and wing-bar, and white below. In summer darker above with chestnut neck and indistinct ear-tufts. Bill black, with yellow base, occasionally all yellow; legs blackish.

STRUCTURE. *Wing length* ML. *Ratios:* wing S; tail VS; neck L; bill M; legs (does not stand).

MOVEMENT. As great crested grebe (p. 190), but walks better.

VOICE. A high-pitched 'keck, keck'.

FIELD MARKS. A smaller edition of the *great crested*, easily told from it in summer by the chestnut neck and lack of head ornaments, and in winter still distinguishable by stockier build, black and yellow bill, lack of stripe over eye, and the dark of the crown coming down below the eye and shading off gradually into the white of the cheeks. Confusion with other grebes and divers unlikely, except for winter *Slavonian*, which is smaller and dumpier and dark of crown not coming below eye, and summer *red-throated*, which is larger, has no wing-bar or white cheeks, and has most of neck grey and red patch only on front. Duck saw-bills are larger, with longer tail, no white cheeks and much more prominent wing-bars.

HABITAT. Salt water, mostly in estuaries and close inshore; occasionally straggles to fresh water.

RANGE AND STATUS. Winter visitor, mainly to E coast, Forth to Kent; usually in small numbers, but after hard weather in Europe sometimes quite common and straying inland.

GREAT SHEARWATER *Puffinus gravis* Plate 98

Greater Shearwater (N America).

PLUMAGE. Brown above, with pale line or mark on wing during moult, and white upper tail-coverts; white of breast extends on to nape to give head a marked cap; underparts white with brown patch on belly. Slightly hooked blackish bill, with tubular nostrils; legs brownish.

STRUCTURE. *Wing length* L. *Ratios:* wing ML; tail MS; neck MS; bill ML; legs (does not stand).

MOVEMENT. Resembles Manx shearwater (p. 169), but flaps more often in flight; dives from both air and water.

VOICE. Feeding birds utter harsh calls.

FIELD MARKS. One of the larger shearwaters, easily told from other sea birds of same size by characteristic flight, and from superficially similar brown immature gulls by white underparts. Dark patch on belly is a poor field mark; more easily told from *sooty* by white underparts, and from *Cory's* by capped effect, white sides of neck and dark bill. Can also be told from markedly smaller *Manx* by capped effect and white at base of tail.

FLOCKING. Often gregarious well out to sea, sometimes with *Manx* and *sooty*.

HABITAT. The open sea, and occasionally inshore.

RANGE AND STATUS. Mainly an autumn visitor, its post-breeding circuit of the Atlantic from Tristan da Cunha (its only known breeding place) taking it N up the W side of the ocean, some, probably mainly non-breeding birds, returning down the E side between August and November. Most often seen off N and W coasts; common off Rockall in June.

CORY'S SHEARWATER *Puffinus diomedea* Plate 98

North Atlantic Great Shearwater.

PLUMAGE. Brown above and on sides of neck, with small white patch on upper tail-coverts; white beneath. Slightly hooked, yellowish bill, with tubular nostrils; pale flesh-coloured legs.

STRUCTURE AND MOVEMENT. As great shearwater (above).

FIELD MARKS. Very similar to *great* (above); can be told from western Mediterranean race of *Manx* (p. 169) by uniform brown upperparts, white underparts and patch at base of tail, yellow bill and larger size.

FLOCKING. Might be seen in small parties.

HABITAT. The open sea.

RANGE AND STATUS. Regular in very small numbers off coasts of SW England and S Ireland in late summer and early autumn; scarce elsewhere.

IVORY GULL *Pagophila eburnea* Plate 104

PLUMAGE. All white, adult with breast suffused pink; immature has forehead, cheeks and throat lead-grey, dark spots on upperparts, wing-tips and tail-bar black. Bill of adult yellow with red tip, of immature, greyish freckled with white tip; legs black; orbital ring vermilion.

STRUCTURE. *Wing length* L. *Ratios:* wing ML; tail MS; neck MS; bill MS; legs M.

MOVEMENT. Flight buoyant and tern-like; swims, runs and walks.

VOICE. Harsh, discordant and tern-like.

FIELD MARKS. The only pure white sea bird, with no grey mantle or wings and no black wing-tips, it looks not unlike a white pigeon, and is smaller than both *glaucous* and *Iceland*, which also have no black wing-tips, but are silver-grey above. Plumage pattern of immature is also unique, no other white sea bird having grey face, or dark spots on white upperparts. Pink tinge on breast of adult fades rapidly after death.

HABITAT. The open sea, but may be driven on to coast or even inland by storms.

RANGE AND STATUS. Rare autumn to spring vagrant, most often in northern isles.

ARCTIC SKUA *Stercorarius parasiticus* Plates 63, 106 and p. 213.

Richardson's Skua; Boatswain or Bosun; Parasitic Jaeger (N America).

PLUMAGE. Dark form and young are all dark brown, except for whitish patch towards wing-tip. Pale form has cheeks, neck and underparts creamy white, and rest dark brown, with cheeks and neck barred dark brown in winter; wide variation in the relative amounts of brown and white. Two common intermediate forms are brown with distinct dark cap and paler cheeks, and brown with yellow neck-ring. Adult has elongated central tail-feathers straight and pointed; immature has them just perceptibly projecting. Slightly hooked blackish bill with black tip (grey-blue with dark tip in juvenile); legs black (blue-grey in juvenile).

STRUCTURE. *Wing length* L. *Ratios:* wing ML/L; tail M/ML; neck MS; bill M; legs S/M.

MOVEMENT. Graceful, buoyant and rather hawk-like flight; habitually chases terns and gulls till they disgorge their food. Swims and walks. Attacks visitors to breeding grounds.

VOICE. On breeding ground has a wailing 'ka-aaow' and a 'tuk-tuk'.

FIELD MARKS. Intermediate in size between *pomarine* and long-tailed skuas, adult can be told from *pomarine* by projecting tail-feathers being straight and pointed, and from *long-tailed* by these being much shorter (see also p. 195). Immatures can only be separated from each other by size, if more than one species should chance to be present (*Arctic* is, however, much the likeliest to be seen). Dark forms and immatures of all skuas can always be told from immature gulls by pale patch towards wing-tip (very variable in *Arctic* and sometimes obscure; beware also exceptional individual gulls with similar patches) and even more readily by their piratical habits; the persistence and skill with which they fly down their victims is quite distinct from the desultory mutual robbery of immature gulls; skuas usually look much darker than gulls.

FLOCKING. Breeds in loose colonies; accompanies migrating flocks of gulls and terns.

HABITAT. Breeds on barren moorlands; at other times at sea, inshore in autumn, but mainly offshore and in open ocean; rare inland except as storm-blown waif.

RANGE AND STATUS. Summer visitor, breeding on Scottish isles S to Inner Hebrides, and on mainland in Caithness; also passage migrant in autumn, commonest on E coast; rare in winter and spring.

POMARINE SKUA, immature See p. 194

WIGEON *Anas penelope* Plates 48, 50, 90, 91 Duck Family

Whew; Whistler; European Widgeon (N America); a surface-feeding duck.

PLUMAGE. Drake is mainly vermiculated grey, with chestnut head, buff crown and forehead, white forewing (absent in first winter drakes), pinkish-brown breast, and black under tail-coverts with white patch in front of them. Duck and juvenile are brown, streaked darker, with greyish forewing. Eclipse drake resembles them but retains white forewing. All have green speculum and white belly; grey-blue bill with black tip; legs variable, grey-blue, greenish-grey or yellowish-brown.

STRUCTURE. *Wing length* L. *Ratios:* wing M; tail S/MS; neck M; bill MS/M; legs S.

MOVEMENT. Flight less swift than teal but faster than mallard, with wing-beats coming more below plane of body; otherwise as mallard (p. 201).

VOICE. Characteristic 'whee-oo' call reveals presence of drake even in fog or at a distance; duck has a purring note.

FIELD MARKS. Drake can be told from all other native ducks by combination of buff crown, chestnut head, white forewing (showing as white patch on closed wing) and grey vermiculated upperparts, and can be picked out at a considerable distance by its shortish bill and conspicuous white forewing; drake common pochard has no buff forehead and no white on wing. Duck can be told from duck mallard by shorter bill, more peaked forehead, more pointed tail, slenderer appearance and green speculum; for distinctions from duck pintail, see p. 200, and from other brown ducks, see mallard (p. 201). Oval white patch on belly is conspicuous in flight.

FLOCKING. Gregarious, often consorting with other surface-feeding ducks; also feeds on eel-grass among brent geese.

HABITAT. Breeds on inland waters in moorland districts, occasionally on coastal marshes; in winter on all kinds of fresh and salt water, but especially large lakes and reservoirs, estuaries and mudflats; flocks will graze in fields.

RANGE AND STATUS. Resident, breeding in many parts of Scotland N of the Forth-Clyde line, and more locally S to the Border; and in N and E England and N Wales; has bred Ireland; otherwise common winter visitor and passage migrant throughout British Isles.

AMERICAN WIGEON or Baldpate *Anas americana* Plate 48

Duck Family

Generally similar to wigeon (above), but drake can be easily told from drake wigeon and both sexes Chiloe wigeon by head pattern (white forehead and crown, broad green stripe from eye back to nape, and speckled buff cheeks and neck), also by darker flanks contrasting more strongly with white patch in front of black under tail-coverts. Duck cannot be told from duck wigeon unless white (not grey) axillaries can be seen. Both sexes can be told from all surface-feeding ducks except wigeons by prominent white forewing in flight. Very rare as genuine vagrant from N America, but not infrequently escapes from waterfowl collections.

COMMON POCHARD *Aythya ferina* Plates 48, 52, 89, 93 Duck Family
Dun-bird; close ally of American Red-head and Canvasback; a diving duck.

PLUMAGE. Drake has bright chestnut head and neck, dark grey vermiculated upperparts, black breast and upper tail-coverts, and whitish underparts. Duck, eclipse drake and juvenile are grey-brown above and paler beneath. Bill grey-blue with blackish base and tip; legs grey; eye red.

STRUCTURE. *Wing length* ML. *Ratios:* wing MS; tail VS; neck M; bill M; legs S.

MOVEMENT. Similar to tufted duck (p. 182).

VOICE. Rather silent, but drake has a wheezy, moaning note, especially when courting, and duck has a harsh 'kurr'.

FIELD MARKS. Drake is the only duck with whole head and neck chestnut and grey upperparts, and lacks the buff crown and white forewing of the drake wigeon; similarly patterned drake scaup has black head and neck. Lack of any salient marking is best distinction of duck, from which duck *tufted* and scaup can be told by their white wing-bar in flight, and by their white underparts and white forehead respectively; also much dumpier than *tufted*.

FLOCKING. Highly gregarious, often associating with *tufted*. Hybrids with *tufted* can be very confusing, resembling scaup.

HABITAT. Breeds on inland waters with good cover; in winter on all kinds of fresh water, including lakes in town parks, but rarely on salt water.

RANGE AND STATUS. Resident, breeding locally in many parts of Scotland and E and S England, also Anglesey and Ireland; otherwise widespread winter visitor.

GOLDENEYE *Bucephala clangula* Plates 47, 51, 88, 91, 93 Duck Family
Morillon; Whistler; American Goldeneye (N America); a diving sea duck.

PLUMAGE. Drake has black head (glossed green) and upperparts, with white face patch. Duck and immature have chocolate brown head and grey-brown upperparts and breast-band. All have neck (grey-brown in immature), hind-wing and underparts white. Blue-black bill, duck having yellow patch at tip; legs orange-yellow; eye yellow.

STRUCTURE. *Wing length* ML. *Ratios:* wing MS; tail S; neck M; bill M; legs S. Drake larger than duck.

MOVEMENT. Similar to other diving ducks (see tufted duck, p. 182), but rises more directly from water, like surface-feeding ducks, and wings make a loud singing or whistling note.

VOICE. Rather silent, but duck has a guttural grunt.

FIELD MARKS. Striking, peaked appearance of head, distinctly more triangular than most other ducks, is outstanding field mark at all ages, but white neck and broad white wing-bars are both important, and prominent white spot between bill and eye distinguishes drake from all other ducks (but beware smaller spot on face of much smaller summer dabchick). Ducks can be told from larger goosander and red-breasted merganser by shape of head, shorter bill and no white chin, while smaller duck smew has white cheeks and more elongated head. Beware local name of 'goldeneye' for tufted duck.

FLOCKING. Gregarious, but does not go much with other ducks.

HABITAT. Coastal and estuarine waters, and large inland lakes, reservoirs and rivers.

RANGE AND STATUS. Winter visitor throughout British Isles, especially Firth of Forth; non-breeders, sometimes summer in Scotland.

FULMAR *Fulmarus glacialis* Plates 61, 101, 104, 107 Shearwater Family
Fulmar Petrel; Mollymawk.

PLUMAGE. White head and underparts, silver-grey upperparts; in worn plumage wings are speckled brown. 'Blue' form has head and underparts dark grey-blue; intermediate forms have head dark with pale grey-blue underparts, or head pale grey-blue with white underparts. Slightly hooked yellow bill, yellowest at tip, with darker tubular nostrils; legs variable, but mostly flesh-coloured.

STRUCTURE. *Wing length* L. *Ratios:* wing ML; tail MS; neck MS; bill M; legs M.

MOVEMENT. Has typical shearwater flight with rigid wings (see Manx shearwater, p. 169), and spends most of time gliding, but flaps more often than shearwaters and rises higher into the air. Habitually follows ships; swims readily, and will both dive and up-end; shuffling gait like shearwaters, but occasionally stands on toes.

VOICE. Various guttural growling, chuckling and grunting sounds, sometimes heard away from the nest.

FIELD MARKS. At first glance is very like silver-grey gulls of *herring* type, but can quickly be told from them by rigid wings, typical shearwater flight, no black wing-tips, and at close range tubular nostrils; can be told from all shearwaters by white head and much paler upperparts. Typical blue fulmars are the only sea birds with dark blue-grey head and underparts, and intermediates can be told from gulls and shearwaters as above.

FLOCKING. Nests in colonies; often in loose parties at sea.

HABITAT. Breeds on cliffs (sometimes quite low ones) and occasionally on crags a few miles inland and even buildings; otherwise seen only at sea, and inland only as a storm-blown waif.

RANGE AND STATUS. Resident, breeding on almost all cliffed coasts, but still very local in SE half of England. Frequents open sea all round British Isles, but mainly on Atlantic side; blue form occurs regularly in Shetland seas in winter, but is a straggler elsewhere.

GREAT CRESTED GREBE *Podiceps cristatus* Plates 47, 99, 110, 111
Diver (Provincial).

PLUMAGE. Grey-brown above with pale wing-bar, white below. Adult has dark double-horned crest and rufous tippets in summer, white cheeks in winter. Juvenile has head, neck and (when quite small) upperparts striped. Red bill and eye; greenish legs.

STRUCTURE. *Wing length* ML. *Ratios:* wing S; tail VS; neck L; bill M/ML; legs (does not stand except on nest).

MOVEMENT. Like other grebes, has rather weak but direct flight, with neck stretched straight out in front and held rather below level of body, and longish legs trailed behind, giving a cigar-shaped outline not unlike saw-bills. Has a pattering take-off; swims, and dives from water. In spring has a characteristic form of display in which two birds face each other on the water and wag their tippeted heads. Has a shuffling gait, but leaves water only to nest or occasionally to sun-bathe at very edge of water.

VOICE. Several harsh trumpeting, barking and grating notes; hunger call of young is a shrill, piping 'pew-pew'.

FIELD MARKS. Unmistakable in summer, when it is the only waterfowl with a double-horned crest and rufous tippets; in winter is substantially smaller than all divers except *red-throated* (p. 200) and larger than all grebes except *red-necked* (p. 184), but beware local name of 'diver'. Has shorter tail and much less conspicuous wing-bars than the saw-bills. The long neck is often not visible when bird is hunched up resting on the water; the wing-bar shows only in flight. The half- and nearly full-grown young are the only waterfowl of their size with striped head and neck.

FLOCKING. In loose associations rather than flocks; exceptionally breeds in colonies.

HABITAT. Breeds on inland waters, including slow-flowing rivers, with plenty of cover, and usually more than 5-7 acres in extent; in winter on all kinds of fresh, brackish and salt water, especially reservoirs and estuaries.

RANGE AND STATUS. Resident, with a breeding population of some 3,000 pairs; breeds almost throughout England and Ireland, but locally in Scotland and Wales and not in Isle of Man; in winter more generally distributed.

SCAUP *Aythya marila* Plates 51, 88, 92, 93 Duck Family
Greater Scaup Duck (N America); a diving duck.

PLUMAGE. Drake has black head, breast, tail and tail-coverts and vermiculated grey back. Duck and immature are brown, with large white patch round base of bill. Eclipse drake is brown, with traces of grey remaining on mantle. All have white wing-bar, flanks and belly. Bill and legs grey-blue; eye yellow.

STRUCTURE. *Wing length* ML. *Ratios:* wing S; tail VS; neck M; bill M; legs S.

MOVEMENT. Similar to tufted duck (p. 182).

VOICE. Rather silent, but duck has a harsh 'karr, karr, karr'.

FIELD MARKS. Black head and breast contrasted with grey back, and white patch round base of bill are hallmarks of drake and duck respectively. Drake can be told from smaller drake *tufted* by grey back, from drake common pochard by black head and neck, and from drake goldeneye by black neck and no white spot on face. Duck can be told from all diving ducks except some duck *tufted* by its white face patch, and from those *tufted* which also have a white face patch by larger size and the fact that the scaup's white extends back nearly to the eye. Immature drakes of the two species can usually be told by their gradual assumption of adult plumage on the back, but immature ducks may not be separable in the field if size comparison is not possible. Beware hybrids between *tufted* and common pochard, which can look like small scaup.

FLOCKING. Highly gregarious, and often with other diving ducks.

HABITAT. The sea, especially shallow bays and estuaries; also not infrequently on inland waters.

RANGE AND STATUS. Winter visitor throughout British Isles, but less common in Wales and England S of Thames; has bred in Outer Hebrides and mainland of N Scotland; summering birds are not infrequent on sea and inland lochs in NW Scotland and W Ireland, and may well occasionally breed.

COMMON SCOTER *Melanitta nigra* Plates 51, 87, 89 Duck Family
Black Duck; Whilk; American Scoter (N America); a diving sea duck.

PLUMAGE. Drake is all black. Duck and young are blackish-brown with a whitish cheek and belly. Bill of drake is black with a knob and an orange patch in the middle of the upper mandible, of duck blackish (sometimes with a narrow orange stripe); legs blackish-brown.

STRUCTURE. *Wing length* ML. *Ratios:* wing MS; tail S; neck M; bill ML; legs S.

MOVEMENT. Similar to eider (p. 203), but much less often on land.

VOICE. Drake has a high, piping note mainly associated with courtship, and duck a typical diving-duck growl.

FIELD MARKS. Drake can be told from all other ducks by all-black plumage relieved only by orange mark on bill; often has tail cocked up on water. Duck can be told from all except ducks of red-crested pochard (which has a white wing-bar) and long-tailed duck (which has much whiter underparts and shorter bill) by whitish face below eye; 'red-head' smews have much whiter face and are white below. Beware other ducks seen against the light, as it is often remarkably hard to be sure how black an apparently black duck really is.

FLOCKING. Gregarious; often accompanied by velvet scoters.

HABITAT. Breeds on inland lochs; in winter frequents coastal waters, often well out at sea, flying low over water in long strings, occasional on fresh water.

RANGE AND STATUS. Resident, breeding in a few places in N Scotland, N Isles and Inner Hebrides, and Lough Erne in Ireland; otherwise common winter visitor on all coasts, occurring inland in small numbers on spring and autumn passage; non-breeding birds regularly summer off E and W coasts Great Britain.

BAHAMA PINTAIL *Anas bahamensis* Plate 49 Duck Family Resembles teal (p. 000) in general appearance and habits, but can be told from all other likely ducks by combination of small size, dark crown and hind-neck, white rest of head and neck, pointed tail, and red patches at base of bill—

the bill patches are sufficient if they can be seen. Resembles brown pintail (p. 200) on the wing, but can be easily told by head pattern and buff tail. A favourite ornamental waterfowl sometimes kept fully-winged.

Red-billed Whistling Duck

WHISTLING, or TREE, DUCKS

Dendrocygna Ornamental waterfowl, notable for long legs and necks, unduck-like upright stance and owl-like flight. Four species sometimes kept full-winged: FULVOUS *D. bicolor* is reddish-brown with white at base of tail and blue-grey bill and legs; JAVAN *D. javanica* is brownish with blue-grey sheen on mantle, and blue-grey legs; WHITE-FACED *D. viduata* is white on head and throat, except for black nape, and has chestnut neck and blackish legs; RED-BILLED *D. autumnalis* is brown, with grey breast and cheeks, black belly, greater part of wing white, and pink bill and legs.

CAROLINA DUCK, Wood Duck or Summer Duck *Aix sponsa* Plates 52, 54

Resembles mandarin duck (p. 183) in general appearance and habits, duck being only distinguishable by more white round eye. Highly distinctive drake is variegated, with mainly green and white head and crest, white throat and foreneck, purplish breast, bronzy green upperparts, blue patch on hindwing and blue wing-tips; for distinctions from drake *mandarin*, harlequin duck and red-breasted goose, see *mandarin*. Escape from waterfowl collections, and is full-winged and breeding in Surrey, Bedfordshire and Gloucestershire.

GADWALL *Anas strepera* Plates 50, 52, 91 Duck Family

A surface-feeding duck.

PLUMAGE. Drake mainly grey-brown, with vermiculations on mantle and crescentic grey bars on breast, white belly, black tail-coverts, and a chestnut patch on the wing. Duck and eclipse drake are pale brown with heavy darker streaks, and white belly. Juvenile similar, but often lacks white belly. All have a black and white speculum. Bill of drake grey, of duck dark horn with orange sides, of juvenile yellow; legs of adult dull orange, of juvenile yellow.

STRUCTURE. *Wing length* L. *Ratios:* wing MS; tail S; neck M; bill M; legs S.

MOVEMENT. Similar to mallard (p. 201), but flight rather more rapid.

VOICE. Drake has a deep, nasal croak, 'nhek'; duck has a softer quack than mallard.

FIELD MARKS. Can be told from all other native ducks by black and white speculum coupled with white belly, both showing up well in flight, and speculum also when wings are moved at rest. Drake also differs from other ducks with vermiculated grey mantles in its grey-brown head (some tending to grey, others to brown) and crescentic marks on breast. Duck is smaller and has more peaked forehead and more pointed wings than duck mallard; for additional distinctions from other brown ducks, see mallard. Beware name of 'gadwall' for duck and young pintail in NE England.

FLOCKING. Gregarious, and often goes with other surface-feeding ducks.

HABITAT. Fresh waters of all kinds; breeds on small lakes, lochs, meres and reservoirs.

RANGE AND STATUS. Resident, breeding in several parts of Scotland, mainly in N and Forth area; in England several colonies of introduced birds, Cumberland, E Anglia, Essex coast, Gloucestershire, Surrey; has bred Ireland; otherwise rather scarce and local winter visitor, and escape from collections of ornamental waterfowl.

SHOVELER *Spatula clypeata* Plates 50, 53, 90, 94 Duck Family

Spoonbill; Shoveller (N America); a surface-feeding duck.

PLUMAGE. Drake has dark green head and neck, white breast and side of mantle, chestnut flanks and belly, and black under tail-coverts with white patch in front of them. Duck and juvenile are brown streaked darker. Eclipse drake is similar, but may keep much chestnut on belly. All have pale blue forewing and green and white speculum. Spatulate, blackish bill, pinkish in juvenile; orange legs; drake has yellow eye.

STRUCTURE. *Wing length* ML. *Ratios:* wing S; tail VS; neck M; bill L; legs S.

MOVEMENT. Not unlike a large, clumsy teal in flight, but big bill always makes it look top-heavy; same effect also apparent on the water, where its typical attitude is with head well forward and bill touching the surface; otherwise as mallard (p. 201).

VOICE. Not a vocal bird, but drake has a call-note, 'took, took', and duck a double quack.

FIELD MARKS. Long, spoon-shaped bill is the shoveler's hallmark at all times, also drake's yellow eye, which no other surface-feeding duck has. Drake's head looks black at a distance, contrasting with the white breast (shared with drake pintail); pale blue forewing, shared only by drake garganey, is also distinctive. Duck closely resembles duck mallard, except for pale blue forewing, green speculum, heavy bill and head-forward attitude; see mallard for distinctions from other brown ducks.

FLOCKING. Gregarious; often goes with other surface-feeding ducks.

HABITAT. Breeds on inland and coastal fresh waters with plenty of cover and shallow muddy water; in winter on any shallow fresh or brackish water, and occasionally on salt water.

RANGE AND STATUS. Resident, breeding locally throughout British Isles, including most English counties; many migrate to Ireland and Continent in winter; also widespread passage migrant and winter visitor, mainly in S.

CHILOE WIGEON *Anas sibilatrix* Plate 53 Duck Family

Resembles wigeon (above) in general appearance and habits, but can be told from all other likely ducks of same size by white face, rest of head and neck black (with dark green patch back from eye to nape), and rufous flanks; both sexes alike. Of other white-faced ducks, female grey-headed shelduck is larger and otherwise mainly buff, drake blue-winged teal is much smaller and has only crescentic white mark on face, and scaup lacks chestnut on flanks and has white on face not extending back as far as eye. Escape from wildfowl collections.

BROWN, or CHILEAN, PINTAIL *Anas georgica* Plate 49 Duck Family

Resembles a small duck pintail (p. 200), but can be told from it by reddish-brown head, dull dark green speculum and pale yellow-green bill. Can be told from yellow-billed teal by reddish-brown head, no black or tan in speculum, and pointed tail; is smaller than the mallard-like African yellow-bills *A. undulata*; see also Bahama pintail (p. 191). Escape from waterfowl collections.

ROSY-BILL *Netta peposaca* Plates 52, 55 Duck Family

Duck resembles duck common pochard (p. 188) in general appearance and habits, but drake can at once be told from all other ducks with black head, breast and upperparts by red bill and knob. Duck is best distinguished from duck common pochard by white wing-bar, darker flanks, and white (not grey) under tail-coverts; from ferruginous duck by area immediately in front of under tail-coverts white instead of brown. Escape from wildfowl collections; full-winged birds breed in the London parks.

POMARINE SKUA *Stercorarius pomarinus* Plate 106

Pomatorhine Skua; Pomarine Jaeger (N America).

PLUMAGE. As Arctic skua (p. 186), but with central tail-feathers of adult twisted as well as elongated. Slightly hooked yellowish-brown bill, with black tip; legs black.

STRUCTURE. *Wing length* L. *Ratios:* wing ML; tail MS (immature); M (adult); neck MS; bill M; legs S/M.

MOVEMENT. As Arctic skua, but flight less quick and agile.

VOICE. A sharp 'which-yew', and other more or less gull-like notes.

FIELD MARKS. Intermediate between *great* and Arctic skuas in size, adult can be told from all other skuas by twisted blunt tail-feathers, but immature is separable only by larger size. Wing patch is less prominent than in *great*; for distinctions from smaller skuas and immature gulls, see *Arctic* (p. 186). Pale form is commoner, dark birds occurring in a ratio of about 1 in 7.

FLOCKING. Accompanies migrating flocks of gulls and terns.

HABITAT. Usually well out to sea, but occasionally inshore, especially after storms; exceptional inland.

RANGE AND STATUS. Uncommon autumn passage migrant through North Sea and English Channel; return passage in spring is well out in Atlantic, and then most often seen Hebridean seas; scarce on W coast and in Ireland.

LONG-TAILED SKUA *Stercorarius longicaudus* Plate 106
Buffon's Skua; Long-tailed Jaeger (N America).

PLUMAGE. Adult as pale form of Arctic skua (p. 186); immature dark brown, with small white patch towards wing-tip. Black bill; grey legs.

STRUCTURE. *Wing length* L. *Ratios:* wing M/ML; tail M (immature), L (adult); neck MS; bill MS; legs S.

MOVEMENT. As Arctic skua, but flight even more graceful.

VOICE. Usually silent.

FIELD MARKS. The smallest skua in bulk, adult is easily told by remarkable length of central tail-feathers, extending 6 or even 10 in. beyond rest of tail, but caution is needed at lower end of tail-range (down to 5 in.) owing to variability of *Arctic* (up to 4 in.). Adult also differs from larger *Arctic* and *pomarine* in having distinctly smaller and less heavy bill, grey legs, smaller white wing patch, and invariable absence of the breast-band which the other two usually have. Immature can only be told from other immature skuas if close enough to be sure of smaller bill, and by size if others are also present. For distinctions from immature gulls, see *Arctic*.

FLOCKING. Accompanies migrating flocks of gulls and terns.

HABITAT. As pomarine skua (above).

RANGE AND STATUS. Scarce and irregular autumn migrant, rare spring and summer; the bulk of the N European breeding birds travel S far out in the Atlantic, but a few pass through the N Sea and English Channel and are seen regularly N Norfolk; extremely rare on other coasts and inland; in spring most often in N and W Ireland.

WATER BIRDS: Long

LESSER BLACK-BACK *Larus fuscus* Plates 63, 64, 108, 109 Gull Family
Lesser Black-backed Gull.

PLUMAGE. White, with slate-grey (slate-black in Scandinavian race) mantle and wings, wings edged white and tipped black with white spots; head streaked greyish in winter. Juvenile is identical with juvenile herring gull (p. 196), and immatures gradually become more like adult until fourth year. Bill and eye as *herring*; legs yellow (flesh-brown in juvenile, not becoming yellow till fourth year); orbital ring vermilion.

STRUCTURE. *Wing length* L. *Ratios:* wing ML; tail MS; neck MS; bill MS/M; legs S.

MOVEMENT. As herring gull.

VOICE. Intermediate between *herring* and great black-back, and has their goblin chuckle.

FIELD MARKS. The two black-backed gulls are the only birds which are all white except for slate-grey or black mantle and wings. *Lesser* can always be told from *great* by smaller size (averaging smaller than *herring*), less stout bill and yellow legs (but beware third- and fourth-year *lessers* which may be adult in everything but leg colour). British race of *lesser* can also normally be told from *great* by paler mantle, contrasting with black wing-tips, and this is the only field mark for separating the British and Scandinavian races of the *lesser*, but owing to the variability of the British race only extreme examples of the Scandinavian, with wings and mantle so dark as to be barely distinguishable from black wing-tips, can be safely set down as such. Plumage of British race ranges from just beyond the upper limit of the *herring's* silver-grey to overlap with the lower limit of the slate-black mantle of the *great*, so that since the effects of light and angle of vision are very tricky, it is unsafe to pronounce on the race of a *lesser* which is not actually at a breeding colony until it has been seen in more than one position.

Juvenile is identical with juvenile *herring*, but immatures become darker each year on wings and mantle, so are easier to distinguish; young *greats* are larger, with heavier bills, and from first winter onwards paler underparts.

HABITAT. Similar to herring gull, but more often occurs inland and is less closely associated with the fishing industry.

RANGE AND STATUS. Summer visitor, breeding extensively on coasts and inland in N England, Wales, Scotland and Ireland, and on S and SW coasts of England, sparsely from Dungeness to S Devon, more commonly thence to Bristol Channel; also widespread passage migrant in spring and autumn, and in recent years has shown increasing tendency to winter near large towns, ports and industrial areas. Some passage and winter birds are of Scandinavian race, which has been most often detected in Lancashire and on E coast England. Non-breeding birds on all coasts in summer.

ICELAND GULL *Larus glaucoides* Plates 61, 62, 63, 104, 107, 108

PLUMAGE. As glaucous gull (p. 209). Bill and legs as *glaucous*, but more extensive dark tip to bill in young, and orbital ring of adult brick-red in summer.

STRUCTURE. *Wing length* VL. *Ratios:* wing ML; tail M; neck MS; bill MS; legs M.

MOVEMENT. Flight has the quicker wing-beats of the smaller gulls, such as *black-headed* and kittiwake; otherwise as *herring* (below).

VOICE. Similar to glaucous gull.

FIELD MARKS. A smaller edition of the *glaucous* (see p. 209); see p. 185 for distinctions from ivory gull.

FLOCKING. Often with other gulls.

HABITAT. As glaucous gull.

RANGE AND STATUS. Scarce winter visitor, mainly to E coast, especially N isles.

LONG-TAILED SKUA, adult See *Water: Medium Long*, p. 195

HERRING GULL *Larus argentatus* Plates 61, 62, 63, 101, 104, 107, 108

Sea Mew.

PLUMAGE. White, with silver-grey mantle and wings; black wing-tips with white spots; head streaked grey in winter. Juvenile is mainly brown with dark bar at tip of tail, and immatures are intermediate, showing increasing amounts of grey above and white below until third winter, third-year birds being completely adult except for white spots on black wing-tips. Bill is yellow, slightly hooked at tip, with red spot towards tip of lower mandible (in juvenile blackish-brown, becoming first pinkish, then yellowish, and not fully adult till third summer); legs pink (tinged brown in young), but yellow in some immigrant races; yellow eye with orange orbital ring in adult.

STRUCTURE. *Wing length* VL. *Ratios:* wing ML; tail MS; neck MS; bill M; legs M.

MOVEMENT. Strong, deliberate flight, frequently soaring and gliding; walks, swims and frequently perches.

VOICE. Has many keening, wailing, chuckling and yelping notes, commonest being 'kee-yow', and in spring a loud, echoing 'gah-gah-gah'.

FIELD MARKS. Very variable in size, the smallest approaching the largest *common*, and the largest almost overlapping with the smallest great black-backs, so that too much reliance should not be placed on size in identifying either *herring* itself or other gulls in reference to it; females average smaller than males, and the difference may be quite striking as they stand side by side. Adult can be told from both *common* and kittiwake by larger size, pink legs, and red spot on stouter, more hooked bill; from kittiwake also by white spots ('mirrors') on black wing-tips. Though easily told from both great and lesser black-backs by much paler mantle, the rare yellow-legged races of the *herring* are darker and might be confused with pale specimens of lesser black-back. For distinctions of glaucous gull, see p. 209, and of Iceland gull, see above. Young *herring* cannot be separated in the field in their early years from the same stages of lesser black-back, but towards maturity (not reached till fourth year) they can be told apart by their gradual approximation to their respective adult plumages. Young great black-backs (p. 208) are likewise mainly separable by size, as also are young *common*, though these have whiter underparts, while young kittiwakes can always be told by their dark colour and striking wing pattern.

FLOCKING. As black-headed gull (p. 175).

HABITAT. Breeds on sea cliffs, sand dunes and marine islands, and exceptionally inland on lochs and bogs and even on buildings; otherwise is pre-eminently the coastal gull, especially at fishing ports, whence it follows the boats to the fishing grounds; also follows other ships. Much less often inland than *black-headed* and *common*, but will feed on farmland, at rubbish dumps and in city parks, and roost on reservoirs.

RANGE AND STATUS. Resident, breeding on all cliffs except the low ones between Humber and Thames, and occasionally inland in Scotland and Ireland. Winter visitors, passage migrants and non-breeders are common on all coasts and far up estuaries; inland mainly in autumn and winter. Yellow-legged birds are very scarce winter visitors from the E Baltic and N Russia.

GLAUCOUS GULL See *Water: Very Long*, p. 209.

SURF SCOTER *Melanitta perspicillata* Plate 87 Duck Family

A diving sea duck.

PLUMAGE. Drake all black with white patches on forehead and nape. Duck and immature are all brown with two pale patches on cheek. Bill of drake reddish-orange with white at sides and square black patches towards base of sides, of duck, blackish; legs orange; eye whitish.

STRUCTURE. *Wing length* ML. *Ratios:* wing S; tail VS; neck M; bill M; legs S.

MOVEMENT AND VOICE. As common scoter (p. 191).

FIELD MARKS. Has curious bill-shape of eider (p. 203), but duck can be told from duck eider by its two face patches. Drake can be told from both common and velvet scoters by nape patch, head shape and bill pattern. Duck *surf* can also be told from duck *common* by the two face patches, and from duck *velvet* by no white on wings; face patches on duck *surf* (but not on immature) are often obscure, when can be told from ducks of both *common* and *velvet* by uniform face. Eider-shaped bill, however, is far the best distinction between this and the two other scoters.

FLOCKING. Likely to consort with common scoters.

HABITAT. Coastal waters.

RANGE AND STATUS. Vagrant from Arctic America, most often in N isles.

VELVET SCOTER *Melanitta fusca* Plates 51, 87, 91 Duck Family

White-winged Scoter (N America); a diving sea duck.

PLUMAGE. Drake is all black except for white patch round eye and white hindwing. Duck and immature are blackish-brown with two whitish face patches and white hindwing. Bill of drake is black with a small knob at the base and bright orange sides to upper mandible, of duck blackish; legs reddish; drake's eye whitish.

STRUCTURE. *Wing length* L. *Ratios:* wing MS; tail S; neck M; bill ML; legs S.

MOVEMENT. Similar to eider (p. 203), but not on land unless oiled.

VOICE. Drake very silent, duck has a harsh growling note.

FIELD MARKS. White hindwing, rarely visible at rest, but easily seen when wings are flapped or in flight, is hall-mark of otherwise uniformly dark velvet scoter. Drake can also be told from smaller drake common scoter by orange sides to bill, whitish eye with a white patch round it, and reddish legs. Duck can also be told from duck *common* by pale patches both behind and in front of eye, and by reddish legs.

FLOCKING. Usually in small parties, or among flocks of common scoter.

HABITAT. Coastal waters, and estuaries containing mussel banks; occasionally on fresh water.

RANGE AND STATUS. Winter visitor, most frequent on E side Great Britain, especially from Angus to Firth of Forth, scarce in the W and rare inland; occasionally summers in northern waters, and may have bred N Scotland.

KING EIDER *Somateria spectabilis* Duck Family

A diving sea duck.

PLUMAGE. Drake has orange forehead, white head (crown and nape tinged grey, cheeks tinged green), breast (tinged buff), upper mantle, sides or rump, forewing and underwing; rest black or blackish. Duck is buffish-brown, streaked and mottled darker, with an obscure small whitish bar on hindwing. Eclipse and immature plumages closely resemble eider (below). Bill and

Drake King Eider

of drake orange, of duck and legs immature greyish.

STRUCTURE. *Wing length* L. *Ratios:* wing MS; tail VS; neck M; bill L (drake), M (duck); legs S.

MOVEMENT AND VOICE. Similar to eider (p. 203).

FIELD MARKS. Drake can be told from all other waterfowl by orange forehead and bill, from drake eider also by black back and white crown. Duck rather buffer or more rufous than duck eider, but can hardly be told from it in the field, except at very close quarters when feathers of forehead can be seen to descend nearly to nostrils while those of lores do not (in eider the reverse is the case).

FLOCKING. Often consorts with eiders.

HABITAT. Offshore waters on low-lying coasts and islands.

RANGE AND STATUS. Vagrants to coasts Scotland, Ireland and E England, most often seen Orkney and Shetland.

GREY-HEADED, or SOUTH AFRICAN, SHELDUCK

Casarca cana Plate 55

Similar to ruddy shelduck (p. 206), but drake has head and neck grey, duck has forehead, cheeks and throat white and rest of head and neck grey. White-faced whistling duck (p. 192) also has a white face, but its chestnut neck and upright stance should suffice to distinguish it; see also ashy-headed goose (p. 205). Escape from waterfowl collections.

RED-CRESTED POCHARD *Netta rufina* Plates 48, 52 Duck Family

A diving duck.

PLUMAGE. Drake has rufous head and neck with crest, grey cheeks, brown mantle, blackish breast and underparts, white flanks and patch on shoulder. Duck and eclipse drake are dull brown, paler beneath, with pale whitish cheeks. All have a white wing-bar. Bill of drake bright red, of duck blackish; legs of drake red, of duck pinkish; drake's eye reddish.

STRUCTURE. *Wing length* L. *Ratios:* wing MS; tail VS; neck M; bill MS/M; legs VS/S.

MOVEMENT. Similar to tufted duck (p. 182), but less awkward on land; feeds by up-ending as well as diving.

VOICE. Rather silent, but duck has a harsh 'kurrr'.

FIELD MARKS. Bright rufous head with crest gives drake a quite different appearance from any native duck, and red bill and legs are additional distinctions. Can also be told from smaller drake common pochard by broad white wing-bar in flight, and from smaller wigeon by dark breast and no buff on crown. Duck is the only uniformly brownish duck with a pale (as distinct from white) cheek, except for duck common scoter, which has no wing-bar.

FLOCKING. Small parties occur.

HABITAT. Mainly inland waters, but has occurred on estuaries.

RANGE AND STATUS. Annual visitor in very small numbers, mainly to Essex in autumn; also escape from waterfowl collections, especially St. James's Park, London; has bred twice E England, probably feral pairs.

PINTAIL *Anas acuta* Plates 50, 52, 90, 94 Duck Family

A surface-feeding duck.

PLUMAGE. Drake is grey, with chocolate head, throat and hind-neck, white on front and sides of neck with streak going up to nape, and underparts white except for black under tail-coverts. Duck, eclipse drake and juvenile are brown, streaked darker. All have obscure bronzy speculum. Bill blue-grey, legs greyish.

STRUCTURE. *Wing length* L. *Ratios:* wing S (drake), MS (duck); tail S (duck), MS (drake); neck M/L; bill M; legs VS/S.

MOVEMENT. Resembles wigeon (p. 187), but flight rather more rapid.

VOICE. Drake rather silent, but has a low, musical croak like a distant moorhen; duck has a low quack.

FIELD MARKS. Drake can easily be told from all other native ducks by pointed and much elongated tail (but see drake long-tailed duck (p. 183), and contrasted dark-light pattern on head and long neck. On the water can also readily be picked out among other ducks by its white breast (though drake shoveler also has this). Duck has more pointed tail and slenderer neck than any native brown duck, though resembles slender duck wigeon, from which it can also be told by narrower wings, indistinct speculum and brown belly. For distinctions from other brown ducks, see mallard (p. 201).

FLOCKING. Gregarious; often with other surface-feeding ducks, especially wigeon.

HABITAT. In breeding season as wigeon; in winter a few large groups on estuaries, more widespread smaller ones on inland waters.

RANGE AND STATUS. Resident, breeding locally in Scotland, chiefly in the E and NE, E England and NE Ireland, and occasionally elsewhere; otherwise rather local winter visitor, mainly to coastal counties.

LONG-TAILED DUCK, drake See *Water: Medium Long*, p. 183

RED-THROATED DIVER *Gavia stellata* Plates 46, 110, 111

Rain Goose; Red-throated Loon (N America).

PLUMAGE. In summer grey head and neck, reddish throat, brown above and white below. Adult winter and young have white cheeks, throat and sides of neck, and brown of upperparts speckled white. Grey bill appears tip-tilted, owing to narrowing of lower mandible towards tip; legs grey and black; eye red.

STRUCTURE. *Wing length* L. *Ratios:* wing MS; tail VS; neck M; bill MS; legs (does not stand).

MOVEMENT. As *great northern* (p. 210), but can take off more easily.

VOICE. Wailing and flight notes similar to *great northern*; also a quacking note.

FIELD MARKS. Intermediate in size between the two larger divers and great crested grebe, from all of which it can always be told by its tip-tilted bill and in summer by its red throat. In summer can also be told from *great northern* by grey head, and from *black-throated* by unspotted upperparts; in winter can also be told from great crested grebe by lack of wing-bar. For distinctions from red-necked grebe see p. 184, and from cormorant, see *great northern.*

FLOCKING. Inclined to be sociable.

HABITAT. Breeds on quite small tarns, feeding on larger lochs and the sea; in winter mainly on coastal waters, but occasionally on lakes and reservoirs inland.

RANGE AND STATUS. Resident, breeding in many parts of Scottish Highlands and islands, and in one locality in Donegal; otherwise winter visitor, especially on E coast.

BRENT GOOSE *Branta bernicla* Plates 56, 95, 96 Duck Family

Brant (N England and N America); a black goose.

PLUMAGE. Head, neck, upper breast and tail black; mantle, rump and wings dark grey-brown; tail-coverts and patch on neck white. Dark-breasted form is slate-grey below; pale-breasted form is pale brown to white below. Immature has white tips to feathers on forewing. Bill and legs black.

STRUCTURE. *Wing length* L. *Ratios:* wing MS; tail VS/S; neck M; bill M; legs S.

MOVEMENT. As greylag goose (p. 161), but flight even quicker than *barnacle*; frequently swims.

VOICE. A croaking 'ruk, gruk, grunk'.

FIELD MARKS. Looks black in flight from front, but grey from side or rear; can be told from all other geese by wholly black head (see below for distinctions from drake paradise shelduck). Is the same size as a drake mallard, whose bottle-green head often looks black against the light but has longer bill and paler body. At reasonable range dark- and pale-breasted races may be separated by the colour of the underparts. White tail-coverts are very prominent in flight and in sunshine.

FLOCKING. Highly gregarious; odd birds may join up with large flocks of grey geese.

HABITAT. Almost exclusively coastal, feeding on estuaries and mudflats and resorting to sandbanks and the open sea at high tide.

RANGE AND STATUS. Winter visitor, now mainly to E coast England, and Ireland; dark-breasted race predominates in E and S England, pale-breasted elsewhere. Full-winged birds may escape from wildfowl collections.

MALLARD *Anas platyrhynchos* Plates 50, 53, 90, 94 Duck Family

Wild Duck; a surface-feeding duck.

PLUMAGE. Drake has green head (glossed violet-purple and turning deep purple for short time just before moult), white collar and tail, dark brown breast (very occasionally spotted black) and centre of back, grey sides of back and underparts, and black rump and tail-coverts (centre coverts curly). In eclipse drake resembles duck, but is rather darker. Duck and juvenile are pale brown, streaked darker, with more uniform head. All have blue speculum, bordered by two narrow black and white lines. Bill of drake is yellow with dark tip, even in eclipse, of duck and juvenile greenish, orange or reddish; legs orange.

STRUCTURE. *Wing length* L. *Ratios:* wing MS; tail VS/S; neck M; bill ML; legs S.

MOVEMENT. Swift, direct flight, with wings not coming much below plane of body, and making a whistling, swishing sound; rises steeply from the water, and descends again in a long glide, finally braking with wings held back, and dropping almost vertically on to it; when alighting on land will sometimes pitch right over. Gait resembles farmyard ducks, but less waddling and more horizontal; does not normally perch on high objects except when nesting in trees, and even then does not stand around on branches. Swims readily, and feeds both by dabbling on the surface and by up-ending in shallow water. Juvenile frequently dives, adult occasionally.

VOICE. Loud quacking sound like farmyard duck is made by duck alone, drake's call-note being softer and higher-pitched, 'quork' or 'quek' compared with duck's 'quark'; courting drake also has a low whistling note.

FIELD MARKS. Can be told at close range in all plumages by blue speculum and large size. Drake's combination of green or purple head, narrow white collar, grey back and underparts and dark brown breast is matched by no other native duck; drake's head often appears black at a distance, giving characteristic contrast with pale upperparts, while similar contrast between dark breast and pale belly is useful when bird flying overhead. Duck is harder to tell from numerous other brown ducks, but its large size and blue speculum are valid against all native species; can also be told from duck gadwall by lack of white in wing, from duck shoveler (which also rides much lower in the water) by bill shape, and from duck wigeon and duck pintail by head shape and shorter and unpointed tail. Mallard almost always go in pairs, so that between late autumn and early summer (when drakes are in full plumage) it is unusual to see two or more plain brown ducks together without a mallard or other drake in attendance. Eclipse (moult) plumages confuse the issue with all surface-feeding ducks, and between June and November all 'duck mallards' should be carefully examined for bill colour and darkness of upperparts; the partial moult plumages should be less confusing as traces of the drakes' summer dress can be detected.

Albinos frequently occur, usually with bright yellow bills and especially in the London area, while parti-coloured farmyard ducks and call ducks from decoys sometimes escape and lead to confusion. One distinctive domestic breed is the Khaki Campbell (Plates 50, 53), which is all khaki brown or *café-au-lait* with a dark brown speculum, greenish bill and orange legs; the drake also has a darker brown head, upper neck and rump and a curly tail. Another is black or glossy green or dark brown with a white patch on the breast. Some escapes can of course fly only very short distances, if at all, but may turn up even on remote coastal marshes or on rivers in large towns.

FLOCKING. Gregarious, almost always in flocks of paired birds, and often with other surface-feeding ducks, especially teal; small 'bachelor parties' of drakes occur while the ducks are incubating.

HABITAT. Breeds near almost every kind of fresh water (including lakes in town parks) and on sea lochs, the nest being often in a pollard tree or under a bramble brake well away from water; afterwards also freely on salt water, especially estuaries and muddy coasts.

RANGE AND STATUS. Resident, breeding throughout British Isles; many also arrive in autumn, some staying the winter.

EIDER *Somateria mollissima* Plates 50, 51, 87, 88, 89, 92 Duck Family
St. Cuthbert's Duck (Northumberland); Common Eider (N America); a diving sea duck.

PLUMAGE. Drake is white, with black crown, tail, wing-tips and underparts, green on nape and side of neck, and occasionally with traces of a black V on the chin. Duck is brown mottled darker all over. Drake in full eclipse is all blackish except for some white on wing; drake moulting into or out of eclipse and young birds present a bewildering variety of different combinations of black, white and mottled brown. Bill and legs yellowish-green.

STRUCTURE. *Wing length* L. *Ratios:* wing MS; tail VS; neck M; bill ML (drake), M (duck); legs VS/S.

MOVEMENT. Slow, rather laboured flight, low over water, with pattering take-off like diving ducks, and in single file when flying together; swims readily and habitually dives; comes to land more often than most sea ducks, when has a rather waddling gait.

VOICE. Drake has a low crooning or cooing note, 'ah-oo' or 'boo-hoo', duck a harsh call like other diving ducks.

FIELD MARKS. Outstanding character, by which it can be told from all other waterfowl except rare surf scoter and duck king eider (p. 198), is remarkable shape of bill, the upper mandible continuing in a straight line from the forehead. Drake is the only waterfowl which is white above and black below. Duck is the only brown duck (apart from very similar duck king eider) with a barred breast. If a large pied duck is seen paired with a brown one, they are almost certainly eiders; birds in eclipse and immature plumages, especially in the transitional stages, can be extremely confusing at a distance too great to see the shape of the bill, but within the eider's range any large duck at sea, which is a mixture of black, white and brown, is likely to be an eider in one of those plumages.

FLOCKING. Gregarious, but not consorting with other waterfowl.

HABITAT. The sea, frequenting both rocky and sandy coasts where there are no high cliffs; also offshore in winter; exceptional on fresh water.

RANGE AND STATUS. Resident, breeding commonly on almost all coasts, in Scotland, S to Northumberland, with important colony on Farne Is., and Lancashire (Walney Is.), and in N Ireland from Donegal to Down; otherwise increasing winter visitor to all coasts, especially E England.

RED-BREASTED MERGANSER *Mergus serrator* Plates 46, 48, 53, 91, 94

A saw-bill. Duck Family

PLUMAGE. Drake has dark green head, crest and upper neck, black mantle and wing-tips, white collar, wing patch and belly, chestnut breast, and grey flanks, rump and tail. Duck, eclipse drake and young closely resemble similar plumage of goosander (p. 206). Slightly hooked and serrated red bill; red legs; eye of adult red, of immature yellow.

STRUCTURE. *Wing length* ML. *Ratios:* wing S; tail VS; neck M; bill M; legs S.

MOVEMENT. Similar to goosander, but wings whistle less in flight.

VOICE. Drake very silent; duck has a harsh 'karr'.

FIELD MARKS. Drake is the only waterfowl with a dark green head (appearing black at any distance) that has a prominent double crest or mane; for distinctions from goosander and grebes and divers, see p. 206.

FLOCKING. Gregarious, in parties rather than flocks.

HABITAT. Breeds on rivers, lochs and low-lying coastal areas; in winter mainly in estuaries and coastal waters, but occasional inland.

RANGE AND STATUS. Resident, breeding commonly in most coastal counties of Scotland, but not S of Aberdeen on E side, also in Cumberland, Anglesey and many parts of Ireland, especially in N and W; elsewhere irregular winter visitor, most frequent E coast England.

GREAT SKUA *Catharacta skua* Plates 63, 106

Bonxie (Shetland); Skua (N America).

PLUMAGE. Dark brown, with a whitish patch towards wing-tip, which may show as a patch on the side at rest. Slightly hooked bill, and legs, are blackish.

STRUCTURE. *Wing length* L. *Ratios:* wing ML; tail MS; neck MS; bill MS/M; legs M.

MOVEMENT. Heavy flight like the larger gulls, but remarkably agile when chasing other birds; also a harrier-like display flight, with wings half raised above back. Swims and walks. Makes fierce attacks on human intruders at its breeding grounds.

VOICE. Calls 'a-er' during display, and a deep 'tuk-tuk' in defence of nest.

FIELD MARKS. Superficially like a large immature gull (but has shorter wings and tail and holds wings more crooked at carpal joint) or even a narrow-winged, short-tailed buzzard, but can easily be told from both by prominent white wing patch, as well as by piratical habits (but see warning under Arctic skua, p. 186). Can be told from dark forms and immatures of the three smaller skuas by more prominent wing patches as well as by large size. A skua chasing a gannet is almost certainly a bonxie.

FLOCKING AND HABITAT. As Arctic skua (p. 186).

RANGE AND STATUS. Summer visitor, breeding in Orkney, Shetland and Outer Hebrides, and has nested N Scotland; in autumn a few pass down North Sea and English Channel and a few more through Hebridean seas *en route* to open Atlantic; rare on other coasts and at other seasons.

SHELDUCK *Tadorna tadorna* Plates 55, 56, 94, 96

Bargander; Bar-goose; Bergander; Burrow Duck; Sheldrake; Shellduck; Sheld-duck.

PLUMAGE. Dark green on head, chestnut band round breast and back; and white elsewhere except for black wing-tips, shoulder patches and centre of belly, and green speculum. In eclipse all colours tend to become browner and whiter, and juvenile is even more so, with forehead, cheeks and whole underparts white. Bill red (greyish-pink in juvenile), drake usually having a knob in summer; legs flesh-colour (whitish in juvenile).

STRUCTURE. *Wing length* L. *Ratios:* wing MS; tail S; neck M; bill ML; legs S.

MOVEMENT. Flight and gait resemble geese more closely than ducks; walks or runs; swims readily, juvenile frequently diving but adult only when wounded.

VOICE. Drake has a whistling flight note 'sostmieu', not unlike sound of some ducks' wing-beats; duck has a rather laughing quack, 'ak-ak-ak. . . .'

FIELD MARKS. Can be told from all other shore-birds by large size, bold black, white and chestnut appearance, and flattish red bill, with or without a knob. Smaller drake shoveler, which has same combination of colours, has spoon-shaped blackish bill, no knob and shorter legs, and sits much lower in the water. Duck is smaller and duller.

FLOCKING. Gregarious, but in small parties and family groups rather than large flocks; rarely consorts with other waterfowl.

HABITAT. Sand dunes, and sandy and muddy coasts and estuaries, but sometimes breeds in rough, heathy places not far from sea and exceptionally even in woods and farmland; on inland waters only casually on migration.

RANGE AND STATUS. Resident, breeding on all suitable coasts and in Cambridgeshire Washes; almost whole adult population migrates to either Heligoland Bight or Bridgwater Bay, Somerset, in July, and odd birds may appear in strange places at this time.

PARADISE, or NEW ZEALAND, SHELDUCK *Casarca variegata*

Plates 55, 56.

General outline and habits as ruddy shelduck (below). Duck differs from *ruddy* and *grey-headed* in having whole head and upper neck white and body much darker; from blue snow goose in having white wing patch and lower neck and under tail-coverts chestnut; from Emperor goose in having white chin, throat and wing patch. Drake differs from brent goose in having white and chestnut wing patches and no white patch on neck; all other waterfowl with black head and neck and grey body are much smaller. Blackish bill and legs. Escape from waterfowl collections.

ASHY-HEADED GOOSE *Chloëphaga poliocephala* Plate 54 Duck Family

Generally resembles magellan goose (p. 208) and its allies, but can at once be told by grey head and neck, chestnut breast, orange on legs and barring on flanks only. Drake grey-headed shelduck, which also has grey head and neck, has buffish breast and unbarred flanks. Short blackish bill; black and orange legs. Escape from waterfowl collections; kept full-winged at Woburn (Beds).

RUDDY SHELDUCK *Casarca ferruginea* Plate 55

Ruddy Sheldrake; Ruddy Sheld-duck; Brahminy Duck (India).

PLUMAGE. Deep buff-brown, with paler head, black tail and wing-tips, green speculum and prominent white wing patch. Drake has a narrow black collar. Bill and legs blackish.

STRUCTURE. *Wing length* L. *Ratios:* wing M; tail S; neck M; bill M; legs S.

MOVEMENT. Similar to common shelduck (above); fond of perching on rocks, walls and trees.

VOICE. A loud double note and a nasal honk.

FIELD MARKS. Can readily be told from all native waterfowl by large size and buffish coloration, but needs to be distinguished from two other shelducks (all three have white wing patches hardly visible at rest but very prominent in flight), viz. *grey-headed* (p. 199), which has a grey head and no black collar, and the duck also a white face; and duck *paradise* (above), which has a white head and upper neck and much darker chestnut plumage barred and freckled with black. For distinctions from Egyptian goose, see p. 210.

FLOCKING. A small party would probably be genuine wild birds.

HABITAT. Margins of coastal and inland waters.

RANGE AND STATUS. Vagrant, exceptionally irrupting in some numbers; odd individuals are most likely to be strays from waterfowl collections.

BLACK-THROATED DIVER *Gavia arctica* Plates 96, 110

Pacific Loon (N America).

PLUMAGE. In summer has head and nape grey, throat black, sides of neck streaked black and white, upperparts black spotted white, and underparts white. Winter adult and young are dark brown above and white below. Bill, legs and eye as great northern diver (p. 210), but bill less stout.

STRUCTURE AND MOVEMENT. As *great northern*, but bill M, and can take off more easily.

VOICE. Wailing and flight notes similar to *great northern.*

FIELD MARKS. In winter closely resembles *great northern* (for distinctions from which and from cormorant, see p. 210); can be told from smaller *red-throated* at all times by straight bill, and in summer also by black throat and speckled upperparts.

FLOCKING. Social gatherings occur in summer.

HABITAT. Breeds on larger inland lochs and visits rivers to fish; in winter mainly on the sea, only rarely on fresh water.

RANGE AND STATUS. Resident, breeding locally in W and Central Highlands and Outer Hebrides; elsewhere uncommon winter visitor, chiefly on E coast.

PINTAIL, drake See p. 200

GOOSANDER *Mergus merganser* Plates 48, 53, 91, 94 Duck Family

A saw-bill; American Merganser (N America).

PLUMAGE. Drake has dark green head and upper neck, black back and wing-tips, grey tail and rump, white lower neck and basal half of wing, and white underparts sometimes tinged pink. Duck and young are grey above and white below, with chestnut head and neck and white hindwing. Eclipse drake is like duck, but retains white forewing. Slightly hooked and serrated red bill; orange legs.

STRUCTURE. *Wing length* L. *Ratios:* wing S; tail S; neck M; bill M; legs S.

MOVEMENT. Saw-bills have a heavy take-off like diving ducks, but swift, direct flight like surface-feeders; wings in flight give a whistling sound; characteristic cigar-shaped appearance in flight, due to holding head straight out in front instead of slightly inclined down like other ducks. Swims and dives readily; will walk either upright like diving ducks or more horizontally like surface-feeders.

VOICE. A harsh 'karr'.

FIELD MARKS. The two larger saw-bills (goosander, red-breasted merganser) are sometimes taken for divers or large grebes, being much the same shape, especially in flight, but no grebe or diver has both the black head and upper neck and the white lower neck and prominent wing patch of the two drakes, nor the head and neck all chestnut except for white chin of the 'red-heads' (duck and young); red-heads can also be told from 'brown-head' goldeneye (which also have white wing-bar and whistling flight) by white chin and long red bill. Best distinctions of the two drakes are merganser's chestnut breast-band and more prominent crest, but goosander is larger, has white (not grey) flanks, and brown (not red) eye. Red-heads are harder to tell apart, best distinction being that white of goosander's chin is much more sharply defined, instead of merging gradually into the chestnut, but merganser is also smaller and is brownish-grey rather than slaty-grey. The longish red bill distinguishes both from other diving ducks.

Emperor Goose

FLOCKING. Gregarious, in parties rather than flocks.

HABITAT. Breeds on lochs and rivers; in winter mainly on fresh water sometimes, on estuaries, rarely on the open sea.

RANGE AND STATUS. Resident, breeding fairly widely in Scottish Highlands locally in Lowlands and N England; elsewhere a winter visitor, uncommon in SW England, Wales and Ireland, but regular on reservoirs in the Thames valley.

EMPEROR GOOSE *Anser canagicus* Duck Family

Not unlike blue snow goose, but has only head and hind-neck white, throat and fore-neck being black. The only goose, except *bean* and *white-fronted*, with yellow legs. Escape from wildfowl collections of ornamental waterfowl.

BLUE-WINGED, or ABYSSINIAN, GOOSE *Cyanochen cyanopterus*
Plate 54 Duck Family
Brown mottled grey, with grey head and neck, its blue-grey forewing with black wing-tips, rump and tail, together with short black bill and black legs, distinguish it from all grey geese. Blue-grey forewing also distinguishes from magellan and ashy-headed geese and their allies and female maned goose *Chenonetta jubata*, which it resembles in its short bill and general outline. Escape from waterfowl collections.

MAGELLAN, BARRED UPLAND or CHILEAN, GOOSE
Chloëphaga picta Plate 54 Duck Family
One of the group known as 'shelgeese' and characterised by short black bills. Magellan gander is much the most likely waterfowl to be seen with head, neck and whole underparts white (radjah sheld-duck *Tadorna radjah* has breast band; Andean goose *Chloëphaga melanoptera* is larger and has red legs). Barred upland gander, a colour form, differs in having whole underparts barred, which distinguishes it from all other white-headed waterfowl. Barred underparts and yellow legs distinguish females of both forms from all waterfowl except ashy-headed goose (p. 205), ruddy-headed goose *C. rubidiceps*, which has breast suffused orange and black and orange legs, and female kelp-goose *C. hybrida*, which has large white wing patch and white tail. Escape from waterfowl collections kept full-winged at Woburn (Beds).

GREAT BLACK-BACK *Larus marinus* Plates 63, 64, 96, 108, 109
Great Black-backed Gull; Saddle-back.

PLUMAGE. Identical with lesser black-back (above), but mantle and wings slate-black like Scandinavian race. Bill and legs as herring gull (p. 196); pearl-grey eye, with orbital ring vermilion in adult.

STRUCTURE. *Wing length* VL. *Ratios:* wing ML; tail M; neck MS; bill MS; legs M.

MOVEMENT. As herring gull, but flight heavier.

VOICE. Similar to *herring*, but deeper and more raucous; has a curious goblin-like chuckle, 'uk-uk-uk', uttered especially when its breeding territory is invaded.

FIELD MARKS. A substantially larger edition of the lesser black-back, but blacker above than its British race, and with a much stouter bill and pink legs; for other differences, see above. See also p. 209 for distinctions from immature glaucous gull.

FLOCKING. Less gregarious than other gulls, though often consorts with them, looking like a Triton among the minnows; does not breed in large colonies.

HABITAT. Much as herring gull, but does not often breed away from sea cliffs and marine islands, and less seen in towns, except fishing ports.

RANGE AND STATUS. Resident, breeding coasts and islands Scotland (not S of

Moray Firth on E side), Ireland (chiefly in W), Wales, and SW England (Dorset to Bristol Channel); also inland to NW England and NW Ireland; widespread on all coasts and estuaries in autumn and winter (including some immigrants), with some non-breeders in summer.

WATER BIRDS: Very Long

GREAT BLACK-BACK See *Water: Long*, above

GLAUCOUS GULL *Larus hyperboreus* Plates 61, 62, 63, 104, 107, 108
Burgomaster.

PLUMAGE. White, with pale silver-grey mantle and wings, and head streaked grey in winter. Juvenile is pale brown-oatmeal or *café-au-lait*, showing an increased admixture of *lait* with each successive moult till adult plumage complete in fifth winter. Bill and legs as herring gull (p. 196), but bill of first-winter bird is creamy-flesh with a dark brown tip that decreases with age, but may be still present in fourth-winter birds otherwise fully adult; adult's orbital ring lemon-yellow in summer.

STRUCTURE. *Wing length* VL. *Ratios:* wing ML; tail MS; neck MS; bill MS; legs S.

MOVEMENT. As herring gull, but flight heavier.

VOICE. Similar to *herring*, but shriller and weaker.

FIELD MARKS. Glaucous and Iceland gulls are the only two sea birds that are all white except for silver-grey wings and mantle unrelieved by any black wing-tips, this last feature at once distinguishing them in all plumages from *herring*, *common* and kittiwake. In immature plumages both are much paler and creamier than any other young gulls. *Glaucous*, however, is extremely variable in size, the smallest birds overlapping with large *herrings* and *Icelands* and the largest overlapping with the largest great black-backs; hence size must be used with great caution in differentiating *glaucous* and *Iceland*, while remembering that typical *glaucous* is roughly the size of a great black-back. Best field mark for separating *glaucous* and *Iceland* in all plumages is relative size of head and neck and stoutness of bill, which make *glaucous* look like an outsize *herring*, while *Iceland* is much more like a rather large *common*; adults can be told apart at close range by colour of orbital ring (yellow in *glaucous*, brick-red in *Iceland*), and immatures by smaller extent of black tip to bill in *glaucous*. Though the wings of the *Iceland* at rest extend farther beyond the tail than those of the *glaucous*, this is a relatively valueless character owing to the large number of moulting birds whose primaries have not yet grown to the full length. In flight a further useful distinction is the much quicker, almost kittiwake-like, flight of the *Iceland*, as against the ponderous wing-beats of the *glaucous* like those of other large gulls. For distinctions from ivory gull, see p. 185. Beware autumn adult *herrings* with black wing-tips much worn.

FLOCKING. As great black-back (above).

HABITAT. Coastal and estuarine waters, sometimes entering fishing harbours

and frequenting rubbish dumps far up estuaries, but distinctly rare inland.
RANGE AND STATUS. Winter visitor, mainly to E coast, Shetland to Suffolk.

MUSCOVY DUCK *Cairina moschata* Plate 54

The wild bird is black, with a prominent white wing-bar; the domesticated race may be black, pied, white or blue-grey. Both have a crest, bare red skin round the eye, and a red knob on the bill. Domesticated birds may often be seen on ponds, but usually near farms, and sometimes in parks; the wild race is very unlikely to be seen, as few are kept in captivity at present.

BAR-HEADED GOOSE *Anser indicus* Plate 56 Duck Family

A pale grey goose, easily told from all other waterfowl by two black bars on white crown (but juvenile has dark brown crown and nape and no bars); yellow bill, orange legs. A popular ornamental waterfowl, often escaping.

EGYPTIAN GOOSE *Alopochen aegyptiacus* Plate 55 Duck Family

PLUMAGE. Dark dun above, paler below and on face, with dark chocolate patches round eye and on lower breast and ring at base of neck (juvenile lacks face patch); chestnut, green and white wing pattern; black tail. Pale pink bill, pink legs.

STRUCTURE. *Wing length* VL. *Ratios:* wing MS; tail MS; neck M; bill M; legs S.

MOVEMENT. Similar to shelduck (p. 205); longer legs give it a more upright appearance than ruddy shelduck and its allies; fond of perching in trees.

VOICE. A monotonous, loud barking quack, 'kek, kek', often uttered on the wing.

FIELD MARKS. Liable to be confused with ruddy shelduck, possibly because has the same prominent white wing patch in flight, but *Egyptian* is dun and *ruddy* orange-buff in general colour; the two also differ in bill and leg colour, while *ruddy* has no dark patches on face or breast, and *Egyptian's* neck ring is brown. *Egyptian* could also be confused with ornamental Orinoco goose *Neochen jubatus*, which has more black on wings, browner underparts, no breast or face patches and still more upright stance.

FLOCKING. Occurs in rather loose parties.

HABITAT. Marshes and inland waters.

RANGE AND STATUS. Escape from waterfowl collections; a well known full-winged breeding colony at Holkham, Norfolk, but not now often seen elsewhere.

GREAT NORTHERN DIVER *Gavia immer* Plates 96, 110, 111

Common Loon (N America).

PLUMAGE. In summer has black head, black and white and dark green bands round the neck, black and white speckled upperparts, and white underparts. Winter adult and immature are dark brown above, white below. Stout bill is blackish-grey in summer, pale grey in winter; legs black and grey; eye red.

STRUCTURE. *Wing length* L. *Ratios:* wing MS; tail VS; neck L; bill M/ML; legs (does not stand).

MOVEMENT. Fast, direct flight, with head stretched out in front, wings set far back and legs stretched out behind tail, head and legs being both held slightly below level of body; swims and dives readily, but takes off from water with difficulty; gait an ungainly shuffle.

VOICE. Has a loud, mournful wail, a loud hoot, and a flight note, 'kwuk-kwuk-kwuk'.

FIELD MARKS. The largest of the true divers; though some individuals overlap with the *black-throated*, it can usually be told from the latter by its stouter bill, and in winter by its less uniform and more speckled appearance; in summer plumage the black head makes identification easy. Is much larger than *red-throated*, and can always be told by its straight bill. Not unlike cormorant and shag at a distance, but can always be told from them on water by holding head straight out (not at an upward angle of 45°) and in flight by slightly depressed head and legs and much shorter tail; adult cormorant also has white face patch and no white on underparts. Rare white-billed diver *G. adamsii* differs in having yellowish or ivory white tip-tilted bill.

FLOCKING. Small parties occur on migration.

HABITAT. Coastal waters, occasionally wandering to lakes and reservoirs inland.

RANGE AND STATUS. Winter visitor, especially in Scotland and E coast England; summers fairly regularly in N Scotland and isles, without breeding.

SHAG *Phalacrocorax aristotelis* Plates 64, 96, 110, 111. Cormorant Family
Green Cormorant.

PLUMAGE. Appears all black (actually dark green), with a recurved crest in summer. Young are brown, with a white chin and paler underparts. Slightly hooked blackish bill, with yellowish base and surrounded by bare yellow skin; legs blackish; yellow skin round adult's green eye, flesh-coloured skin round juvenile's pale yellow eye.

STRUCTURE. *Wing length* ML. *Ratios:* wing S; tail S; neck L; bill M; legs S.

MOVEMENT. Similar to cormorant (below), but rather more rapid and graceful; perches on rocks rather than posts; more often jumps up in water before diving.

VOICE. A harsh croak, only heard at nest.

FIELD MARKS. A smaller edition of the cormorant, from which adult can be told by green tinge, crest in summer, and no white patches, and young by darker underparts and less thick bill. Can be told from divers and grebes by uniform colouring (except for white chin of young) and upward slant of head and bill when swimming.

FLOCKING. Breeds in colonies; in winter sometimes in small parties.

HABITAT. Rocky coasts, rarely wandering inland or to muddy or sandy shores.

RANGE AND STATUS. Resident, breeding commonly on most suitable coasts and islands, but local on E coasts Scotland and Ireland, and in England only on Farne Is. (Northumberland), St. Bees Head (Cumberland) and from Isle of Wight to Lundy (Bristol Channel); in winter does not wander far from breeding haunts, but may be storm-blown inland.

CORMORANT *Phalacrocorax carbo* Plates 64, 96, 110, 111

European Cormorant (N America).

PLUMAGE. Appears all black (actually blue-black head, neck and underparts, with bronze-green wings and tail) with white patch on face and in summer also on thigh. Some old birds have head and neck predominantly white or whitish (this is very often found in southern race in spring). Young are brownish with whitish chin and more or less white underparts; occasional birds breed in this plumage. Slightly hooked bill is horn-coloured, yellowish at the base and surrounded by bright yellow skin; legs black; eye of adult green, of juvenile blue-grey.

STRUCTURE. *Wing length* L. *Ratios:* wing S; tail S; neck L; bill M; legs VS/S.

MOVEMENT. Fast, direct flight, with head and neck straight out in front and legs not visible behind tail; sometimes glides and even soars; takes off from the water heavily. Swims low, usually holding its head and bill at an angle of 45°, and dives frequently; regularly perches on posts, buoys, etc., and stretches wings out, as if drying them.

VOICE. Rarely heard away from nest, where it has a good many guttural notes.

FIELD MARKS. Can be told from all birds of similar shape by white face patch and in summer also white thigh patch; has no crest like summer shag. From divers can be told on the water by characteristic upward tilt of head, and in flight by longer tail and broader wings; is much bigger than any grebe. Young can be told from same plumages of shag by white underparts. Extreme white-headed examples of southern race can be identified in the field only by those familiar with the range of variation in the head of the native bird.

FLOCKING. Breeds in colonies; in winter sometimes in small parties.

HABITAT. Sea coasts of all kinds, sandy, muddy and rocky, but rarely far from shore; breeds on cliffs and marine islands, and exceptionally inland and in trees; non-breeding birds fairly regular on some inland waters.

RANGE AND STATUS. Resident, breeding on most stretches of cliff, but absent from much of E coasts of both Great Britain and Ireland; inland colonies in Merioneth and Wigtownshire; elsewhere common in winter round coasts, especially in estuaries, and not infrequent inland in Scotland, Ireland, the London area, the Cheshire and Shropshire meres and elsewhere. The southern race is occasional (perhaps regular) on S and E coasts England.

GANNET *Sula bassana* Plates 58, 86, 109, 110, 112 Booby Family

Solan Goose.

PLUMAGE. White with black wing-tips and yellow-buff head and neck. Juvenile dark brown speckled white; immatures show all stages of intermediacy between juvenile and adult plumages. Stout bill of adult bluish-white, of juvenile dark horn; legs blackish-brown; eye grey, with blue orbital ring and surrounded by grey skin in adult, brown skin in juvenile.

STRUCTURE. *Wing length* VL. *Ratios:* wing MS; tail S; neck M; bill M; legs S.

MOVEMENT. Direct flight, but will glide and soar; heavy, flapping take-off from water. Swims readily, but always dives like a plummet from the air, often from a height of over 100 ft., with wings folded like an arrow-head; rather ungainly on land.

VOICE. Harsh, and heard only at nest.

FIELD MARKS. Our biggest sea bird, its large size, white plumage, black wing-tips and unique method of diving enable adult to be identified at great distances. Young birds in various stages of chequer-board and piebald plumage are puzzling at first, but once the characteristic cigar-shape is known, there should be no possibility of confusion with other large birds, especially if they plunge.

FLOCKING. Breeds in colonies; in winter sometimes in small parties.

HABITAT. The sea; breeds on marine islands, and frequents both inshore and offshore waters, but rarely estuaries; inland as a storm-blown wanderer only.

RANGE AND STATUS. Resident, breeding in large colonies on St. Kilda and Sula Sgeir (Outer Hebrides), Sule Stack (Orkney), Hermaness and Noss (Shetland), Bass Rock (Firth of Forth), Ailsa Craig (Firth of Clyde), Grassholm (Pembrokeshire), Little Skellig and Bull Rock (SW Ireland) and a few small colonies elsewhere; also off western coasts at all seasons and off eastern and southern coasts on migration and in winter.

COSCOROBA SWAN *Coscoroba coscoroba* Duck Family

Like a small swan with black wing-tips; red bill and pink legs. Bill less stout and neck longer than snow goose. Escape from waterfowl collections.

CHINESE, or SWAN, GOOSE *Anser cygnoides* Plate 57 Duck Family

Much browner than other geese, with distinctive dark brown crown and hind-neck, and white cheeks; occurs in two races, domesticated with a red bill and knob, wild (swan-goose) with a black bill; legs orange. Domesticated race is widely kept on farms, and both races in collections of ornamental waterfowl; full-winged birds in Regent's Park (London), New Grounds (Glos) and elsewhere.

CANADA GOOSE See *Water: Huge*, below

WATER BIRDS: Huge

CANADA GOOSE *Branta canadensis* Plates 56, 95, 96 Duck Family

PLUMAGE. Grey-brown, barred paler, with black head, neck, rump, tail and wing-tips, and white cheeks and tail-coverts. Juvenile has both black and white tinged brown. Black bill, grey-black legs.

STRUCTURE. *Wing length* VL. *Ratios:* wing MS; tail S; neck L; bill M; legs S.

MOVEMENT. Similar to greylag goose (p. 161); often swims.

VOICE. A loud double trumpeting note; in flight a loud honking cackle, 'ker-honk'; especially noisy when pairing in spring.

FIELD MARKS. Any large goose seen S of the Great Glen in summer, especially inland, is most likely to be a *Canada*. Can be told from the *barnacle* (for which it is often taken, though *barnacle* hardly ever occurs inland) by its large size, longer neck, brownish plumage including grey-brown breast, and smaller extent of white on face. Is slightly larger than the grey geese, from which its black and white head and neck at once distinguish it.

FLOCKING. Gregarious, but not often directly consorting with other waterfowl.

HABITAT. Mainly inland, ponds, lakes and meres in lowland districts, and adjacent parks, pastures and grass marshes; in winter will resort to coast and the type of habitat favoured by white-fronted geese (p. 159), but except in hard weather usually remains fairly close to its breeding locality.

RANGE AND STATUS. Resident, as a result of escapes from private collections over the past 200 years and recent large-scale population transfers; breeds in many parts of England, notably Home Counties, E. Anglia, Northants, and the W Midlands N to Cheshire; less common in N and SW England and in Wales; in Scotland in Dumfries, Tay, Forth and Moray areas; occurs in Ireland; in winter, especially in hard weather, wanders to districts where does not breed, especially Beauly Firth; in far W occasional birds believed to be genuine transatlantic vagrants are seen.

BLACK SWAN *Chenopsis atrata* Plate 58 Duck Family

Similar to mute swan (below), but brownish-black, paler below, with white wing-tips and a white-tipped pinkish-red bill. The only almost completely black bird of its size and the only one at all which is black except for white wing-tips. A popular ornamental waterfowl; some were put down on the Thames many years ago, and still survive in London, especially in the Docks.

BEWICK'S SWAN *Cygnus columbianus* Plate 58 Duck Family

PLUMAGE. Adult all white, immature ash-brown and white. Bill of adult black at tip and yellow at base and on lores, of immature dirty-white with blackish nail; legs of adult black, of immature dirty-white.

STRUCTURE. *Wing length* VL. *Ratios:* wing S; tail VS; neck VL; bill ML; legs VS/S.

MOVEMENT. As whooper swan (below).

VOICE. Softer and higher pitched than whooper swan; various notes, including 'hoo', 'ho' and a honking note.

FIELD MARKS. Adult can best be told from larger *whooper* by yellow on bill ending bluntly above nostrils; for other distinctions see below; distinctions from larger *mute* are similar to those of *Whooper*; for distinctions from rare snow goose, see p. 160; for distinctions from other large white birds, see mute swan (below).

FLOCKING. Gregarious, consorting with mute and whooper swans.

HABITAT. As whooper swan, but has not bred.

RANGE AND STATUS. Winter visitor, commonest in Ireland and S England, especially the Cambridgeshire Washes.

WHOOPER SWAN *Cygnus cygnus* Plates 58, 86 Duck Family

Whistling Swan (Provincial name; not N America).

PLUMAGE. Adult all white; young ash-brown and white. Bill of adult yellow at base and on lores, of young flesh-coloured, all with black tip; legs of adult black, of young grey.

STRUCTURE. *Wing length* H. *Ratios:* wing S; tail VS; neck VL; bill ML; legs VS/S.

MOVEMENT. As mute swan (below), but wings in flight are silent, on water carries neck in characteristic stiff attitude instead of graceful curve of mute.

VOICE. A loud, clanging 'ahng-ha', often on the wing, more goose-like than Bewick's.

FIELD MARKS. Adult can be told from *mute* by yellow at base instead of orange at tip of bill, and has no knob at base of bill. Young can be told from young *mutes* by flesh-coloured bill. Can be told from *mute* at all ages by upright carriage of neck, tendency to call on the wing and more silent flight. Adult can be told from adult *Bewick's* by greater extent of yellow on bill, reaching below the nostril in an acute angle. Can be told from *Bewick's* at all ages by larger size (a tricky point unless both species are present) and different call-note; for distinctions from other large white birds, see mute swan.

FLOCKING. Gregarious, consorting with mute and Bewick's swans.

HABITAT. Breeds on lochs; in winter on all kinds of fresh and sheltered salt water, e.g. lakes, reservoirs, estuaries.

ANGE AND STATUS. Winter visitor, commonest in Scotland (especially Outer Hebrides), Ireland and N England; during 1918-39 a few pairs bred in the Scottish Highlands, but though a few still seem to summer, it is uncertain whether they still breed, at any rate successfully.

MUTE SWAN *Cygnus olor* Plates 58, 86 Duck Family

Cob (male); pen (female); cygnet (young).

PLUMAGE. Adult all white, as are young in rare variety, known as 'Polish swan'. Normal cygnets are ash-brown, becoming white as they grow older; nestling a downy ash-brown. Bill of adult is orange with black base and knob, of cygnet blackish-grey to dark flesh with no knob; legs dark grey.

STRUCTURE. *Wing length* H. *Ratios:* wing S; tail VS; neck VL; bill ML; legs VS/S.

MOVEMENT. Flight is laboured but majestic, with a distinctive, loud, throbbing 'fair, fair, fair', and neck fully extended in flight. Ungainly and waddling on land, but swims with grace and ease, often arching up wings and slightly erecting the tail (a mannerism not shared by *whooper* and *Bewick's*); thrashes the water as it takes off, and creates a bow-wave when it lands again.

VOICE. Not as silent as its name suggests, but is less vocal than either *whooper* or *Bewick's*; has a twangy trumpeting note, and will snort or hiss when annoyed.

FIELD MARKS. Adult can best be told from *whooper* and *Bewick's* by orange at tip of bill; for other distinctions, see above. Can be told from other large white birds by lack of legs trailed in flight by spoonbill and white stork, of black wings of white stork, and of black wing-tips of immature spoonbill, snow goose and gannet. All swans are liable to get rusty-coloured heads and necks through feeding in water stained with iron compounds or algae.

FLOCKING. Gregarious, but does not (except at Abbotsbury and Weymouth, Dorset) breed in colonies; consorts with other swans in winter, often in large flocks on estuaries.

HABITAT. All kinds of fresh water (lakes, ponds, reservoirs, rivers) and sheltered salt water (estuaries, bays, sea lochs); a common town bird, both on waters in parks and on tidal and non-tidal rivers.

RANGE AND STATUS. Resident, breeding almost throughout British Isles; most are probably feral descendants of medieval semi-domesticated stock, which may itself have derived from the original wild population of eastern England, and there are a few wild migrants from Europe in winter.

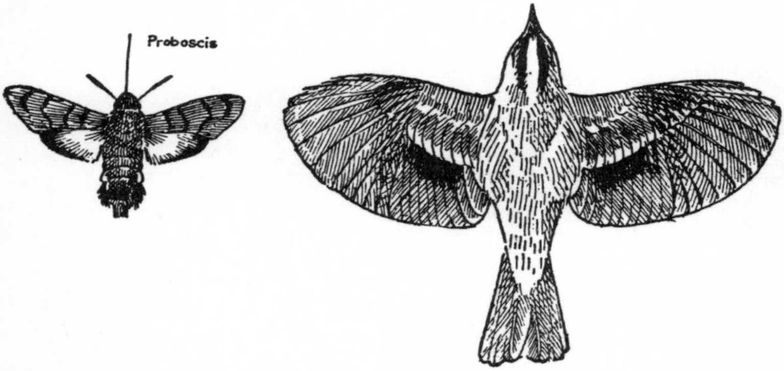

The Humming-bird Hawk-moth, often taken for a real Humming-bird, shown in comparison with the Goldcrest, the smallest British bird

THE KEY

ARRANGEMENT

The key is arranged in four main divisions:

Plumage, subdivided into:
- Plumage Features arranged by Colours (p. 219).
- Barred, Spotted, Streaked and Striped Effects (p. 238).
- Darker or Paler Effects (p. 240).
- Single Bars, Lines, Patches, Spots, Streaks and Stripes (p. 241).

Structural Features, dealing with the sizes and shapes of bill, head, neck, wing, tail and legs (p. 251).

Behaviour Features, covering flight, stance, swimming, diving, voice and social habits (p. 255).

Habitats, divided into three broad groups: Land, Waterside, Water (p. 259).

The names of the birds are printed in three types: ordinary type for land birds, *italics* for waterside birds, and SMALL CAPITAL LETTERS for water birds. For definitions of these habitat groupings, see p. 6 of the Introduction.

Within each subsection, the birds are divided into the eight size-groupings based on length, as described and defined on pp. 10-11. The groups are abbreviated as follows:

VS	Very Short	**ML**	Medium Long
S	Short	**L**	Long
MS	Medium Short	**VL**	Very Long
M	Medium	**H**	Huge

ABBREVIATIONS

ad	adult	imm	immature	sum	summer
aut	autumn	juv	juvenile	win	winter
esp	especially	m	male	y	young (immature and juvenile)
f	female	occ	occasional		

Index to the Key is given on page 286.

HOW TO USE THE KEY

The key is not intended to be exhaustive. It is meant to help you by making suggestions as to which birds have the features which you happen to have been able to see in the brief view which was all you had before the bird disappeared. Therefore it is arranged in the form of lists of birds which have various more or less striking characteristics, such as a red bill, white underparts, a hovering flight, a tendency to dive from a perch, a liking for stony mountain tops and so forth.

Let us suppose, for instance, that one day in January you are on a country walk when, in a ploughed field just over the hedge, you notice a flock of black birds. On closer inspection you see that they all have a grey patch on the nape of the neck, but are otherwise black all over. They are larger than starlings, but smaller than rooks, i.e. medium size. You turn to the **PLUMAGE** section of the Key, and under **Black or Blackish—General Appearance** on page 219 you will find four medium size land birds (distinguished from water and waterside birds by being in ordinary type, not italics), viz. Ring ouzel, Blackbird, Jackdaw and Red Grouse. Next look up 'grey patches or spots' on page 246, and under 'patch on nape' you will find only one medium size bird, the Jackdaw. Thus you have eliminated the three other birds. For confirmation, there are still three clues you can follow up. The birds were seen in a flock; turn therefore to **BEHAVIOUR FEATURES** starting on page 255; under **Social Habits—Flocking** on page 258, against 'M' for medium size, you will find the Jackdaw included. The birds were seen on farmland; therefore turn to **HABITATS—Farmland** on page 260, and you will see the Jackdaw again appears against the letter M. Finally by turning to the migration table beginning on page 266, you can see that the Jackdaw is not listed as a migratory bird, so it is quite in order for you to have seen it in January.

Thus the key endeavours to make the most of whatever field marks you may have seen. It cannot, of course, give you an answer if all you have seen is a small brown bird diving into a hedge, but if you have also been able to see that the bird had a white throat or rufous tail, then a look at the sections on pages 236 and 227 will considerably narrow the field. The key represents, in fact, an analysis of the field marks of birds into those which are most likely to be of use to bird watchers in their early stages. In order to reduce it to manageable proportions, some categories, which seemed to be unlikely to be of much help, such as brown mantles and white bellies, have been omitted. It must not, therefore, be assumed that because a heading, such as 'Brown bills', is not there, there are no birds that might have been included in it.

The key covers all the birds described in detail in the text. The vagrants, rarer birds and ornamental escapes that are described only briefly have, however, been omitted to simplify and reduce the length of the key.

The major part of the key consists of the analysis of plumage characters by colours. Each colour begins with 'general appearance', and follows with 'upperparts' with its subdivisions and 'underparts' and its subdivisions. Each of these main headings is inclusive of those that go before. Thus 'black upperparts' does not repeat those birds with black upperparts that have already been listed under 'general appearance, black', nor does 'black mantle' repeat the birds with black mantles that have been shown under 'black upperparts'. After the three main headings under each colour, the parts of the body shown are only those which stand out as different in colour from the neighbouring parts of the body. Thus 'black crown' includes only birds like the common tern and the marsh tit, the rest of whose heads are a different colour, and not birds like the rook and the blackbird whose black crowns are the same colour as their whole heads.

Immediately following each colour, are a group of headings for that colour in combination with another colour, such as 'Black and white' or 'Grey and yellow'.

After the main colour sections of the plumage analysis are three smaller sections, covering (1) barred, spotted, streaked and striped effects, (2) darker and paler effects within the same general colour, and (3) single bars, lines, patches, spots, streaks and stripes. This last section is of great importance, for an eyestripe or a wing-bar, for instance, can often be picked out in even a brief view of a bird, and at the same time is often one of the best clues to its identity. A small brown bird in a reed-bed might be three or four species, but if it has a prominent buff stripe over the eye it can only be a sedge warbler. Again, the only bird of any kind with a red patch on the nape (as distinct from the crown) is a male pied woodpecker.

The lists in the habitat section show only those birds which are fairly typical of the habitat in the British Isles. Almost any bird can at some time or another be seen in almost any habitat—I have seen a mallard in a suburban back yard and a wryneck in a heap of barbed wire on a bleak Shetland moor—but no purpose would be served by listing all the possible birds that might occur in every habitat. By the same token, there is no point in listing birds under habitats that they commonly frequent on the Continent but not in Britain.

PLUMAGE

Plumage Features arranged by Colours

BLACK OR BLACKISH

(*=blackish)

General Appearance. S: Black redstart m sum (*m win), *swift, *STORM PETREL; **MS:** *Starling ad (green & purple gloss), **purple sandpiper*, *F/T PETREL; **M:** *Ring-ouzel, blackbird m (*imm m), jackdaw, *red grouse, **spotted redshank* sum, *MOORHEN ad, BLACK GUILLEMOT sum (at rest); **ML:** Chough, g/b woodpecker, rook, carrion crow, COOT ad, *SOOTY SHEARWATER, COM SCOTER m (*f); **L:** Black grouse m (at rest), raven, **glossy ibis*, SURF SCOTER m (*f), VELVET SCOTER m (*f), *EIDER m eclipse; **VL:** *Capercaillie m, SHAG ad (*y), CORMORANT ad (*y). N.B.—Many birds have occasional blackish (melanic) forms, notably: **M:** *London pigeon*; **ML:** Montagu's harrier; **L:** Com pheasant.

Upperparts. VS: Pied flycatcher m sum, stonechat m sum (*m win & f); **MS:** Pied wagtail m sum, swallow (blue-black), LIT AUK; **M:** Lapwing, *lit bittern* m, MANX SHEARWATER, PUFFIN, B/N GREBE, SLAVONIAN GREBE, *BLACK GUILLEMOT juv; **ML:** RAZORBILL, GUILLEMOT, TUFTED DUCK m, R/N GREBE sum, GOLDENEYE m; **L:** LESSER BLACK-BACK ad (at rest), *B/T DIVER win & y, GT BLACK-BACK ad (at rest).

Head. VS: Stonechat ad, house martin ad (blue-black); **S:** Brambling m, Lapland bunting m, *reed bunting* m; **MS:** Rosy starling ad, LIT AUK sum; **M:** *W/w black tern* sum, *black tern* sum, LIT GULL sum; **ML:** Magpie, hooded crow, *oystercatcher*, RAZORBILL sum, GUILLEMOT sum, TUFTED DUCK m (& neck), GOLDENEYE m (green & purple gloss), SCAUP m (& neck); **L:** BRENT GOOSE (& neck), SHELDUCK (& neck); **VL:** G/N DIVER sum (& neck).

Crown or Cap. VS: Coal tit, marsh tit, willow tit, goldfinch ad, siskin m; **S:** Blackcap m, gt tit, bullfinch ad, *brambling f, *l/r plover* ad, *Kentish plover* m, *shore lark*, R/N PHALAROPE juv; **MS:** Pied wagtail m win & f & imm, white wagtail m & f sum, pied woodpecker ad, *ringed plover* ad, *GREY PHALAROPE f sum; **M:** Lapwing, *w/w black tern* win, *black tern* win, *lit tern*, *com tern*, *arctic tern*, *roseate tern*, *g/b tern* sum, *LIT GULL imm, *BLACK GUILLEMOT juv, *B/H GULL ad moulting; **ML:** *Stilt*, *Sandwich tern* sum & juv, *avocet* ad, *GARGANEY m, *L/T DUCK f, R/N GREBE sum, ARCTIC SKUA pale form, G/C GREBE ad & imm, POMARINE SKUA pale form, L/T SKUA; **L:** *Night heron* ad, *barnacle goose*, *MALLARD m eclipse (unstreaked), EIDER m (with white streak); **VL:** *Bittern*, *purple heron* ad; **H:** CANADA GOOSE.

Crest. MS: Rosy starling ad; **M:** Lapwing; **ML:** *Sandwich tern* sum, TUFTED DUCK m (*f & y); **L:** R/B MERGANSER m; **VL:** Purple heron ad, SHAG ad.

Bill. VS: *Goldcrest, firecrest, *willow warbler, *chiffchaff, coal tit, crested tit, blue tit, marsh tit, willow tit, pied flycatcher, Dartford warbler, whinchat, stonechat, house martin, *sand martin*; **S:** *Lesser whitethroat, *blackcap, spotted flycatcher, com redstart, black redstart, nuthatch, gt tit, l/t tit, *tree sparrow, house sparrow m sum, bullfinch, wheatear, *hedgesparrow, *barred woodpecker, swift, r/b shrike m, woodchat (bluish), *lit stint*, **l/r plover*, *Kentish plover*, **rock & water pipits*, *snow bunting* sum, *kingfisher*, STORM PETREL, *R/N PHALAROPE; **MS:** Pied & white wagtails, waxwing, swallow, scops owl (bluish), *alpine swift, *redwing, dotterel, **dipper*, *dunlin*, **curlew sandpiper*, **wood sandpiper*, *sanderling*, **purple sandpiper*, **green sandpiper*, *turnstone*, F/T PETREL, GREY PHALAROPE m, LIT AUK; **M:** *G/g shrike, blackbird imm m, *nightjar, *turtle dove, bee-eater, golden plover, *roller, lapwing, nutcracker, *green woodpecker, jackdaw, jay, l/e owl, ptarmigan, *red grouse, *w/w black tern* (tinged red), *black tern*, *knot*, *grey plover*, **ruff*, *com tern* win, *arctic tern* win, *roseate tern* win & juv, *g/b tern*, *MANX SHEARWATER, DABCHICK ad, *LIT GULL win & imm, *SABINE'S GULL imm, BLACK GUILLEMOT; **ML:** *Black grouse, Montagu's harrier, hen-harrier, magpie, rook, carrion crow, hooded crow, honey buzzard, *stilt*, *Sandwich tern* (yellow tip), *avocet*, *marsh harrier*, *osprey*, *FERRUGINOUS DUCK, *SOOTY SHEARWATER, *COM GULL y, KITTIWAKE juv, RAZORBILL, GUILLEMOT,

*L/T DUCK f, GT SHEARWATER, IVORY GULL (streaked white), *ARCTIC SKUA ad, GOLDENEYE (bluish), *COM SCOTER f, *SHOVELER m, L/T SKUA; **L:** Snowy owl, raven, *barnacle goose*, *LESSER BLACK-BACK y, *HERRING GULL y, *VELVET SCOTER f, *R/C POCHARD f, BRENT GOOSE, GT SKUA, *RUDDY SHELDUCK, B/T DIVER sum, *GT BLACK-BACK y; **VL:** Golden eagle, *spoonbill* ad, G/N DIVER sum; **H:** CANADA GOOSE, MUTE SWAN juv.

Neck (see also Head). **M:** B/N GREBE sum; **ML:** Lit bustard m sum (white stripe); **L:** *Barnacle goose*; **H:** CANADA GOOSE.

Mantle. **VS:** House martin ad (blue-black; & wings); **S:** *Brambling f, woodchat (& wings), *snow bunting* m sum, *bearded tit* juv; **MS:** Pied woodpecker; **M:** *W/w black tern* sum, *LIT GULL imm; **ML:** Magpie (& wings), *stilt* m, *oystercatcher*, SMEW m; **L:** *Night heron* ad, LESSER BLACK-BACK ad (& wings), R/B MERGANSER m, GOOSANDER m, GT BLACK-BACK ad (& wings).

Rump. **S:** Barred woodpecker; **MS:** Pied wagtail ad (*juv), pied woodpecker (& tail), *jack snipe*; **ML:** **Bl/t godwit*, COM POCHARD m, GOLDENEYE f & imm, SCAUP, GADWALL m; **L:** *Barnacle goose* (& tail), L/T DUCK m, *KING EIDER m (& tail), R/C POCHARD m, MALLARD m, EIDER m (& tail), RUDDY SHELDUCK (& tail); **H:** CANADA GOOSE (& tail).

Tail (see also Rump) (w.f.=white feathers in) **VS:** Goldfinch (pale tip), pied flycatcher (w.f.), Dartford warbler, house martin (brown-black); **S:** Nuthatch, l/t tit (w.f.), bullfinch, brambling (w.f.), chaffinch (w.f.), woodchat (w.f.); **MS:** Pied and white wagtails (w.f.), rosy starling; **M:** Golden oriole m (pale tip), g/g shrike (w.f.), *fieldfare, turtle dove (white at tip), r/f falcon m, nutcracker (pale tip), jay, woodcock, *lit bittern*, BLACK GUILLEMOT win & y; **ML:** Magpie, hooded crow, MANDARIN DUCK m, G/C GREBE; **L:** BRENT GOOSE, *SHELDUCK juv; **VL:** EGYPTIAN GOOSE.

Wings (see also Mantle). **VS:** Pied flycatcher; **S:** Bullfinch, *wheatear; **MS:** Rosy starling ad; **M:** Golden oriole m, g/g shrike, *nutcracker, **lit bittern* f; **ML:** Hooded crow, *stilt*; **H:** White stork ad (*imm).

Underparts. **M:** Golden plover sum, *w/w black tern* sum, *black tern* m sum, *grey plover* sum.

Throat. **VS:** Coal tit ad, crested tit ad, blue tit ad, marsh tit, willow tit, siskin; **S:** Com redstart m sum (in win & imm m edged white), gt tit, tree sparrow, house sparrow m, cirl bunting m, hawfinch ad, *bluethroat* m win, *reed bunting* m; **MS:** Pied & white wagtails sum, waxwing, rosy starling ad (& breast), *grey wagtail* m sum, LIT AUK sum (& breast); **M:** Lapwing sum (& breast); **ML:** Magpie (& breast), *oystercatcher* sum (& breast), GARGANEY m, TUFTED DUCK m (& breast), WIGEON m, SCAUP m (& breast); **L:** *Barnacle goose* (& breast), BRENT GOOSE (& breast), B/T DIVER sum; **H:** **Com crane* ad.

Breast (see also Throat). **S:** Gt tit ad; **MS:** **Turnstone*; **ML:** COM POCHARD m; **L:** R/C POCHARD m.

Flanks. **L:** KING EIDER m (& belly), EIDER m (& belly); **VL:** *Heron* ad.

Belly (see also Flanks). **S:** *Dunlin* sum; **MS:** Dotterel sum; **L:** R/C POCHARD ad, SHELDUCK ad; **VL:** *Purple heron* ad.

Legs and Feet. **VS:** Pied flycatcher, whinchat, stonechat, *sand martin*; **S:** Spotted flycatcher, com redstart, black redstart, nuthatch, *l/t tit ad, wheatear, swift, *woodchat, *lit stint*, *snow bunting*, *shore lark*, *yellow wagtails*, STORM PETREL; **MS:** Pied & white wagtails, waxwing, swallow, *dipper*, *sanderling*, F/T PETREL; **M:** G/g shrike, nutcracker, jackdaw, *arctic tern* win, *g/b tern*; **ML:** Magpie, rook, carrion crow, hooded crow; **bl/t godwit*, *Sandwich tern*, FERRUGINOUS DUCK m, *KITTIWAKE ad, RAZORBILL, IVORY GULL, ARCTIC SKUA ad, COM SCOTER m, POMARINE SKUA, L/T; **L:** Raven, *barnacle goose*, R/T DIVER, BRENT GOOSE, *GT SKUA, *RUDDY SHELDUCK, B/T DIVER; **VL:** *Spoonbill* ad, G/N DIVER, *SHAG CORMORANT; **H:** *Com crane*, BEWICK'S SWAN ad, WHOOPER SWAN ad.

BLACK AND BLUE

Wings. **M:** Roller (in flight).

BLACK AND BUFF

General Appearance. **M:** Golden plover sum (golden-buff), *lit bittern*.

BLACK AND CHESTNUT

General Appearance. **VS:** Stonechat m; **S:** Com redstart m, tree sparrow, house sparrow m sum, brambling m, Lapland bunting m sum, *reed bunting* m; **MS:** Swallow (blue-black), *dunlin* sum, *turnstone* sum; **M:** SLAVONIAN GREBE sum.

Head. **S:** Woodchat; **M:** B/N GREBE sum (golden chestnut).

BLACK AND GREY

General Appearance. **MS:** Pied & white wagtails; **M:** G/g shrike, jackdaw, *black tern* sum, *grey plover* sum, *London pigeon* (grey-blue); **ML:** Hooded crow; **L:** *Night heron* ad, BRENT GOOSE; **VL:** *Heron* (in flight).

Upperparts. **ML:** Scaup m.

Head. **S:** R/b shrike m (grey-blue); **M:** PUFFIN.

Bill. **ML:** COM POCHARD.

Tail. **MS:** Waxwing; **M:** Woodcock; **ML:** Woodpigeon.

Wings. **M:** LIT GULL m; **ML:** *Marsh harrier* m (grey-brown): both in flight.

BLACK AND PINK

General Appearance. **S:** Bullfinch m; **MS:** Rosy starling ad.

Upperparts. **S:** L/t tit ad.

Bill. **M:** *Com redshank* sum, *spotted redshank*; **ML:** *Ba/t godwit*; **L:** *P/f goose*.

BLACK AND WHITE

General Appearance. **VS:** Pied flycatcher m sum, house martin (blue-black); **S:** L/t tit ad, barred woodpecker, woodchat, *snow bunting* m sum; **MS:** Pied &

white wagtails, swallow (blue-black), pied woodpecker, *green sandpiper* (in flight), *turnstone*, LIT AUK; **M:** G/g shrike, ring ouzel m, hoopoe (in flight), lapwing, *w/w black tern* sum, *spotted redshank* sum (black spotted white), *London pigeon*, MANX SHEARWATER, LIT GULL imm, PUFFIN, B/N GREBE, SLAVONIAN GREBE win & juv, BLACK GUILLEMOT; **ML:** Magpie, *stilt*, *avocet*, *oystercatcher*, *Greenland falcon* (white spotted or streaked black), COOT juv, SMEW, RAZORBILL, GUILLEMOT, TUFTED DUCK m, R/N GREBE, IVORY GULL imm (white flecked black), GOLDENEYE m, SCAUP m, SHOVELER m; **L:** Black grouse m (in flight), snowy owl (barred), *barnacle goose*, LESSER BLACK-BACK ad, KING EIDER m, BRENT GOOSE, EIDER m, R/B MERGANSER m, SHELDUCK, B/T DIVER sum (black spotted white), GOOSANDER m, GT BLACK-BACK ad; **VL:** G/N DIVER sum (black spotted white), CORMORANT sum, GANNET imm; **H:** White stork (in flight).

Head. VS: Coal tit ad, crested tit; **S:** Gt tit ad; **M:** Hobby; **H:** CANADA GOOSE.

Crown or Cap. M: Jay (white streaked black).

Tail. S: Wheatear, r/b shrike; **M:** Turtle dove, hoopoe, collared dove (underside); **ML:** *Bl/t godwit*; **L:** L/T DUCK m, MALLARD m.

Wings. M: Hoopoe, *lit bittern* m; **ML:** Stone curlew, lit bustard; **L:** RUDDY SHELDUCK: all in flight.

Underparts. M: Golden plover sum; **L:** R/C POCHARD m; **VL:** *Heron.*

BLACK AND YELLOW

(including orange)

General Appearance. S: Gt tit; **M:** Golden oriole m, golden plover sum (golden buff).

Head. VS: Coal tit juv; **S:** Cirl bunting m, *shore lark.*

Bill. MS: *Ringed plover*, GREY PHALAROPE; **M:** *Com redshank* win (orange), *roseate tern* sum (orange); **ML:** Stone curlew, R/N GREBE, COM SCOTER m (yellow or orange), GADWALL f (orange); **L:** L/T DUCK m (orange), VELVET SCOTER m (orange); **VL:** *Bean goose* (orange); **H:** BEWICK'S SWAN ad, WHOOPER SWAN ad, MUTE SWAN ad (orange).

BLUE

(including blue-green and purple)

General Appearance. VS: Blue tit; **MS:** Starling sum (purple gloss).

Upperparts. VS: House martin (blue-black); **S:** *Kingfisher*; **MS:** Swallow (blue-black).

Underparts. M: Bee-eater, roller.

Head. M: Roller (blue-green); **ML:** GOLDENEYE m (purple gloss).

Crown or Cap. ML: MANDARIN DUCK m (purple).

Mantle. MS: *Purple sandpiper* (purple gloss).

Rump. M: Roller (deep purplish-blue); **VL:** Com pheasant m.

Tail. M: Roller (blue-green with blackish centre).

Throat. S: *Bluethroat* m; **ML:** MANDARIN DUCK m (purple); **VL:** Com pheasant m (purple).

Breast. M: Turtle dove ad (purplish-pink), stock dove (purplish-brown); **ML:** Woodpigeon (purplish-brown), MANDARIN DUCK m (purple); **L:** MALLARD m (purplish-brown).

BLUE AND BLACK: See Black and Blue (above, p. 182)

BLUE AND CHESTNUT

General Appearance. S: *Kingfisher*; **M:** Bee-eater, roller.

BLUE AND WHITE

Head. VS: Blue tit.

BLUE AND YELLOW

General Appearance. VS: Blue tit.

BROWN

(including dark brown, olive-brown, yellowish brown)

See Blue (for purplish brown); Chestnut (for rufous brown); Green (for greenish brown); Grey-Brown; Pink (for pinkish brown)

General Appearance. VS: Coal tit juv (olive), crested tit, goldfinch juv, siskin juv, redpolls, treecreeper, grasshopper warbler, Dartford warbler juv (ad dark), whinchat, stonechat (not m sum), *reed warbler, marsh warbler, sedge warbler*; **S:** Linnet (not m sum), twite, lit bunting, com whitethroat, garden warbler, blackcap (olive), spotted flycatcher juv, robin (olive), tree sparrow, house sparrow, scarlet grosbeak f & imm, brambling m win & f, chaffinch f & juv (yellowish), hedge sparrow, meadow pipit, tree pipit, woodlark, Lapland bunting, ortolan cirl bunting f & juv, yellowhammer f & juv, crossbill juv, wryneck, nightingale, tawny pipit, *bluethroat, reed bunting, rock pipit, shore lark, bearded tit* juv (yellowish); **MS:** Corn bunting, skylark, Richard's pipit, quail, starling juv, rosy starling juv, redwing (olive), song thrush (olive), *lit crake* f, *pectoral sandpiper, jack snipe, wood sandpiper* sum, *sanderling* sum, *spotted crake*; **M:** Ring ouzel juv, blackbird juv (f & imm dark), nightjar, corncrake, turtle dove juv, golden plover win, merlin f & y, sparrowhawk f (dark), hobby juv (imm dark), com partridge, nutcracker, l/e owl, woodcock, red grouse (dark), r/l partridge, s/e owl, *com snipe, gt snipe, ruff* m win & f, *lit bittern* f, MAURETANIAN SHEARWATER (dark), DABCHICK, MOORHEN y (olive), TEAL f & juv; **ML:** Tawny owl, peregrine y (dark), stone curlew, black grouse f & juv, Montagu's harrier f, hen-harrier f & y, lit bustard (at rest), com buzzard, r/l buzzard (at rest), honey buzzard, *ba/t godwit* sum, *whimbrel, marsh harrier*, GARGANEY f & juv,

ARCTIC SKUA dark form & imm (dark), WIGEON f & juv, COM POCHARD f & juv, COM SCOTER f & juv, GADWALL f & juv, SHOVELER f & juv, POMARINE SKUA dark form & imm (dark), L/T SKUA imm (dark); **L:** Com pheasant f & juv, capercaillie f & y, kite, *curlew*, *night heron* imm, ICELAND GULL imm (pale), SURF SCOTER f, VELVET SCOTER f, KING EIDER f, R/C POCHARD f, PINTAIL f & juv, MALLARD f & juv, EIDER f & juv, GT SKUA (dark); **VL:** Golden eagle (dark), *sea eagle*, *bittern*, *purple heron* imm, GLAUCOUS GULL imm (pale), SHAG y, CORMORANT y, GANNET juv (dark).

Upperparts. VS: Pied flycatcher (not m sum) (olive), *sand martin*; **S:** L/t tit juv, *Temminck's stint* sum, *l/r plover*, *Kentish plover*; **MS:** Alpine swift, *dipper* ad, *Baillon's crake*, *lit crake* m, *pectoral sandpiper*, *ringed plover*, GREY PHALAROPE sum; **M:** Ptarmigan sum, *water rail*, MOORHEN ad (olive); **ML:** *Bl/t godwit* sum, *osprey* (dark), GARGANEY m, GUILLEMOT (dark), TUFTED DUCK f & y, L/T DUCK sum & f win, GT SHEARWATER, CORY'S SHEARWATER, ARCTIC SKUA pale form (dark), SCAUP f, POMARINE SKUA pale form (dark), L/T SKUA ad (dark); **L:** R/T DIVER, B/T DIVER win & imm; **VL:** G/N DIVER win & imm, CORMORANT y, GANNET y.

Head. VS: House martin juv, *sand martin*; **M:** B/H GULL sum; **ML:** GUILLEMOT sum (& neck), GOLDENEYE f & imm (& neck), GADWALL (& neck); **L:** PINTAIL m (& neck); **H:** *Com crane* imm (& neck).

Crown or Cap. S: *L/r plover* juv, *Kentish plover*, *snow bunting* win & imm; **MS:** *Lit crake*, *ringed plover* f & juv; **M:** Turtle dove juv, nutcracker (unspotted), B/H GULL juv; **ML:** Lit bustard m sum, *avocet* imm, GT SHEARWATER (dark); **L:** SHELDUCK juv.

Crest. S: Woodlark; **MS:** Skylark; **ML:** SMEW f & imm (very slight), MANDARIN DUCK f; **VL:** *Purple heron* imm.

BROWN AND GREY

General Appearance. S: Hedgesparrow; **MS:** *Baillon's crake*, *lit crake* m; **M:** Com partridge, *lit tern* juv, *water rail*, *com tern* juv, *arctic tern* juv, MOORHEN ad, TEAL m; **ML:** *Sandwich tern* juv, GARGANEY m; **L:** MALLARD m.

BROWN AND PINK

General Appearance. S: Bullfinch f & juv, chaffinch m (pinkish-brown); **ML:** *Ba/t godwit* m sum (pinkish-brown), *bl/t godwit* sum (pinkish-brown).

BROWN AND RED

General Appearance. S: Robin ad, crossbill m; **MS:** GREY PHALAROPE sum.

BROWN AND WHITE

General Appearance. VS: Pied flycatcher (not m sum), house martin juv, *sand martin*; **S:** L/t tit juv, *Temminck's stint* sum, *l/r plover*, *Kentish plover*, *snow bunting* f & imm; **MS:** Alpine swift, *dipper, pectoral sandpiper, ringed plover*; **M:** Golden plover win, ptarmigan sum & juv, MAURETANIAN SHEARWATER, B/H GULL y; **ML:** Lit bustard (in flight), r/l buzzard, *Sandwich tern* juv, *osprey*, GUILLEMOT, TUFTED DUCK f & juv, L/T DUCK, GT SHEARWATER, CORY'S SHEARWATER, ARCTIC SKUA pale form, FULMAR (worn plumage), SCAUP f, POMARINE SKUA pale form, L/T SKUA; **L:** R/T DIVER win & imm, SHELDUCK juv, B/T DIVER win & imm; **VL:** G/N DIVER win and imm, CORMORANT y.

BUFF

General Appearance. **L:** RUDDY SHELDUCK.

Upperparts. **S:** *Lit stint* sum; **MS:** *Dunlin* juv; **M:** Golden plover (golden-buff mottled darker), barn owl (golden-buff mottled grey).

Head. **S:** *Snow bunting* f (speckled black); **ML:** *Squacco heron* (& neck); **VL:** EGYPTIAN GOOSE (& neck).

Crown or Cap. **ML:** WIGEON m.

Neck (see also Head). **M:** *Lit bittern.*

Underparts. **VS:** Coal tit ad, whinchat ad (juv speckled), stonechat juv (speckled); **S:** Com redstart f (orange-buff) & juv (speckled), nuthatch, wheatear, *yellow wagtail* juv; **MS:** Swallow, *lit crake* f; **M:** Blackbird f & y (speckled darker), barn owl (dark-breasted form), *lit bittern* m.

Throat. **VS:** Wren (& breast), r/b flycatcher f & imm, house martin juv; **S:** Brambling f (deep buff; & breast), wheatear (deep buff, esp Greenland race), *bluethroat* imm m (deep buff), *reed bunting* f & juv, *kingfisher*; **MS:** *Grey wagtail, ruff* imm; **M:** R/f falcon f; **ML:** *Squacco heron* (& breast), *marsh harrier*, MANDARIN DUCK m (streaked white); **L:** Capercaillie f (deep buff; & breast).

Breast (see also Throat). **M:** *Ruff* win & imm; **L:** KING EIDER m.

Flanks. **VS:** Goldfinch, house martin juv; **ML:** MANDARIN DUCK m.

BUFF AND BLACK: See Black and Buff (above, p. 182)

BUFF AND CHESTNUT

Head and Neck. **ML:** WIGEON m.

Underparts. **S:** Nuthatch.

BUFF AND WHITE

General Appearance. **S:** *Lit stint* sum; **MS:** *Dunlin* juv; **M:** Barn owl; **ML:** *Squacco heron* (at rest).

CHESTNUT

(including rufous and reddish-brown)

General Appearance. **VS:** Wren, *reed warbler* juv, *marsh warbler* juv; **S:** Linnet m, blackcap juv, hawfinch, nightingale ad, r/b shrike f & juv, *bearded tit* ad;

MS: Scops owl; **M:** Corncrake (in flight), kestrel, woodcock; **ML:** FERRUGINOUS DUCK; **VL:** Com pheasant m. N.B.—Some birds have occasional rufous or erythristic forms, notably: **M:** Cuckoo f, com partridge.

Upperparts (all streaked or mottled darker). **S:** Cirl bunting m, yellowhammer m; **MS:** *Dunlin* sum, *turnstone* sum; **M:** Turtle dove.

Head and Neck. **S:** COOT nestling; **M:** Com partridge; **ML:** COM POCHARD m; **L:** *Glossy ibis* sum, R/C POCHARD m, R/B MERGANSER f & y, GOOSANDER f & y; **H:** SWANS (after feeding in discoloured water).

Crown or Cap. **S:** Lit bunting, blackcap f & juv, tree sparrow, woodchat; **MS:** Waxwing; **M:** Bee-eater, r/f falcon f.

Crest. **L:** R/B MERGANSER f & y, GOOSANDER f & y.

Bill. **S:** Ortolan; **M:** LIT GULL sum; **ML:** MANDARIN DUCK m; **L:** MALLARD juv.

Neck (see also Head). **MS:** GREY PHALAROPE sum; **M:** SLAVONIAN GREBE sum; **ML:** R/N GREBE sum; **VL:** *Purple heron* ad (striped black).

Mantle. **VS:** Goldfinch ad; **S:** Tree sparrow, house sparrow m, chaffinch m, r/b shrike; **M:** Fieldfare (dark), bee-eater, roller, *knot* sum; **L:** SHELDUCK ad.

Rump. **VS:** Treecreeper. **S:** Com redstart (& tail), black redstart (& tail), yellowhammer, *bluethroat.*

Tail. **S:** Redstarts (see Rump), nightingale; **M:** Com partridge, r/l partridge; **L:** Kite.

Wings. **S:** Com whitethroat, r/b shrike; **M:** Corncrake, kestrel.

Underparts. **VS:** Stonechat ad; **S:** Com redstart m, *kingfisher,* GREY PHALAROPE sum; **M:** R/f falcon f; **ML:** Montagu's harrier y; **L:** *Glossy ibis* sum (dark).

Throat. **S:** R/N PHALAROPE sum; **MS:** Swallow; **M:** DABCHICK sum.

Breast. **S:** Brambling m; **MS:** Dotterel sum; **L:** Capercaillie y, R/B MERGANSER m; **VL:** *Purple heron* ad.

Flanks. **S:** Nuthatch; **MS:** Redwing (reddish); **M:** B/N GREBE sum, SLAVONIAN GREBE sum; **ML:** SHOVELER m.

Belly. **MS:** *Dipper* ad; **M:** R/l partridge ad; **ML:** *Marsh harrier,* SHOVELER m.

Legs and Feet. **S:** Ortolan; **MS:** Starling; **M:** *Black tern* (dark), BLACK GUILLEMOT y.

CHESTNUT AND BLACK: See Black and Chestnut (p. 222)

CHESTNUT AND BLUE: See Blue and Chestnut (p. 224)

CHESTNUT AND BUFF: See Buff and Chestnut (p. 226)

CHESTNUT AND GREEN

Head and Neck. **M:** TEAL m.

CHESTNUT AND GREY

General Appearance. **S:** Nuthatch, r/b shrike m; **MS:** *Curlew sandpiper* sum; **M:** Fieldfare, turtle dove ad, r/f falcon f, kestrel m, barn owl (dark-breasted form), *knot* sum; **ML:** COM POCHARD m.

CHESTNUT AND WHITE

General Appearance. **L:** SHELDUCK ad.
Head and Neck. **ML:** GARGANEY m (or dark brown), SMEW f & imm.
Underparts. **S:** *Bearded tit* ad.

CHESTNUT AND YELLOW

General Appearance. **S:** Cirl bunting m, yellowhammer m.

GREEN

(including greenish-brown, greenish-grey, olive-green and yellowish-green). See also Blue (for blue-green)

General Appearance. **VS:** Goldcrest ad (yellowish)& juv (brownish), firecrest (yellowish), y/b warbler (brownish), willow warbler (brownish), chiffchaff (brownish), serin m (yellowish) & f (brownish), siskin m (yellowish) & f (brownish); **S:** Greenfinch ad (yellowish) & juv (brownish), crossbill f (yellowish) & juv (brownish); **MS:** Starling ad (gloss); **M:** Golden oriole f (yellowish), green woodpecker; **VL:** Com pheasant m (melanic form), SHAG ad (dark).
Upperparts. **VS:** Wood warbler (brownish); **S:** Gt tit (yellowish), *yellow wagtails* (brownish).
Head. **S:** Ortolan ad (olive); **ML:** GOLDENEYE m (dark), SCAUP m (dark; & neck), SHOVELER m (do); **L:** MALLARD m (do), R/B MERGANSER m (do), SHELDUCK ad (do), GOOSANDER m (do); **VL:** Com pheasant m (do).
Crown or Cap. **S:** Cirl bunting m (greyish).
Bill. **S:** *Yellow wagtails* (greyish); **MS:** Lit owl (yellowish), *grey wagtail, Baillon's crake, lit crake, pectoral sandpiper* (greyish); **M:** Com partridge (brownish), MOORHEN y (brownish); **ML:** Tawny owl (pale yellowish), *squacco heron* (yellowish), COM GULL ad (yellowish), KITTIWAKE win (yellowish) & imm (dull), MANDARIN DUCK f (greyish), SHOVELER f (brownish); **L:** Com pheasant (pale yellowish), *night heron* (greyish), SURF SCOTER f (greyish), KING EIDER f (greyish), MALLARD m (yellowish) & f (olive), EIDER m win & f (greyish); **VL:** *G/l goose* juv (greyish or yellowish), *bittern* (yellowish); **H:** *Com crane* (brownish).
Eye. **VL:** SHAG ad, CORMORANT.
Neck. See Head.
Mantle: **VS:** Blue tit (& rump); **ML:** MANDARIN DUCK m (olive; & rump).
Rump (see also Mantle). (All yellowish.) **VS:** Blue tit ad; **S:** Chaffinch, cirl bunting (olive), *b/h wagtail, g/h wagtail*; **MS:** *Grey wagtail*; **M:** Green woodpecker.

Tail. **M:** Bee-eater; **ML:** Magpie (dark), MANDARIN DUCK m (olive).
Throat. **M:** Green woodpecker (greyish); **VL:** Capercaillie m.
Legs and Feet. **S:** Barred woodpecker (greyish), r/b shrike (greyish), *Temminck's stint*; **MS:** Pied woodpecker (greyish), *lit crake*, *dunlin* (olive), *curlew sandpiper* (olive), *jack snipe* (greyish), *com sandpiper* (greyish), *wood sandpiper* (olive), *green sandpiper* (olive), *spotted crake* (olive); **M:** Golden plover (greyish), *knot* (olive), *com snipe* (dull), *gt snipe* (greyish), *ruff*, *greenshank* (olive), *lit bittern* (yellow soles), DABCHICK (greyish), B/N GREBE (greyish), SLAVONIAN GREBE (greyish), MOORHEN, TEAL (greyish); **ML:** *Ba/t godwit* (greyish), *whimbrel* (greyish), *squacco heron*, (yellowish), *Greenland falcon* imm (greyish), *osprey*, COOT, FERRUGINOUS DUCK f (greyish), COM GULL ad (yellowish), MANDARIN DUCK f (greyish), R/N GREBE, G/C GREBE; **L:** *Glossy ibis* (brownish), *curlew* (greyish), *night heron* imm (greyish), KING EIDER f (greyish), PINTAIL f & juv (greyish), EIDER; **VL:** *Bittern* (yellow soles).

GREEN AND CHESTNUT: See Chestnut and Green (p. 187)

GREEN AND PURPLE

Upperparts. **MS:** Starling ad (gloss); **M:** Lapwing (dark); **L:** *Glossy ibis* (dark).

GREEN AND YELLOW

General Appearance. (All greenish-brown.) **VS:** Wood warbler; **S:** *Yellow wagtails* (not m sum).

GREY
(including blue-grey)
See also Green (for greenish-grey) and Grey-brown

General Appearance. **VS:** Coal tit ad (olive); **S:** Black redstart m win (dark), *snow bunting* juv; **MS:** Pied wagtail juv; **M:** r/f falcon m, cuckoo ad, stock dove (bluish), *rock dove* (bluish), *London pigeon* (bluish); **ML:** Wood pigeon (at rest), Montagu's harrier m, hen-harrier m, *Greenland falcon*, WIGEON m, FULMAR blue form; **L:** PINTAIL m; **VL:** *Purple heron* (dark), *heron* (at rest); **H:** *Com crane.*
Upperparts. **S:** Nuthatch (bluish), R/N PHALAROPE win; **MS:** Pied wagtail imm, white wagtail, *grey wagtail* ad, *sanderling* win, GREY PHALAROPE win; **M:** G/g shrike, merlin m (bluish), sparrowhawk ad (dark), hobby ad, ptarmigan aut, *w/w black tern* win, *black tern* win (sum, dark), *lit tern* ad (at rest), *knot* win, *grey plover* sum, *com tern* ad (at rest), *arctic tern* ad (at rest), *roseate tern* ad (at rest), *g/b tern* (at rest), LIT GULL win & imm (at rest), TEAL m (vermiculated), B/H GULL ad & imm (at rest); **ML:** *Sandwich tern* ad (at rest), SMEW f & imm, COM GULL ad (at rest), KITTIWAKE ad (at rest), COM POCHARD m (vermiculated), FULMAR; **L:** *Barnacle goose* (barred), LESSER BLACK-BACK ad (dark; at rest), ICELAND GULL ad (at rest), HERRING GULL ad (at rest), R/B MERGANSER f & y, GOOSANDER f & y; **VL:** GLAUCOUS GULL ad (at rest).
Head. **VS:** R/b flycatcher m, Dartford warbler m (dark); **S:** Linnet m, *water*

pipit sum, *g/h wagtail* ad, *bearded tit* m; **MS:** *Grey wagtail* ad; **M:** Fieldfare (bluish), kestrel (bluish), ptarmigan aut; **L:** R/T DIVER sum, B/T DIVER sum; **VL:** Capercaillie m win.

Crown or Cap. S. Lesser whitethroat ad (crown only), com whitethroat m sum (crown & nape), com redstart m, house sparrow m, chaffinch m (bluish), r/b shrike m (bluish), *b/h wagtail* m sum (bluish); **MS:** White wagtail f win; **M:** Turtle dove ad (bluish), *lit tern* juv, *com tern* juv, *arctic tern* juv, *g/b tern* win; **ML:** *Stilt, Sandwich tern* win; **L:** KING EIDER m, R/T DIVER win & imm.

Crest. VL: *Heron* y.

Bill. S: Twite sum & juv, com whitethroat (olive), brambling sum (bluish), chaffinch m sum (bluish), yellowhammer (bluish), hawfinch sum (bluish), *yellow wagtail* (dark); **MS:** Quail, pied woodpecker, *grey wagtail* (dark); **M:** Merlin (bluish), sparrowhawk, r/f falcon f & imm (bluish), hobby (bluish), kestrel (bluish), *greenshank* (bluish), *rock dove, London pigeon,* B/N GREBE (bluish), SLAVONIAN GREBE (bluish), TEAL ad (dark); **ML:** Peregrine (bluish), lit bustard (bluish), *Greenland falcon* (bluish), GARGANEY ad (dark), SMEW, TUFTED DUCK f (m, bluish), ARCTIC SKUA juv (bluish), WIGEON (bluish), SCAUP (bluish), GADWALL; **L:** PINTAIL (bluish), R/T DIVER (pale), R/T DIVER win & imm; **VL:** G/N DIVER win & imm, GANNET ad (bluish).

Eyes. M: Jackdaw; **L:** GT BLACK-BACK ad; **VL:** GANNET (pale); **H:** *White stork.*

Mantle. S: Com redstart m sum, bullfinch m; **MS:** Pied wagtail m win & f; **M:** *Lit tern* ad (& wings), *com tern* ad (& wings), *arctic tern* ad (& wings), *roseate tern* ad (& wings), *g/b tern* ad (& wings), LIT GULL ad (& wings), B/H GULL ad (& wings); **ML:** Hooded crow (& rump), *Sandwich tern* ad (& wings), COM GULL imm (ad, & wings), KITTIWAKE ad (& wings), SCAUP m (vermiculated), GADWALL m (vermiculated); **L:** LESSER BLACK-BACK imm (ad, & wings), ICELAND GULL imm (ad, & wings), HERRING GULL imm (ad, & wings); **VL:** GLAUCOUS GULL imm (ad, & wings).

Rump. VS: Blue tit ad (bluish); **S:** Gt tit juv, house sparrow m, r/b shrike m (bluish), *reed bunting*; **MS:** White wagtail, waxwing, GREY PHALAROPE sum; **M:** Fieldfare (bluish), merlin, kestrel ad (bluish); **ML:** Woodpigeon (bluish), hooded crow; **L:** *Night heron* ad (& tail), GOOSANDER m (& tail).

Tail (see also Rump). (Geese with white tip.) **VS:** Blue tit (bluish); **S:** Gt tit (bluish); **ML:** *Stilt, marsh harrier* m, GOLDENEYE m; **L:** *Lesser white-front, p/f goose, w/f goose*; **VL:** *G/l goose, bean goose.*

Wings (see also Mantle). **S:** Gt tit (bluish); **M:** *W/w black tern* sum; **L:** *Night heron* ad, MALLARD m.

Underparts. S: Hedgesparrow ad; **MS:** *Baillon's crake, lit crake* m; **M:** *Black tern* (dark), *water-rail* ad, MOORHEN ad (dark); **ML:** Hooded crow; **L:** MALLARD, m.

Throat. S: Blackcap; **M:** Cuckoo ad (& breast), PUFFIN; **ML:** Lit bustard m (bluish), rook (bare skin), IVORY GULL imm.

Breast. S: Temminck's stint win (pale); **M:** Golden plover win (yellowish), com partridge (with brown horseshoe), cuckoo ad, ptarmigan aut, r/l partridge ad, *spotted redshank* win; **ML:** *Stilt* imm, SMEW f & imm; **L:** R/B MERGANSER f & y.

Flanks. S: Black redstart m, robin ad (bluish); **M:** TEAL m (vermiculated); **ML:**

SMEW f (m vermiculated), WIGEON m (vermiculated); **L:** PINTAIL m (vermiculated), R/B MERGANSER (m vermiculated), GOOSANDER, f & y.

Underwing. M: LITTLE GULL.

Legs and Feet. VS: Y/b warbler (brownish), coal tit (bluish), crested tit (olive), blue tit (bluish), marsh tit (bluish), willow tit (bluish), *sedge warbler*; **S:** Lesser whitethroat (bluish), garden warbler (brownish), blackcap (dark), gt tit (bluish), barred warbler (brownish), nightingale (brownish), *Kentish plover*, R/N PHALAROPE ad (bluish); **MS:** Scops owl, *jack snipe* (bluish), LIT AUK; **M:** Golden oriole (dark), hoopoe, com partridge, green woodpecker (olive), *grey plover*, B/N GREBE (bluish), SLAVONIAN GREBE (bluish), SABINE'S GULL; **ML:** Peregrine y (bluish), g/b woodpecker, lit bustard (yellowish), *bl/t godwit*, *avocet* (bluish), *oystercatcher* juv (pale), *Greenland falcon* imm (bluish), GARGANEY, SMEW, SOOTY SHEARWATER, COM GULL imm, TUFTED DUCK f (m bluish), ARCTIC SKUA juv (bluish), WIGEON (bluish), COM POCHARD, FULMAR (bluish), SCAUP (bluish), L/T SKUA; **L:** Com pheasant (brownish), PINTAIL m, SHELDUCK juv (pale); **VL:** *G/l goose* juv, *spoonbill* imm; **H:** CANADA GOOSE (dark), BEWICK'S SWAN imm, WHOOPER SWAN y, MUTE SWAN.

GREY AND BLACK: See Black and Grey (p. 183)

GREY AND BROWN: See Brown and Grey (p. 185)

GREY AND CHESTNUT: See Chestnut and Grey (p. 187)

GREY AND WHITE

General Appearance. S: R/N PHALAROPE; **MS:** White wagtail y, *sanderling* win, GREY PHALAROPE win; **M:** Ptarmigan aut, *w/w black tern* win, *black tern* win, *lit tern*, *knot* win, *grey plover* win, *com tern*, *arctic tern*, *roseate tern*, *g/b tern*, LIT GULL, B/H GULL; **ML:** Woodpigeon (in flight), *Sandwich tern*, SMEW f & imm, COM GULL ad, KITTIWAKE, FULMAR; **L:** LESSER BLACK-BACK ad (dark grey), ICELAND GULL ad, HERRING GULL ad, R/B MERGANSER f & y, GOOSANDER f & y; **VL:** GLAUCOUS GULL ad.

Head. S: Lesser whitethroat ad, com whitethroat m sum, *b/h wagtail* m sum.

Tail. M: Cuckoo; **L & VL:** *Geese* (see under Grey).

GREY AND YELLOW

General Appearance. S: *B/h wagtail* m sum, *g/h wagtail* m sum; **MS:** *Grey wagtail.*

GREY BROWN

General Appearance. VS: Chiffchaff (northern races), r/b flycatcher; **S:** Lesser whitethroat, com whitethroat m sum, blackcap m, spotted flycatcher ad, com and black redstarts f & y, wheatear f & y, barred warbler, wryneck, *rock pipit*, *water pipit* sum; **MS:** Scops owl, dotterel, lit owl, *wood sandpiper*; **M:** Ring ouzel juv, mistle thrush, cuckoo juv, collared dove, l/e owl juv, *com redshank* (at rest); **ML:** Tawny owl, Montagu's harrier m (worn plumage) & imm m, hen-harrier m (worn plumage) & imm m, *ba/t godwit* win, *bl/t godwit* win, COM GULL juv, MANDARIN DUCK f, GADWALL m; **L:** *Lesser white-front*, *p/f goose*, *w/f goose*, LESSER BLACK-BACK y, HERRING GULL y, R/T DIVER win & imm, GT BLACK-BACK y; **VL:** *G/l goose*, *bean goose*, EGYPTIAN GOOSE; **H:** CANADA GOOSE, BEWICK'S SWAN imm, WHOOPER SWAN y, MUTE SWAN y.

Upperparts. **S:** *Temminck's stint* win, *lit stint* win, *snow bunting* m win & f & imm; **MS:** *Grey wagtail* juv, *dipper* juv, *dunlin* win, *curlew sandpiper* win, *com sandpiper*, *green sandpiper* (at rest); **M:** Sparrowhawk f, *knot* win, *grey plover* win, *spotted redshank* win, *greenshank* (at rest), SABINE'S GULL imm; **ML:** Woodpigeon, R/N GREBE win, COM POCHARD f, GOLDENEYE, G/C GREBE; **L:** BRENT GOOSE, R/B MERGANSER f & y, GOOSANDER f & y; **VL:** *Snow goose* imm, *purple heron*.

Crown or Cap. **S:** Com redstart m win, R/N PHALAROPE f sum; **L:** B/T DIVER win & imm.

Mantle. **S:** Com redstart m win.

Wings. **MS:** *Dunlin*; **ML:** *Marsh harrier* m.

Underparts. **L:** BRENT GOOSE pale-breasted form.

Throat and Breast. **M:** Turtle dove juv, *Grey plover* win (breast only).

GREY-BROWN AND BLACK: See Black and Grey (p. 183)

GREY-BROWN AND WHITE

General Appearance. **S:** *Temminck's stint* win, *lit stint* win; **MS:** *Dipper* juv, *dunlin* win, *curlew sandpiper* win, *com sandpiper*, *green sandpiper*; **M:** *Knot* win, *com redshank* (in flight), *spotted redshank* win, *greenshank*, SABINE'S GULL imm; **ML:** R/N GREBE win, GOLDENEYE f & imm, G/C GREBE; **L:** GT BLACK-BACK imm; **VL:** *Snow goose* imm; **H:** BEWICK'S SWAN imm. WHOOPER SWAN imm, MUTE SWAN imm.

ORANGE: See Red (p. 193)

ORANGE AND BLACK: See Black and Yellow (p. 183)

PINK

(including flesh and pinkish-brown)
See also Red

General Appearance. (All pinkish-brown.) **MS:** Waxwing, *curlew sandpiper* sum; **M:** Hoopoe, jay, *London pigeon*.

Upperparts. **MS:** *Dunlin* sum (brownish).

Head and Neck. (All pinkish-brown.) **M:** *Knot* sum; **ML:** *Ba/t godwit* m sum, *bl/t godwit* sum.

Crown or Cap. **S:** *Kentish plover* m sum (brownish); **L:** R/C POCHARD m (brownish).
Crest. (All pinkish-brown.) **MS:** Waxwing; **M:** Hoopoe (black tips); **L:** R/C POCHARD.
Bill. (Mostly flesh.) **VS:** Goldfinch (whitish); **S:** Greenfinch (whitish); **MS:** Rosy starling sum, *jack snipe* (pale); **M:** Golden oriole (dark), barn owl (whitish), woodcock (dull), TEAL juv, B/H GULL y (dull); **ML:** SHOVELER juv; **L:** *Lesser white-front* ad (imm greyish), *w/f goose* ad (imm greyish), SHELDUCK juv; **VL:** *Spoonbill* imm, *heron*, GLAUCOUS GULL imm, EGYPTIAN GOOSE; **H:** BEWICK'S SWAN imm (dull), WHOOPER SWAN y.
Eye. **M:** B/N GREBE (orange-pink), SLAVONIAN GREBE.
Mantle. **MS:** Rosy starling ad (& rump); **ML:** *Squacco heron* (brownish).
Rump. **VS:** Redpolls m; **S:** Twite m, l/t tit ad; **MS:** Rosy starling ad.
Underparts. **VS:** Dartford warbler (brownish); **S:** Bullfinch, chaffinch m (brownish), ortolan (brownish), r/b shrike m; **MS:** Rosy starling ad; **M:** *Knot* sum (brownish); **ML:** *Ba/t godwit* m sum (brownish); **L:** GOOSANDER m.
Throat and Breast. **VS:** Redpolls ad; **S:** *Water pipit* sum; **M:** Turtle dove ad (purplish), collared dove (breast), *roseate tern* sum; **ML:** WIGEON m (breast); **ML:** IVORY GULL ad.
Flanks and Belly. **S:** L/t tit ad (flanks only); **ML:** SHOVELER m (deep).
Legs and Feet. **VS:** Wren (brownish), goldfinch (pale), grasshopper warbler, house martin, *marsh warbler*; **S:** Linnet (brownish), l/t tit juv (dull), greenfinch (pale), brambling (brownish), hedgesparrow (brownish), meadow pipit y, tree pipit (brownish), woodlark (brownish), cirl bunting (brownish), yellowhammer (brownish), hawfinch (brownish), nightingale (livid), *l/r plover, rock and water pipits* (brownish), kingfisher juv (brownish), R/N PHALAROPE juv (bluish); **MS:** Richard's pipit, quail, alpine swift (dark), rosy starling, song thrush (pale), *grey wagtail* (brownish), *Baillon's crake* (greyish); **M:** Nightjar (brownish), corncrake (pale), turtle dove (dark), lapwing (brownish), collared dove, stock dove (mauve), woodcock (greyish), r/l partridge juv, *water rail* (brownish), *ruff*, MANX SHEARWATERS (pale), LIT GULL win & imm, PUFFIN juv, B/H GULL juv (yellowish); **ML:** Woodpigeon, *oystercatcher* ad, COM GULL y (yellowish), GT SHEARWATER (whitish), CORY'S SHEARWATER; **L:** *P/f goose*, LESSER BLACK-BACK imm, ICELAND GULL, HERRING GULL, R/C POCHARD f, SHELDUCK ad (reddish), GT BLACK-BACK (livid bluish); **VL:** *G/l goose* ad, *heron*, GLAUCOUS GULL, EGYPTIAN GOOSE.

PINK AND BLACK: See Black and Pink (p. 183)

PINK AND BROWN: See Brown and Pink (p. 185)

PINK AND WHITE

Upperparts: **M:** *London pigeon* (pinkish-brown).
Underparts. **S:** L/t tit; **M:** *Roseate tern* sum; **ML:** IVORY GULL ad.

PURPLE: See Blue (p. 184)

RED
(including orange)
See also Chestnut, Pink

General Appearance. S: Crossbill m (imm m, orange).

Crown or Cap. S: Barred woodpecker juv; **MS:** Pied woodpecker m & juv; **M:** Green woodpecker; **ML:** G/b woodpecker; **L:** *Glossy ibis* (reddish-purple gloss on reddish-brown); **H:** *Com crane* ad.

Crest. VS: Goldcrest (orange) back of crest, firecrest m (reddish-orange) & f (orange-yellow); **ML:** G/b woodpecker.

Bill. M: R/f falcon m (orange), r/l partridge ad, *w/w black tern, com tern* sum (vermilion with black tip), *arctic tern* sum (crimson), B/H GULL ad (vermilion) & y (orange); **ML:** Chough, *oystercatcher* (orange), G/C GREBE; **L:** *W/f goose* Greenland race (orange), SURF SCOTER m (orange), KING EIDER m (orange), R/C POCHARD m, R/B MERGANSER, SHELDUCK ad, GOOSANDER; **VL:** *Snow goose, g/l goose* (orange), *bean goose* (orange), *heron*; **H:** White stork ad, MUTE SWAN ad (orange).

Eye. S: Barred woodpecker; **MS:** Pied woodpecker, *Baillon's crake, lit crake*; **M:** Golden oriole (dark), bee-eater, *water rail, rock dove & London pigeon* (orange), DABCHICK, B/N GREBE (orange-pink), MOORHEN ad; **ML:** *Stilt, avocet* m, COOT, SMEW, COM POCHARD m sum, G/C GREBE, SHOVELER m (orange); **L:** *Night heron* ad, R/C POCHARD m, R/T DIVER, R/B MERGANSER ad, B/T DIVER; **VL:** *Spoonbill*, G/N DIVER; **H:** *Com crane.*

Tail. S: Com redstart, black redstart.

Underparts. S: Bullfinch m.

Throat. VS: R/b flycatcher m (orange); **S:** Robin ad (reddish-orange; & breast); **L:** R/T DIVER sum.

Breast. S: Linnet m sum, robin ad (reddish-orange).

Legs and Feet. S: *Kingfisher* (imm, orange); **MS:** *Turnstone* (orange); **M:** R/f falcon (orange), r/l partridge ad, *w/w black tern, lit tern* ad (orange), *ruff* (orange), *com redshank* ad (reddish-orange) & juv (orange-yellow), *spotted redshank* sum (dark purplish) & win & juv (orange), *rock dove & London pigeon* (dull), *com tern* (juv orange), *arctic tern* sum (juv orange), *roseate tern*, LIT GULL, PUFFIN (autumn orange), BLACK GUILLEMOT ad, B/H GULL ad; **ML:** Chough, *stilt*, MANDARIN DUCK (orange), GOLDENEYE m (orange), GADWALL ad (orange), SHOVELER (orange); **L:** *Lesser white-front* (orange), *w/f goose* (orange), SURF SCOTER (orange), VELVET SCOTER, KING EIDER m (orange), R/C POCHARD m, MALLARD (orange), R/B MERGANSER, SHELDUCK ad (pinkish), GOOSANDER ad; **VL:** *Snow goose* (purplish), *bean goose* (orange), *heron*; **H:** White stork.

RED AND BROWN: See Brown and Red (p. 186)

WHITE OR WHITISH

(*=whitish)

General Appearance. (Gulls and terns included under Grey and White (p. 191) look white at a distance. **MS:** *Sanderling* win; **M:** Barn owl (in flight), ptarmigan win; **ML:** *Squacco heron* ad (in flight), *Greenland falcon*, SMEW m, IVORY GULL; **L:** Snowy owl, *ICELAND GULL imm; **VL:** *Snow goose* ad, *spoonbill*, *GLAUCOUS GULL imm, GANNET ad (at rest); **H:** White stork (at rest), BEWICK'S SWAN ad, WHOOPER SWAN ad, MUTE SWAN ad. N.B.—Many birds have occasional whitish (albino) forms, notably: **S:** House sparrow; **M:** Blackbird, *London pigeon*; **L:** **Com pheasant*, *p/f goose*.

Upperparts. **L:** EIDER m.

Head and Neck. **S:** *Snow bunting* m sum; **M:** B/H GULL win; **ML:** *Stilt* m win & f, *osprey* (streaked black), COM GULL ad & imm, KITTIWAKE sum & y, L/T DUCK win, FULMAR; **L:** LESSER BLACK-BACK ad & imm, ICELAND GULL, HERRING GULL ad & imm, KING EIDER m, GT BLACK-BACK ad & imm; **VL:** **Sea eagle* (head only), *heron* ad, GLAUCOUS GULL, CORMORANT sum, GANNET imm.

Crown or Cap. **S:** L/t tit ad (*juv), *barred woodpecker, R/N PHALAROPE win; **MS:** GREY PHALAROPE win; **ML:** **Marsh harrier* f & y, IVORY GULL imm.

Crest. **L:** *Night heron* ad; **VL:** *Spoonbill* sum (yellowish).

Bill. **ML:** G/b woodpecker, COOT ad.

Eye. **M:** Green woodpecker, jay (bluish); **ML:** FERRUGINOUS DUCK m; **VL:** SHAG juv (yellowish).

Neck (see also Head). **ML:** GOLDENEYE m; **L:** PINTAIL m, EIDER m.

Mantle. **ML:** *Avocet* (& rump); **L:** L/T DUCK m win, KING EIDER m, SHELDUCK ad (& rump).

Rump (see also Sides of Rump, p. 207). **VS:** *Mealy redpoll, house martin; **S:** Bullfinch, brambling, wheatear, woodchat, **snow bunting* m, STORM PETREL; **MS:** *Curlew sandpiper* win (*sum), *wood sandpiper*, *green sandpiper*, *turnstone*, F/T PETREL; **M:** Hoopoe, lapwing, jay, *w/w black tern* sum (& tail), *com redshank*, *spotted redshank*, *greenshank*, *rock dove*, *London pigeon*, *com tern* sum, *arctic tern* ad & juv, LIT GULL (& tail), SABINE'S GULL imm (& tail), B/H GULL (& tail); **ML:** Montagu's harrier f & imm, hen-harrier, lit bustard, *stilt*, *ba/t godwit*, *whimbrel*, *bl/t godwit*, *Sandwich tern* (& tail), *avocet* (& tail), *oystercatcher*, COM GULL ad (& tail), KITTIWAKE (& tail); **L:** *Curlew*, *lesser white-front*, *barnacle goose*, *p/f goose*, *w/f goose*, LESSER BLACK-BACK ad (& tail), ICELAND GULL ad (& tail), HERRING GULL (& tail), BRENT GOOSE, SHELDUCK ad (& tail), GT BLACK-BACK ad (& tail); **VL:** *G/l goose*, *bean goose*, GLAUCOUS GULL ad (& tail); **H:** CANADA GOOSE.

Tail (see also Rump). **S:** Snow bunting m (black feathers in centre); **M:** Collared dove (underside), *Water rail* (tail-coverts), MOORHEN (tail-coverts); **ML:** R/l buzzard; **VL:** Golden eagle y, *sea eagle* ad.

Wings. **S:** *Snow bunting* m; **M:** Ptarmigan sum & aut; **ML:** Lit bustard.

Underparts. **VS:** *Y/b warbler, *chiffchaff (northern races), *treecreeper, pied flycatcher, wood warbler, house martin, *sand martin*; **S:** *Lesser whitethroat, l/t tit, *tree sparrow, *house sparrow, *barred woodpecker, barred warbler imm, *woodchat, *bluethroat* ad, *Temminck's stint*, *lit stint*, *reed bunting* m, *l/r plover*, *Kentish plover*, *snow bunting*, *bearded tit* ad, R/N PHALAROPE; **MS:** Pied & white wagtails, *swallow, alpine swift, *pied woodpecker, *dunlin* win & juv, *curlew sandpiper* win, *ringed plover*, *com sandpiper*, GREY PHALAROPE win, LIT AUK; **M:** G/g shrike, barn owl, *w/w black tern* win, *black tern* win, *lit tern*, *knot* win, *grey plover* win, *spotted redshank* win, *greenshank* win, *com tern*, *arctic tern* win (*sum), *roseate tern*, *g/b tern*, MANX SHEARWATER (*Mauretanian race), LIT GULL, PUFFIN, B/N GREBE, SLAVONIAN GREBE win, SABINE'S GULL imm, BLACK GUILLEMOT win & y, B/H GULL; **ML:** Lit bustard m sum, magpie, *stilt*, *Sandwich tern*, *avocet*, *squacco heron*, *osprey*, SMEW, COM GULL ad (*juv), KITTIWAKE, RAZORBILL, GUILLEMOT, L/T DUCK win, *R/N GREBE, GT SHEARWATER, CORY'S SHEARWATER, IVORY GULL imm, ARCTIC SKUA pale form, GOLDENEYE, FULMAR, G/C GREBE ad & imm, POMARINE SKUA pale form, L/T SKUA ad; **L:** **Night heron* ad, *barnacle goose*, LESSER BLACK-BACK ad (*imm), ICELAND GULL ad, HERRING GULL ad (*imm), PINTAIL m, R/T DIVER, *BRENT GOOSE pale-breasted form, SHELDUCK juv, B/T DIVER, GOOSANDER, GT BLACK-BACK ad (*imm); **VL:** GLAUCOUS GULL ad, G/N DIVER, CORMORANT y, GANNET imm; **H:** White stork, BEWICK'S SWAN imm, WHOOPER SWAN y, MUTE SWAN y.

Throat. **VS:** *Willow warbler, *chiffchaff, *grasshopper warbler, *reed warbler*, *marsh warbler*, *sedge warbler*; **S:** Lesser whitethroat, com whitethroat, *wheatear juv, Lapland bunting f, swift juv (*ad), *r/b shrike f, **bluethroat* imm m, **bearded tit* juv, **kingfisher*; **MS:** *Pied wagtail juv, *quail, dotterel sum, *pied woodpecker, *dipper* (& breast), **lit crake* f, **purple sandpiper*, *turnstone*; **M:** Hobby, lapwing win, jay, *kestrel, r/l partridge, *ruff* win, MOORHEN y; **ML:** Peregrine, stone curlew, *ba/t godwit* (not m sum), *oystercatcher* win, *squacco heron*, *COOT juv, GARGANEY f & juv, MANDARIN DUCK f; **L:** Snowy owl, *barnacle goose*, R/B MERGANSER f, GOOSANDER f; **VL:** SHAG juv; **H:** CANADA GOOSE.

Breast. **VS:** Crested tit, goldfinch ad; **MS:** *Dipper* ad (*juv); **M:** Ring ouzel m sum (*m win & f & imm); **ML:** SHOVELER m; **L:** EIDER m, SHELDUCK; **VL:** *Heron*.

Flanks. **M:** Golden plover sum; **ML:** TUFTED DUCK (& belly), SCAUP (& belly); **L:** R/C POCHARD m (& belly), BRENT GOOSE; **VL:** Capercaillie m.

WHITE AND BLACK: See Black and White (p. 222)

WHITE AND BLUE: See Blue and White (p. 224)

WHITE AND BROWN: See Brown and White (p. 225)

WHITE AND BUFF: See Buff and White (p. 226)

WHITE AND CHESTNUT: See Chestnut and White (p. 228)

WHITE AND GREY: See Grey and White (p. 231)

WHITE AND GREY-BROWN: See Grey-Brown and White (p. 192)

WHITE AND PINK: See Pink and White (p. 193)

YELLOW OR YELLOWISH

See also Brown (for yellowish-brown), Buff, Green (for yellowish-green) and Red (for orange)
(*=yellowish; o=orange-yellow)

General Appearance. S: *Yellow wagtail* m sum.

Head. S: Yellowhammer m; **M:** Golden oriole m; **VL:** *GANNET ad (& neck).

Crown or Cap. VS: Serin m.

Crest. VS: Goldcrest, firecrest f (o); **VL:** **Spoonbill.*

Bill. VS: Redpolls; **S:** Twite win, brambling win, Lapland bunting, hawfinch win & juv, **snow bunting* win, *bearded tit* m; **MS:** Starling sum, GREY PHALAROPE f; **M:** Ring ouzel, blackbird m (o) & *imm m *f, fieldfare, *barn owl, *lit tern, lit bittern*; **ML:** *COOT juv, KITTIWAKE sum, FULMAR, GADWALL juv; **L:** *W/f goose* Greenland race, LESSER BLACK-BACK ad, ICELAND GULL ad, HERRING GULL ad, MALLARD m, EIDER m sum, GT BLACK-BACK ad; **VL:** *Sea eagle* ad (pale), *heron*, GLAUCOUS GULL ad.

Eye. S: Barred warbler, *bearded tit*; **MS:** *Quail, Scops owl, lit owl; **M:** Turtle dove, sparrowhawk, cuckoo (o), l/e owl (o), s/e owl (o), *lit bittern*; **ML:** Stone curlew, woodpigeon, Montagu's harrier m, hen-harrier, g/b woodpecker, lit bustard, honey buzzard, *squacco heron*, **marsh harrier*, *osprey*, TUFTED DUCK m, GOLDENEYE, SCAUP, SHOVELER m; **L:** Snowy owl, kite, LESSER BLACK-BACK, ICELAND GULL, HERRING GULL, SURF SCOTER, R/B MERGANSER imm, GT BLACK-BACK; **VL:** *Sea eagle* ad, *bittern*, *purple heron*, *heron*, GLAUCOUS GULL, EGYPTIAN GOOSE, SHAG juv.

Neck. ML: ARCTIC SKUA sum (pale form), POMARINE SKUA sum (pale form), L/T SKUA sum; **VL:** *GANNET ad.

Mantle. M: Golden oriole m (& rump).

Rump. VS: *Goldcrest ad, serin, siskin ad; **S:** Greenfinch ad, *crossbill f & juv; **M:** Golden oriole, bee-eater, green woodpecker.

Underparts. VS: Willow warbler (esp juv), chiffchaff (esp juv), coal tit juv, blue tit; **S:** Cirl bunting m, yellowhammer, *yellow wagtails* ad; **MS:** *Grey wagtail* ad.

Throat. VS: Serin, wood warbler; **S:** Ortolan, hawfinch juv, *shore lark*; **M:** Bee-eater.

Breast. VS: Serin m.

Legs and Feet. VS: Dartford warbler; **S:** Tawny pipit; **MS:** Corn bunting, dotterel, *ringed plover*, *purple sandpiper*; **M:** Merlin, sparrowhawk, hobby, *roller, com partridge juv, cuckoo, kestrel, *gt snipe* (pale), PUFFIN win; **ML:** Peregrine ad, stone curlew, Montagu's harrier, hen-harrier, lit bustard (greyish), com buzzard, r/l buzzard (feet), honey buzzard, *marsh harrier*, *Greenland falcon* ad, GUILLEMOT, GADWALL juv; **L:** Kite, *night heron* ad (pale), **p/f goose* imm, LESSER

BLACK-BACK ad, GOOSANDER juv (dull); **VL:** Golden eagle (feet), *sea eagle, spoonbill* imm (pale).

YELLOW AND BLACK: See Black and Yellow (p. 223)

YELLOW AND BLUE: See Blue and Yellow (p. 224)

YELLOW AND CHESTNUT: See Chestnut and Yellow, (p. 228)

YELLOW AND GREEN: See Green and Yellow (p. 229)

YELLOW AND GREY: See Grey and Yellow (p. 231)

BARRED, SPOTTED, STREAKED AND STRIPED EFFECTS

Barred Effects

General Appearance. VS: Wren; **S:** R/b shrike juv; **M:** Hobby juv, cuckoo juv, kestrel f & y, l/e owl juv, woodcock, s/e owl juv; **ML:** Tawny owl juv; **L:** Snowy owl (esp f), *lesser white-front, p/f goose, w/f goose*; **VL:** *G/l goose, bean goose*; **H:** CANADA GOOSE.

Upperparts. M: BLACK GUILLEMOT win & imm; **L:** *Barnacle goose.*

Crown or Cap. S: *Kingfisher.*

Neck. ML: ARCTIC SKUA win (pale form), POMARINE SKUA win (pale form), L/T SKUA win.

Mantle. S: Barred woodpecker; **M:** Hoopoe.

Rump. M: *Knot.*

Tail. MS: *Wood sandpiper, green sandpiper* (tip only); **M:** Merlin f & y, sparrowhawk, r/f falcon f & imm, kestrel f & y, l/e owl, s/e owl, *com redshank, spotted redshank, greenshank*; **ML:** Tawny owl, peregrine, Montagu's harrier f, hen-harrier f & y, goshawk, com buzzard, honey buzzard, *ba/t godwit, whimbrel, Greenland falcon*; **L:** *Curlew*; **VL:** Com pheasant m, golden eagle ad.

Underparts. S: Barred warbler ad, hawfinch juv, r/b shrike f & juv; **MS:** *Spotted crake*; **M:** Corncrake, sparrowhawk, green woodpecker, juv, cuckoo, water rail y; **ML:** Peregrine ad, black grouse f & y, com buzzard, r/l buzzard, honey buzzard, ARCTIC SKUA imm (pale form), POMARINE SKUA imm (pale form), L/T SKUA imm; **L:** *Lesser white-front* ad, *w/f goose* ad.

Breast. M: G/g shrike f & imm; **ML:** *Bl/t godwit* sum (& belly), GARGANEY m, GADWALL m (crescentic bars).

Flanks. S: R/b shrike f; **MS:** *Baillon's crake*; **M:** Com partridge (rufous bars), r/l partridge (barred black, white & chestnut), *water rail.*

Belly. MS: *Baillon's crake*; **M:** Green woodpecker f, *water rail*; **ML:** *Bl/t godwit* sum (& breast).

SPOTTED EFFECTS

(Dark spots on pale ground, except where otherwise stated)

General Appearance. (All pale spots.) **MS:** Starling ad, lit owl, *spotted crake*; **M:** Nutcracker; **VL:** GANNET juv.

Upperparts. (Pale spots.) **L:** B/T DIVER sum; **VL:** G/N DIVER sum.

Mantle. M: Kestrel m.

Tail. (All pale spots.) **VS:** Goldfinch; **M:** Barred woodpecker; **MS:** Swallow, pied woodpecker; **M:** Cuckoo; **VL:** Capercaillie m.

Wings. MS: Pied woodpecker (pale); **M:** Kestrel m.

Underparts. VS: Pied flycatcher juv; **S:** Spotted flycatcher juv, wryneck, nightingale juv, *snow bunting* juv; **MS:** Song thrush; **M:** Ring ouzel juv, fieldfare, mistle thrush, barn owl; **VL:** *G/l goose* (sparse).

Throat. VL: *Purple heron* imm, *heron.*

Breast. S: Wheatear juv; **MS:** *Purple sandpiper*; **M:** R/l partridge, TEAL; **L:** R/B MERGANSER m; **VL:** *Purple heron* imm.

STREAKED AND STRIPED EFFECTS

(Dark streaks, except where otherwise stated)

General Appearance. VS: Serin, goldfinch juv, siskin f & juv, redpolls, treecreeper (pale), grasshopper warbler, whinchat, stonechat (not m sum), *sedge warbler*; **S:** Linnet (not m sum), twite, lit bunting, black redstart juv, tree sparrow, house sparrow, greenfinch juv, scarlet grosbeak f & juv, hedge sparrow, meadow pipit, tree pipit, woodlark, Lapland bunting, ortolan, cirl bunting f & juv, yellowhammer f & juv, crossbill f & juv, *reed bunting, rock pipit, water pipit* sum, *snow bunting* juv; **MS:** Corn bunting, skylark, Richard's pipit, scops owl, song thrush juv (pale), *lit crake, jack snipe*; **M:** Ring ouzel juv (pale), blackbird juv (pale), l/e owl, s/e owl, *com snipe, gt snipe*; **ML:** Tawny owl, stone curlew, *ba/t godwit* win, *whimbrel, bl/t godwit* win, *Greenland falcon*; **L:** Kite (pale), curlew, *night heron* imm (pale); **VL:** Com pheasant m, *bittern.*

Upperparts. S: Cirl bunting m, yellowhammer m, *Temminck's stint* sum, *lit stint* sum, *snow bunting* m win & f & imm; **MS:** *Baillon's crake, dunlin* sum & juv, *curlew sandpiper* sum, *pectoral sandpiper*; **M:** Ptarmigan (aut), *water rail*; **ML:** *Bl/t godwit* sum.

Underparts. S: Spotted flycatcher ad, meadow pipit, tree pipit, *rock pipit, water pipit* win; **MS:** Redwing; **M:** Merlin, hobby, kestrel, *lit bittern* f; **ML:** Peregrine y, Montagu's harrier f, hen-harrier f & y; **L:** Kite ad (pale); **VL:** *Heron* y.

Throat. MS: *Grey wagtail* f sum, *dipper* juv, *dunlin, green sandpiper*; **M:** Sparrowhawk, *greenshank* sum.

Breast. S: *Temminck's stint* sum, *lit stint* sum; **MS:** *Grey wagtail* juv, *dipper* juv, *dunlin* sum, *pectoral sandpiper, green sandpiper*; **M:** Fieldfare, ptarmigan sum & aut, *knot* win, *ruff* win, *greenshank* sum; **ML:** *Marsh harrier* m; **VL:** *Purple heron* ad.

Flanks. **VS:** Siskin ad, redpolls, grasshopper warbler; **S:** Lit bunting, brambling, barred woodpecker, *reed bunting*; **M:** Hoopoe, BLACK GUILLEMOT juv; **ML:** Montagu's harrier m, GUILLEMOT ad.

DARKER OR PALER EFFECTS

(Same Colour, but Darker or Paler than Other Parts of Body)

Head and Neck (darker than body). **ML:** COOT; **L:** *P/f goose*; **VL:** *Bean goose*.

Head (paler than body). **ML:** R/l buzzard, *marsh harrier* f & y, *osprey*; **L:** Kite, RUDDY SHELDUCK (& neck); **VL:** Golden eagle, *sea eagle*.

Crown (darker than rest of head). **MS:** Dotterel, *dunlin* sum, *curlew sandpiper* sum; **M:** *Knot* sum; **ML:** GADWALL; **L:** MALLARD m.

Cheeks (paler than rest of face). **MS:** Song thrush; **M:** Mistle thrush ad, merlin, sparrowhawk, *spotted redshank* win; **VL:** EGYPTIAN GOOSE.

Nape (paler than upperparts). **S:** Hawfinch ad; **M:** Merlin f & y, jackdaw.

Mantle (darker than upperparts). **MS:** Waxwing.

Rump (paler than mantle). **VS:** Coal tit ad, crested tit, goldfinch, redpolls f & juv; **S:** Hawfinch juv; **M:** G/g shrike, magpie, *roseate tern* sum; **ML:** Montagu's harrier m, COM GULL y, GT SHEARWATER; **L:** *Night heron* imm, LESSER BLACK-BACK y, HERRING GULL y, GT BLACK-BACK y.

Tail (darker than mantle). **VS:** Goldcrest, firecrest, coal tit, crested tit, marsh tit, willow tit; **S:** Woodlark, crossbill, *yellow wagtails*.

Wings (darker than mantle). **VS:** Crested tit, siskin; **S:** Com redstart, crossbill, *yellow wagtails*; **MS:** Rosy starling juv, grey wagtail; **M:** Golden oriole y. (Paler than mantle.) **M:** Ring ouzel.

Underparts (paler than upperparts). **VS:** Goldcrest, firecrest, willow warbler, chiffchaff, crested tit, marsh tit, willow tit, r/b flycatcher f & y, grasshopper warbler, Dartford warbler juv, whinchat sum, *reed warbler*, *marsh warbler*, *sedge warbler*; **S:** Lit bunting, com whitethroat, garden warbler, blackcap, spotted flycatcher, black redstart f & imm, house sparrow f & juv, chaffinch f & juv, hawfinch, nightingale, tawny pipit, *water pipit* sum, *shore lark*; **MS:** Richard's pipit, waxwing, rosy starling juv; **M:** R/f falcon m, green woodpecker, stock dove, *rock dove*, *London pigeon*, MAURETANIAN SHEARWATER, DAB-CHICK; **ML:** Woodpigeon, Montagu's harrier m, hen-harrier m, *ba/t godwit* m win & f, *bl/t godwit* win, COM POCHARD f & y; **L:** R/C POCHARD f, R/B MERGANSER f & y, GOOSANDER f & y; **VL:** *Purple heron* imm, EGYPTIAN GOOSE, SHAG y, CORMORANT y.

Throat (paler than head). **S:** Linnet m sum; wryneck; **MS:** Starling juv; **M:** Golden oriole f & y, corncrake; **ML:** *Bl/t godwit* win.

Belly (paler than breast). **VS:** Serin, siskin m; **MS:** Corn bunting, pied wagtail juv; **M:** Turtle dove; **ML:** COM SCOTER f & y.

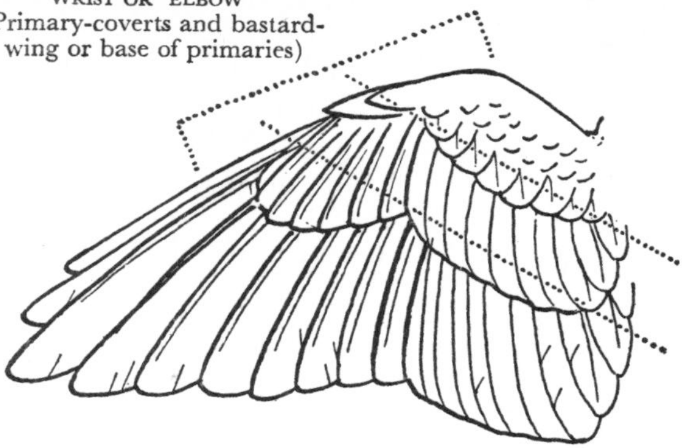

The Topography of a Wing

SINGLE BARS, LINES, PATCHES, SPOTS, STREAKS AND STRIPES

(Arranged by Colours)

BLACK OR BLACKISH BARS OR BANDS

Neck Collar. **S:** *L/r plover*; **MS:** *Ringed plover*; **M:** Collared dove, PUFFIN; **ML:** Lit bustard m sum, KITTIWAKE y (incomplete), COM POCHARD m; **L:** R/C POCHARD m, RUDDY SHELDUCK m (narrow); **VL:** G/N DIVER sum (dark green).

Wing Bars. (1) **Forewing.** **M:** LIT GULL imm; **ML:** *Avocet*, KITTIWAKE y, COM POCHARD. (2) **Midwing.** **S:** Brambling, chaffinch, *bearded tit*; **VL:** EGYPTIAN GOOSE. (3) **Hindwing.** **VS:** Goldcrest, firecrest; **M:** Stock dove (two short bars), *rock dove* (two long bars), *London pigeon* (two long bars); **ML:** Stone curlew, Montagu's harrier m; **L:** MALLARD (black & white lines at either end of blue patch). For definitions, see illustration on p. 200.

Bar on Rump. **MS:** F/T PETREL (dark vertical bar).

Bar at Tip of Tail. **VS:** Siskin; **S:** *Bluethroat*; **MS:** *Turnstone*; **M:** Merlin m, lapwing, stock dove, kestrel, ptarmigan, *rock dove, London pigeon*, LIT GULL imm, SABINE'S GULL imm, B/H GULL y; **ML:** Stone curlew, woodpigeon, r/l buzzard, *bl/t godwit*, COM GULL y, KITTIWAKE imm, IVORY GULL imm; **L:** LESSER BLACK-BACK y, HERRING GULL y, GT BLACK-BACK y; **VL:** Golden eagle.

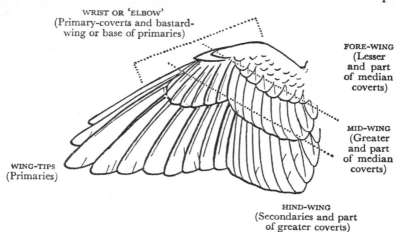

Breast Band. **VS:** Blue tit (dark vertical bar); **S:** Great tit (black vertical bar),

Bluethroat f & imm, *l/r plover* ad, *Kentish plover* m (incomplete), *shore lark*, *yellow wagtail* juv; **MS:** Pied wagtail win & juv, quail m, swallow (blue-black), dotterel sum, *ringed plover* ad; **M:** Bee-eater, r/l partridge ad; **ML:** Lit bustard, L/T DUCK f & imm, ARCTIC SKUA pale form, POMARINE SKUA pale form.

BLACK OR BLACKISH LINES, STREAKS OR STRIPES

(dts=down to shoulders)

Eyestripe above Eye. **VS:** Goldcrest ad, firecrest (& white); **S:** Barred woodpecker; **VL:** *Heron.*

Eyestripe through Eye. **VS:** Firecrest, y/b warbler, crested tit (behind eye only), blue tit; **S:** Nuthatch, l/t tit ad, cirl bunting m, r/b shrike m, woodchat, *Kentish plover* m, R/N PHALAROPE win & juv; **MS:** Waxwing, *jack snipe*, *turnstone* sum (dts), GREY PHALAROPE win; **M:** G/g shrike, woodcock, ptarmigan m win, r/l partridge ad (dts), *lit tern* ad, *com snipe*, *gt snipe*, PUFFIN, TEAL f; **ML:** *Osprey* (dts), GUILLEMOT win.

Eyestripe below Eye. **S:** Wheatear, barred woodpecker (dts), *l/r plover* ad, *bearded tit* (dts); **MS:** Pied woodpecker (dts), *ringed plover* ad, *turnstone* sum (dts); **M:** Bee-eater, r/f falcon f, hobby (dts), lapwing, green woodpecker (dts), jay (dts), LIT GULL imm (dts), Peregrine (thick, dts), stone curlew; **VL:** Bittern (dts), *purple heron* ad.

Line between Cheeks and Nape. **VS:** Crested tit ad; **MS:** Pied woodpecker.

Stripes on Neck. **M:** B/N GREBE juv, SLAVONIAN GREBE juv; **ML:** G/C GREBE juv; **VL:** *Purple heron* ad.

Line on Shoulders. **ML:** SMEW m (two lines); KITTIWAKE y.

Stripe at Side of Mantle. **ML:** *Avocet*; **L:** PINTAIL m.

Single Feathers on Tail. **S:** *Temminck's stint*, *lit stint*, *snow bunting*; **MS:** *Pectoral sandpiper*, *sanderling*, *purple sandpiper*; **M:** Roller, *ruff*; **L:** L/T DUCK m, PINTAIL m.

Line between Throat and Breast. **VS:** Blue tit juv; **MS:** Quail m; **M:** R/l partridge ad, PUFFIN.

Line between Breast and Flanks. **ML:** MANDARIN DUCK m (two lines).

Two Stripes on Throat. **MS:** Quail m.

BLACK OR BLACKISH PATCHES OR SPOTS

Forehead. **S:** Chaffinch m, woodchat; **MS:** Waxwing; **VL:** *Purple heron* imm; **H:** *Com crane* ad.

Tip of Bill. **MS:** *Ringed plover*, *jack snipe*, GREY PHALAROPE f; **M:** Woodcock, *lit tern*, *com redshank*, *spotted redshank*, *com tern* sum, *arctic tern* (spring & aut), *roseate tern* sum, B/H GULL y; **ML:** Stone curlew, g/b woodpecker, *ba/t godwit*, *bl/t godwit*, *squacco heron*, KITTIWAKE imm, R/N GREBE, ARCTIC SKUA, WIGEON, COM POCHARD, POMARINE SKUA; **L:** Kite; **H:** BEWICK'S SWAN, WHOOPER SWAN.

Base of Bill. **ML:** IVORY GULL ad, COM POCHARD; **L:** L/T DUCK m, SURF SCOTER m, VELVET SCOTER; **VL:** *Bean goose*; **H:** MUTE SWAN ad.

Cheeks and area round Eye. **VS:** Crested tit (L-shaped patch); **S:** Lesser whitethroat, com redstart m, tree sparrow (patch), wheatear m, r/b shrike m, woodchat, *l/r plover* ad, *shore lark,* R/N PHALAROPE win (round eye); **MS:** *Ringed plover* ad, GREY PHALAROPE win (round eye); **M:** G/g shrike, bee-eater, golden plover, roller (round eye), lapwing win (patch), green woodpecker, *grey plover,* MANX SHEARWATER, LIT GULL (patch), SLAVONIAN GREBE sum, B/H GULL win (patch); **H:** White stork (round eye).

Patch on Nape. **ML:** SMEW m.

Patch on Wing. **M:** *Grey plover* (under wing), TEAL (hindwing); **ML:** Lit bustard (elbow), WIGEON (hindwing), GADWALL (hindwing).

Wing Tips. **S:** Hawfinch, *Temminck's stint, lit stint, l/r plover, snow bunting,* R/N PHALAROPE; **MS:** Waxwing, swallow, dotterel, *dunlin, curlew sandpiper, pectoral sandpiper, ringed plover, sanderling,* GREY PHALAROPE; **M:** Turtle dove, golden plover, merlin, r/f falcon f, hobby, roller, collared dove, stock dove, kestrel, ptarmigan juv, red grouse, *knot, grey plover, com redshank, spotted redshank, greenshank, rock dove, London pigeon,* SABINE'S GULL imm, TEAL, B/H GULL; **ML:** Stone curlew, woodpigeon, Montagu's harrier m, hen-harrier m, *ba/t godwit, whimbrel, bl/t godwit, avocet, marsh harrier,* SMEW, COM GULL y (ad, & white), KITTIWAKE, IVORY GULL imm; **L:** *Curlew,* LESSER BLACK-BACK y (ad, & white), HERRING GULL y (ad, & white), R/T DIVER, EIDER m, R/B MERGANSER, SHELDUCK, RUDDY SHELDUCK, B/T DIVER, GOOSANDER, GT BLACK-BACK y (ad, & white); **VL:** Com pheasant m, *snow goose, purple heron, spoonbill* imm, *heron,* EGYPTIAN GOOSE, G/N DIVER, GANNET; **H:** *Com crane.*

Patch at Side of Breast. **S:** *Kentish plover*; **M:** *Black tern* win.

Patch on Belly. **ML:** GT SHEARWATER. (Beware other sea birds when oiled.)

BLUE BARS OR BANDS

Breast Band. **S:** *Bluethroat* m & imm m (occ f); **MS:** Swallow (blue-black).

Wing Bar. **M:** Collared dove (blue-grey, on leading edge).

BLUE STRIPES

Eyestripe below Eye. **S:** *Bluethroat* m win & imm & f sum.

BLUE OR PURPLE PATCHES OR SPOTS

Cheeks and area round Eye. **VL:** Com pheasant m (purple).

Patch on Neck (all purple shot with green). **M:** Stock dove, *rock dove, London pigeon*; **ML:** Woodpigeon.

Shoulders. **M:** Roller.

Patch on Wing. **M:** Jay (midwing); **ML:** GARGANEY m (blue-grey; forewing), MANDARIN DUCK m (hindwing), SHOVELER (forewing); **L:** MALLARD (hindwing); **VL:** Com pheasant m (forewing).

BROWN BARS OR BANDS

Neck Collar. VL: EGYPTIAN GOOSE, G/N DIVER win & imm.
Bar at Tip of Tail. MS: *Green sandpiper* (barred); **ML:** Com buzzard (dark).
Breast Band. VS: *Sand martin*; **S:** *L/r plover* juv, *Kentish plover* f (incomplete); **MS:** Alpine swift, *curlew sandpiper* (faint streaks), *ringed plover* juv; **ML:** *Osprey* (pale to rusty).

BROWN LINES, STREAKS OR STRIPES

Stripes on Crown. MS: *Jack snipe* (3 dark & 2 pale); **M:** *Com snipe* (2 dark & 1 pale), *gt snipe* (do); **ML:** *Whimbrel* (do).
Eyestripe through Eye. S: *Kentish plover* f; **MS:** Quail (dts).
Eyestripe below Eye (dts). **S:** *Bluethroat* f & imm m (dts), *reed bunting* f & juv (dts), *l/r plover* juv; **MS:** Richard's pipit (dts), *ringed plover* juv; **ML:** Peregrine y (thick).

BROWN PATCHES OR SPOTS

Cheeks and area round Eye. VL: EGYPTIAN GOOSE.
Patch on Neck. ML: L/T DUCK win (dark).
Patch on Breast. VL: EGYPTIAN GOOSE.

BUFF BARS OR BANDS

Bar at Tip of Tail. M: Merlin f & y, hobby (esp y).
Breast Band. M: Cuckoo f.

BUFF LINES, STREAKS OR STRIPES

Stripe on Crown. S: Woodlark (line between crown & nape; actually eyestripes meeting); **MS:** Quail.
Eyestripe above Eye. VS: Wren, willow warbler ad, chiffchaff, redpolls, grasshopper warbler (faint), whinchat juv, *reed warbler*, *marsh warbler*, *sedge warbler* (conspicuous); **S:** Meadow pipit, tree pipit, woodlark, tawny pipit, *bluethroat*, *reed bunting* f & juv, *yellow wagtail*; **MS:** Skylark, Richard's pipit, quail, redwing (conspicuous), dotterel win, *grey wagtail*, *pectoral sandpiper* (faint), *jack snipe*; **M:** Lapwing win, *com snipe*, *gt snipe*, TEAL m; **ML:** *Ba/t godwit* win, *whimbrel*, *bl/t godwit* win.
Eyestripe below Eye (and, except for TEAL, down to shoulders). **S:** *Bluethroat* f & imm m, *reed bunting* f & juv; **MS:** Richard's pipit, redwing; **M:** TEAL m.
Stripes on Mantle. M: *Com snipe*, *gt snipe*.

BUFF PATCHES OR SPOTS

Tip of Bill. ML: MANDARIN DUCK m.
Shoulders. S: Brambling (deep buff).
Patch on Wing. M: *Lit bittern* m (forewing).

CHESTNUT BARS OR BANDS

Wing Bar. S: Brambling (midwing).
Breast Band. S: Yellowhammer m, *bluethroat* m; **MS:** Quail f (spots); **L:** SHELDUCK ad.

CHESTNUT LINES, STREAKS OR STRIPES

Eyestripe through Eye. M: B/N GREBE sum (golden-chestnut, down to shoulders), SLAVONIAN GREBE sum.
Eyestripe below Eye. M: R/f falcon f.

CHESTNUT PATCHES OR SPOTS

Forehead. MS: Swallow.
Cheeks and area round Eye. S: Lit bunting, *reed bunting* f & juv, *kingfisher*; **M:** Sparrowhawk m, barn-owl, DABCHICK sum; **VL:** *Purple heron* ad.
Nape. S: Lapland bunting; **M:** R/l partridge ad.
Sides of Neck. S: R/N PHALAROPE sum.
Sides of Rump. M: B/N GREBE sum, SLAVONIAN GREBE sum.
Patch on Wing. ML: GADWALL m (midwing; obscure in f); **L:** Capercaillie m (forewing), SHELDUCK (hindwing).
Spot on Throat. S: *Bluethroat* m.
Patch on Breast. M: Com partridge (horseshoe-shaped).

GREEN BARS OR BANDS

Breast Band. S: Cirl bunting (olive); **VL:** Capercaillie m.

GREEN LINES, STREAKS OR STRIPES

Line between Forehead and Crown. M: Bee-eater.
Eyestripe through Eye. VS: Wood warbler (brownish); **M:** TEAL m.
Eyestripe below Eye. S: Ortolan (olive; & down to shoulders).

GREEN PATCHES OR SPOTS

Forehead. ML: MANDARIN DUCK m; **L:** *Glossy ibis* (gloss).
Tip of Bill. MS: *Spotted crake.*

Cheeks and area round Eye. **M:** Hobby juv (pale), sparrowhawk (pale); **L:** KING EIDER m.

Patch on Nape. **L:** EIDER m.

Patch on Neck. (All shot with purple.) **M:** Stock dove, *rock dove, London pigeon*; **ML:** Woodpigeon; **L:** EIDER m.

Patch on Wing. (All hindwing.) **M:** TEAL; **ML:** GARGANEY, WIGEON, SHOVELER; **L:** PINTAIL (bronzy), SHELDUCK, RUDDY SHELDUCK; **VL:** EGYPTIAN GOOSE (bronzy).

GREY BARS OR BANDS

Bar at Tip of Tail. **M:** Woodcock.

Breast Band. **ML:** GOLDENEYE f & imm.

GREY LINES, STREAKS OR STRIPES

Eyestripe above Eye. **M:** Corncrake.

Eyestripe through Eye. **M:** *Knot* win.

Stripe at Side of Mantle. **ML:** GARGANEY m.

Single Feathers in Tail. **S:** *Rock pipit.*

GREY PATCHES OR SPOTS

Forehead. **M:** R/l partridge ad; **ML:** Rook ad (bare skin), IVORY GULL imm.

Cheeks and area round Eye. **S:** Lesser whitethroat (dark brownish), blackcap, house sparrow m, brambling f (brownish), *b/h wagtail* m sum (bluish); **MS:** *Baillon's crake, lit crake* m; **M:** Merlin, hobby juv, green woodpecker ad, jackdaw, *water rail, grey plover* win (brownish), PUFFIN; **ML:** Peregrine juv, lit bustard m (bluish), R/N GREBE sum, IVORY GULL imm; **L:** *Night heron.*

Patch on Nape. **S:** Blackcap m, brambling, R/N PHALAROPE win (bluish); **MS:** GREY PHALAROPE win (dark); **M:** Jackdaw; **L:** *Night heron* ad, B/T DIVER sum.

Patch on Wing. (All forewing.) **MS:** *Curlew sandpiper* sum; **M:** *Knot* sum; **ML:** GARGANEY m (bluish), WIGEON f; **L:** *P/f goose*, R/B MERGANSER f & y, GOOSANDER f & y; **VL:** *G/l goose.*

Wing Tips. **M:** Jay, *lit tern* juv, *com tern* juv, *arctic tern* juv, *roseate tern* juv; **ML:** *Sandwich tern* juv.

RED LINES, STREAKS OR STRIPES

Eyestripe below Eye (and down to shoulders). **M:** Green woodpecker m (ad & juv).

RED, PINK AND ORANGE PATCHES AND SPOTS

Forehead. **VS:** Goldfinch ad (red), redpolls ad (red); **S:** Linnet m sum (red), robin ad (reddish-orange); **M:** MOORHEN ad (red frontal shield).

Tip of Bill. **M:** PUFFIN (red); **ML:** IVORY GULL ad (red); **L:** L/T DUCK m (red, orange), VELVET SCOTER m (orange); **VL:** *Bean goose* (orange).

Patch on Bill. **ML:** COM SCOTER m (orange).

Red Spot on Bill. **L:** LESSER BLACK-BACK ad, ICELAND GULL ad, HERRING GULL ad, GT BLACK-BACK ad; **VL:** GLAUCOUS GULL ad.

Base of Bill. **MS:** *Lit crake* (red), *spotted crake* (red); **M:** R/f falcon (orange cere), stock dove (pink), *water rail* (red), *com redshank* sum (red) & win (orange), *spotted redshank* (red), *com tern* win (red), *arctic tern* win (red), *roseate tern* sum (red), MOORHEN (red); **ML:** Woodpigeon (pink), *ba/t godwit* (pink), *bl/t godwit* (pink), COM GULL y (pink); **L:** LESSER BLACK-BACK y (pink), ICELAND GULL imm (pink), HERRING GULL y (pink), VELVET SCOTER m (orange), GT BLACK-BACK y (pink); **VL:** GLAUCOUS GULL imm (pink).

Eyelids or Orbital Ring. **VS:** Dartford warbler (red); **S:** L/t tit (pink); **MS:** *Lit crake* (red); **M:** R/l partridge (red), PUFFIN (red; sum, with blue-grey appendages), B/H GULL ad (red); **ML:** COM GULL ad (red), KITTIWAKE (orange), IVORY GULL ad (red); **L:** LESSER BLACK-BACK ad (red), ICELAND GULL ad (red), HERRING GULL ad (orange), GT BLACK-BACK ad (red) & y (orange); **VL:** *G/l goose* (pink), SHAG (orange).

Cheeks and area round Eye. **VS:** Goldfinch ad (red); **S:** Robin ad (orange); **M:** Turtle dove (pink), r/f falcon (orange), com partridge (red), ptarmigan (red), red grouse (red), r/l partridge (red); **L:** Black grouse m (red), R/C POCHARD m (pinkish-brown); **VL:** Com pheasant m (red), capercaillie m (red), *spoonbill* imm (pink).

Patch on Nape. **S:** *Shore lark* (pinkish-brown); **MS:** Pied woodpecker m.

Patch on Wing. **MS:** Waxwing (red; hindwing).

Chin. **VS:** Goldfinch ad (red).

Under Tail-Coverts. **MS:** Pied woodpecker (red); **M:** Lapwing (pinkish-brown).

Garter on Leg. **M:** MOORHEN ad (red).

WHITE OR WHITISH BARS OR BANDS
(*=whitish)

Neck Collar. **S:** *Reed bunting, l/r plover, Kentish plover*; **MS:** *Ringed plover*; **M:** *W/w black tern* win, *black tern* win; **ML:** Woodpigeon ad (incomplete), lit bustard m sum, ARCTIC SKUA pale form, GOLDENEYE f, POMARINE SKUA pale form, L/T SKUA; **L:** MALLARD m (narrow), R/B MERGANSER m, GOOSANDER imm m; **VL:** Com pheasant m, G/N DIVER sum (alternate black & white stripes).

Wing Bars, Single. (1) **Forewing.** **M:** B/H GULL ad. (2) **Midwing.** **VS:** Blue tit, pied flycatcher; **S:** Gt tit, brambling, *hawfinch, **Temminck's stint*, **lit stint*, **Kentish plover*, *STORM PETREL, R/N PHALAROPE; **MS:** *Dotterel, **dunlin*, **curlew sandpiper, ringed plover, com sandpiper, sanderling*, **purple sandpiper, turnstone*, GREY PHALAROPE; **M:** **Knot*, **grey plover*, **ruff*, TEAL; **ML:** SHOVELER; **L:** KING EIDER f, PINTAIL, MALLARD, EIDER f. (3) **Hindwing** (outer edge except where stated). **S:** *Linnet; **MS:** LIT AUK; **M:** BLACK GUILLEMOT; **ML:** Black grouse (inner edge), *bl/t godwit* (do), *oystercatcher* (do), COOT ad (do), COM GULL ad,

KITTIWAKE, RAZORBILL, GUILLEMOT; **L:** LESSER BLACK-BACK ad, ICELAND GULL ad, HERRING GULL ad, GT BLACK-BACK ad; **VL:** GLAUCOUS GULL ad.

Wing Bars, Double. **VS:** *Goldcrest, *firecrest, *y/b warbler, coal tit, *redpolls; **S:** Tree sparrow, *scarlet grosbeak imm, *chaffinch, **yellow wagtails*; **MS:** Pied & white wagtails, *turnstone*; **M:** G/g shrike; **ML:** Stone curlew, R/N GREBE (in flight), G/C GREBE (do); **L:** MALLARD (black & white lines at either end of blue patch).

Bar at Tip of Tail. **S:** Woodlark, hawfinch, woodchat, *l/r plover*; **MS:** *Ringed plover, com sandpiper*; **M:** Nutcracker, cuckoo, collared dove, *kestrel; **L:** *Lesser white-front, p/f goose, w/f goose*, R/T DIVER, SHELDUCK juv, B/T DIVER; **VL:** *G/l goose, bean goose*, G/N DIVER.

Bar across Middle of Tail. **M:** Hoopoe.

Edging to Tail. **M:** Turtle dove.

Breast Band. **S:** *Bluethroat* m & imm m; **MS:** Dotterel (narrow in win); **M:** Ring-ouzel m sum (*m win & f); **ML:** Lit bustard.

WHITE OR WHITISH LINES, STREAKS OR STRIPES

(*=whitish)

Stripe on Crown. **VS:** Blue tit ad (line between crown & nape); **L:** EIDER m.

Line on Bill. **ML:** RAZORBILL ad.

Eyestripe above Eye. **VS:** Firecrest, blue tit, *treecreeper, whinchat ad; **S:** Com redstart m, wheatear m (*f & imm), *meadow pipit, r/b shrike m, **lit stint*, **rock pipit*, *water pipit* sum, *b/h wagtail* m sum (*m win), R/N PHALAROPE; **MS:** *Pied wagtail, dotterel, *grey wagtail*, **dunlin* sum, **curlew sandpiper* win, **com sandpiper*, **wood sandpiper*, **green sandpiper*, *turnstone* sum; **M:** G/g shrike, golden plover sum, sparrowhawk f, r/l partridge ad, **knot* win, *grey plover* sum, **spotted redshank* win; **ML:** GARGANEY m, G/C GREBE ad; **L:** *Night heron* ad.

Eyestripe through Eye. **S:** Lapland bunting m, *r/b shrike f, *l/r plover* (behind eye only); **MS:** *Ringed plover* (do); **M:** LIT GULL juv; **ML:** RAZORBILL ad, GUILLEMOT bridled form sum, *MANDARIN DUCK f, R/N GREBE sum (down to shoulders); **L:** KING EIDER m (do); **H:** *Com crane* ad (do).

Eyestripe below Eye and down to shoulders. **S:** Barred woodpecker, *reed bunting* m, *b/h wagtail* m sum; **MS:** Pied woodpecker, *grey wagtail* m sum.

Line between Cheeks and Nape. **M:** Golden plover sum, *grey plover* sum; **L:** EIDER m.

Stripes on Neck. **M:** Turtle dove ad (black & white streaks), golden plover sum; **ML:** Lit bustard m sum; **L:** PINTAIL m, EIDER m, B/T DIVER sum (black and white streaks); **H:** *Com crane* ad.

Stripe at Side of Mantle. **S:** Woodchat; **MS:** Pied woodpecker, *Baillon's crake, lit crake*, LIT AUK (streaks); **M:** G/g shrike, TEAL m; **ML:** Tawny owl, magpie, WIGEON m, SHOVELER m; **L:** L/T DUCK m win.

Single Feathers in Tail. **VS:** Pied flycatcher; **S:** Lit bunting, lesser whitethroat, com whitethroat, gt tit, l/t tit, brambling, chaffinch, meadow pipit, tree pipit, Lapland bunting, ortolan, cirl bunting, yellowhammer, tawny pipit, woodchat, *reed bunting*, **rock pipit*, *water pipit*, *yellow wagtails*; **MS:** Skylark, Richard's pipit, pied & white wagtails, *grey wagtail*; **M:** G/g shrike, **w/w black tern*, *com snipe*; **ML:** Stone curlew, lit bustard.

Line between Throat and Breast. VS: Whinchat.

Stripe at Side of Breast. M: Golden plover sum, *grey plover* sum; **ML:** MANDARIN DUCK (two stripes).

Stripe on Flanks. M: MOORHEN ad (*y).

WHITE OR WHITISH PATCHES OR SPOTS

(*=whitish)

Forehead. VS: Blue tit ad, pied flycatcher m; **S:** Com redstart m, wheatear m, *barred woodpecker, *lit stint, l/r plover, Kentish plover*, R/N PHALAROPE juv; **MS:** Pied wagtail ad (*imm), *white wagtail m & f sum, *pied woodpecker, *ringed plover, sanderling* win, *turnstone* sum; **M:** Bee-eater, golden plover sum, **kestrel, w/w black tern* win, *black tern* win, *lit tern* ad, *grey plover, com tern* win & juv, *arctic tern* win & juv, *roseate tern* win & imm, LIT GULL win & imm, B/H GULL juv; **ML:** *Stilt* m sum & imm, *Sandwich tern* win & imm, COOT ad (frontal shield), KITTIWAKE win, SCAUP f; **L:** *Night heron* ad, *lesser white-front* ad, *barnacle goose, w/f goose* ad, SURF SCOTER m, SHELDUCK juv.

Patch on Bill. L: SURF SCOTER m.

Patch at Base of Bill (Cere). **M:** Stock dove, *rock dove, London pigeon*; **ML:** Woodpigeon.

Eyelids and Orbital Ring. ML: GUILLEMOT bridled form; **VL:** **G/l goose* juv.

Cheeks and area round Eye. VS: Coal tit ad, *crested tit, blue tit ad, *marsh tit, *willow tit, goldfinch ad; **S:** Nuthatch, gt tit ad, *l/t tit, tree sparrow, *house sparrow m, *barred woodpecker, **lit stint* win, *Kentish plover, snow bunting* m, R/N PHALAROPE win & juv (sum, patch); **MS:** Pied wagtail ad (*juv), white wagtail ad, pied woodpecker, *curlew sandpiper* win, *com sandpiper, sanderling* win, GREY PHALAROPE win (sum, patch), LIT AUK win; **M:** Lapwing sum, *green woodpecker juv, *lit tern, knot* win, *com tern, arctic tern, roseate tern, g/b tern*, SLAVONIAN GREBE win, BLACK GUILLEMOT juv; **ML:** *Montagu's harrier f (round eye), *hen-harrier f & y (round eye), *Sandwich tern*, COOT juv, SMEW f & imm, KITTIWAKE win, RAZORBILL win & juv, GUILLEMOT win & juv, MANDARIN DUCK m (f, round eye), R/N GREBE win, G/C GREBE sum & juv (*win), *COM SCOTER f; **L:** *Barnacle goose*, L/T DUCK m sum, SURF SCOTER f (two patches), VELVET SCOTER m (round eye) & f (two patches), *R/C POCHARD f, R/T DIVER win & imm, EIDER m, *SHELDUCK juv; **VL:** CORMORANT ad (patch); **H:** *Com crane* ad, CANADA GOOSE.

Spot on Face. M: DABCHICK sum; **ML:** GOLDENEYE m.

Patch on Nape. VS: Coal tit ad, *blue tit; **S:** *Reed bunting* m, *snow bunting* m; **MS:** Dotterel (eyestripes meeting), *turnstone* sum; **M:** Lapwing (eyestripes meeting), cuckoo juv, *LIT GULL imm, B/H GULL sum; **ML:** *GT SHEARWATER; **L:** SURF SCOTER m (white).

Patch on Neck. MS: Pied woodpecker; **ML:** Woodpigeon ad; **L:** BRENT GOOSE.

Shoulders. VS: Stonechat m; **S:** Chaffinch, *kingfisher*; **MS:** Pied wagtail ad; **M:** Hobby, *w/w black tern* sum; **ML:** Peregrine; **L:** R/C POCHARD m.

Sides of Rump. S: *Temminck's stint, lit stint, l/r plover, Kentish plover,* R/N PHALAROPE; **MS:** *Dunlin, pectoral sandpiper, ringed plover, com sandpiper, sanderling, purple sandpiper,* GREY PHALAROPE; **M:** *Ruff*; **ML:** L/T DUCK, WIGEON m, SHOVELER m; **L:** *Barnacle goose,* KING EIDER m, *PINTAIL m, BRENT GOOSE, EIDER m.

Sides of Tail. VS: R/b flycatcher, Dartford warbler, whinchat; **S:** Wheatear, r/b shrike, *Temminck's stint, l/r plover, Kentish plover, snow bunting*; **MS:** *Ringed plover, com sandpiper*; **M:** *Mistle thrush (tips only), nightjar m (do), turtle dove, hoopoe, *gt snipe, ruff*; **ML:** *Bl/t godwit*; **L:** L/T DUCK m, MALLARD m.

Spots on Tail. MS: Swallow.

Patch on Wing. (1) **Forewing. S:** *Snow bunting*; **MS:** *Turnstone* (inner half); **M:** *W/w black tern* sum; **ML:** SMEW, WIGEON m, GOLDENEYE; **L:** KING EIDER m, EIDER m, R/B MERGANSER m, RUDDY SHELDUCK, GOOSANDER m. (2) **Midwing. VS:** Whinchat, stonechat; **MS:** Pied woodpecker; **M:** *Lit bittern* m; **ML:** Woodpigeon. (3) **Hindwing. VS:** *Willow tit; **S:** Black redstart m, l/t tit; **M:** Jay, *com redshank,* B/N GREBE, SLAVONIAN GREBE, SABINE'S GULL imm; **ML:** FERRUGINOUS DUCK, TUFTED DUCK, R/N GREBE, GOLDENEYE, G/C GREBE, SCAUP, GADWALL, SHOVELER; **L:** VELVET SCOTER, R/C POCHARD, R/B MERGANSER, GOOSANDER. (4) **Elbow. S:** Woodchat; **MS:** Waxwing; **ML:** *ARCTIC SKUA, *FULMAR, *POMARINE SKUA, *L/T SKUA; **L:** *GT SKUA.

Wing Tips. S: *Bearded tit*; **M:** Ptarmigan sum, *London pigeon*; **ML:** COM GULL ad; **L:** LESSER BLACK-BACK ad, HERRING GULL ad, GT BLACK-BACK ad.

Spot on Breast. S: *Bluethroat* m.

Patch on Flanks. VL: CORMORANT sum.

YELLOW BARS OR BANDS

Wing Bars. VS: Siskin (midwing), goldfinch (double); **S:** Greenfinch (hindwing).

Bar at Tip of Tail. MS: Waxwing; **M:** Golden oriole.

Breast Band. VL: *Spoonbill* sum.

YELLOW LINES, STREAKS OR STRIPES

Line between Crown and Nape. VS: Blue tit juv.

Eyestripe above Eye. VS: Y/b warbler, willow warbler juv, serin m, siskin m, wood warbler; **S:** Cirl bunting m, *shore lark, yellow wagtail.*

Eyestripe below Eye. S: Ortolan (& down to shoulders).

YELLOW OR YELLOWISH PATCHES OR SPOTS

(*=yellowish)

Forehead. VS: Blue tit juv; **S:** *Shore lark*; **M:** Golden plover sum (pale golden); **ML:** *COOT juv.

Tip of Bill. S: House sparrow juv; **M:** PUFFIN win, MOORHEN ad; **ML:** Woodpigeon, *Sandwich tern,* COM GULL imm, GOLDENEYE f; **L:** LESSER BLACK-BACK imm, ICELAND GULL imm, HERRING GULL imm, GT BLACK-BACK imm; **VL:** *Spoonbill* ad, GLAUCOUS GULL imm.

Patch on Bill. ML: IVORY GULL ad, COM SCOTER m.

Base of Bill (c=cere). **MS:** *Spotted crake*, GREY PHALAROPE m; **M:** Merlin ad (c), sparrowhawk (c), r/f falcon f & imm, hobby ad (c), kestrel (c), *com tern* juv; **ML:** Peregrine ad (c), stone curlew, Montagu's harrier (c), hen-harrier ad (c), com buzzard ad (c), r/l buzzard (c), honey buzzard (c), *marsh harrier* (c), *Greenland falcon* ad (c), R/N GREBE; **L:** Kite (c); **VL:** Golden eagle (c), *sea eagle* ad (c), SHAG, CORMORANT; **H:** BEWICK'S SWAN ad, WHOOPER SWAN ad.

Eyelids and Orbital Ring. S: Ortolan, *l/r plover*; **M:** Blackbird, cuckoo; **L:** *Lesser white-front*, GT BLACK-BACK y; **VL:** GLAUCOUS GULL ad, SHAG.

Cheeks and area round Eye. VS: Coal tit juv (& Irish race), blue tit juv, siskin m, *wood warbler; **M:** Hobby ad (round eye), kestrel (round eye); **ML:** Peregrine ad (round eye), ARCTIC SKUA pale form, POMARINE SKUA pale form, L/T SKUA; **L:** Kite (round eye); **VL:** *Spoonbill* ad (round eye).

Patch on Nape. VS: Coal tit juv (& Irish race), blue tit (pale); **S:** Gt tit ad (greenish) & juv (pale).

Sides of Tail. S: Greenfinch.

Patch on Wing, VS: Goldfinch (midwing); **M:** Golden oriole m.

Garter on Leg. M: MOORHEN y.

STRUCTURAL FEATURES

BILL FEATURES

Crossed bill

Crossed Bill. S: Crossbill.

Bill Curved Up. ML: *Ba/t godwit* (slightly), *avocet*.

Bill Curved Down. VS: Treecreeper; **MS:** *Dunlin* (very slightly), *curlew-sandpiper* (slightly); **M:** Bee-eater (slightly), hoopoe; **ML:** Chough, *whimbrel*; **L:** *Glossy ibis*, *curlew*.

Bill Hooked (markedly). **MS:** Scops owl, lit owl; **M:** Merlin, sparrowhawk, r/f falcon, hobby, kestrel, barn owl, l/e owl, s/e owl; **ML:** Tawny owl, peregrine, Montagu's harrier, hen-harrier, goshawk, com buzzard, r/l buzzard, honey buzzard, *marsh harrier*, *Greenland falcon*, *osprey*; **L:** Snowy owl, kite; **VL:** Golden eagle, *sea eagle*.

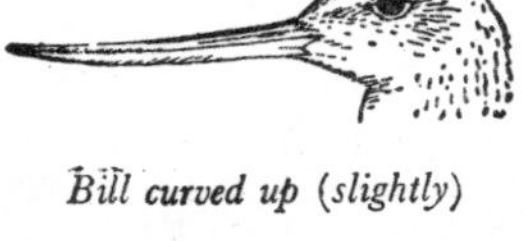

Bill curved up (slightly)

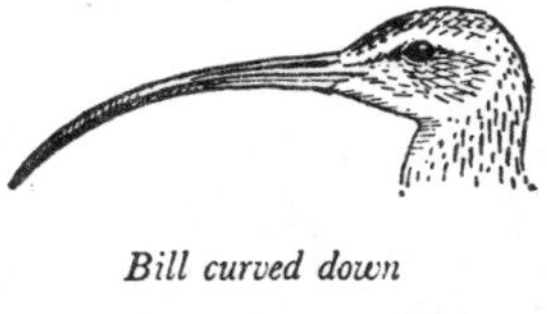

Bill curved down

Bill hooked (markedly)

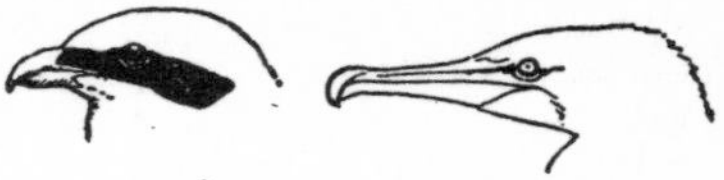

Bill hooked (slightly)

Knob at base of bill

Bill long

Bill Hooked (slightly). **S:** R/b shrike, woodchat; **M:** G/g shrike, roller; **ML:** SMEW; **L:** R/B MERGANSER, GOOSANDER; **VL:** SHAG, CORMORANT.

Knob at Base of Bill. ML: COM SCOTER (black); **L:** KING EIDER m sum (orange), SHELDUCK m sum (red); **H:** MUTE SWAN (black).

Tubular nostrils

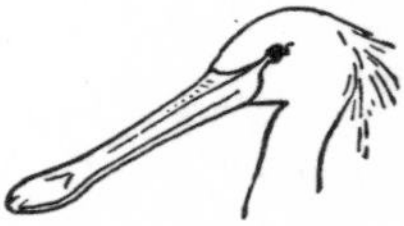

Bill spatulate

Bill stout

Tip-tilted

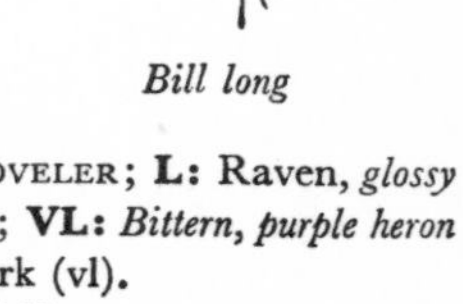

Bill long

Long (vl=very long). **VS:** Treecreeper; **S:** *Temminck's stint, lit stint, kingfisher*; **MS:** *Dunlin, curlew-sandpiper, pectoral sandpiper, jack snipe* (vl), *com sandpiper, wood sandpiper, sanderling, purple sandpiper, green sandpiper*; **M:** Bee-eater (vl) hoopoe (vl), nutcracker, green woodpecker, woodcock (vl), *knot, com snipe* (vl), *gt snipe* (vl), *water rail, ruff, com redshank, spotted redshank* (vl), *greenshank, lit bittern*; **ML:** Chough, g/b woodpecker, *stilt* (vl), *ba/t godwit* (vl), *whimbrel* (vl), *bl/t godwit* (vl), *Sandwich tern, avocet* (vl), *oystercatcher, squacco heron,* GUILLEMOT, SHOVELER; **L:** Raven, *glossy ibis* (vl), *curlew* (vl), *night heron,* R/T DIVER, B/T DIVER; **VL:** *Bittern, purple heron* (vl), *spoonbill* (vl), *heron* (vl), G/N DIVER; **H:** White stork (vl).

Spatulate (spoon-shaped). **ML:** SHOVELER; **VL:** *Spoonbill.*

Stout (vs=very stout). **VS:** Serin, goldfinch, siskin, redpolls; **S:** Linnet, twite, lit bunting, tree sparrow, house sparrow, greenfinch, bullfinch (vs), scarlet grosbeak (vs), brambling, chaffinch, Lapland bunting, ortolan, cirl bunting, yellowhammer, crossbill, hawfinch (vs), *kingfisher*; **MS:** Corn bunting; **M:**

Roller, nutcracker, green woodpecker, PUFFIN; **ML:** G/b woodpecker, rook, carrion crow, hooded crow, RAZORBILL; **L:** Raven, LESSER BLACK-BACK, HERRING GULL, GT BLACK-BACK; **VL:** GLAUCOUS GULL, G/N DIVER, GANNET. (N.B.—Almost all ducks, geese and swans have stout, flattened bills.)

Tip-tilted. **M:** B/N GREBE; **L:** R/T DIVER.

Tubular Nostrils. **S:** STORM PETREL; **MS:** F/T PETREL; **M:** MANX SHEARWATERS; **ML:** SOOTY SHEARWATER, GT SHEARWATER, CORY'S SHEARWATER, FULMAR.

HEAD FEATURES

Crest. (Same Colour as Head or Crown.) **VS:** Crested tit; **S:** Woodlark; **MS:** Skylark, waxwing, rosy starling ad; **M:** Hoopoe (with black tips), lapwing; **ML:** G/b woodpecker, *Sandwich tern* sum, *squacco heron*, SMEW f & imm (very slight), TUFTED DUCK, MANDARIN DUCK f; **L:** R/C POCHARD, R/B MERGANSER, GOOSANDER f & y; **VL:** *Purple heron* imm, *spoonbill* sum, *heron* y, SHAG ad.

Crest. (Different Colour from Head or Crown.) **VS:** Goldcrest, firecrest; **M:** Jay; **ML:** SMEW m, MANDARIN DUCK m; **L:** *Night heron* ad; **VL:** *Purple heron* ad, *spoonbill* sum, *heron* ad.

Crest (same colour as head)

Crest (different colour from head) and Ears and Horns

Facial disc

'Ears' or 'Horns'. **S:** *Shore lark* (black); **MS:** Scops owl (brown); **M:** L/e owl (brown), s/e owl (brown, indistinct), *ruff* m sum (black, white or brown), B/N GREBE sum (golden chestnut), SLAVONIAN GREBE sum (chestnut); **ML:** R/N GREBE ad (much longer in summer), G/C GREBE (do).

Facial Discs. **MS:** Scops owl (greyish or reddish-brown), lit owl (grey-brown & white); **M:** Barn owl (white with rufous patch round eye; rusty buff in dark-breasted form), l/e owl (buff), s/e owl (buff); **ML:** Tawny owl (grey-white to rufous), Montagu's harrier m (grey) & f & y (brownish), hen-harrier m (grey) & f & y (brownish); **L:** Snowy owl (white).

NECK FEATURES

Ruffs. **M:** *Ruff* m sum (black, white & chestnut, plain or in combination); **ML:** MANDARIN DUCK m (orange-chestnut), G/C GREBE sum (chestnut).

Long (vl=very long). **ML:** *Squacco heron*, R/N GREBE, G/C GREBE; **L:** *Glossy ibis, night heron, lesser white-front, p/f goose, w/f goose*, PINTAIL, R/T DIVER, B/T DIVER; **VL:** *Snow goose, g/l goose, bean goose, bittern* (vl), *purple heron* (vl), *spoonbill* (vl), *heron*, G/N DIVER, SHAG, CORMORANT; **H:** White stork (vl), *com crane* (vl), CANADA GOOSE (vl), BEWICK'S SWAN (vl), WHOOPER SWAN (vl), MUTE SWAN (vl).

Ruffs

Long neck

WING FEATURES

Rounded wings

Rounded Wings. MS: Scops owl, lit owl; **M:** Hoopoe, sparrowhawk, lapwing, barn owl, l/e owl, s/e owl; **ML:** Tawny owl, goshawk; **L:** Snowy owl, *glossy ibis, night heron*; **VL:** *Bittern, purple heron, heron.*

Wing Fans. ML: MANDARIN DUCK m (orange-chestnut fans with black & white shoulder plumes).

TAIL FEATURES

Central Feathers Projecting. M: Bee-eater; **ML:** ARCTIC SKUA ad, POMARINE SKUA ad, L/T SKUA ad.

Curly. L: MALLARD m.

Cleft Tail. VS: Serin, goldfinch, siskin, redpolls; **S:** Linnet, twite, lit bunting, greenfinch, bullfinch, scarlet grosbeak, brambling, chaffinch, Lapland bunting, ortolan, cirl bunting, yellowhammer, crossbill, hawfinch, *reed bunting, snow bunting*; **MS:** Corn bunting; **M:** LIT GULL imm; **ML:** KITTIWAKE juv.

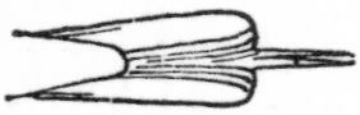

Central feathers projecting

Tail curly

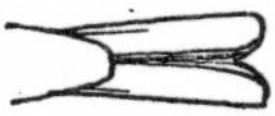

Tail cleft

Forked Tail. VS: House martin, *sand martin*; **S:** Swift; **MS:** Swallow, alpine swift, F/T PETREL; **M:** *W/w black tern, black tern, lit tern, com tern, arctic tern, roseate tern, g/b tern,* SABINE'S GULL; **ML:** Black grouse f, *Sandwich tern*; **L:** Kite.

Lyre-shaped Tail. L: Black grouse m.

Long (vl=very long). **VS:** Dartford warbler; **S:** L/t tit (vl), barred warbler, wryneck, tawny pipit, r/b shrike, woodchat, *yellow wagtails, bearded tit*; **MS:** Richard's pipit, pied & white wagtails, swallow (ad, vl), *grey wagtail*; **M:** G/g shrike, blackbird, bee-eater, merlin, sparrowhawk, r/f falcon, cuckoo, kestrel, *com tern, arctic tern, roseate tern*; **ML:** Montagu's harrier, hen-harrier, magpie

Tail forked

Tail lyre-shaped

Tail long (or graduated)

(vl), *marsh harrier*, POMARINE SKUA ad, L/T SKUA ad (vl); **L:** Com pheasant (vl), kite, L/T DUCK m, PINTAIL (m, vl).

Tail Often Cocked Up. **VS:** Wren, Dartford warbler; **MS:** *Dipper*; **M:** Blackbird (when alighting).

LEG FEATURES

Feathered Legs and Feet. **VS:** House martin (white); **MS:** Lit owl (white); **M:** Barn owl (white), l/e owl (buff), ptarmigan (white), red grouse (whitish), s/e owl (buff); **ML:** Tawny owl (whitish), black grouse (whitish, legs only), g/b woodpecker (black, front of legs only), r/l buzzard (brown, legs only); **L:** Snowy owl (white), capercaillie (grey-brown, legs only); **VL:** Golden eagle (brown, legs only).

Legs feathered

Long (vl=very long). **MS:** *Baillon's crake, lit crake, spotted crake*; **M:** Golden plover, lapwing, *water rail, grey plover, ruff, com redshank, spotted redshank* (vl), *greenshank, lit bittern*, MOORHEN; **ML:** Stone curlew, Montagu's harrier, hen-harrier, lit bustard, *stilt* (vl), *b/t godwit* (vl), *whimbrel, bl/t godwit, avocet* (vl), *oystercatcher, squacco heron*, COOT; **L:** *Glossy ibis* (vl), *curlew, night heron*; **VL:** *Bittern, purple heron, spoonbill, heron*; **H:** White stork (vl), *com crane* (vl).

Long legs

BEHAVIOUR FEATURES

FLIGHT FEATURES

Circular Flight. **M:** Stock dove (display), and see p. 258, below.

Flycatching from a Perch. **VS:** Y/b warbler, willow warbler, chiffchaff, r/b flycatcher, pied flycatcher, wood warbler, whinchat, stonechat; **S:** Spotted flycatcher, com redstart, black redstart, house sparrow, wheatear, r/b shrike, *yellow wagtails*; **MS:** Pied & white wagtails, *grey wagtail*; **M:** G/g shrike, bee-eater.

Hovering (see also Flycatching above, and Singing in Flight, p. 215). **S:** *Kingfisher*; **M:** Merlin (occ), r/f falcon, kestrel (most often); **ML:** Com buzzard, r/l buzzard, honey buzzard (occ), *osprey*.

Gliding, alternately showing upper and under sides. **M:** MANX SHEARWATER; **ML:** SOOTY SHEARWATER, GT SHEARWATER, CORY'S SHEARWATER, FULMAR.

Following Ships. **S:** STORM PETREL; **M:** B/H GULL; **ML:** COM GULL, KITTIWAKE, FULMAR; **L:** LESSER BLACK-BACK, HERRING GULL, GT BLACK-BACK.

Legs Dangling. **MS:** Corn bunting, *Baillon's crake, lit crake, spotted crake*; **M:** Corncrake, *water rail*, MOORHEN. Also pipits and skylark when alighting from song-flight.

Legs dangling: Corn-bunting in flight

Musical or Whistling Flight (not to be confused with the frou-frou or feather-rustle of, e.g., a swift or a flock of starlings). **ML:** Lit bustard, GOLDENEYE; **L:** MALLARD, R/B MERGANSER, GOOSANDER; **H:** MUTE SWAN.

Pursuit of Other Birds (to make them disgorge food). **ML:** COM GULL, ARCTIC SKUA, POMARINE SKUA, L/T SKUA; **L:** LESSER BLACK-BACK, HERRING GULL, GT SKUA, GT BLACK-BACK; **VL:** GLAUCOUS GULL. (N.B.—The skuas are much more persistent than the gulls.)

Singing in Flight. See p. 258 below.

Soaring Flight. **M:** Merlin, sparrowhawk, hobby, kestrel, s/e owl; **ML:** Peregrine, Montagu's harrier, hen-harrier, goshawk, com buzzard, r/l buzzard, honey buzzard, *marsh harrier, osprey*; **L:** Kite, raven; **VL:** Golden eagle, *sea eagle.*

Pursuit of other birds: Arctic Skua chasing Sandwich Tern

Undulating or Dipping Flight. **VS:** Goldcrest, firecrest, coal tit, crested tit, blue tit, marsh tit, willow tit, r/b flycatcher, serin, goldfinch, redpolls, pied flycatcher, Dartford warbler; **S:** Linnet, twite, lit bunting, spotted flycatcher, nuthatch, gt tit, l/t tit, greenfinch, bullfinch, scarlet grosbeak, brambling, chaffinch, barred woodpecker, meadow pipit, tree pipit, woodlark, Lapland bunting, ortolan, cirl bunting, yellowhammer, crossbill, hawfinch, wryneck, tawny pipit, r/b shrike, woodchat, *reed bunting, rock and water pipits, snow bunting, shore lark, yellow wagtails, bearded tit*; **MS:** Corn bunting, skylark, Richard's pipit, pied & white wagtails, waxwing, lit owl, pied woodpecker, *grey wagtail*; **M:** Golden oriole, g/g shrike, nutcracker, green woodpecker, jay. N.B.—Warblers have a flitting rather than dipping flight.)

Somersaults in Flight. **ML:** Chough; **L:** Raven. Also birds of prey when sparring.

V-Formation Flight. M: TEAL; **ML:** WIGEON; **L:** *Curlew, barnacle goose, p/f goose, w/f goose,* BRENT GOOSE, MALLARD, SHELDUCK; **VL:** *G/l goose, bean goose.* Also GULLS going to roost.

Zigzag Flight. MS: *Jack snipe*; **M:** *Com snipe.*

Steep Up and Glide Down Display Flight. M: Turtle dove, collared dove; **ML:** Woodpigeon.

STANCE FEATURES

Head on One Side, Listening. MS: Redwing, song thrush; **M:** Blackbird, fieldfare, mistle thrush.

Wings Outspread. VL: SHAG, CORMORANT.

Tail Often Cocked Up. See p. 212.

SWIMMING

MS: *Baillon's crake, lit crake, spotted crake*; **M:** *W/w black tern, black tern, lit tern, water rail, com tern, arctic tern, g/b tern*; **ML:** *Sandwich tern.* (N.B.—All the foregoing and nearly all *waders* occasionally swim a short distance, the *terns* only when young and when bathing.) **L:** *Lesser white-front, barnacle goose, p/f goose, w/f goose*; **VL:** *Snow goose, g/l goose, bean goose.* (N.B.—All WATER BIRDS swim.)

DIVING METHODS

From Air. S: *Kingfisher*; **M:** *Lit tern, com tern, arctic tern, roseate tern*; **ML:** *Sandwich tern, osprey*; **VL:** *Sea eagle,* GANNET.

Dipping down to Surface of Water but not immersing. **VS:** House martin, *sand martin*; **S:** Swift; **MS:** Swallow, F/T PETREL; **M:** *W/w black tern, black tern, g/b tern,* LIT GULL, SABINE'S GULL.

From a Perch. S: *Kingfisher*; **MS:** *Dipper.*

From Surface of Water. MS: *Dipper, Baillon's crake, lit crake,* LIT AUK; **M:** MANX SHEARWATERS, DABCHICK, PUFFIN, B/N GREBE, SLAVONIAN GREBE, MOORHEN, BLACK GUILLEMOT, TEAL juv, B/H GULL (occ); **ML:** COOT, FERRUGINOUS DUCK, SMEW, SOOTY SHEARWATER, RAZORBILL, GUILLEMOT, TUFTED DUCK, L/T DUCK, R/N GREBE, GT SHEARWATER, CORY'S SHEARWATER, COM POCHARD, GOLDENEYE, G/C GREBE, SCAUP, COM SCOTER, GADWALL juv, SHOVELER (occ); **L:** SURF SCOTER, VELVET SCOTER, KING EIDER, R/C POCHARD, R/T DIVER, MALLARD (esp juv), EIDER, R/B MERGANSER, B/T DIVER GOOSANDER; **VL:** G/N DIVER, SHAG, CORMORANT, GANNET. (N.B.—All young and wounded *waders* and WATER BIRDS will dive when alarmed.)

Walking on Bed of Stream. MS: *Dipper.*

VOICE FEATURES

Communal Song. VS: Lesser redpoll; **S:** Linnet, twite, tree sparrow, house sparrow; **MS:** Starling, redwing; **M:** Fieldfare.

Mimicry of other birds in song. **VS:** Whinchat, *reed warbler, marsh warbler, sedge warbler*; **S:** Garden warbler (occ), blackcap, com redstart; **MS:** Starling, R/b shrike; **M:** Blackbird (occ), jay. (N.B.—Some other song birds will occasionally mimic in their songs.)

Singing in Flight. (a) **Direct Flight.** **VS:** Lesser redpoll, grasshopper warbler (occ), house martin, *sand martin, reed warbler* (occ), *marsh warbler* (occ); **S:** Linnet, twite, lesser whitethroat (occ), chaffinch, woodlark (occ), crossbill, *l/r plover, Kentish plover, snow bunting, yellow wagtails*; **MS:** Corn bunting (occ), pied & white wagtails, swallow, song thrush (occ), *grey wagtail, ringed plover*; **M:** Golden plover, cuckoo, *com redshank*; **M:** *Bl/t godwit.* (N.B.—Some other song birds occasionally sing in flight.)

(b) **Circular Flight.** **VS:** Siskin, lesser redpoll; **S:** Greenfinch, woodlark; **MS:** *Dunlin, com sandpiper*; **ML:** *Whimbrel.*

(c) **Hovering.** **VS:** Stonechat; **S:** Com whitethroat; **MS:** Skylark, dunlin; **L:** *Curlew.*

(d) **Descending.** **VS:** Dartford warbler, *sedge warbler*; **S:** Com whitethroat, meadow pipit, tree pipit, *rock pipit*; **M:** Lapwing, *com snipe, greenshank.*

Singing at Night. **VS:** Grasshopper warbler, *reed warbler, marsh warbler* (occ), *sedge warbler*; **S:** Woodlark, crossbill (occ), nightingale; **MS:** Scops owl, lit owl, song thrush (occ); **M:** Nightjar, barn owl, l/e owl, s/e owl; **ML:** Tawny owl, stone curlew. (N.B.—All these, except the owls, more normally sing by day; most song birds will occasionally sing a few bars at night.)

SOCIAL HABITS

Flocking (birds commonly found, away from breeding grounds, in parties of a score or more, not necessarily all of one species). **VS:** Goldfinch, siskin, redpolls, house martin, *sand martin*; **S:** Linnet, twite, tree sparrow, house sparrow, greenfinch, brambling, chaffinch, meadow pipit, yellowhammer, swift, *reed bunting, snow bunting, shore lark*; **MS:** Skylark, swallow, starling, redwing, song thrush, *dunlin, ringed plover, sanderling, turnstone*; **M:** Blackbird, fieldfare, mistle thrush, turtle dove, golden plover, lapwing, jackdaw, collared dove, stock dove, *black tern, lit tern, knot, com snipe, com redshank, London pigeon, com tern, arctic tern,* MANX SHEARWATERS, PUFFIN, MOORHEN, TEAL, B/H GULL; **ML:** Woodpigeon, rook, *ba/t godwit, bl/t godwit, Sandwich tern, oystercatcher,* COOT, COM GULL, KITTIWAKE, GUILLEMOT, TUFTED DUCK, WIGEON, COM POCHARD, COM SCOTER, SHOVELER; **L:** *Curlew, barnacle goose, p/f goose, w/f goose,* LESSER BLACK-BACK, HERRING GULL, PINTAIL, BRENT GOOSE, MALLARD, GT BLACK-BACK; **VL:** *G/l goose, bean goose*; **H:** CANADA GOOSE, MUTE SWAN.

Flocking (birds, in addition to the above, commonly found in parties of 5-20; not counting odd individuals attached to flocks of other species). **VS:** Coal tit, crested tit, blue tit, marsh tit, Dartford warbler; **S:** Gt tit, l/t tit, bullfinch, woodlark, Lapland bunting, cirl bunting, crossbill, *lit stint, yellow wagtail, bearded tit*; **MS:** Corn bunting, pied & white wagtails, waxwing, dotterel, *curlew sandpiper, com sandpiper, wood sandpiper,* LIT AUK; **M:** Ring ouzel, bee-eater, com partridge, jay, ptarmigan, red grouse, r/l partridge, s/e owl, *grey plover,* *rock dove, roseate tern*, DABCHICK, BLACK GUILLEMOT; **ML:** Chough, stone curlew, black grouse, magpie, carrion crow, hooded crow, *whimbrel, avocet*, GARGANEY, SMEW, RAZORBILL, MANDARIN DUCK, GOLDENEYE, SCAUP, GADWALL; **L:** Capercaillie, raven, *glossy ibis*, VELVET SCOTER, EIDER, R/B MERGANSER, SHELDUCK, GOOSANDER; **VL:** *Heron*, GLAUCOUS GULL, SHAG, CORMORANT, GANNET; **H:** BEWICK'S SWAN, WHOOPER SWAN.

Nesting in Colonies. **VS:** House martin, *sand martin, reed warbler*; **S:** Linnet (loose colony), tree sparrow, house sparrow, greenfinch (loose colony), swift, STORM PETREL, R/N PHALAROPE; **MS:** F/T PETREL; **M:** Jackdaw, stock dove, *lit tern, rock dove, London pigeon, com tern, arctic tern, roseate tern*, MANX SHEARWATER, PUFFIN, B/N GREBE, SLAVONIAN GREBE, B/H GULL; **ML:** Rook, *Sandwich tern, avocet*, COM GULL, KITTIWAKE, RAZORBILL, GUILLEMOT, ARCTIC SKUA, FULMAR; **L:** LESSER BLACK-BACK, HERRING GULL, GT SKUA, GT BLACK-BACK; **VL:** *Heron*, SHAG, CORMORANT, GANNET; **H:** MUTE SWAN (only at Abbotsbury and Weymouth, Dorset). (N.B.—Some other birds might have been included under the heading of 'loose colonies', as the restricted amount of habitat available, e.g. in a reed-bed, often forces birds to nest closer together than normal.)

Roosting Gregariously away from Nests. Most birds listed under the three previous headings are more or less gregarious roosters, at any rate out of the breeding season. The following are particularly fond of so roosting in *trees and bushes*: **S:** Linnet, tree sparrow, house sparrow, greenfinch, brambling, chaffinch, yellowhammer; **MS:** Starling, redwing, song thrush; **M:** Blackbird, fieldfare, mistle thrush, jackdaw, l/e owl; **ML:** Woodpigeon, rook, carrion crow, hooded crow.

Birds that commonly roost gregariously in *reed-beds*: **VS:** *Sand martin*; **S:** *Yellow wagtails*; **MS:** Pied wagtail, swallow, starling.

Birds that commonly roost gregariously on *buildings*: **MS:** Starling; **M:** *London pigeon.*

Waders, geese DUCKS and GULLS roost together on mudflats, sandbanks, fresh and salt water.

HABITATS

LAND

Built-up Areas (towns and industrial sites). **VS:** House martin; **S:** Black redstart, house sparrow, swift; **MS:** Pied wagtail, swallow, starling; **M:** Jackdaw, kestrel, *London pigeon*, B/H GULL; **ML:** Carrion crow.

Town Parks and Squares. **VS:** Wren, willow warbler, coal tit, blue tit, serin, treecreeper, house martin; **S:** Spotted flycatcher, robin, gt tit, house sparrow, greenfinch, chaffinch, hedge sparrow, swift; **MS:** Pied wagtail, waxwing, swallow, scops owl, starling, redwing (hard weather), song thrush, pied woodpecker; **M:** Blackbird, mistle thrush, sparrowhawk (local), jackdaw (local), collared dove, stock dove (local), kestrel, jay, *London pigeon*, MOORHEN, B/H GULL; **ML:** Tawny owl, woodpigeon, carrion crow, COOT (local), COM GULL, TUFTED

DUCK, COM POCHARD; **L:** HERRING GULL, MALLARD; **H:** CANADA GOOSE, MUTE SWAN.

Gardens and Orchards. VS: Goldcrest, wren, willow warbler, chiffchaff, coal tit, blue tit, marsh tit, serin, goldfinch, lesser redpoll (local), treecreeper, house martin; **S:** Linnet, lesser whitethroat, blackcap, spotted flycatcher, com redstart, robin, nuthatch, gt tit, tree sparrow, house sparrow, greenfinch, bullfinch, chaffinch, hedge sparrow, barred woodpecker, cirl bunting, hawfinch, wryneck, swift; **MS:** Pied wagtail, waxwing, swallow, scops owl, starling, lit owl, song thrush, pied woodpecker; **M:** Golden oriole, blackbird, mistle thrush, turtle dove, hoopoe, sparrowhawk, green woodpecker, cuckoo, jackdaw, collared dove, stock dove, kestrel, jay, barn owl, B/H GULL; **ML:** Tawny owl, woodpigeon, carrion crow; **L:** Com pheasant (large gardens only).

Farmland. VS: Goldfinch, house martin; **S:** Linnet, com whitethroat, tree sparrow, house sparrow, greenfinch, brambling, chaffinch, meadow pipit, cirl bunting, yellowhammer, swift, *reed bunting, yellow wagtails*; **MS:** Corn bunting, skylark, pied wagtail, quail, swallow, starling, rosy starling, redwing, lit owl, song thrush, pied woodpecker (uncommon); **M:** Blackbird, fieldfare, mistle thrush, corncrake, turtle dove, golden plover, sparrowhawk, hobby, lapwing, com partridge, green woodpecker, cuckoo, jackdaw, stock dove, kestrel, barn owl, red grouse (stubbles), r/l partridge, s/e owl (win), gt snipe, MOORHEN, B/H GULL; **ML:** Tawny owl, stone curlew, woodpigeon, magpie, rook, carrion crow, hooded crow, *oystercatcher*, COM GULL, WIGEON; **L:** Com pheasant, *curlew, lesser white-front, barnacle goose, p/f goose, w/f goose*, LESSER BLACK-BACK, HERRING GULL; **VL:** *Snow goose, g/l goose, bean goose*; **H:** White stork.

Downland. VS: Goldfinch, Dartford warbler (gorse), stonechat; **S:** Linnet, wheatear, meadow pipit, tree pipit, woodlark, yellowhammer; **MS:** Corn bunting, skylark, quail, starling, dotterel (on passage); **M:** Mistle thrush, sparrowhawk, hobby, lapwing, com partridge, cuckoo, kestrel, r/l partridge, s/e owl, B/H GULL; **ML:** Stone curlew, woodpigeon, Montagu's harrier, hen-harrier (win), magpie, rook, carrion crow, r/l buzzard, COM GULL; **L:** HERRING GULL.

Lowland Moors and Open Heaths. VS: Wren, willow warbler, siskin (in birches), redpolls (do), grasshopper warbler, Dartford warbler (gorse, heather), whinchat, stonechat; **S:** Linnet (esp in gorse), twite, com whitethroat, wheatear, hedgesparrow, meadow pipit, tree pipit, woodlark, crossbill (conifers), r/b shrike, *yellow wagtails*; **MS:** Skylark, dotterel (on passage), *dunlin, ringed plover* (E Anglia); **M:** G/g shrike, blackbird, nightjar, golden plover (Ireland), merlin, sparrowhawk, hobby, lapwing, com partridge, cuckoo, kestrel, l/e owl, woodcock, r/l partridge, s/e owl, *com snipe, gt snipe, com redshank, greenshank*, TEAL, B/H GULL; **ML:** Stone curlew, black grouse, Montagu's harrier, hen-harrier, carrion crow, hooded crow, r/l buzzard, COM GULL, ARCTIC SKUA (N Scotland); **L:** Snowy owl, *curlew*, LESSER BLACK-BACK, HERRING GULL (nr sea), MALLARD, GT SKUA (nr sea, Shetland).

Upland Moors and Rough Grazings. Wren, grasshopper warbler, whinchat, stonechat, *sand martin*; **S:** Twite, wheatear, hedgesparrow, meadow pipit, Lapland bunting, swift, *reed bunting, snow bunting*; **MS:** Skylark, swallow, starling, rosy starling, dotterel, *dunlin*; **M:** Ring ouzel, blackbird, mistle thrush, nightjar, corncrake, golden plover, merlin, lapwing, cuckoo, kestrel, woodcock, red grouse, s/e owl, com snipe (Scotland), gt snipe, com redshank (Scotland), greenshank (Scotland), B/H GULL; **ML:** Peregrine, black grouse, hen-harrier, carrion crow, hooded crow, com buzzard, r/l buzzard, *whimbrel*, COM GULL, ARCTIC SKUA (N Scotland), WIGEON, COM SCOTER; **L:** Snowy owl, capercaillie, kite, raven, *curlew*, LESSER BLACK-BACK, HERRING GULL (nr sea), R/T DIVER, MALLARD, GT SKUA (nr sea, Shetland), B/T DIVER; **VL:** Golden eagle, *G/l goose* (N Scotland).

Mountain Tops, Stony. **VS:** Wren; **S:** Wheatear, *snow bunting*; **MS:** Dotterel; **M:** Golden plover, ptarmigan; **ML:** Peregrine; **VL:** Golden eagle.

Inland Cliffs, Quarries, Sand-pits and Gravel-pits. **VS:** *Sand martin*; **S:** Tree sparrow, *l/r plover*; **MS:** Pied wagtail, starling, *ringed plover*; **M:** Bee-eater, jackdaw, stock dove, kestrel, *London pigeon*; **ML:** Chough, peregrine, carrion crow, hooded crow; **L:** Raven.

Woodland, Broad-leaved. **VS:** Goldcrest, wren, willow warbler, chiffchaff, coal tit, blue tit, marsh tit, willow tit, lesser redpoll (alder), treecreeper, pied flycatcher, wood warbler; **S:** Garden warbler, blackcap, spotted flycatcher, com redstart, robin, nuthatch, gt tit, l/t tit, bullfinch, brambling (esp beeches), chaffinch, hedgesparrow, barred woodpecker, hawfinch, wryneck, nightingale; **MS:** Starling, song thrush, pied woodpecker; **M:** Golden oriole, blackbird, mistle thrush, nightjar, turtle dove, sparrowhawk, hobby, green woodpecker, cuckoo, stock dove, jay, l/e owl, woodcock; **ML:** Tawny owl, woodpigeon, g/b woodpecker, goshawk, com buzzard, honey buzzard, MANDARIN DUCK; **L:** Com pheasant, capercaillie (local), kite, MALLARD.

Woodland, Coniferous. **VS:** Goldcrest, wren, willow warbler, coal tit, crested tit, willow tit, goldfinch, siskin, treecreeper, wood warbler; **S:** Spotted flycatcher, com redstart, robin, gt tit, l/t, brambling, chaffinch, crossbill; **MS:** Song thrush, pied woodpecker; **M:** Mistle thrush, nightjar, sparrowhawk, cuckoo, jay, l/e owl, woodcock; **ML:** Tawny owl, woodpigeon, Montagu's harrier (young plantations), goshawk; **L:** Capercaillie.

Areas of Scattered Timber (wood-clearings, wood-edges, sites of felled woodland, well-timbered parks and commons, overgrown hedgerows). **VS:** Goldcrest (esp conifer), firecrest, wren, willow warbler, chiffchaff, coal tit (esp conifers), blue tit, marsh tit, willow tit, serin, goldfinch, siskin, redpolls, treecreeper, pied flycatcher, wood warbler, grasshopper warbler; **S:** Linnet, lesser whitethroat, com whitethroat, garden warbler, blackcap, spotted flycatcher, com redstart, robin, nuthatch, gt tit, l/t tit, tree sparrow, greenfinch, bullfinch, chaffinch, hedgesparrow, barred woodpecker, tree pipit, woodlark, cirl bunting, yellowhammer, crossbill (conifers), hawfinch, wryneck, nightingale, r/b shrike, woodchat; **MS:** Waxwing, scops owl, starling, redwing, lit owl, song thrush, pied woodpecker; **M:** Golden oriole, g/g shrike, blackbird, fieldfare, mistle thrush, nightjar, turtle dove, hoopoe, sparrowhawk, hobby, roller, nutcracker, green woodpecker, cuckoo, jackdaw, stock dove, kestrel, jay, barn owl, l/e owl, woodcock; **ML:** Tawny owl, woodpigeon, black grouse, g/b woodpecker, magpie, rook, carrion crow, hooded crow, goshawk, com buzzard, honey buzzard; **L:** Com pheasant, kite, MALLARD, R/B MERGANSER, GOOSANDER.

WATERSIDE

Rivers and Streams, Lowland. **VS:** House martin, *sand martin, reed warbler, sedge warbler*; **S:** Swift, *kingfisher*; **MS:** Pied wagtail, swallow, *grey wagtail, com sandpiper, green sandpiper*; **M:** DABCHICK, MOORHEN, TEAL, B/H GULL; **ML:** COM GULL, WIGEON, GOLDENEYE, GADWALL; **L:** LESSER BLACK-BACK, HERRING GULL, MALLARD, R/B MERGANSER, GOOSANDER; **VL:** *Heron*; **H:** CANADA GOOSE, BEWICK'S SWAN, WHOOPER SWAN, MUTE SWAN.

Rivers and Streams, Upland. **VS:** *Sand martin*; **MS:** *Grey wagtail, dipper, com sandpiper*; **M:** *Com tern*, B/H GULL; **ML:** *Oystercatcher*, COM GULL, WIGEON; **L:** R/B MERGANSER, GOOSANDER.

Freshwater Margins. All River (above) and Lake (p. 264) birds, with the following: **VS:** Wren (in sedge), blue tit (in willows), goldfinch (in alders), siskin (do), redpolls (do); **S:** Meadow pipit, *Temminck's stint, lit stint, reed bunting, l/r plover, Kentish plover, water pipit, yellow wagtails*; **MS:** Starling, *dunlin, curlew sandpiper, pectoral sandpiper, ringed plover, jack snipe, wood sandpiper, sanderling, turnstone, spotted crake*; **M:** Lapwing, woodcock, *knot, com snipe, gt snipe, ruff, com redshank, spotted redshank, greenshank, London pigeon*, LIT GULL, SABINE'S GULL; **ML:** Carrion crow, hooded crow, *stilt, bl/t godwit, squacco heron*; **L:** *Glossy ibis, curlew, night heron*; **VL:** *Purple heron, spoonbill*; **H:** White stork.

Damp Grassland in Valleys. **VS:** Grasshopper warbler, whinchat, house martin, *sand martin*; **S:** Meadow pipit, swift, *reed bunting, yellow wagtails*; **MS:** Swallow, starling, redwing; **M:** Fieldfare, corncrake, jackdaw, *com snipe, gt snipe, com redshank*, MOORHEN, TEAL, B/H GULL; **ML:** Black grouse, magpie, rook, carrion crow, hooded crow, COM GULL, SHOVELER; **L:** Com pheasant, *curlew*, HERRING GULL, MALLARD; **VL:** *Heron.*

Fresh Grass Marshes. **VS:** House martin, *sand martin*; **S:** Meadow pipit, swift, *reed bunting, yellow wagtails*, R/N PHALAROPE; **MS:** Corn bunting, skylark, swallow, starling, redwing, *dunlin, jack snipe*; **M:** Fieldfare, golden plover, lapwing, com partridge, cuckoo, jackdaw, kestrel, *com snipe, gt snipe, ruff, com redshank*, MOORHEN, TEAL, B/H GULL; **ML:** Hen-harrier, rook, carrion crow, hooded crow, bl/t godwit, COM GULL, WIGEON; **L:** *Curlew, lesser white-front, barnacle goose, p/f goose, w/f goose*, LESSER BLACK-BACK, HERRING GULL, MALLARD, SHELDUCK, GT BLACK-BACK; **VL:** *Snow goose, g/l goose, bean goose, heron*, EGYPTIAN GOOSE; **H:** White stork, *com crane*, CANADA GOOSE.

Reed-beds. **VS:** Grasshopper warbler, house martin (roosting), *sand martin* (roosting); *reed warbler, marsh warbler* (osiers), *sedge warbler*; **S:** *Reed bunting, yellow wagtails* (roosting), *bearded tit*; **MS:** Pied wagtail (roosting), swallow (roosting), starling (roosting), *Baillon's crake, lit crake, spotted crake*; **M:** *Com snipe water rail, lit bittern*, MOORHEN, TEAL; **ML:** Montagu's harrier, *squacco heron, marsh harrier*, COOT, GARGANEY, TUFTED DUCK, COM POCHARD, SHOVELER; **L:** Com pheasant, *night heron*, MALLARD; **VL:** *Bittern, purple heron*; **H:** *Com crane.*

Bogs and Swamps. **VS:** Grasshopper warbler, *sedge warbler*; **S:** Twite, meadow pipit, *reed bunting*, R/N PHALAROPE; **MS:** Skylark, *Baillon's crake, lit crake, dunlin, jack snipe, spotted crake*; **M:** Merlin, woodcock, red grouse, s/e owl, *com snipe*, *gt snipe, water rail, lit bittern,* MOORHEN, TEAL, B/H GULL; **ML:** *Squacco heron, marsh harrier,* COM GULL, TUFTED DUCK, SHOVELER; **L:** *Curlew, night heron, p/f goose, w/f goose,* LESSER BLACK-BACK, MALLARD; **VL:** *G/l goose, bean goose, bittern, purple heron, heron*; **H:** *Com crane.*

Sewage Farms. **VS:** *House martin, sand martin, sedge warbler*; **S:** Linnet, black redstart, house sparrow, greenfinch, meadow pipit, swift, *Temminck's stint, lit stint, reed bunting, l/r plover, Kentish plover, water pipit, yellow wagtails*; **MS:** Pied & white wagtails, swallow, starling, *grey wagtail, dunlin, curlew sandpiper, pectoral sandpiper, ringed plover, jack snipe, com sandpiper, wood sandpiper, sanderling, green sandpiper, turnstone,* GREY PHALAROPE; **M:** Golden plover, lapwing, *w/w black tern, black tern, knot, com snipe, gt snipe, water rail, ruff, com redshank, spotted redshank, greenshank, com tern, arctic tern,* LIT GULL, MOORHEN, TEAL, B/H GULL; **ML:** Carrion crow, hooded crow, *stilt, bl/t godwit,* COM GULL, SHOVELER; **L:** LESSER BLACK-BACK, HERRING GULL, MALLARD, GT BLACK-BACK; **VL:** *Heron*; **H:** MUTE SWAN.

Sea Cliffs. **VS:** House martin (local); **S:** *Rock pipit*; **MS:** Starling; **M:** Jackdaw, stock dove, kestrel, *rock dove,* PUFFIN, BLACK GUILLEMOT; **ML:** Chough, peregrine, carrion crow, hooded crow, com buzzard, *Greenland falcon,* KITTIWAKE, RAZORBILL, GUILLEMOT, FULMAR; **L:** Raven, LESSER BLACK-BACK, HERRING GULL, GT BLACK-BACK; **VL:** *Sea eagle,* SHAG, CORMORANT, GANNET.

Sea Shores, Rocky. **S:** Black redstart (win), *rock pipit, kingfisher* (win), STORM PETREL (sum); **MS:** *Purple sandpiper, turnstone,* F/T PETREL (sum); **M:** *Com tern, arctic tern, roseate tern,* MANX SHEARWATER (sum), BLACK GUILLEMOT; **ML:** *Oystercatcher,* KITTIWAKE, RAZORBILL; **L:** LESSER BLACK-BACK, HERRING GULL, EIDER, GT BLACK-BACK; **VL:** SHAG, CORMORANT, GANNET (local).

Sea Shores, Sandy. **S:** Meadow pipit, *rock pipit, snow bunting, shore lark*; **MS:** Pied & white wagtails, *dunlin, ringed plover, sanderling*; **M:** Merlin, lapwing, *lit tern, knot, com redshank, com tern, arctic tern, roseate tern,* LIT GULL, SABINE'S GULL, B/H GULL; **ML:** Peregrine, *ba/t godwit, whimbrel, Sandwich tern, oystercatcher,* COM GULL, ARCTIC SKUA; **L:** *Curlew,* LESSER BLACK-BACK, HERRING GULL, EIDER, SHELDUCK, GT BLACK-BACK.

Sea Shores and Estuaries, Muddy. **S:** Meadow pipit, *Temminck's stint, lit stint, rock & water pipits, kingfisher* (win); **MS:** Starling, *dunlin, curlew sandpiper, pectoral sandpiper, ringed plover, com sandpiper, turnstone*; **M:** Golden plover, merlin, lapwing, jackdaw, *lit tern, knot, grey plover, ruff, com redshank, spotted redshank, greenshank, London pigeon, com tern, arctic tern, g/b tern,* DABCHICK, LIT GULL, B/N GREBE, SLAVONIAN GREBE, SABINE'S GULL, TEAL, B/H GULL; **ML:** Peregrine, rook, carrion crow, hooded crow, *ba/t godwit, whimbrel, bl/t godwit, avocet, oystercatcher,* COOT, SMEW, COM GULL, R/N GREBE, ARCTIC SKUA, WIGEON, GOLDENEYE, G/C GREBE, SCAUP; **L:** *Glossy ibis, curlew, lesser white-front, barnacle goose, p/f goose, w/f goose,* LESSER BLACK-BACK, ICELAND GULL, HERRING GULL, VELVET SCOTER, R/T DIVER, BRENT GOOSE, MALLARD, R/B MERGANSER, SHELDUCK, B/T DIVER, GOOSANDER, GT BLACK-BACK; **VL:** *Snow goose, g/l goose, bean goose, spoonbill, heron,* GLAUCOUS GULL, G/N DIVER, CORMORANT; **H:** BEWICK'S SWAN, WHOOPER SWAN, MUTE SWAN.

Shingle Tracts, Sand Dunes, Salt-marshes and Sea-walls. **VS:** Goldcrest, y/b warbler, r/b flycatcher, pied flycatcher, grasshopper warbler, stonechat;

S: Linnet, twite, lit bunting, greenfinch, scarlet, grosbeak, wheatear, meadow pipit, barred warbler, Lapland bunting, ortolan, tawny pipit, *bluethroat, Temminck's stint, lit stint, reed bunting, Kentish plover, rock & water pipits, snow bunting, shore lark, yellow wagtails*; **MS:** Skylark, Richard's pipit, starling, dotterel (on passage), *dunlin, curlew sandpiper, ringed plover, jack snipe, com sandpiper, wood sandpiper, green sandpiper*; **M:** Nightjar (dunes), merlin, com partridge, cuckoo, stock dove, kestrel, l/e owl, r/l partridge, *s/e owl, lit tern, com snipe, gt snipe, ruff, com redshank, spotted redshank, greenshank, com tern, arctic tern, roseate tern, g/b tern,* B/H GULL; **ML:** Peregrine, stone curlew (shingle), Montagu's harrier, hen-harrier, r/l buzzard, *Sandwich tern, avocet, oystercatcher, Greenland falcon*; **L:** *Snowy owl, barnacle goose,* HERRING GULL, PINTAIL (dunes), EIDER, SHELDUCK; **VL:** *Sea eagle.*

Docks and Harbours. **S:** House sparrow; **M:** *London pigeon,* B/H GULL; **ML:** COM GULL; **L:** LESSER BLACK-BACK, ICELAND GULL, HERRING GULL, MALLARD, GT BLACK-BACK; **VL:** GLAUCOUS GULL; **H:** MUTE SWAN.

WATER

Lakes, Ponds and Reservoirs. **VS:** House martin, *sand martin*; **S:** Swift, *kingfisher,* R/N PHALAROPE; **MS:** Swallow, GREY PHALAROPE; **M:** *W/w black tern, black tern, lit tern, com tern, arctic tern, g/b tern,* DABCHICK, LIT GULL, B/N GREBE, SLAVONIAN GREBE, MOORHEN, SABINE'S GULL, TEAL, B/H GULL; **ML:** *Marsh harrier, osprey,* COOT, GARGANEY, FERRUGINOUS DUCK, SMEW, COM GULL, TUFTED DUCK, MANDARIN DUCK, WIGEON, COM POCHARD, GOLDENEYE, G/C GREBE, SCAUP, COM SCOTER, GADWALL, SHOVELER; **L:** LESSER BLACK-BACK, HERRING GULL, R/C POCHARD, PINTAIL, R/T DIVER, MALLARD, R/B MERGANSER, SHELDUCK, RUDDY SHELDUCK, B/T DIVER, GOOSANDER, GT BLACK-BACK; **VL:** *G/l goose,* EGYPTIAN GOOSE, G/N DIVER, CORMORANT; **H:** CANADA GOOSE, BEWICK'S SWAN, WHOOPER SWAN, MUTE SWAN.

The Sea, Inshore Waters. **S:** R/N PHALAROPE; **MS:** GREY PHALAROPE, LIT AUK; **M:** *Black tern, lit tern, com tern, arctic tern, roseate tern, g/b tern,* MANX SHEARWATERS, LIT GULL, PUFFIN, SABINE'S GULL, BLACK GUILLEMOT, B/H GULL; **ML:** *Sandwich tern,* COM GULL, KITTIWAKE, RAZORBILL, GUILLEMOT, L/T DUCK, IVORY GULL, ARCTIC SKUA, WIGEON, GOLDENEYE, FULMAR, SCAUP, COM SCOTER, POMARINE SKUA, L/T SKUA; **L:** *Barnacle goose, p/f goose, w/f goose,* LESSER BLACK-BACK, ICELAND GULL, HERRING GULL, SURF SCOTER, VELVET SCOTER, KING EIDER, PINTAIL, R/T DIVER, BRENT GOOSE, MALLARD, EIDER, R/B MERGANSER, GT SKUA, SHELDUCK, B/T DIVER, GT BLACK-BACK; **VL:** *G/l goose, bean goose,* GLAUCOUS GULL, G/N DIVER, SHAG, CORMORANT, GANNET; **H:** BEWICK'S SWAN, WHOOPER SWAN, MUTE SWAN.

The Sea, Offshore Waters. **S:** STORM PETREL, R/N PHALAROPE; **MS:** F/T PETREL, GREY PHALAROPE, LIT AUK; **M:** MANX SHEARWATERS, PUFFIN, SABINE'S GULL; **ML:** SOOTY SHEARWATER, KITTIWAKE, RAZORBILL, GUILLEMOT, GT SHEARWATER, CORY'S SHEARWATER, IVORY GULL, ARCTIC SKUA, FULMAR, POMARINE SKUA, L/T SKUA; **L:** LESSER BLACK-BACK, ICELAND GULL, HERRING GULL, KING EIDER, EIDER, GT SKUA, GT BLACK-BACK; **VL:** GLAUCOUS GULL, GANNET.

APPENDIX I—MIGRATION TABLE

The table shows the times of year when the more frequent migratory birds can be seen in the British Isles, omitting those which, like the robin and skylark, can be seen at all times of year in good numbers. Each month is divided into equal thirds, and the symbol '×' indicates that the bird is present in some part of the British Isles in full force, while '○' shows the periods when only small numbers occur. The dividing line between '×' and '○' and between '○' and no entry at all is inevitably an arbitrary one and particularly at the beginning and end of the migration season needs adjustment to fit local circumstances. Generally speaking, for the South of England there will be a shift of one place to the left for spring arrivals and departures, and a shift of one place to the right for autumn arrivals and departures. For Scotland, conversely, there will be a corresponding shift of one place to the right for spring movements, and one place to the left for autumn movements. The symbols '×' and '○' must not be compared as between species, e.g. '×' stands for very different numbers with the chiffchaff on the one hand and the yellow-browed warbler on the other. No account is taken of occasional wintering in SW England by such birds as the chiffchaff.

	Jan			Feb			March			April			May			June			July			Aug			Sept			Oct			Nov			Dec		
	1	2	3	1	2	3	1	2	3	1	2	3	1	2	3	1	2	3	1	2	3	1	2	3	1	2	3	1	2	3	1	2	3	1	2	3
LAND BIRDS																																				
VS																																				
Firecrest	×	×	×	×	×	×	×	×	×	×	×														O	O	O	O	O	×	×	×	×	×	×	×
Yellow-browed Warbler											O	O	O	O										O	O	×	×	×	×	×	O	O				
Willow Warbler								O	×	×	×	×	×	×	×	×	×	×	×	×	×	×	×	×	×	×	×	O	O	O						
Red-breasted Flycatcher												O	O	O	O	O								O	×	×	×	×	×	×	O					
Chiffchaff							O	×	×	×	×	×	×	×	×	×	×	×	×	×	×	×	×	×	×	×	×	×	O	O						
Siskin (S England)	×	×	×	×	×	×	×	×	×	O																		O	×	×	×	×	×	×	×	×
Pied Flycatcher											O	×	×	×	×	×	×	×	×	×	×	×	×	×	×	×	×	×	×	O						
Wood Warbler											O	×	×	×	×	×	×	×	×	×	×	×	×	×	O	O	O									
Grasshopper Warbler											O	×	×	×	×	×	×	×	×	×	×	×	×	×	×	×	×	O								
Whinchat										O	×	×	×	×	×	×	×	×	×	×	×	×	×	×	×	×	×	O	O							
House Martin									O	O	×	×	×	×	×	×	×	×	×	×	×	×	×	×	×	×	×	×	×	×	O	O	O	O		
S																																				
Little Bunting												O	O	O											O	×	×	×	×	×	O					
Melodious Warbler																O	O	O				O	O	×	×	×	×	O								
Icterine Warbler																O	O	O					O	O	×	×	×	×	O							
Lesser Whitethroat										O	×	×	×	×	×	×	×	×	×	×	×	×	×	×	×	×	×	×	O	O						
Common Whitethroat									O	O	×	×	×	×	×	×	×	×	×	×	×	×	×	×	×	×	×	×	O	O						
Garden Warbler											O	×	×	×	×	×	×	×	×	×	×	×	×	×	×	×	×	×	O	O						
Blackcap									O	O	×	×	×	×	×	×	×	×	×	×	×	×	×	×	×	×	×	×	O	O	O					
Spotted Flycatcher											O	O	×	×	×	×	×	×	×	×	×	×	×	×	×	×	×	O								
Common Redstart										O	×	×	×	×	×	×	×	×	×	×	×	×	×	×	×	×	×	×	O	O						
Scarlet Grosbeak																								O	O	O	O									
Brambling	×	×	×	×	×	×	×	×	×	×	O	O	O	O													O	O	×	×	×	×	×	×	×	×
Wheatear							O	×	×	×	×	×	×	×	×	×	×	×	×	×	×	×	×	×	×	×	×	×	O	O	O	O				
Tree Pipit										O	×	×	×	×	×	×	×	×	×	×	×	×	×	×	×	×	×	O	O							
Barred Warbler																							O	O	×	×	×	×	O	O	O					
Lapland Bunting									O	O	O	O	O	O	O									O	×	×	×	×	×	O	O	O	O	O	O	O
Ortolan												O	O	O	O	O								O	×	×	×	O								
Wryneck									O	×	×	×	×	×	×	×	×	×	×	×	×	×	×	×	×	×	O									
Nightingale										O	×	×	×	×	×	×	×	×	×	×	×	×	×	×	O	O	O									
Tawny Pipit													O	O										O	O	O	O	O								
Swift											O	×	×	×	×	×	×	×	×	×	×	×	×	×	×	O	O	O								

Red-backed Shrike											O	×	×	×	×	×	×	×	×	×	×	×	×	×	×	O	O								
Woodchat											O	×	×	×	×	O	O					O	O	O	O	O	O								
MS																																				
Richard's Pipit																								O	O	O	O	O	O	O	O	O	O	O	O
White Wagtail								O	O	×	×	×	×	×	×	O							O	×	×	×	×	×	O							
Waxwing	×	×	×	×	×	×	×	×	×	O	O																			O	×	×	×	×	×	×
Quail												O	O	×	×	×	×	×	×	×	×	×	×	×	×	×	×	O	O	O						
Swallow								O	O	×	×	×	×	×	×	×	×	×	×	×	×	×	×	×	×	×	×	×	×	×	O	O	O	O		
Alpine Swift										O	O	O	O	O	O	O				O	O	O	O	O	O	O	O	O	O	O						
Rosy Starling										O	O	O	O	O	O	×	×	×	×	×	×	×	×	×	O	O	O	O	O	O	O	O	O			
Redwing	×	×	×	×	×	×	×	×	×	O	O																O	O	×	×	×	×	×	×	×	×
Dotterel											O	O	×	×	×	×	×	×	×	×	×	×	×	×	×	×	×	×	O	O	O					
M																																				
Golden Oriole											O	O	×	×	×	O	O	O	O	O	O															
Great Grey Shrike	×	×	×	×	×	×	×	×	×	×	O	O	O	O											O	O	O	×	×	×	×	×	×	×	×	×
Ring Ouzel							O	O	×	×	×	×	×	×	×	×	×	×	×	×	×	×	×	×	×	×	×	×	O	O	O					
Fieldfare	×	×	×	×	×	×	×	×	×	×	×	×	O	O													O	O	×	×	×	×	×	×	×	×
Nightjar												O	O	×	×	×	×	×	×	×	×	×	×	×	×	O	O									
Corncrake											O	O	×	×	×	×	×	×	×	×	×	×	×	×	×	×	×	O	O							
Turtle Dove											O	×	×	×	×	×	×	×	×	×	×	×	×	×	×	×	×	O								
Bee-eater												O	O	O	O	O	O	O				O	O	O	O	O	O	O	O	O						
Hoopoe								O	×	×	×	×	×	×	×	×	O	O	O	O	×	×	×	×	×	×	×	O	O							
Golden Plover (S England)	×	×	×	×	×	×	×	×	×	×	×	×	×	×	O					O	×	×	×	×	×	×	×	×	×	×	×	×	×	×	×
Hobby											O	O	×	×	×	×	×	×	×	×	×	×	×	×	×	×	×	O	O	O						
Roller												O	O	O	O	O	O				O	O	O	O	O	O	O	O								
Nutcracker																												O	O	O	O	O	O	O	O	O
Cuckoo									O	O	×	×	×	×	×	×	×	×	×	×	×	×	×	×	×	O	O									
ML																																				
Stone Curlew								O	O	×	×	×	×	×	×	×	×	×	×	×	×	×	×	×	×	×	×	×	×	O	O	O				
Montagu's Harrier											O	O	×	×	×	×	×	×	×	×	×	×	×	×	×	×	×	×	O	O						
Hen-Harrier (S England)	×	×	×	×	×	×	×	×	×	O	O	O												O	O	O	O	×	×	×	×	×	×	×	×	×
Rough-legged Buzzard	×	×	×	×	×	×	×	×	×	O	O	O	O												O	O	O	O	×	×	×	×	×	×	×	×
Honey Buzzard													O	O	O	O	O	O							×	×	×	×	×	×	O	O	O			
L																																				
Snowy Owl	×	×	×	×	×	×	×	×	×	×	×	×	O	O												O	O	O	×	×	×	×	×	×	×	×

	Jan			Feb			March			April			May			June			July			Aug			Sept			Oct			Nov			Dec		
	1	2	3	1	2	3	1	2	3	1	2	3	1	2	3	1	2	3	1	2	3	1	2	3	1	2	3	1	2	3	1	2	3	1	2	3
WATERSIDE BIRDS																																				
VS																																				
Sand Martin								O	×	×	×	×	×	×	×	×	×	×	×	×	×	×	×	×	×	×	×	×	×	O						
Reed Warbler											O	×	×	×	×	×	×	×	×	×	×	×	×	×	×	×	×	O								
Marsh Warbler														O	×	×	×	×	×	×	×	×	×	×	O	O	O									
Sedge Warbler										O	×	×	×	×	×	×	×	×	×	×	×	×	×	×	×	×	×	O								
S																																				
Bluethroat												O	O	O	O	O								O	×	×	×	×	O	O						
Temminck's Stint												O	O	×	×	O						O	×	×	×	×	×	×	O	O	O					
Little Stint												O	O	O	×	×	O					O	×	×	×	×	×	×	×	O	O	O				
Little Ringed Plover									O	O	×	×	×	×	×	×	×	×	×	×	×	×	×	×	×	×	O									
Kentish Plover										O	×	×	×	×	×	O	O	O	O	O	O	×	×	×	×	×	O	O	O	O						
Water Pipit	O	O	O	O	O	O	O	O	O	O															O	O	O	O	O	O	O	O	O	O	O	O
Snow Bunting (England)	×	×	×	×	×	×	×	×	×	O	O														O	O	O	×	×	×	×	×	×	×	×	×
Shore Lark	×	×	×	×	×	×	×	×	×	×	×	O																O	×	×	×	×	×	×	×	×
Yellow Wagtail									O	×	×	×	×	×	×	×	×	×	×	×	×	×	×	×	×	×	×	O								
MS																																				
Curlew Sandpiper											O	×	×	×	×	O				O	O	×	×	×	×	×	×	×	O	O	O					
Pectoral Sandpiper								O	O													O	O	O	×	×	×	×	×	O						
Jack Snipe	×	×	×	×	×	×	×	×	×	O	O	O	O													O	O	O	×	×	×	×	×	×	×	×
Common Sandpiper	O	O	O	O	O	O	O	O	O	×	×	×	×	×	×	×	×	×	×	×	×	×	×	×	×	×	×	×	O	O	O	O	O	O	O	O
Wood Sandpiper											O	O	O	O	O	O	O	O	O	×	×	×	×	×	×	×	×	O								
Sanderling	×	×	×	×	×	×	×	×	×	×	×	×	×	×	×	×	O	O	O	×	×	×	×	×	×	×	×	×	×	×	×	×	×	×	×	×
Purple Sandpiper	×	×	×	×	×	×	×	×	×	×	×	×	×	×	×	×	O	O	O	O	O	×	×	×	×	×	×	×	×	×	×	×	×	×	×	×
Green Sandpiper	O	O	O	O	O	O	O	O	O	×	×	×	×	×	O	O	O	O	O	×	×	×	×	×	×	×	×	×	O	O	O	O	O	O	O	O
Turnstone	×	×	×	×	×	×	×	×	×	×	×	×	×	×	×	×	O	O	×	×	×	×	×	×	×	×	×	×	×	×	×	×	×	×	×	×
Spotted Crake								O	O	O	O	O	O	O	O	O	O	O	O	O	O	O	×	×	×	×	×	×	×	×	×	O	O	O	O	O
M																																				
White-winged Black Tern												O	×	×	×	O	O	O			O	O	O	O	O	O	O	O	O	O						
Black Tern											O	O	×	×	×	×	O	O	O	O	×	×	×	×	×	×	×	O	O	O	O					
Little Tern											O	×	×	×	×	×	×	×	×	×	×	×	×	×	×	×	O	O								

Knot	Great Snipe	Grey Plover	Ruff	Spotted Redshank	Greenshank	Little Bittern	Common Tern	Arctic Tern	Roseate Tern	Gull-billed Tern	ML Stilt	Bar-tailed Godwit	Whimbrel	Black-tailed Godwit	Sandwich Tern	Avocet	Marsh Harrier	Greenland Falcon	Osprey	L Glossy Ibis	Night Heron	Lesser White-front	Barnacle Goose	Pink-footed Goose	White-fronted Goose	VL Snow Goose	Greylag Goose (not N Scotland)	Bean Goose	Sea Eagle	Purple Heron
×		×	O		O							×		O				O				O	×	×	×	O	×	×	O	
×		×	O		O						O	×		O				O				O	×	×	×	O	×	×	O	
×		×	O		O						O	×		O				O					×	×	×	O	×	×	O	
×		×	O	O	O						O	×		×				O		O	O		×	×	×	O	×	×	O	
×	O	×	O	O	O						O	×		×				O	O	O	O		×	×	×	O	×	×	O	
×	O	×	O	O	O						O	×		×				O	O	O	O		×	×	×	O	×	×	O	
×	O	×	O	O	O			O			O	×	O	×					O	O	O		×	×	×	O	×	×	O	O
×	×	×	O	O	O	O		O			O	×	O	×					×	O	O		×	×	×	O	×	×		O
×	×	×	O	×	×	O	O	O			O	×	O	×		O			×	O	O		O	×	×	O	×	×		O
×	×	×	×	×	×	O	O	O			O	×	O	×	×	O	O		×	O			O	×	O		O	O		O
×	×	×	×	×	×	O	×	×	O	O	O	×	O	×	×	×	×		×	O			O	×						O
×	×	×	×	×	×	O	×	×	×	O	O	×	×	×	×	×	×		×	O				O						O
×	×	×	×	×	×	O	×	×	×	O	O	×	×	×	×	×	×		×	O				O						O
×	O	×	×	×	×	O	×	×	×	O	O	×	×	×	×	×	×		O	O										O
×	O	×	×	×	×		×	×	×	O	O	×	×	×	×	×	×		O	O										O
×		×	×	O	×		×	×	×	O	O	O	×	O	×	×	×		O											O
O		O	O	O	×		×	×	×	O	O	O	O	O	×	×	×		O											O
O		O	O		×		×	×	×	O	O	O	O	O	×	×	×		O											O
O		O	O		×		×	×	×	O	O	O	O	O	×	×	×		O		O									O
O		O	O		×	O	×	×	×	O	O	O	O	O	×	×	×		O		O									O
O		×	O	O	×	O	×	×	×	O	O	O	×	O	×	×	×		×	O	O									O
×		×	×	O	×	O	×	×	×	O	O	×	×	×	×	×	×		×	O	O				O					O
×	O	×	×	O	×	O	×	×	×	O	O	×	×	×	×	×	×		×	O	O		O		O					O
×	O	×	×	O	×	O	×	×	×	O	O	×	×	×	×	×	×	O	×	O	O		O	O	O		O	O		O
×	O	×	×	O	×	O	×	O	O	O	O	×	O	×	×	×	×	O	×	O			O	O	×		O	O		O
×	O	×	×		×	O	×			O	O	×	O	×	×	×	×	O	O				×	×	×		O	O		O
×	O	×	×		×		O					×		O	O	×	O	O	O				×	×	×		×	×	O	O
×	O	×	×		×							×		O	O	O		O	O				×	×	×	O	×	×	O	
×	O	×	O		×							×		O				O					×	×	×	O	×	×	O	
×		×	O		O							×		O				O				O	×	×	×	O	×	×	O	
×		×	O		O							×		O				O				O	×	×	×	O	×	×	O	
×		×	O		O							×		O				O				O	×	×	×	O	×	×	O	
×		×	O		O							×		O				O				O	×	×	×	O	×	×	O	
×		×	O		O							×		O				O				O	×	×	×	O	×	×	O	
×		×	O		O							×		O				O				O	×	×	×	O	×	×	O	
×		×	O		O							×		O				O				O	×	×	×	O	×	×	O	

	Jan			Feb			March			April			May			June			July			Aug			Sept			Oct			Nov			Dec		
	1	2	3	1	2	3	1	2	3	1	2	3	1	2	3	1	2	3	1	2	3	1	2	3	1	2	3	1	2	3	1	2	3	1	2	3
WATER BIRDS																																				
S																																				
Storm Petrel	O	O	O	O	O	O	O	O	O	×	×	×	×	×	×	×	×	×	×	×	×	×	×	×	×	×	×	×	×	×	×	×	×	O	O	O
Red-necked Phalarope												O	O	×	×	×	×	×	×	×	×	×	×	×	×	×	O	O	O	O						
Fork-tailed Petrel	O	O	O	O	O	O	O	O	O	O	O	×	×	×	×	×	×	×	×	×	×	×	×	×	×	×	×	×	×	×	×	×	×	×	O	O
Grey Phalarope																							O	O	×	×	×	×	×	×	×	O	O	O	O	O
Little Auk	×	×	×	×	×	O	O	O																					O	O	×	×	×	×	×	×
MS																																				
Manx Shearwater	O	O	O	O	O	×	×	×	×	×	×	×	×	×	×	×	×	×	×	×	×	×	×	×	×	×	×	×	×	O	O	O	O	O	O	O
Little Gull	O	O	O	O	O	O	O	O	O	O	O	×	×	×	O							O	×	×	×	×	×	×	×	×	×	×	O	O	O	O
Puffin	O	O	O	O	O	O	O	O	O	×	×	×	×	×	×	×	×	×	×	×	×	×	×	×	×	×	×	×	×	×	×	O	O	O	O	O
Black-necked Grebe	×	×	×	×	×	×	×	×	×	×	×	O	O	O	O	O	O	O	O	O	O	×	×	×	×	×	×	×	×	×	×	×	×	×	×	×
Slavonian Grebe	×	×	×	×	×	×	×	×	×	×	×	O	O	O	O	O	O	O	O	O	O	O	O	O	O	O	×	×	×	×	×	×	×	×	×	×
Sabine's Gull													O	O											O	O	O	O	O	O	O	O	O	O		
ML																																				
Garganey									O	×	×	×	×	×	×	×	×	×	×	×	×	×	×	×	×	×	O	O	O	O						
Mediterranean Gull	×	×	×	×	×	×	×	×	×	O	O	O										O	O	O	O	O	O	×	×	×	×	×	×	×	×	×
Ferruginous Duck	×	×	×	×	×	×	×	×	O	O																			O	O	O	O	O	×	×	×
Smew	×	×	×	×	×	×	×	×	×	O	O	O	O																	O	O	O	×	×	×	×
Sooty Shearwater																				O	O	×	×	×	×	×	×	×	×	×	O	O				
Long-tailed Duck	×	×	×	×	×	×	×	×	×	×	O	O	O	O	O	O	O	O	O	O	O	O	O	O	O	O	O	×	×	×	×	×	×	×	×	×
Red-necked Grebe	×	×	×	×	×	×	×	×	×	O	O	O												O	O	O	O	×	×	×	×	×	×	×	×	×
Great Shearwater																O	O	O	O	O	O	×	×	×	×	×	×	×	×	×	O	O	O			
Cory's Shearwater																								O	O	O	O	O	O							
Arctic Skua													O	×	×	×	×	×	×	×	×	×	×	×	×	×	×	×	×	O						
Goldeneye	×	×	×	×	×	×	×	×	×	×	O	O	O													O	O	O	×	×	×	×	×	×	×	×
Scaup	×	×	×	×	×	×	×	×	×	×	O	O	O													O	O	×	×	×	×	×	×	×	×	×
Common Scoter	×	×	×	×	×	×	×	×	×	×	×	×	×	O	O	O	O	O	O	O	O	O	O	O	×	×	×	×	×	×	×	×	×	×	×	×
Pomarine Skua														O	O								O	O	×	×	×	×	×	×	×	×	O	O	O	O
Long-tailed Skua												O	O										O	O	×	×	×	×	×	×	O	O				

Lesser Black-back	O	O	O	O	O	×	×	×	×	×	×	×	×	×	×	×	×	×	×	×	×	×	×	×	×	×	×	×	×	×	×	×	×	O	O	O	O	O
Iceland Gull	×	×	×	×	×	×	×	×	O	O	O	O	O															O	O	O	×	×	×	×	×	×	×	×
Velvet Scoter	×	×	×	×	×	×	×	×	×	×	×	O	O	O	O													O	O	×	×	×	×	×	×	×	×	×
Red-crested Pochard	O	O	O	O	O	O	O	O																				O	O	O	O	O	O	O	O	O	O	O
Red-throated Diver (England)	×	×	×	×	×	×	×	×	×	×	×	O	O	O														O	O	×	×	×	×	×	×	×	×	×
Brent Goose	×	×	×	×	×	×	×	×	×	×	O	O	O	O													O	O	O	O	O	O	×	×	×	×	×	×
Red-breasted Merganser (England)	×	×	×	×	×	×	×	×	×	×	O	O	O	O													O	O	O	×	×	×	×	×	×	×	×	×
Great Skua	O	O	O	O	O	O	O	O	O	O	×	×	×	×	×	×	×	×	×	×	×	×	×	×	×	×	×	×	×	×	×	×	O	O	O	O	O	O
Black-throated Diver (England)	×	×	×	×	×	×	×	×	×	×	×	O	O	O																	O	O	×	×	×	×	×	×
Goosander (S England)		×	×	×	×	×	×	×	×	×	×	×	O	O															O	O	O	×	×	×	×	×	×	×
VL																																						
Glaucous Gull	×	×	×	×	×	×	×	×	×	×	O	O																O	O	O	×	×	×	×	×	×	×	×
Great Northern Diver	×	×	×	×	×	×	×	×	×	×	×	×	O	O	O													O	O	O	×	×	×	×	×	×	×	×
H																																						
Bewick's Swan	×	×	×	×	×	×	×	×	×	O	O	O																		O	O	O	×	×	×	×	×	×
Whooper Swan	×	×	×	×	×	×	×	×	×	×	×	×	O	O	O	O	O	O	O	O	O	O	O	O	O	O	O	O	O	×	×	×	×	×	×	×	×	×

NOCTULE

PIPISTRELLE

SWIFT

HOUSE-MARTIN

BATS AND BIRDS. *Everything that flies is not a bird. These are the largest (noctule) and smallest (pipistrelle) bats likely to be seen flying by day, compared with a swift and a house-martin respectively.*

APPENDIX II—GEOGRAPHICAL RACES

THE PROBLEM of geographical races is not one that need concern a bird watcher in the early stages of his interest, but as races have been mentioned from time to time in the text, some explanation seems desirable. It is now well known that the plumage of many birds is not constant over the whole of their range, but varies, sometimes grading in what is known as a 'cline' from one extreme to another, sometimes existing in well-marked distinct populations, which are known as races or subspecies. Owing to their relative isolation, island populations are particularly prone to geographical variation, so that many British resident birds have become sufficiently different from their Continental counterparts to be given a separate racial name, and even some bird populations on particular islands or groups of islands off Scotland have evolved to this stage. In most cases where separate names have been given, as for instance with the British and Continental robin and chaffinch, the differences between the two forms can be detected only in the hand, and not in the field, and as this book is primarily concerned with field identification such races are not mentioned in it. However, in a good many cases, such as those of the wagtails *Motacilla alba* and *M. flava*, the racial distinctions are usually clear in the field.

Zoologists have solved the problem of naming these races by adding a third to the two Latin names already described on p. 9. Thus the robin, meaning a robin from any part of its range, which extends from Co. Kerry to the Urals, is *Erithacus rubecula*, but a robin of the British race is distinguished as *Erithacus rubecula melophilus*, or *E.r.melophilus* for short, and one of the race found over most of the continent of Europe, as *Erithacus rubecula rubecula*. The following list contains the third names to be added on to those of all the birds in this book which have geographical races identifiable in the field and occurring with reasonable regularity in the British Isles, either as migrants or as regional residents.

English Name	*Breeding Race(s)*	*Migrant Race(s)*
	LAND BIRDS	
Willow warbler	*trochilus*	*acredula* (northern)
Chiffchaff	*collybita*	**abietinus* (Scandinavian)
		**tristis* (Siberian)
Coal Tit	*britannicus*	
	hibernicus (Irish)	
Serin and Canary		*serinus* (serin)
		canarius (canary)
Redpolls	*cabaret* (lesser)	*flammea* (mealy)
		rostrata (Greenland)

English Name	*Breeding Race(s)*	*Migrant Race(s)*
Bullfinch	*nesa*	*pyrrhula* (northern)
Wheatear	*oenanthe*	*leucorrhoa* (Greenland)
Pied and White Wagtails	*yarrellii* (pied)	*alba* (white)
Starling	*vulgaris* *zetlandicus* (Shetland)	
Golden Plover	*apricarius* (southern)	*altifrons* (northern)
Barn Owl	*alba*	*guttata* (dark-breasted)
Common Pheasant	*colchicus* ('Old English') *torquatus* (Chinese)	
	WATERSIDE BIRDS	
Bluethroat		*svecica* (red-spotted) *cyanecula* (white-spotted)
Rock and Water Pipits	*petrosus* (rock)	*spinoletta* (water)
Yellow Wagtails	*flavissima* (yellow)	*flava* (blue-headed) *thunbergi* (grey-headed)
Dipper	*gularis*	*cinclus* (black-bellied)
Dunlin	*schinzii* (southern)	*alpina* (northern)
Gyrfalcons		*islandus* (Iceland) *candicans* (Greenland)
Snow and Blue Snow Geese		*atlanticus* (greater snow) *caerulescens* (lesser snow and blue snow)
	WATER BIRDS	
Manx Shearwaters	*puffinus* (Manx)	*mauretanicus* (western Mediterranean)
Teal	*crecca*	*carolinensis* (American green-winged)
Guillemot	*aalge* (northern) *albionis* (southern)	
Lesser Black-back	*graellsii*	*fuscus* (Scandinavian)
Herring Gull	*argentatus*	**omissus* (Scandinavian) **heuglini* (N Russian)
Brent Goose		*bernicla* (dark-breasted) *hrota* (pale-breasted)
Cormorant	*carbo*	*sinensis*

* Pairs of races starred thus are not distinguishable from each other in the field, but can be told collectively from the breeding race in the preceding column.

APPENDIX III—ORDER OF FAMILIES

In the text the English names only of bird families are given, and it is assumed that if no family is shown the bird belongs to the family to which it gives its own name, e.g. the song thrush to the Thrush Family. Here the English and Latin names of the various families are listed in their correct systematic order.

Diver Family	*Gaviidae*
Grebe Family	*Podicipitidae* (*Podicipedidae*)
Albatross Family	*Diomedeidae*
Shearwater Family	*Procellariidae*
Booby Family	*Sulidae*
Cormorant Family	*Phalacrocoracidae*
Frigate-Bird Family	*Fregatidae*
Heron Family	*Ardeidae*
Stork Family	*Ciconiidae*
Spoonbill Family	*Plataleidae*
Flamingo Family	*Phoenicopteridae*
Duck Family	*Anatidae*
Vulture Family	*Aegypiidae*
Falcon Family	*Falconidae*
Hawk Family	*Accipitridae*
Osprey Family	*Pandionidae*
Grouse Family	*Tetraonidae*
Pheasant Family	*Phasianidae*
Crane Family	*Balearicidae*
Rail Family	*Rallidae*
Bustard Family	*Otididae*
Oystercatcher Family	*Haematopodidae*
Plover Family	*Charadriidae*
Sandpiper Family	*Scolopacidae*
Avocet Family	*Recurvirostridae*
Phalarope Family	*Phalaropidae*
Stone-Curlew Family	*Burhinidae*
Pratincole Family	*Glareolidae*
Skua Family	*Stercorariidae*
Gull Family	*Laridae*
Auk Family	*Alcidae*
Sand-Grouse Family	*Pteroclidae*
Dove Family	*Columbidae*
Cuckoo Family	*Cuculidae*
Owl Family	*Strigidae*

Nightjar Family	*Caprimulgidae*
Swift Family	*Apodidae*
Kingfisher Family	*Alcedinidae*
Bee-eater Family	*Meropidae*
Roller Family	*Coraciidae*
Hooper Family	*Upupidae*
Woodpecker Family	*Picidae*
Lark Family	*Alaudidae*
Swallow Family	*Hirundinidae*
Oriole Family	*Oriolidae*
Crow Family	*Corvidae*
Tit Family	*Paridae*
Nuthatch Family	*Sittidae*
Creeper Family	*Certhiidae*
Wren Family	*Troglodytidae*
Dipper Family	*Cinclidae*
Thrush Family	*Turdidae*
Warbler Family	*Sylviidae*
Kinglet Family	*Regulidae*
Flycatcher Family	*Muscicapidae*
Wagtail Family	*Motacillidae*
Waxwing Family	*Bombycillidae*
Shrike Family	*Laniidae*
Vireo Family	*Vireonidae*
Starling Family	*Sturnidae*
American Wood Warbler Family	*Parulidae*
American Oriole Family	*Icteridae*
Tanager Family	*Thraupidae*
Accentor Family	*Prunellidae*
Finch Family	*Fringillidae*
Sparrow Family	*Passeridae*

APPENDIX IV—LIST OF RARE BIRDS

For the sake of completeness, a list is given of all other birds, not mentioned anywhere in the text, which are officially accepted as having appeared in the British Isles at least once up to the end of 1964, and which there is no positive reason for supposing to have escaped from captivity. Full details of the majority of them appear either in *The Handbook of British Birds* or in *The Popular Handbook of Rarer British Birds*. Races of birds already mentioned are not included.

*White-billed Diver	*Gavia adamsii*
†*Pied-billed Grebe	*Podilymbus podiceps*
Black-browed Albatross	*Diomedea melanophrys*
Wilson's Petrel	*Oceanites oceanicus*
Madeiran Petrel	*Oceanodroma castro*
Frigate Petrel	*Pelagodroma marina*
*Little Shearwater	*Puffinus baroli*
Audubon's Shearwater	*P. l'herminieri*
Bulwer's Petrel	*Bulweria bulwerii*
Kermadec Petrel	*Pterodroma neglecta*
Collared Petrel	*P. leucoptera*
†Capped Petrel	*P. hasitata*
†Man o' War Bird	*Fregata magnificens*
Great White Heron	*Egretta alba*
†*Black Duck	*Anas rubripes*
Baikal Teal	*A. formosa*
†*Ring-necked Duck	*Aythya collaris*
†*Bufflehead	*Bucephala albeola*
Harlequin Duck	*Histrionicus histrionicus*
*Steller's Eider	*Polysticta stelleri*
†Hooded Merganser	*Mergus cucullatus*
Egyptian Vulture	*Neophron percnopterus*
Griffon Vulture	*Gyps fulvus*
Spotted Eagle	*Aquila clanga*
Pallid Harrier	*Circus macrourus*
Lesser Kestrel	*Falco naumanni*
†Sora Rail	*Porzana carolina*
†*American Purple Gallinule	*Porphyrula martinica*
*Houbara Bustard	*Chlamydotis undulata*
*Sociable Plover	*Chettusia gregaria*
†*Killdeer Plover	*Charadrius vociferus*
Caspian Plover	*C. asiaticus*
*Lesser Golden Plover	*C. dominicus*
†*Upland Sandpiper	*Bartramia longicauda*
†Eskimo Curlew	*Numenius borealis*
†*Solitary Sandpiper	*Tringa solitaria*
*Marsh Sandpiper	*T. stagnatilis*
*Terek Sandpiper	*T. terek*
†*Least Sandpiper	*Calidris minutilla*

*Has occurred since 1958. †Of transatlantic origin.

†*Baird's Sandpiper	*C. bairdii*
*Sharp-tailed Sandpiper	*C. acuminata*
†*Semipalmated Sandpiper	*C. pusilla*
†*Western Sandpiper	*C. mauri*
†*Stilt Sandpiper	*Micropalama himantopus*
Great Black-headed Gull	*Larus ichthyaëtus*
*†Laughing Gull	*L. atricilla*
*†Bonaparte's Gull	*L. philadelphia*
*Slender-billed Gull	*L. genei*
*Ross's Gull	*Rhodostethia rosea*
*Sooty Tern	*Sterna fuscata*
*Bridled Tern	*S. anaethetus*
†Royal Tern	*S. maxima*
*Brünnich's Guillemot	*Uria lomvia*
ΦPallas's Sand-grouse	*Syrrhaptes paradoxus*
*Rufous Turtle Dove	*Streptopelia orientalis*
*Great Spotted Cuckoo	*Clamator glandarius*
Eagle Owl	*Bubo bubo*
*Hawk Owl	*Surnia ulula*
†Nighthawk	*Chordeiles minor*
Red-necked Nightjar	*Caprimulgus ruficollis*
Egyptian Nightjar	*C. aegyptius*
Needle-tailed Swift	*Chaetura caudacuta*
Blue-cheeked Bee-eater	*Merops superciliosus*
*Calandra Lark	*Melanocorypha calandra*
*Bimaculated Lark	*M. bimaculata*
White-winged Lark	*M. leucoptera*
*Lesser Short-toed Lark	*Calandrella rufescens*
*Crested Lark	*Galerida cristata*
*Red-rumped Swallow	*Hirundo daurica*
*Penduline Tit	*Remiz pendulinus*
Wallcreeper	*Tichodroma muraria*
*Eye-browed Thrush	*Turdus obscurus*
*Dusky Thrush	*T. euonomus*
Black-throated Thrush	*T. ruficollis*
Siberian Thrush	*T. sibiricus*
†*American Robin	*T. migratorius*
*Rock Thrush	*Monticola saxatilis*
†Olive-backed Thrush	*Hylocichla ustulata*
†*Gray-cheeked Thrush	*H. minima*
*Desert Wheatear	*Oenanthe deserti*
Pied Wheatear	*Oe. leucomela*
Isabelline Wheatear	*Oe. isabellina*
Black Wheatear	*Oe. leucura*
*Red-flanked Bluetail	*Tarsiger cyanurus*
*Sprosser	*Luscinia luscinia*
*Cetti's Warbler	*Cettia cetti*
*Lanceolated Warbler	*Locustella lanceolata*
*River Warbler	*L. fluviatilis*
Pallas's Grasshopper Warbler	*L. certhiola*
ΦMoustached Warbler	*Lusciniola melanopogon*
Thick-billed Warbler	*Phragmaticola aedon*
Blyth's Reed Warbler	*Acrocephalus dumetorum*
Paddyfield Warbler	*A. agricola*
*Olivaceous Warbler	*Hippolais pallida*

*Has occurred since 1958 †Of transatlantic origin. ΦHas bred.

*Booted Warbler	*H. caligata*
Orphean Warbler	*Sylvia hortensis*
Sardinian Warbler	*S. melanocephala*
*Rufous Warbler	*Agrobates galactotes*
*Bonelli's Warbler	*Phylloscopus bonelli*
*Pallas's Warbler	*P. proregulus*
*Dusky Warbler	*P. fuscatus*
*Radde's Warbler	*P. schwarzi*
Brown Flycatcher	*Muscicapa latirostris*
*Collared Flycatcher	*M. albicollis*
*Olive-backed Pipit	*Anthus hodgsoni*
*Yellow-headed or Citrine Wagtail	*Motacilla citreola*
†*Red-eyed Vireo	*Vireo olivaceus*
†Black-and-White Warbler	*Mniotilta varia*
†*Yellow Warbler	*Dendroica petechia*
†*Myrtle Warbler	*D. coronata*
†*Northern Waterthrush	*Seiurus noveboracensis*
†Yellowthroat	*Geothlypis trichas*
†*Bobolink	*Dolichonyx oryzivorus*
†*Baltimore Oriole	*Icterus galbula*
†Summer Tanager	*Piranga rubra*
†*Rose-breasted Grosbeak	*Pheucticus ludovicianus*
†Slate-coloured Junco	*Junco hyemalis*
Citril Finch	*Carduelis citrinella*
*Parrot Crossbill	*Loxia pytyopsittacus*
†*White-throated Sparrow	*Zonotrichia albicollis*
†*Fox Sparrow	*Passerella iliaca*
†*Song Sparrow	*Melospiza melodia*
Pine Bunting	*Emberiza leucocephala*
*Black-headed Bunting	*E. melanocephala*
*Yellow-breasted Bunting	*E. aureola*
*Rock Bunting	*E. cia*

*Has occurred since 1958. †Of transatlantic origin. ΦHas bred.

INDEX

Figures in heavy type refer to plates. Where more than one page reference is given, the first is the principal one.

INDEX TO KEY

INDEX TO KEY

N
45
MILES TO
SCILLY IS.
0
25
MILES